Legend

vol. 3

Kara · Woo SooJung

Yen
Press

CONTENTS

21

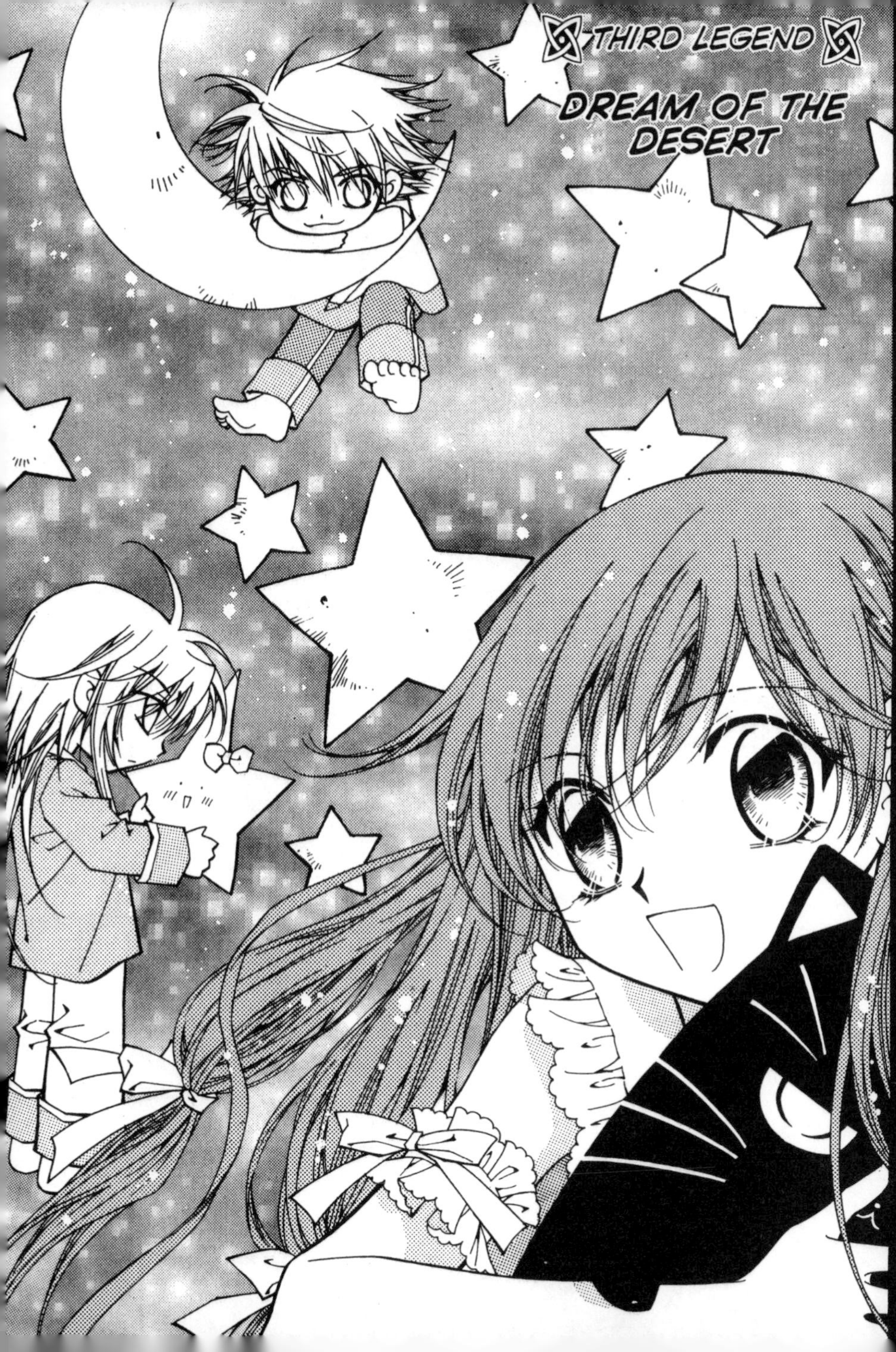
THIRD LEGEND
DREAM OF THE DESERT

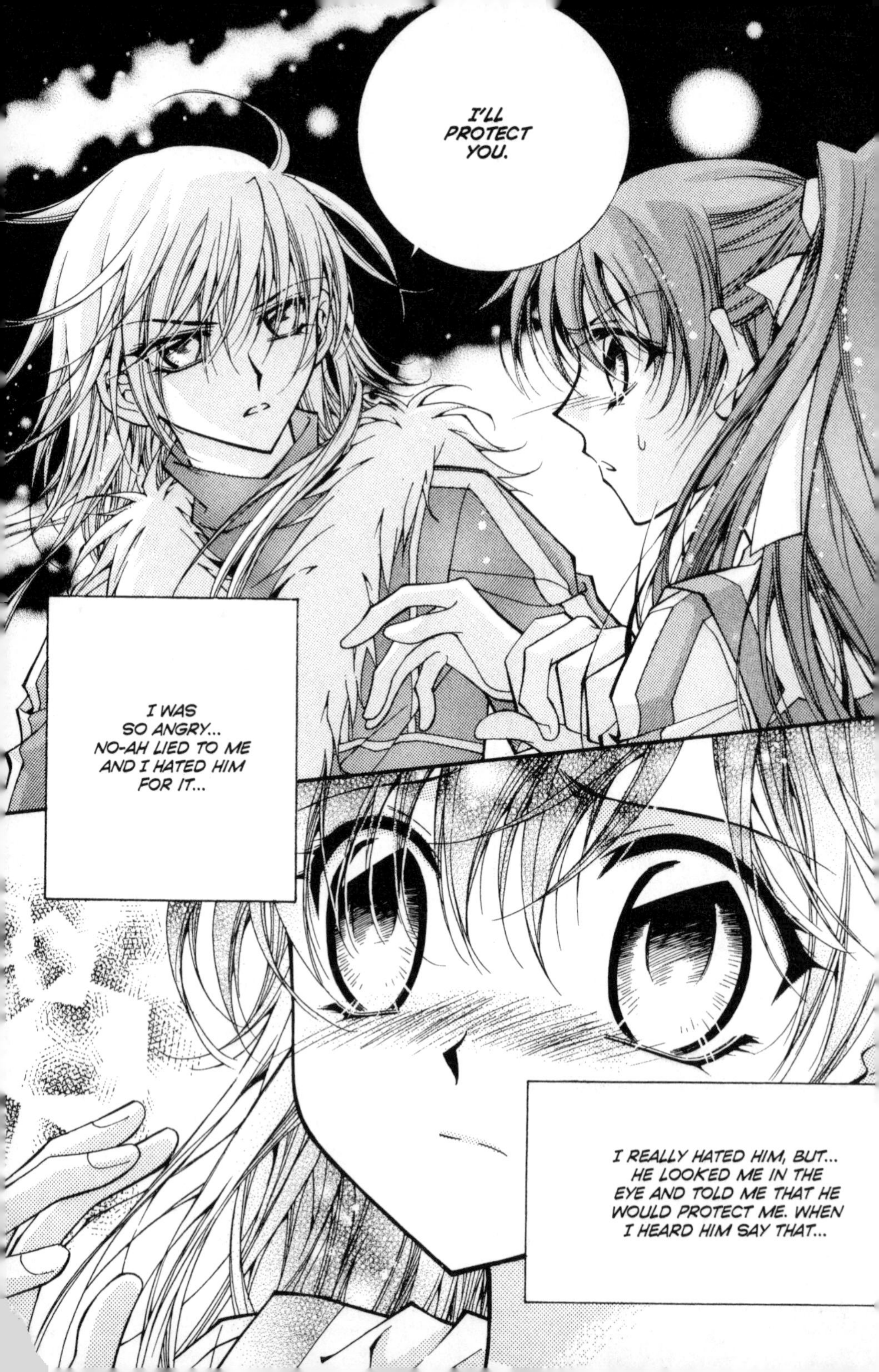
I'LL PROTECT YOU.
I WAS SO ANGRY... NO-AH LIED TO ME AND I HATED HIM FOR IT...
I REALLY HATED HIM, BUT... HE LOOKED ME IN THE EYE AND TOLD ME THAT HE WOULD PROTECT ME. WHEN I HEARD HIM SAY THAT...

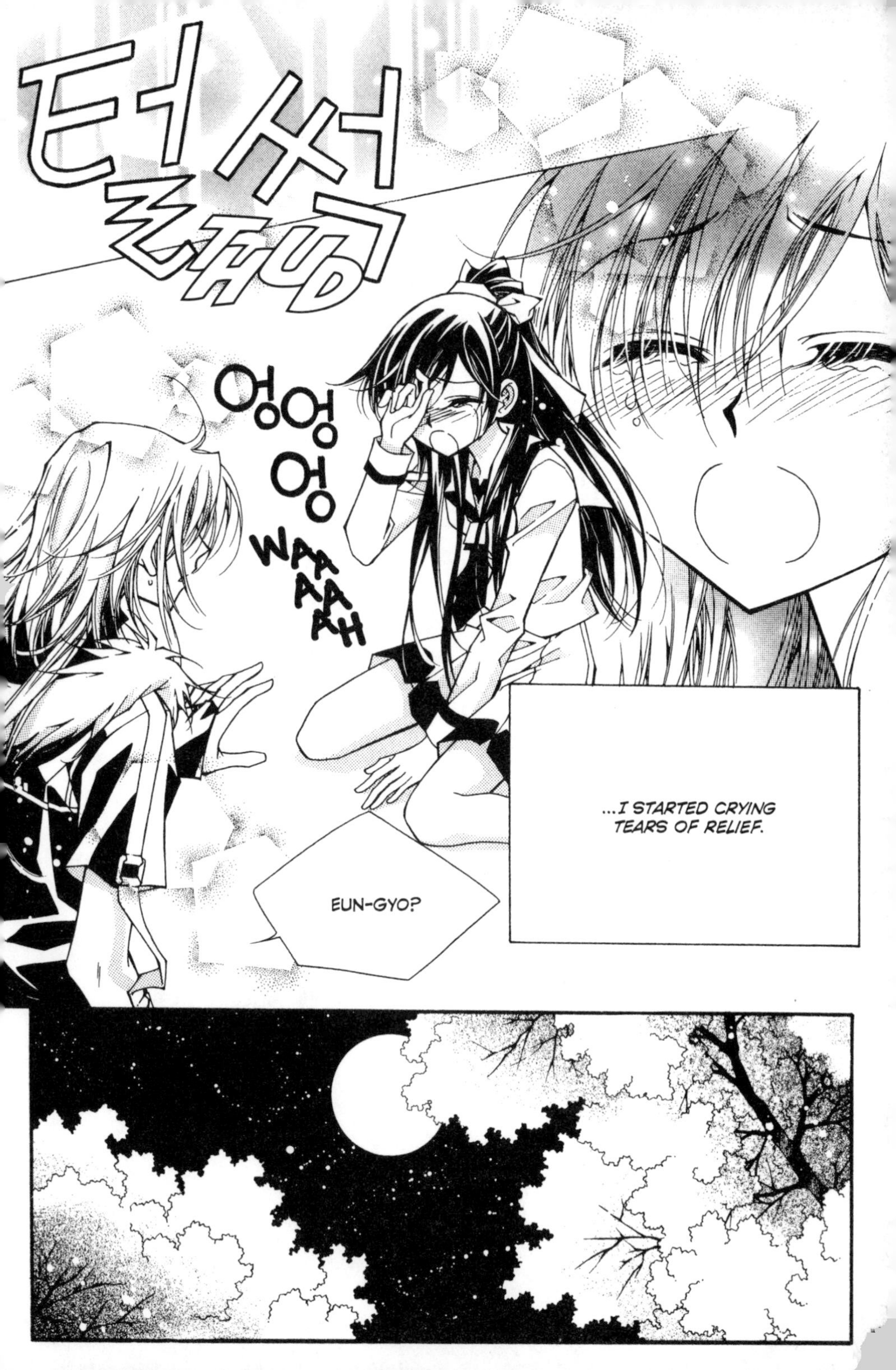
털썩
THUD
엉엉엉
WAAAAAH
...I STARTED CRYING TEARS OF RELIEF.
EUN-GYO?

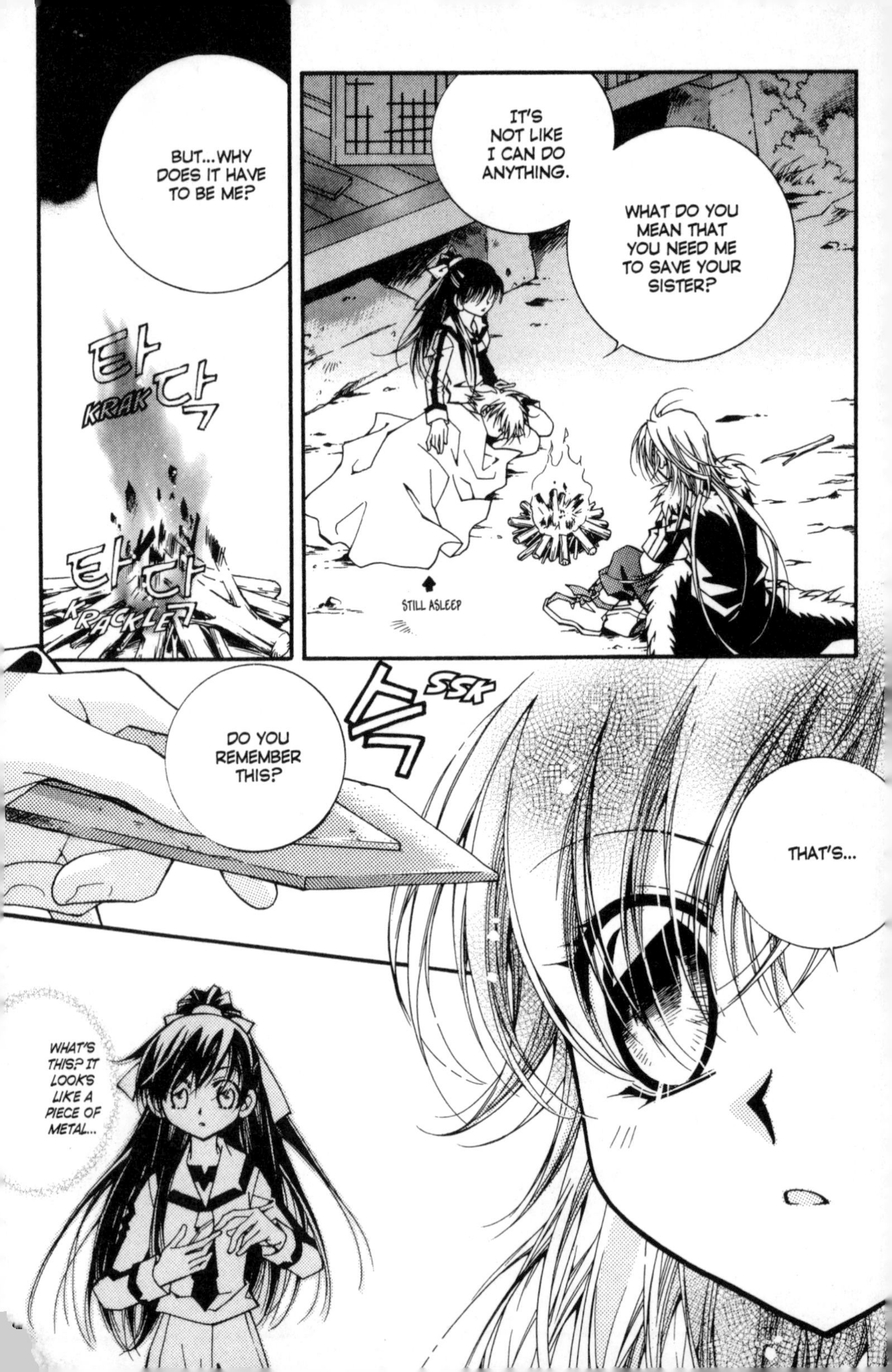

BUT...WHY DOES IT HAVE TO BE ME?
KRAK
KRACKLE
IT'S NOT LIKE I CAN DO ANYTHING.
WHAT DO YOU MEAN THAT YOU NEED ME TO SAVE YOUR SISTER?
STILL ASLEEP
DO YOU REMEMBER THIS?
SSK
THAT'S...
WHAT'S THIS? IT LOOKS LIKE A PIECE OF METAL...

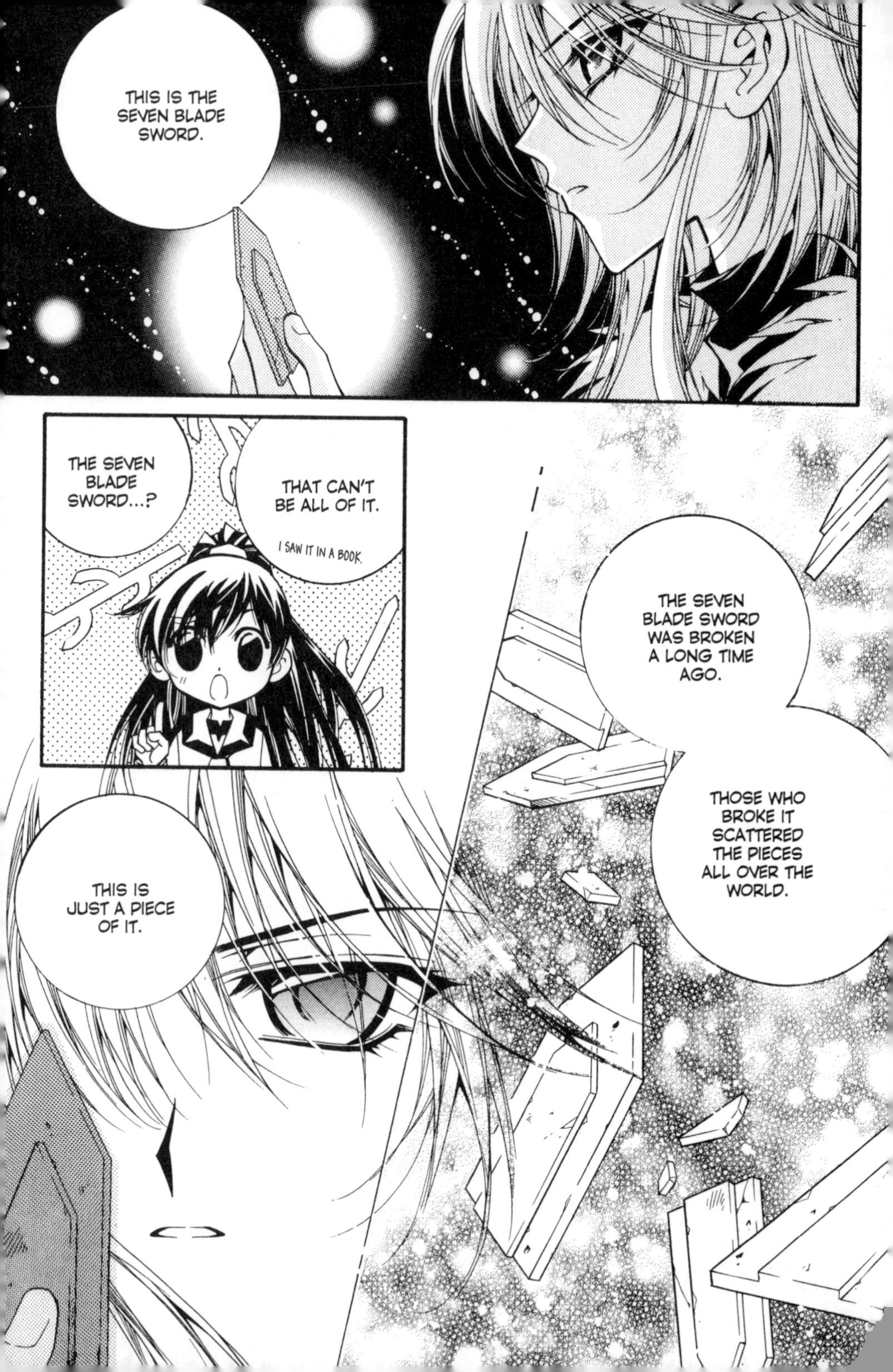
THIS IS THE SEVEN BLADE SWORD.
THE SEVEN BLADE SWORD...?
THAT CAN'T BE ALL OF IT.
I SAW IT IN A BOOK.
THE SEVEN BLADE SWORD WAS BROKEN A LONG TIME AGO.
THOSE WHO BROKE IT SCATTERED THE PIECES ALL OVER THE WORLD.
THIS IS JUST A PIECE OF IT.

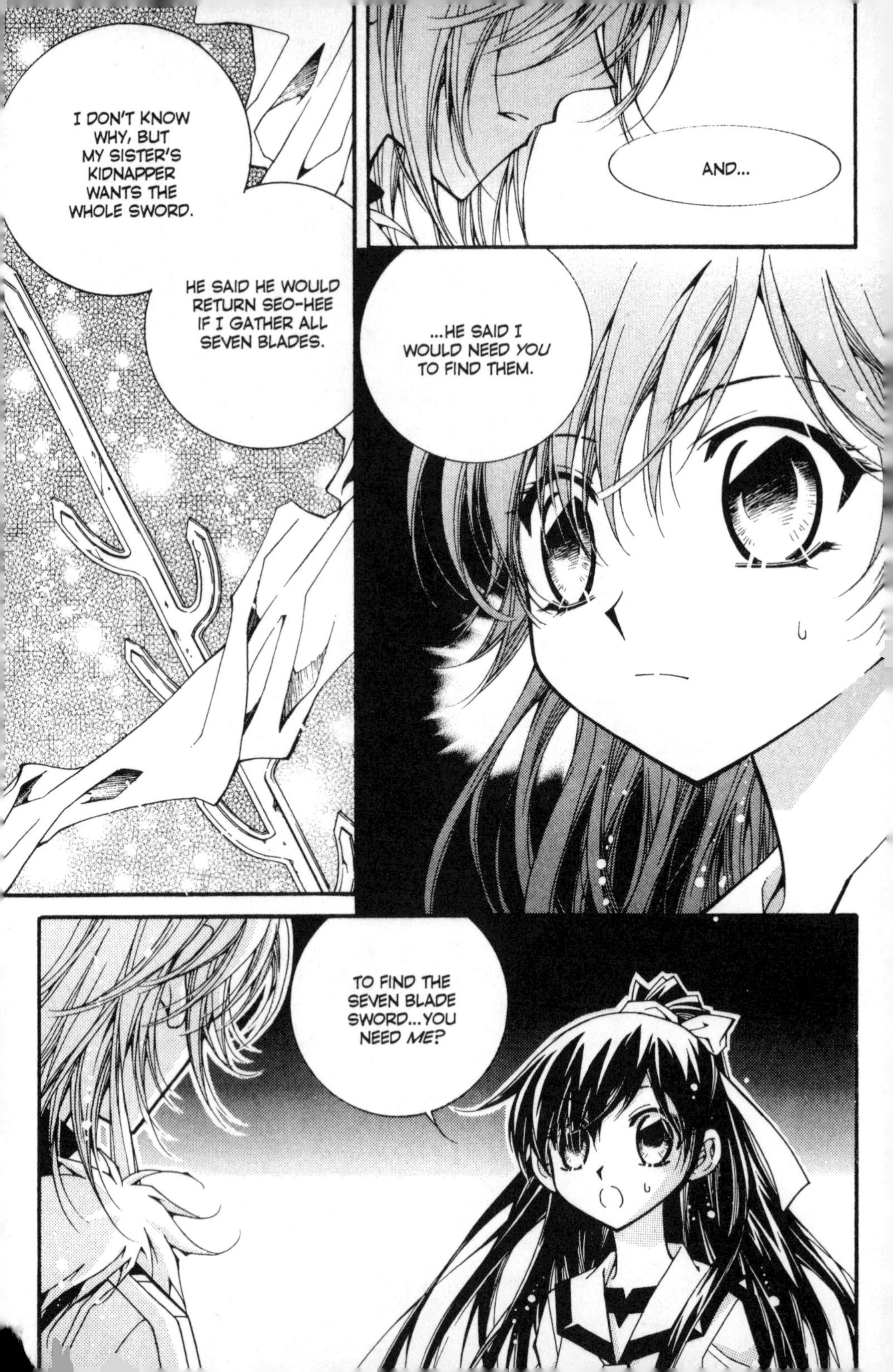
I DON'T KNOW WHY, BUT MY SISTER'S KIDNAPPER WANTS THE WHOLE SWORD.
HE SAID HE WOULD RETURN SEO-HEE IF I GATHER ALL SEVEN BLADES.
AND...
...HE SAID I WOULD NEED *YOU* TO FIND THEM.
TO FIND THE SEVEN BLADE SWORD...YOU NEED *ME*?

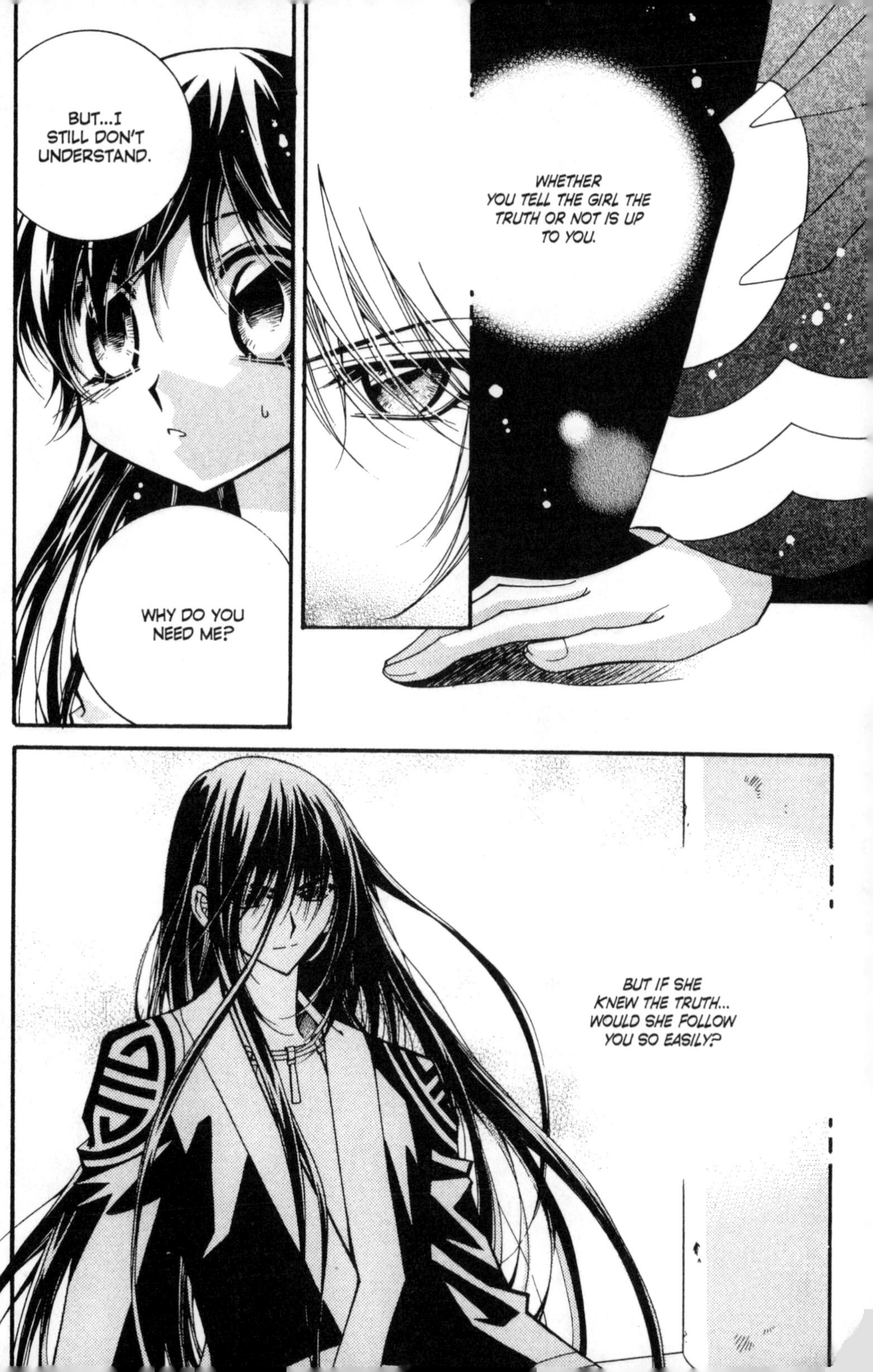
BUT...I STILL DON'T UNDERSTAND.
WHY DO YOU NEED ME?
WHETHER YOU TELL THE GIRL THE TRUTH OR NOT IS UP TO YOU.
BUT IF SHE KNEW THE TRUTH... WOULD SHE FOLLOW YOU SO EASILY?

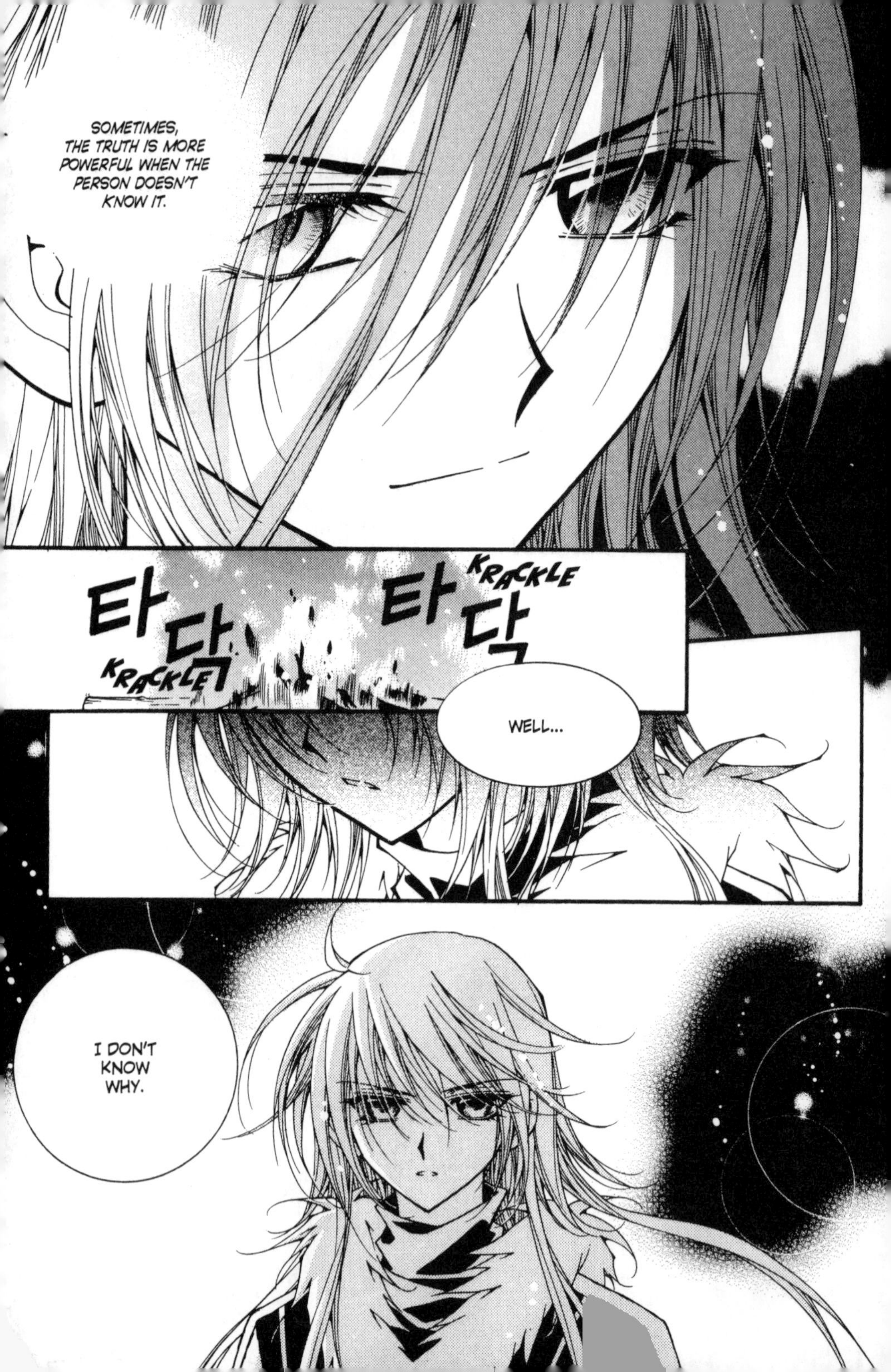
SOMETIMES, THE TRUTH IS MORE POWERFUL WHEN THE PERSON DOESN'T KNOW IT.
타닥
KRACKLE
타닥
KRACKLE
WELL...
I DON'T KNOW WHY.

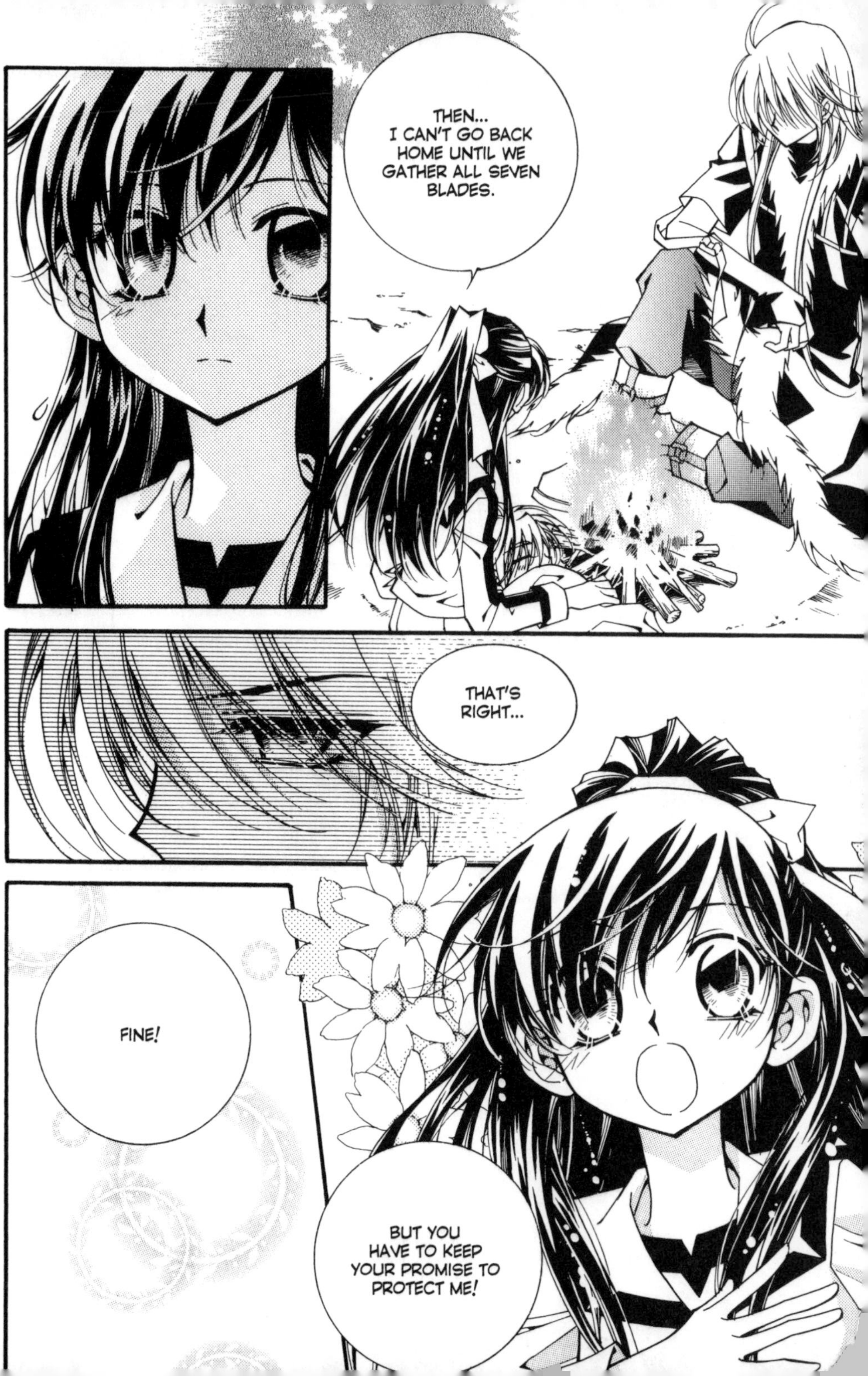
THEN... I CAN'T GO BACK HOME UNTIL WE GATHER ALL SEVEN BLADES.
THAT'S RIGHT...
FINE!
BUT YOU HAVE TO KEEP YOUR PROMISE TO PROTECT ME!

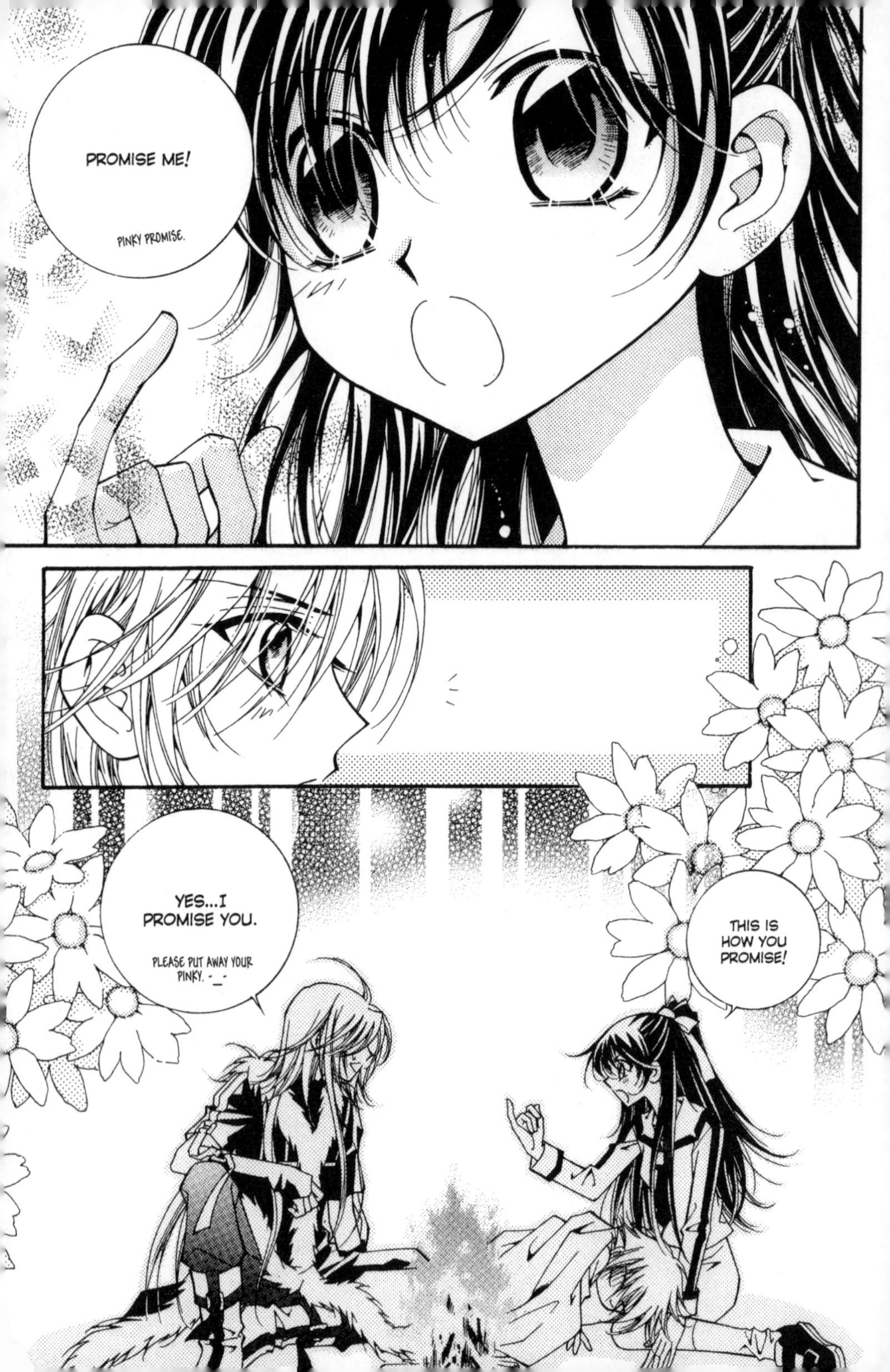
PROMISE ME!
PINKY PROMISE.
YES...I PROMISE YOU.
PLEASE PUT AWAY YOUR PINKY. -_-
THIS IS HOW YOU PROMISE!

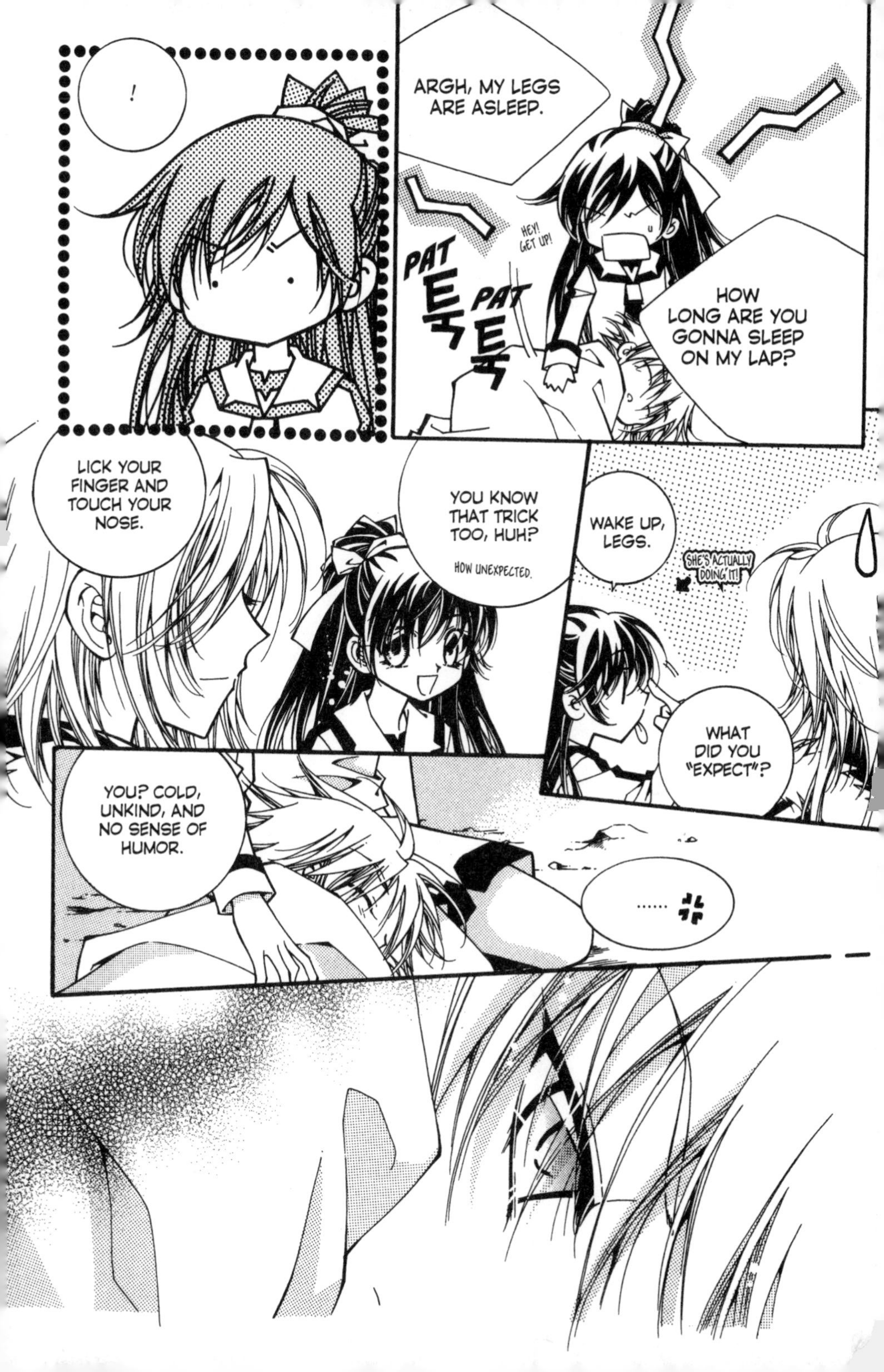
!
ARGH, MY LEGS ARE ASLEEP.
HEY! GET UP!
PAT 툭
PAT 툭
HOW LONG ARE YOU GONNA SLEEP ON MY LAP?
LICK YOUR FINGER AND TOUCH YOUR NOSE.
YOU KNOW THAT TRICK TOO, HUH?
HOW UNEXPECTED.
WAKE UP, LEGS.
SHE'S ACTUALLY DOING IT!
WHAT DID YOU "EXPECT"?
YOU? COLD, UNKIND, AND NO SENSE OF HUMOR.
......

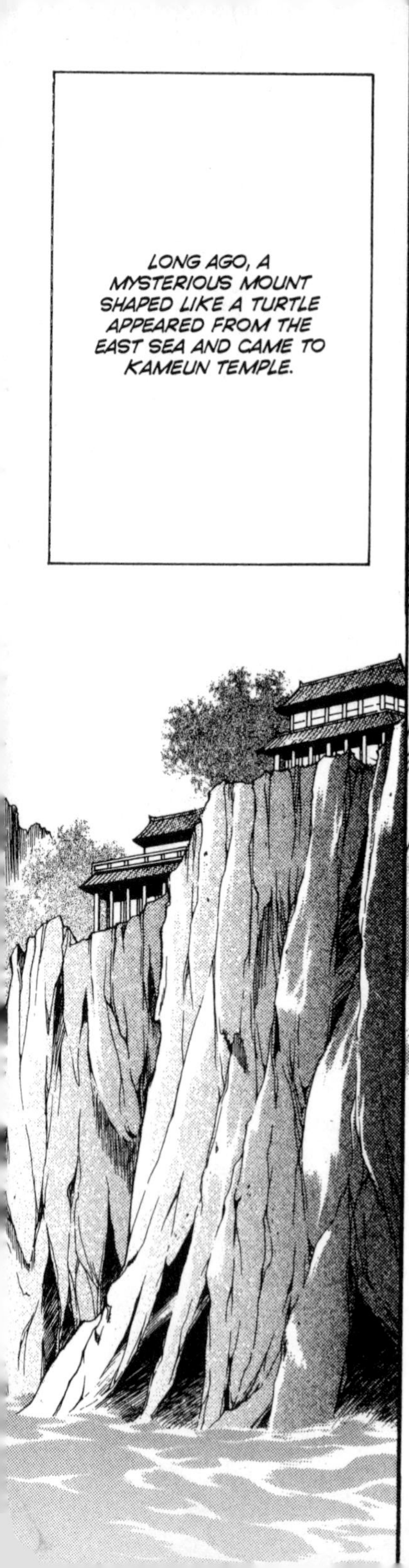
LONG AGO, A MYSTERIOUS MOUNT SHAPED LIKE A TURTLE APPEARED FROM THE EAST SEA AND CAME TO KAMEUN TEMPLE.
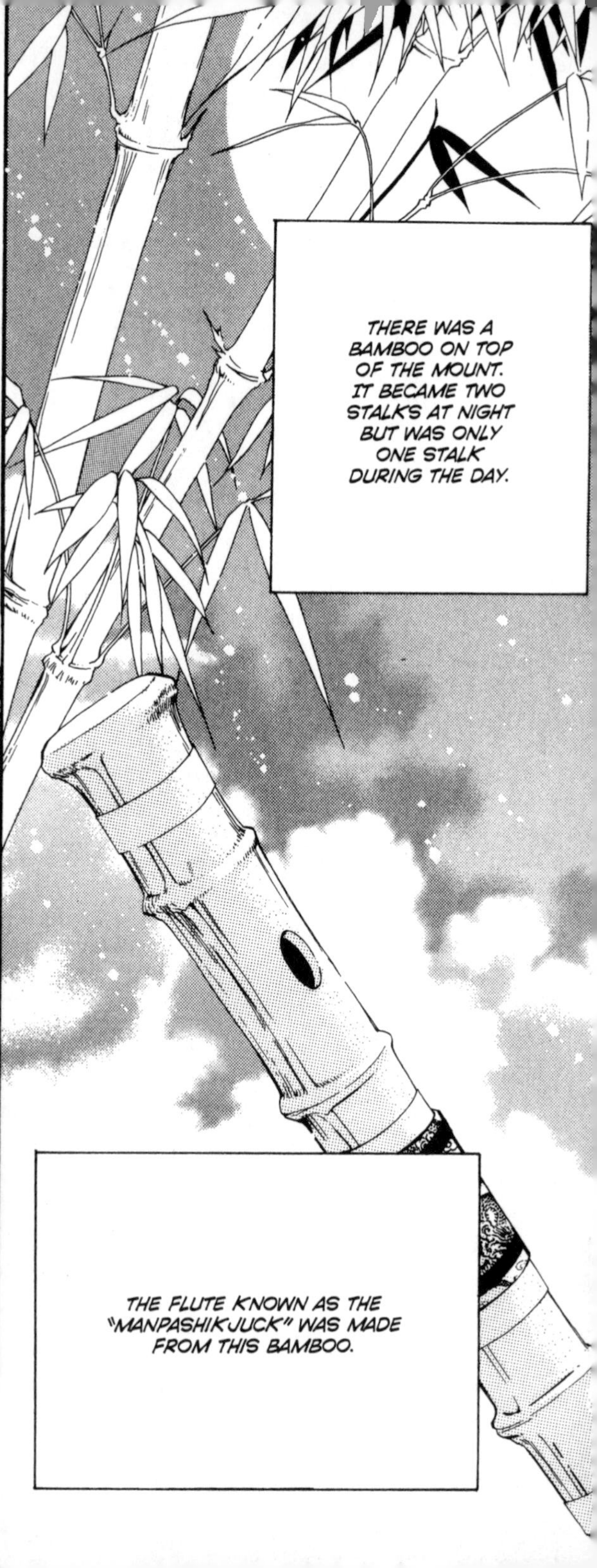
THERE WAS A BAMBOO ON TOP OF THE MOUNT. IT BECAME TWO STALKS AT NIGHT BUT WAS ONLY ONE STALK DURING THE DAY.
THE FLUTE KNOWN AS THE "MANPASHIKJUCK" WAS MADE FROM THIS BAMBOO.

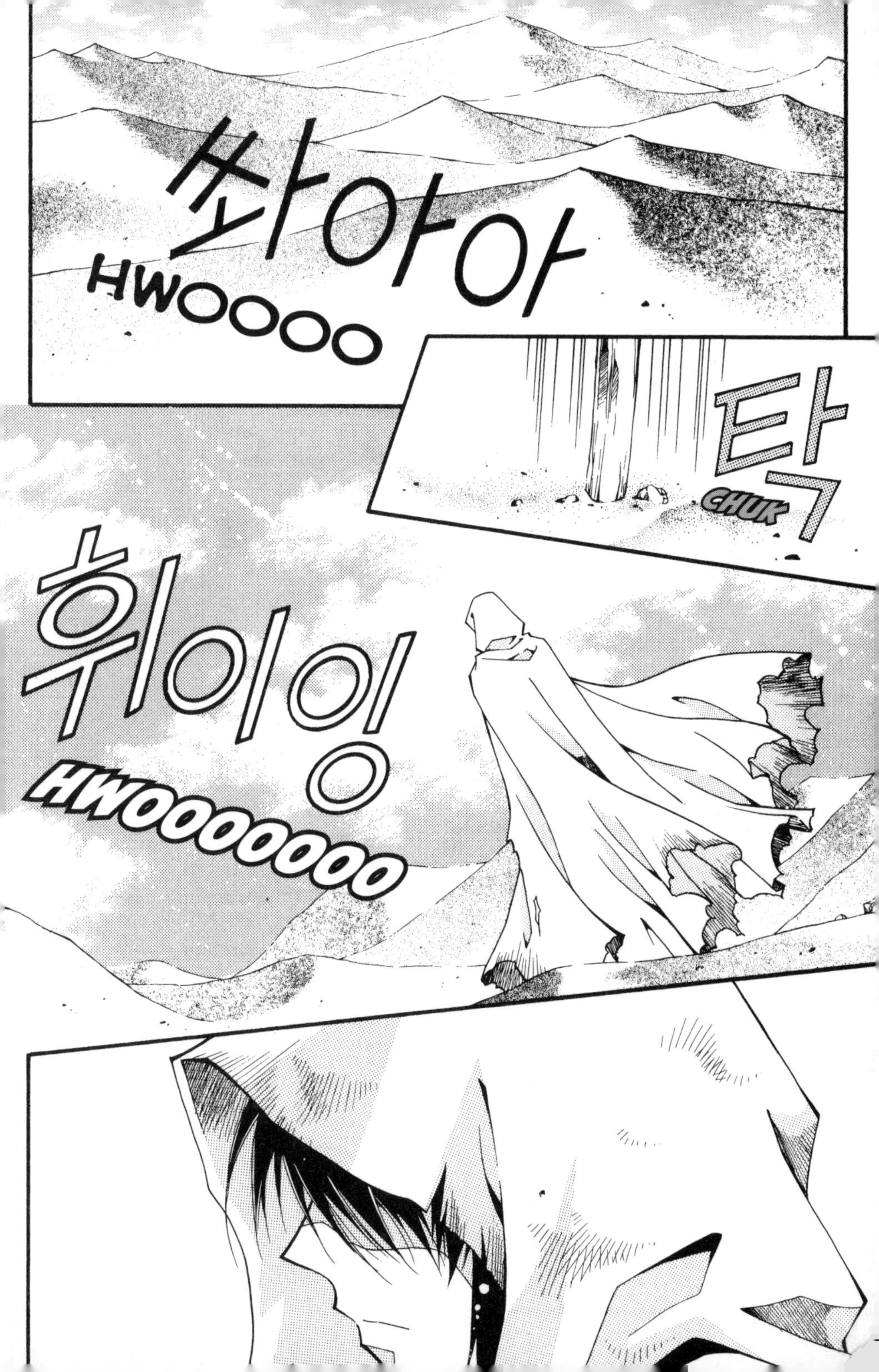
쏴아아
HWOOOO
탁
CHUK
휘이잉
HWOOOOOOOO

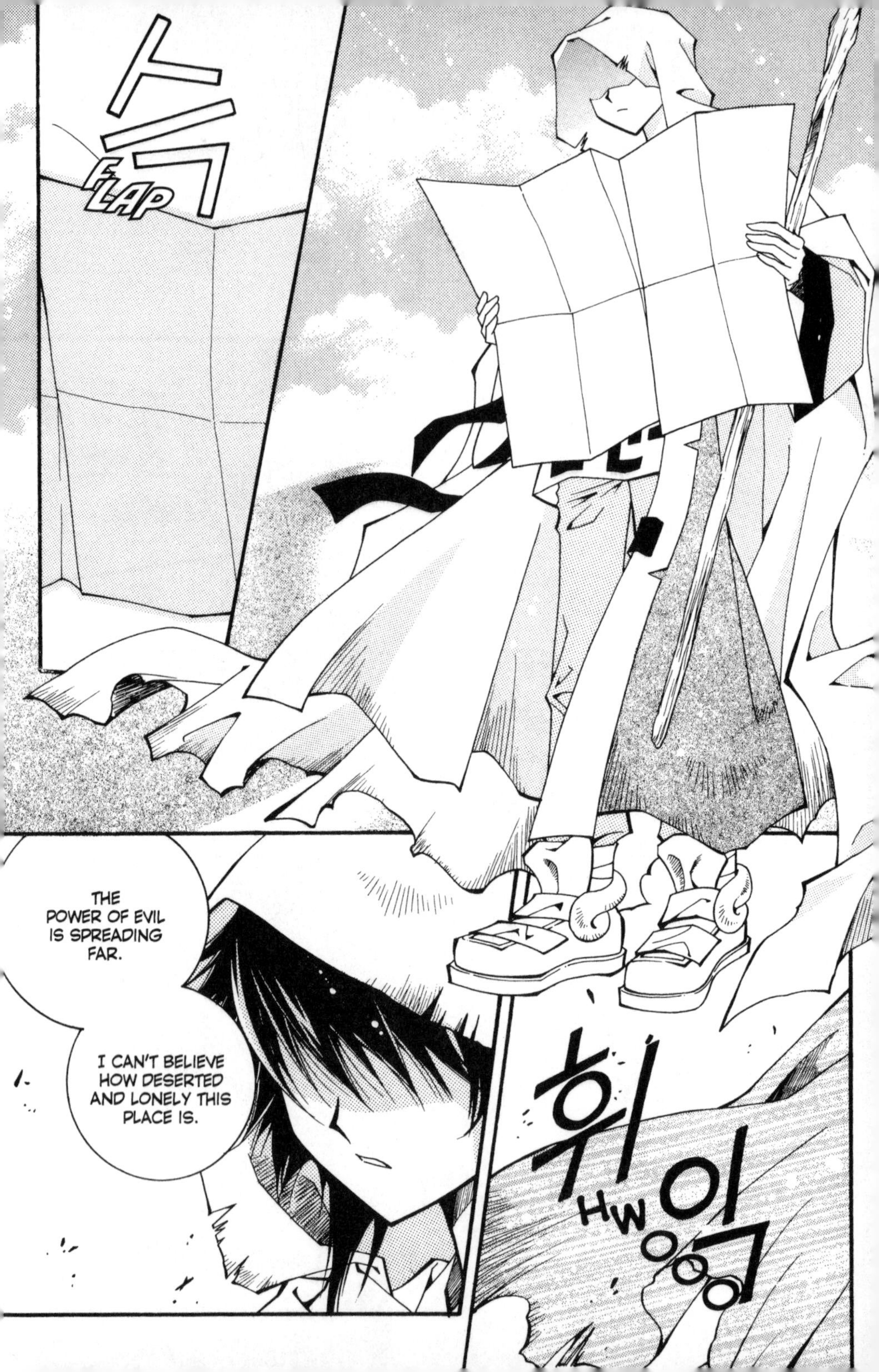
FLAP
THE POWER OF EVIL IS SPREADING FAR.
I CAN'T BELIEVE HOW DESERTED AND LONELY THIS PLACE IS.
휘이
HWOOOO

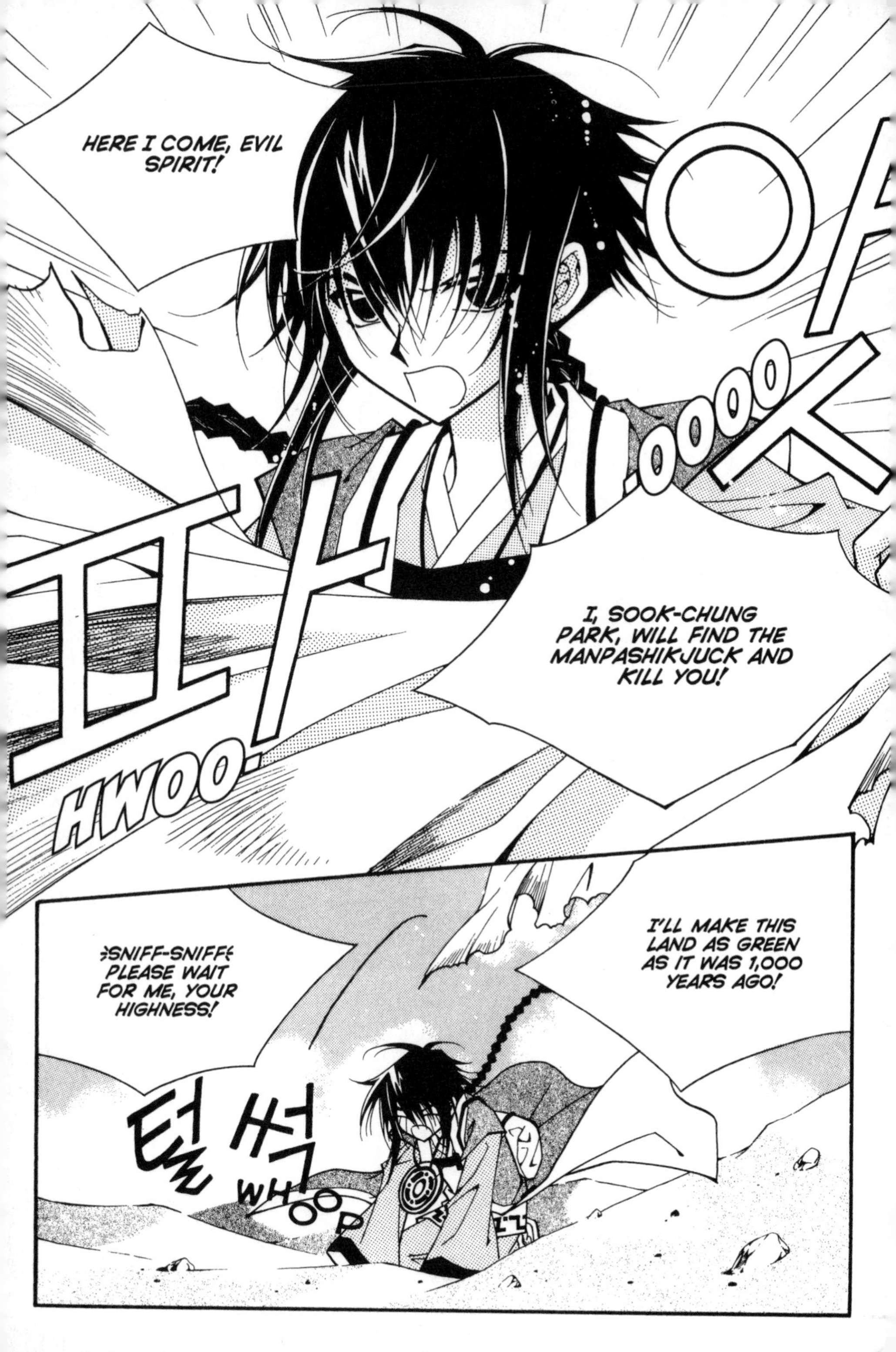
HERE I COME, EVIL SPIRIT!
파
HWOO...
아
...OOOO
I, SOOK-CHUNG PARK, WILL FIND THE MANPASHIKJUCK AND KILL YOU!
≻SNIFF-SNIFF≺ PLEASE WAIT FOR ME, YOUR HIGHNESS!
I'LL MAKE THIS LAND AS GREEN AS IT WAS 1,000 YEARS AGO!
터벅
WHOOP

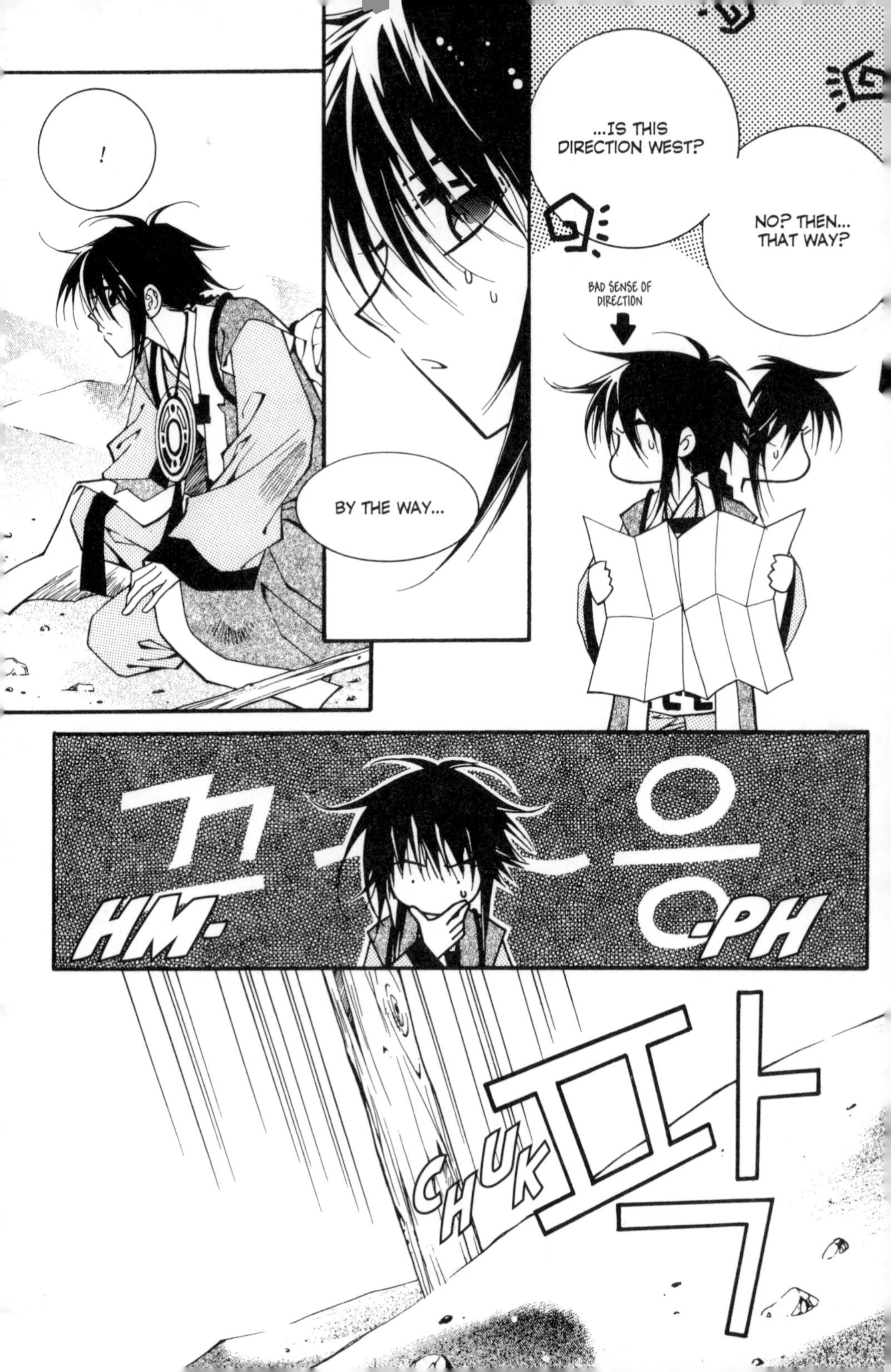
!
BY THE WAY...
...IS THIS DIRECTION WEST?
NO? THEN... THAT WAY?
BAD SENSE OF DIRECTION
HM-
-PH
CHUK

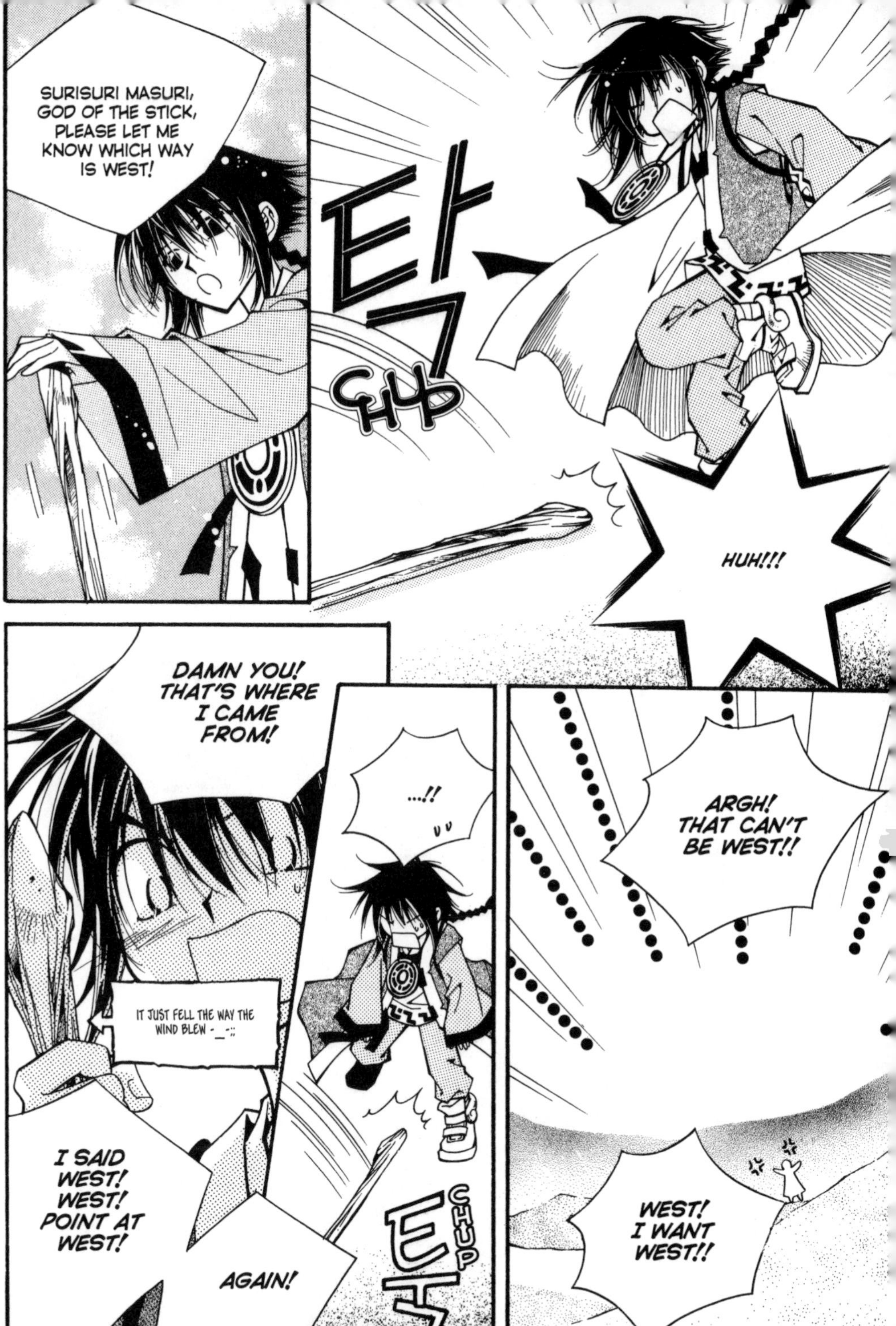
SURISURI MASURI, GOD OF THE STICK, PLEASE LET ME KNOW WHICH WAY IS WEST!
CHUP
HUH!!!
DAMN YOU! THAT'S WHERE I CAME FROM!
IT JUST FELL THE WAY THE WIND BLEW -_-;;
I SAID WEST! WEST! POINT AT WEST!
AGAIN!
...!!
CHUP
ARGH! THAT CAN'T BE WEST!!
WEST! I WANT WEST!!

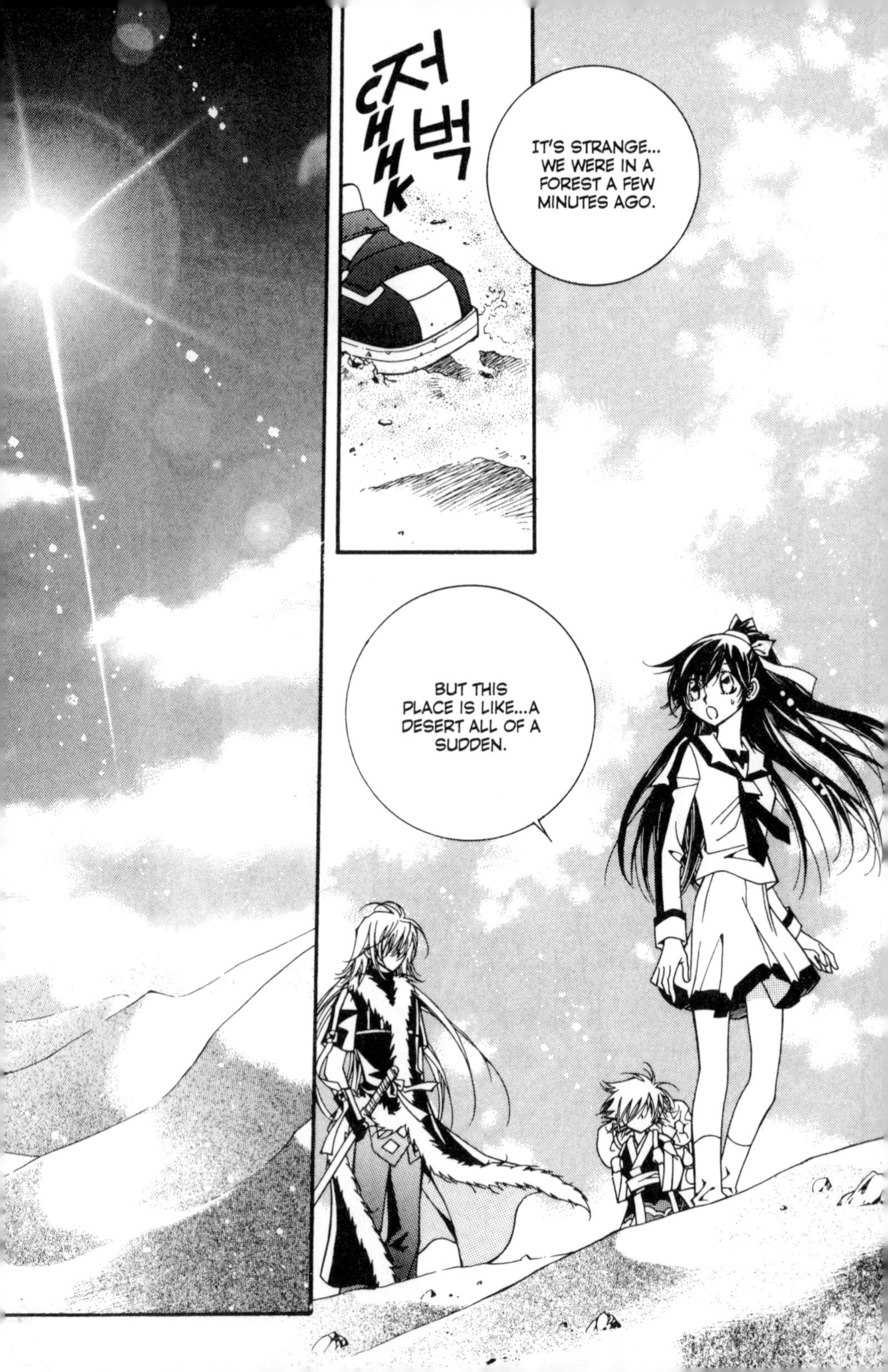
저벅
CHHK
IT'S STRANGE... WE WERE IN A FOREST A FEW MINUTES AGO.
BUT THIS PLACE IS LIKE...A DESERT ALL OF A SUDDEN.

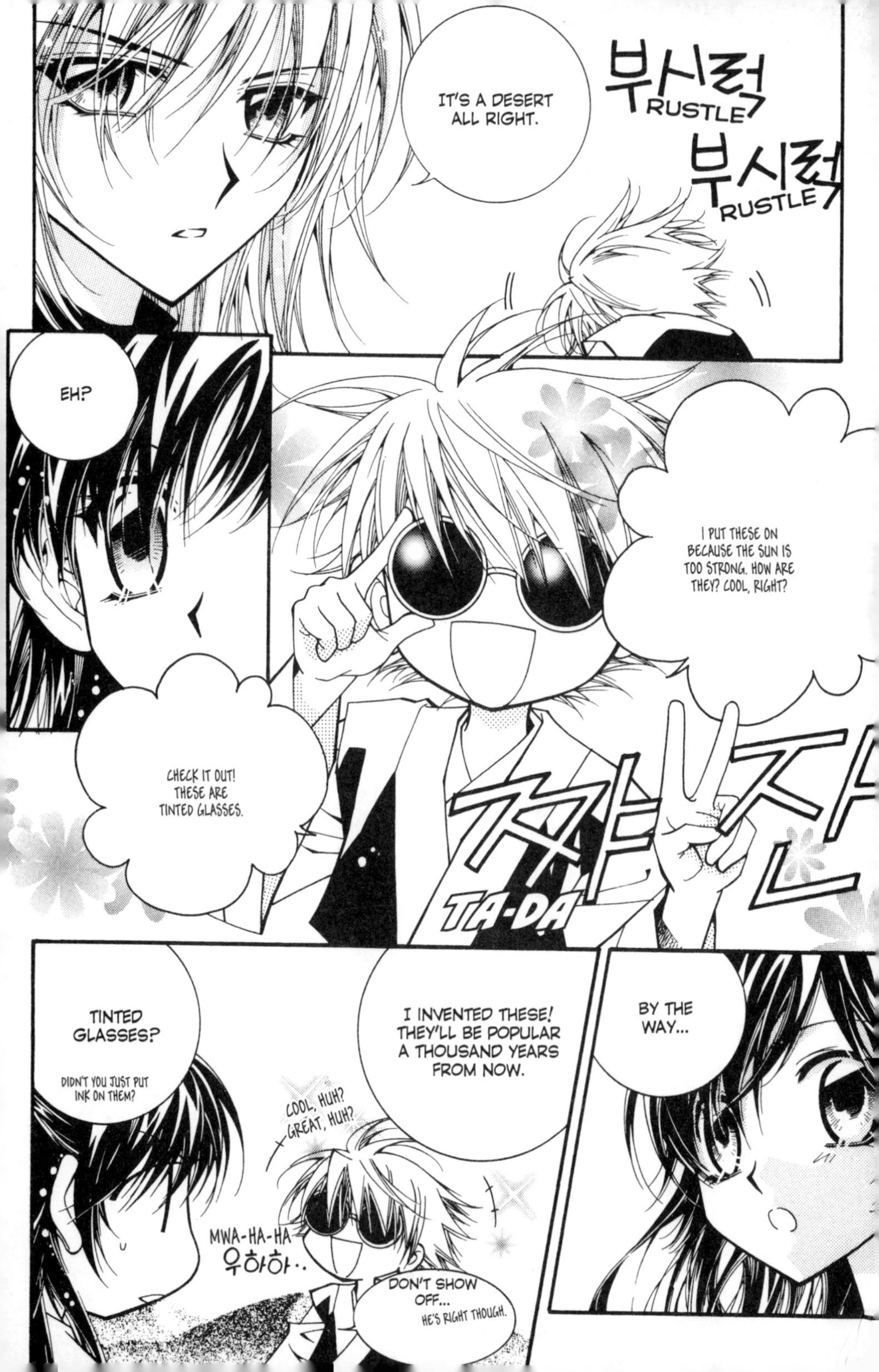
IT'S A DESERT ALL RIGHT.
부시럭
RUSTLE
부시럭
RUSTLE
EH?
CHECK IT OUT! THESE ARE TINTED GLASSES.
I PUT THESE ON BECAUSE THE SUN IS TOO STRONG. HOW ARE THEY? COOL, RIGHT?
짜잔
TA-DA
TINTED GLASSES?
DIDN'T YOU JUST PUT INK ON THEM?
I INVENTED THESE! THEY'LL BE POPULAR A THOUSAND YEARS FROM NOW.
COOL, HUH? GREAT, HUH?
MWA-HA-HA
우하하..
DON'T SHOW OFF...
HE'S RIGHT THOUGH.
BY THE WAY...

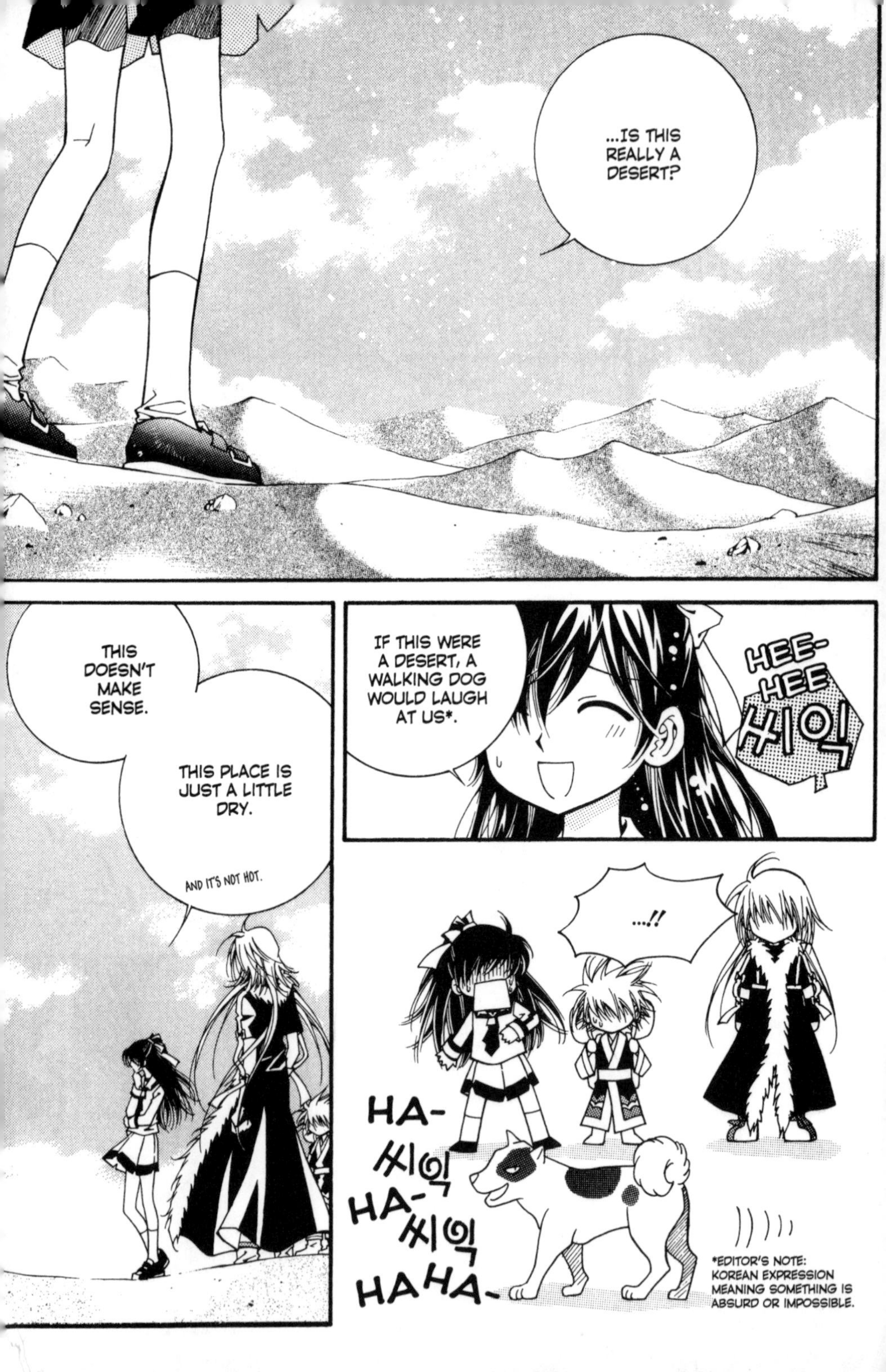
...IS THIS REALLY A DESERT?
THIS DOESN'T MAKE SENSE.
THIS PLACE IS JUST A LITTLE DRY.
AND IT'S NOT HOT.
IF THIS WERE A DESERT, A WALKING DOG WOULD LAUGH AT US*.
HEE-HEE 씨익
...!!
HA- 씨익 HA- 씨익 HAHA-

*EDITOR'S NOTE: KOREAN EXPRESSION MEANING SOMETHING IS ABSURD OR IMPOSSIBLE.

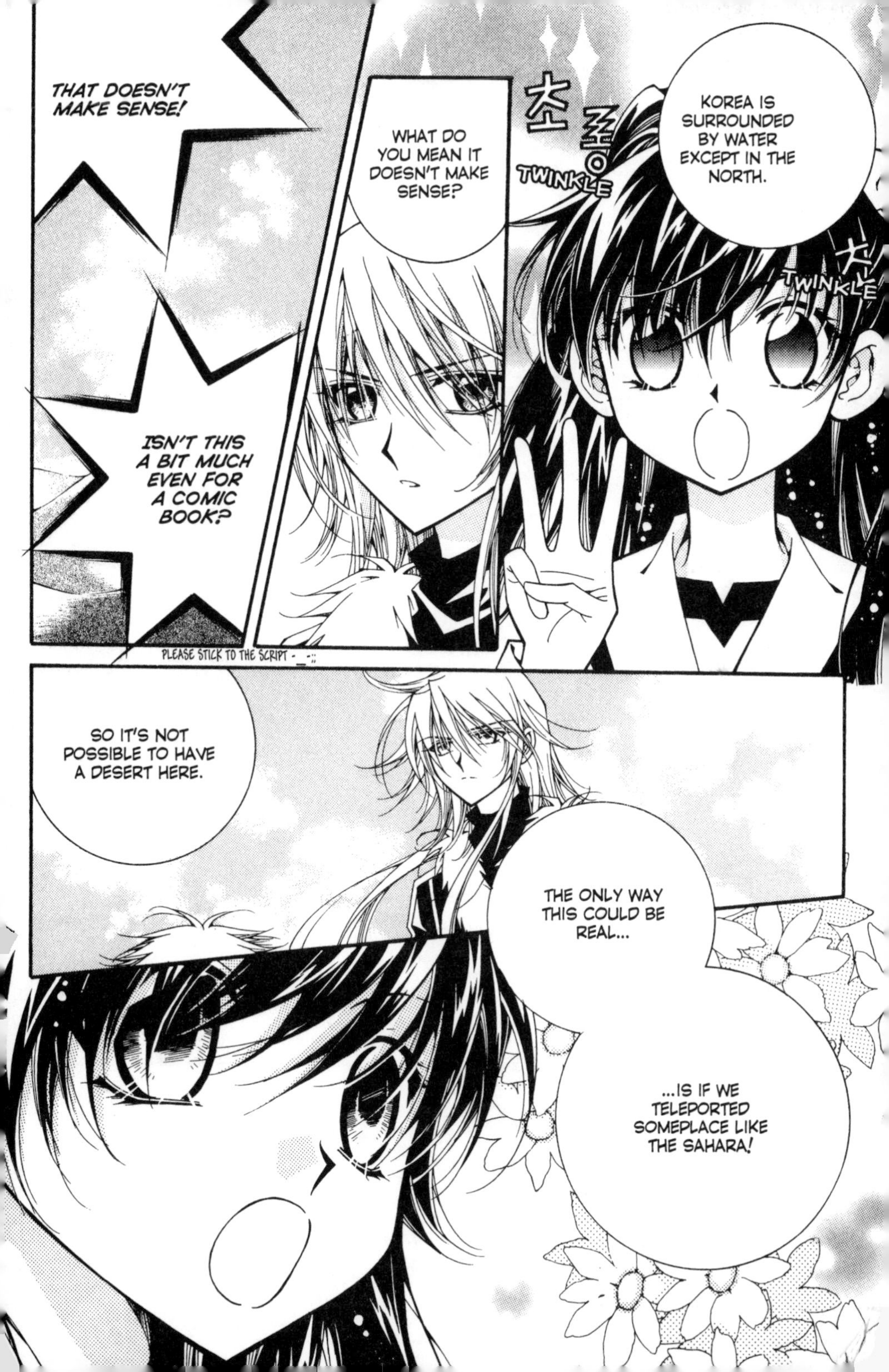
THAT DOESN'T MAKE SENSE!
ISN'T THIS A BIT MUCH EVEN FOR A COMIC BOOK?
WHAT DO YOU MEAN IT DOESN'T MAKE SENSE?
초롱
TWINKLE
KOREA IS SURROUNDED BY WATER EXCEPT IN THE NORTH.
TWINKLE
PLEASE STICK TO THE SCRIPT -_-;;
SO IT'S NOT POSSIBLE TO HAVE A DESERT HERE.
THE ONLY WAY THIS COULD BE REAL...
...IS IF WE TELEPORTED SOMEPLACE LIKE THE SAHARA!

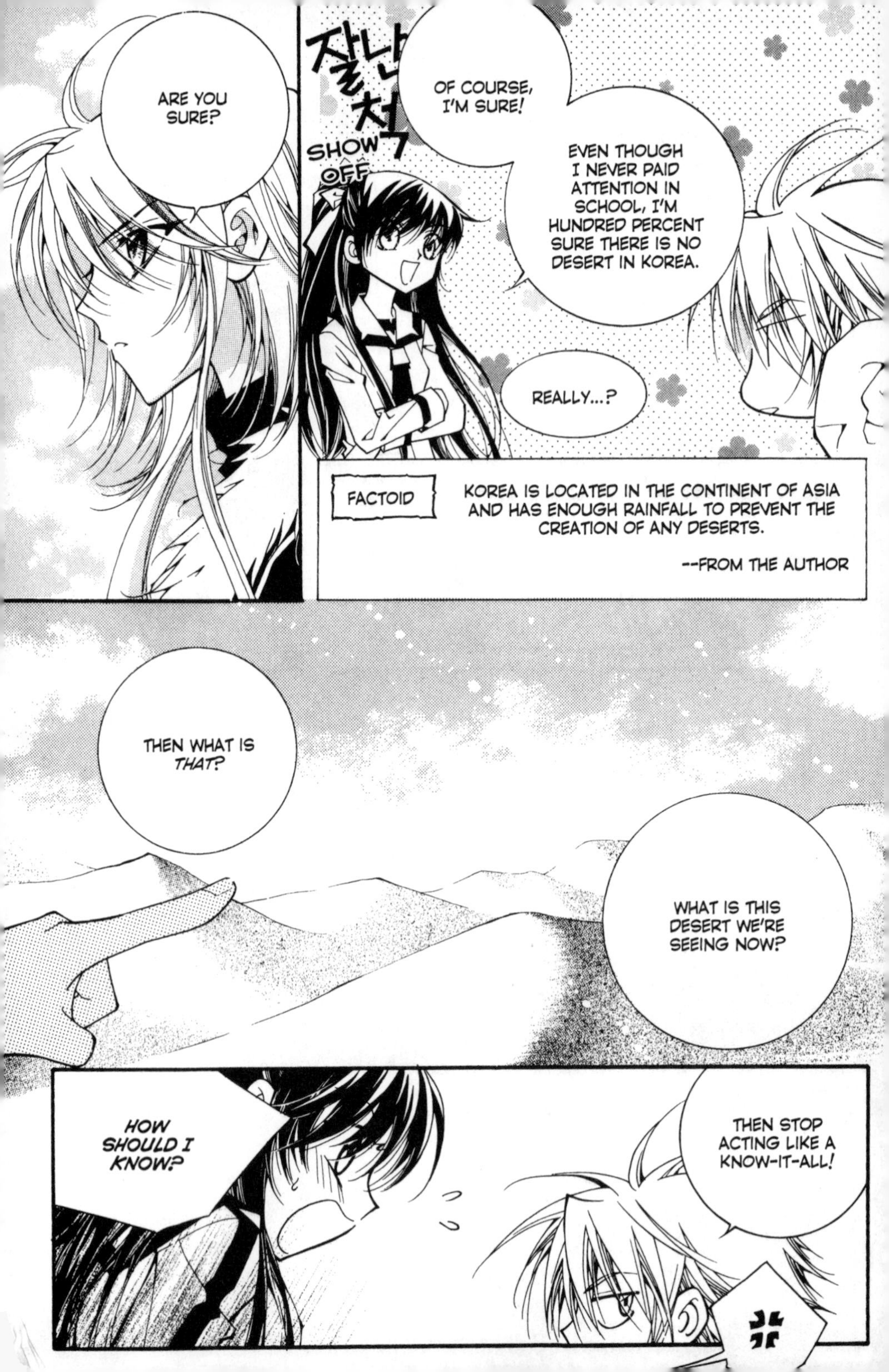
ARE YOU SURE?
잘난척
SHOW OFF
OF COURSE, I'M SURE!
EVEN THOUGH I NEVER PAID ATTENTION IN SCHOOL, I'M HUNDRED PERCENT SURE THERE IS NO DESERT IN KOREA.
REALLY...?
FACTOID
KOREA IS LOCATED IN THE CONTINENT OF ASIA AND HAS ENOUGH RAINFALL TO PREVENT THE CREATION OF ANY DESERTS.
--FROM THE AUTHOR
THEN WHAT IS *THAT*?
WHAT IS THIS DESERT WE'RE SEEING NOW?
HOW SHOULD I KNOW?
THEN STOP ACTING LIKE A KNOW-IT-ALL!

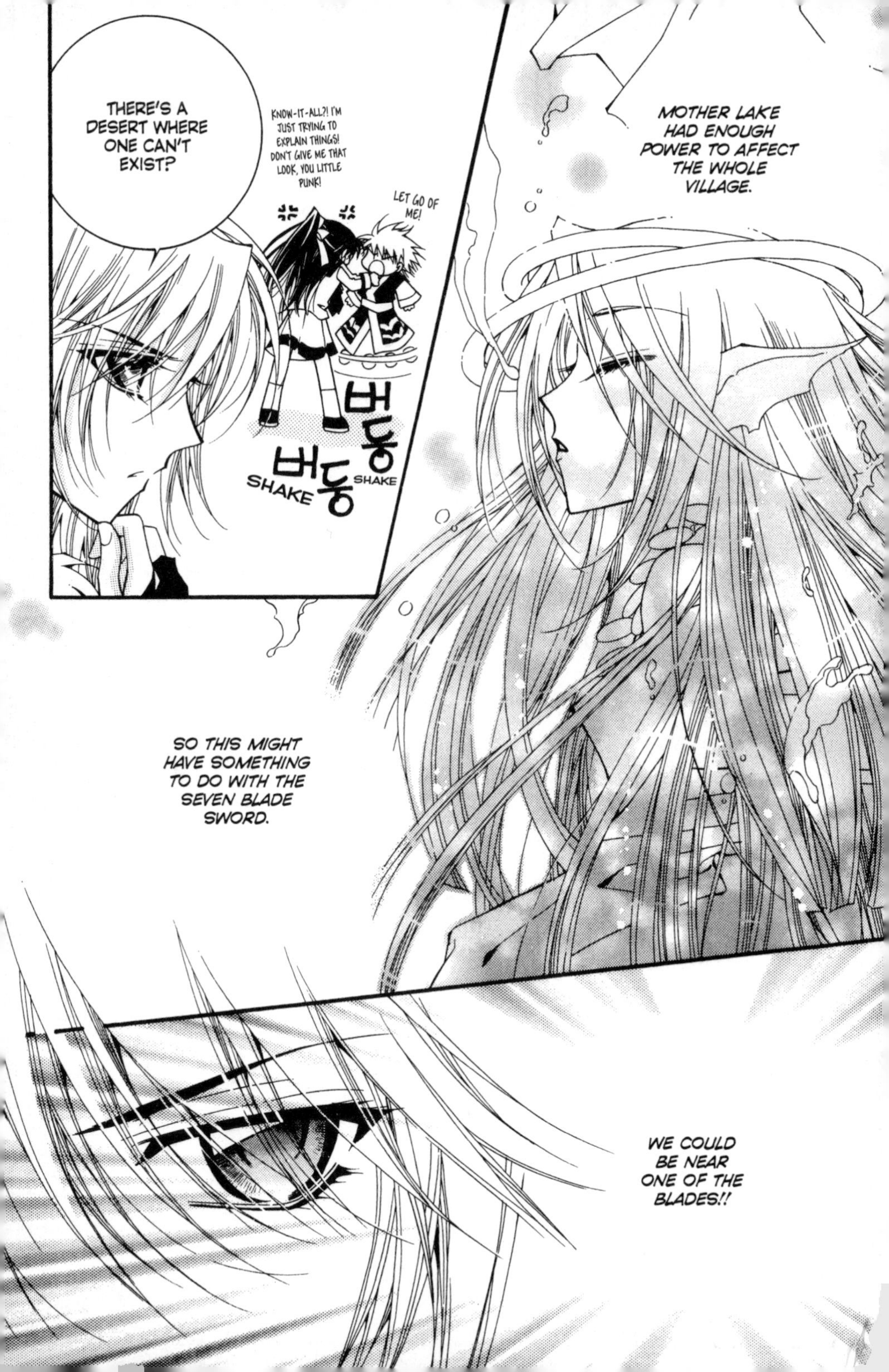

THERE'S A DESERT WHERE ONE CAN'T EXIST?
KNOW-IT-ALL?! I'M JUST TRYING TO EXPLAIN THINGS! DON'T GIVE ME THAT LOOK, YOU LITTLE PUNK!
LET GO OF ME!
버둥 버둥
SHAKE SHAKE
MOTHER LAKE HAD ENOUGH POWER TO AFFECT THE WHOLE VILLAGE.
SO THIS MIGHT HAVE SOMETHING TO DO WITH THE SEVEN BLADE SWORD.
WE COULD BE NEAR ONE OF THE BLADES!!

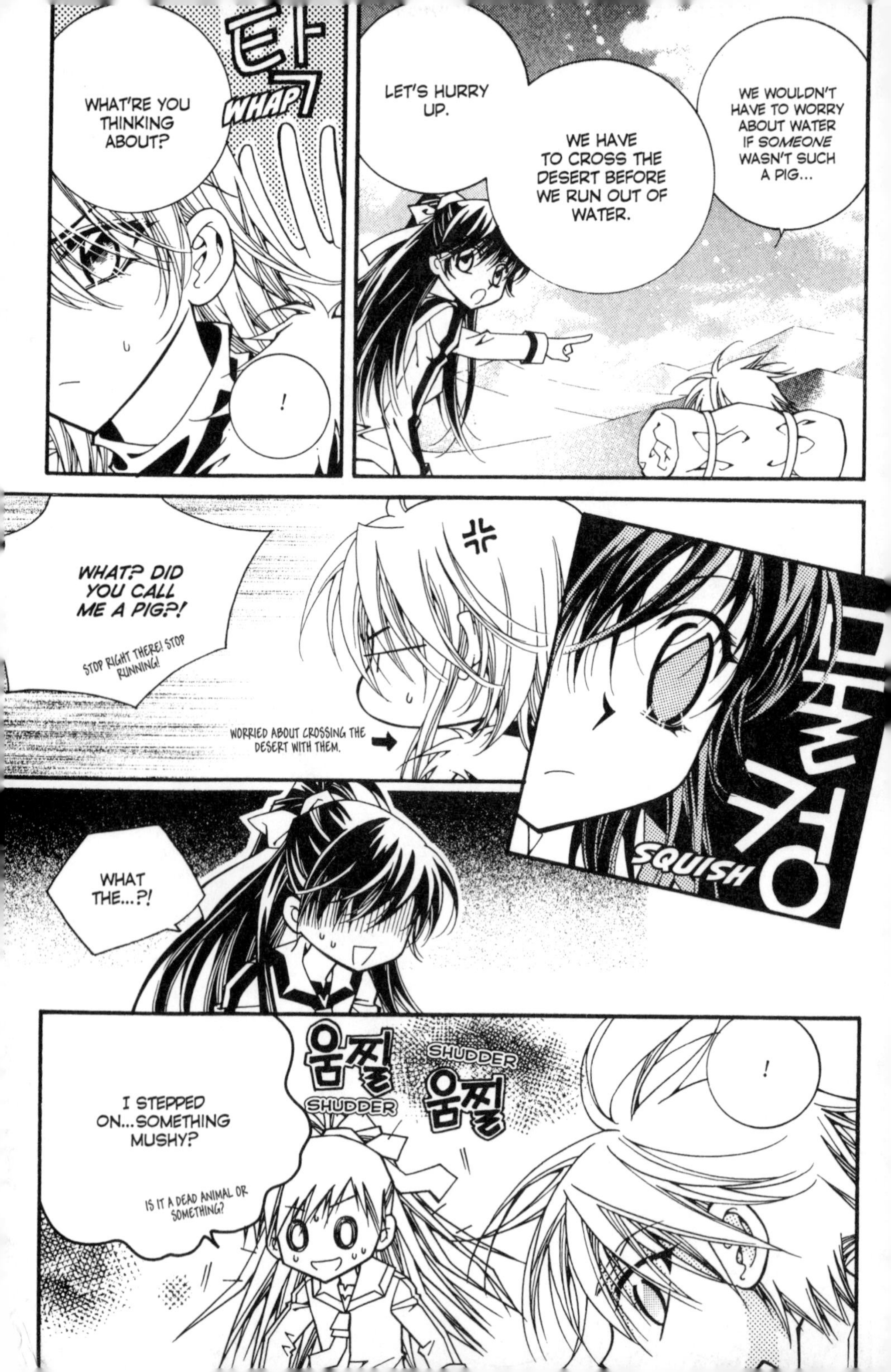

탁
WHAP
WHAT'RE YOU THINKING ABOUT?
!
LET'S HURRY UP.
WE HAVE TO CROSS THE DESERT BEFORE WE RUN OUT OF WATER.
WE WOULDN'T HAVE TO WORRY ABOUT WATER IF *SOMEONE* WASN'T SUCH A PIG...
WHAT? DID YOU CALL ME A PIG?!
STOP RIGHT THERE! STOP RUNNING!
WORRIED ABOUT CROSSING THE DESERT WITH THEM.
SQUISH
WHAT THE...?!
I STEPPED ON...SOMETHING MUSHY?
IS IT A DEAD ANIMAL OR SOMETHING?
움찔
SHUDDER
움찔
SHUDDER
!

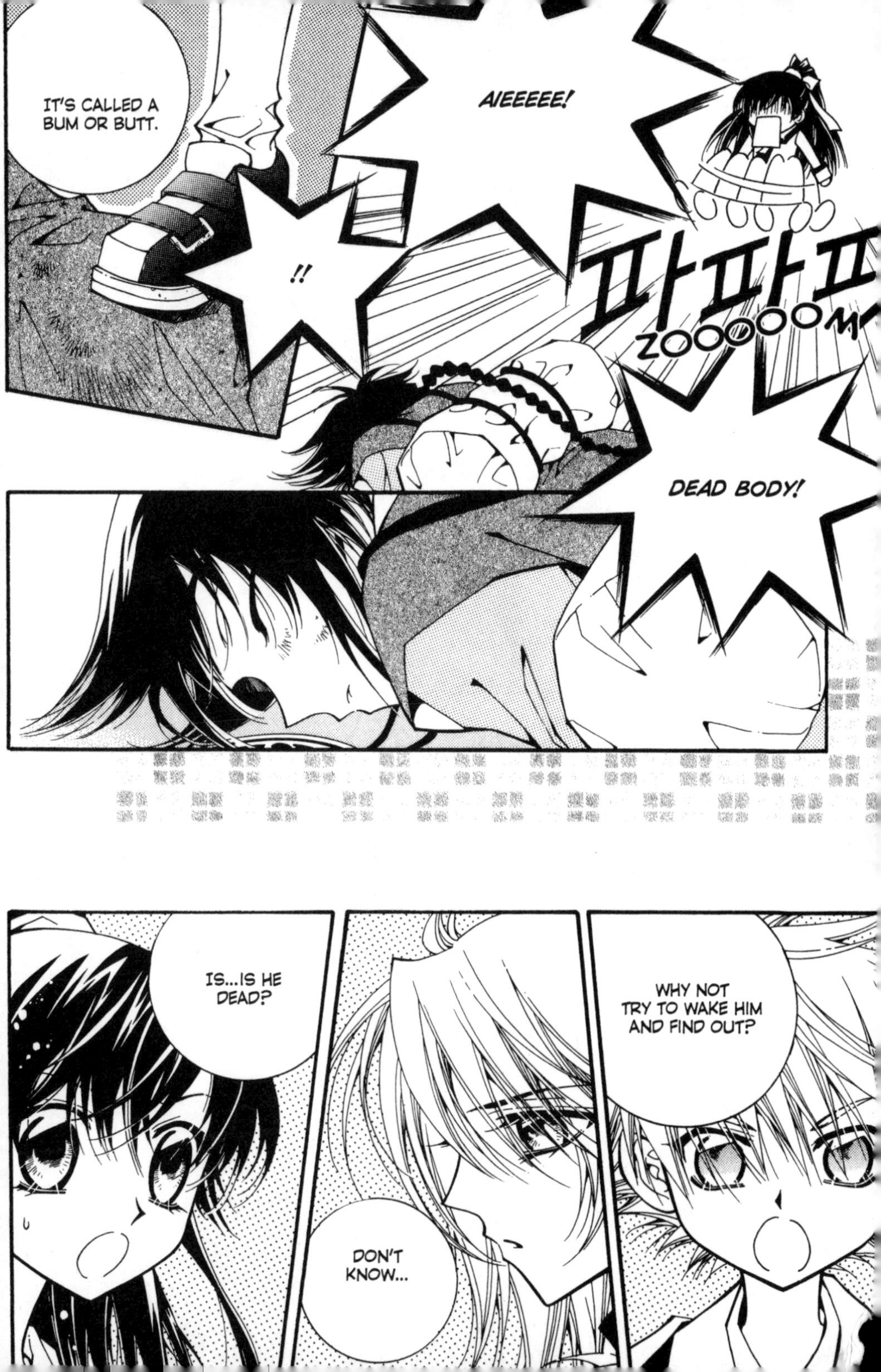

IT'S CALLED A BUM OR BUTT.
!!
AIEEEEE!
ZOOOOOM
DEAD BODY!
IS...IS HE DEAD?
DON'T KNOW...
WHY NOT TRY TO WAKE HIM AND FIND OUT?

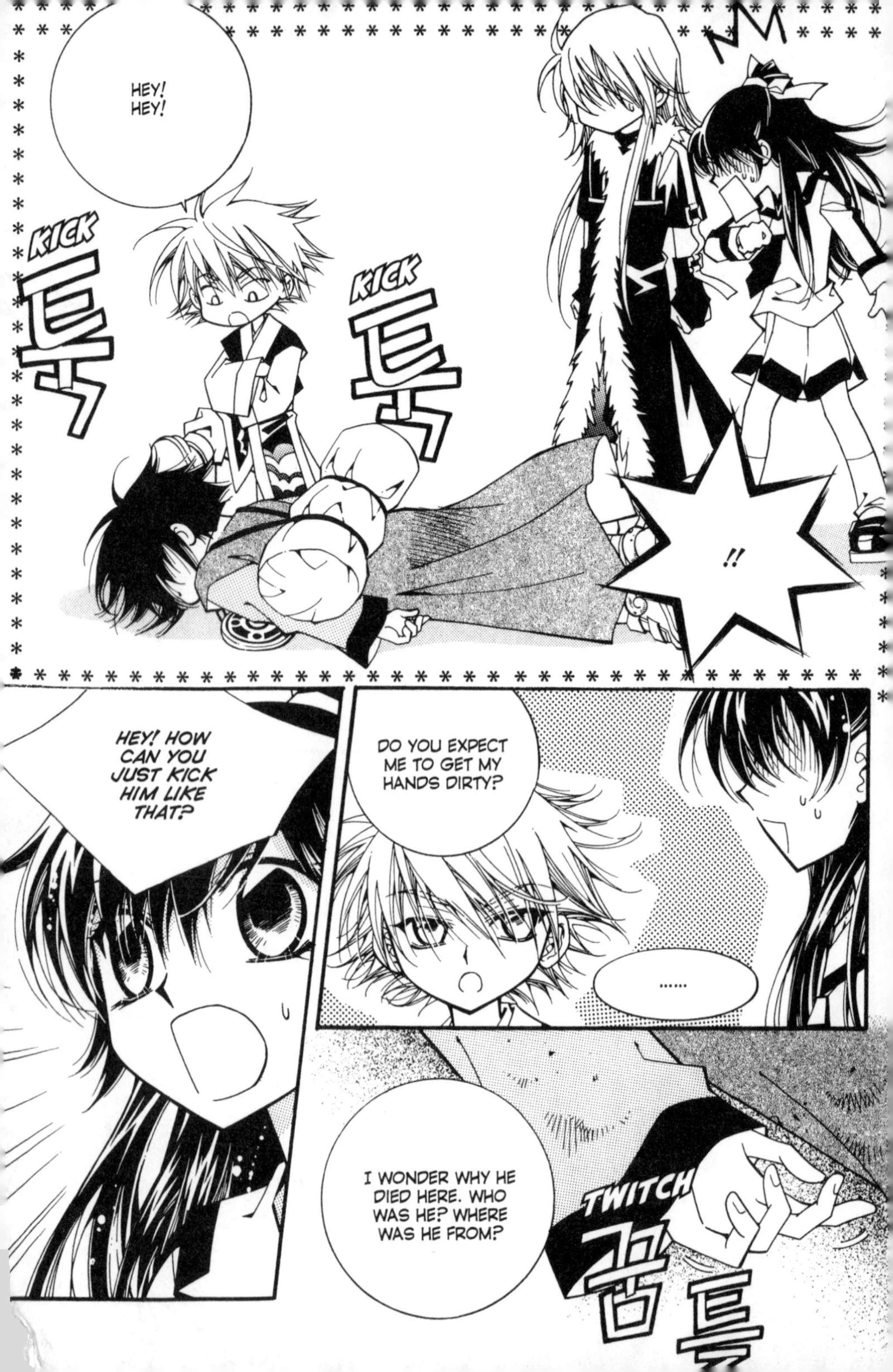
HEY! HEY!
KICK
툭
KICK
툭
!!
HEY! HOW CAN YOU JUST KICK HIM LIKE THAT?
DO YOU EXPECT ME TO GET MY HANDS DIRTY?
......
I WONDER WHY HE DIED HERE. WHO WAS HE? WHERE WAS HE FROM?
TWITCH
꿈틀

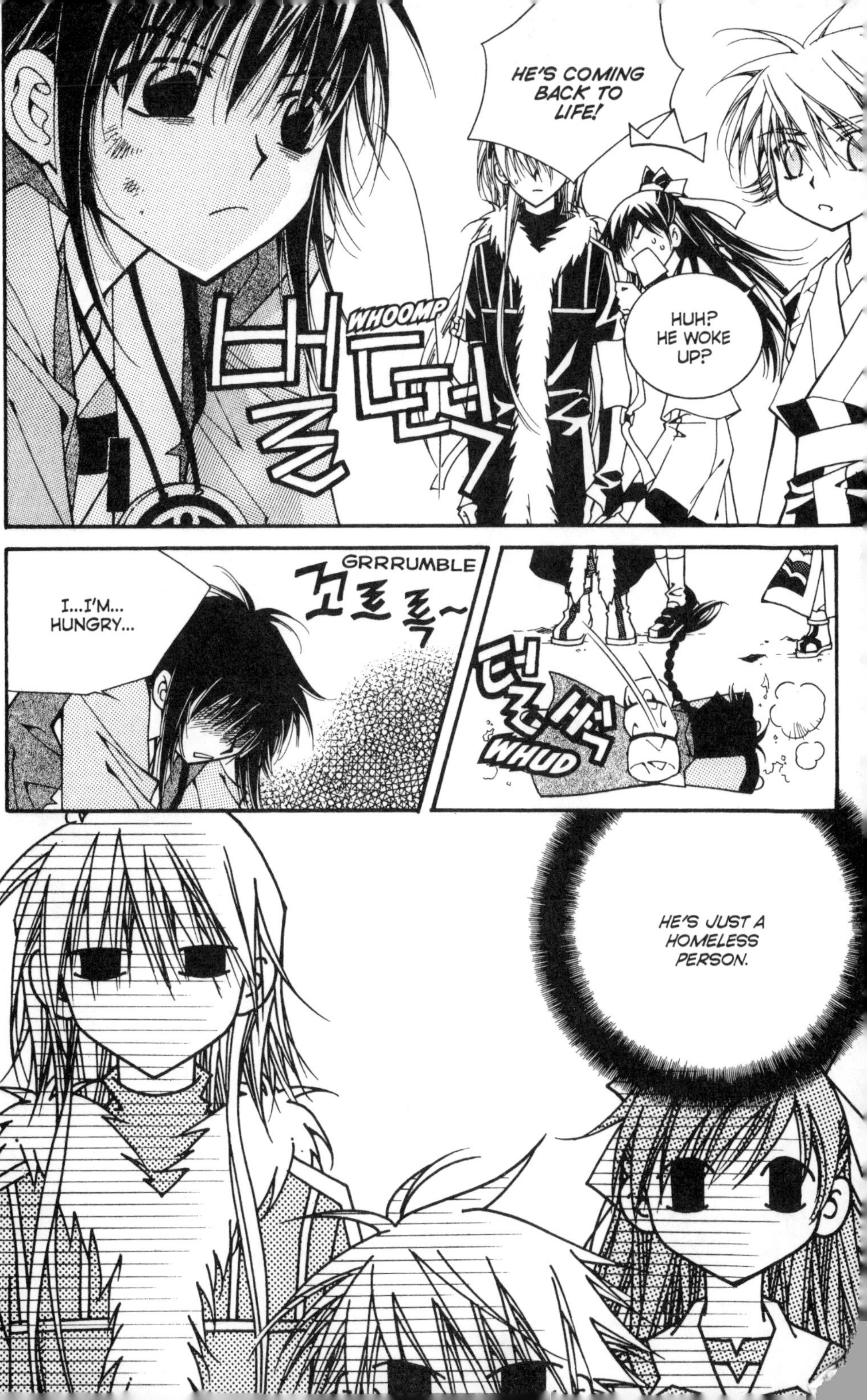
WHOOMP
HE'S COMING BACK TO LIFE!
HUH? HE WOKE UP?
I...I'M... HUNGRY...
GRRRUMBLE
꼬르륵~
WHUD
HE'S JUST A HOMELESS PERSON.

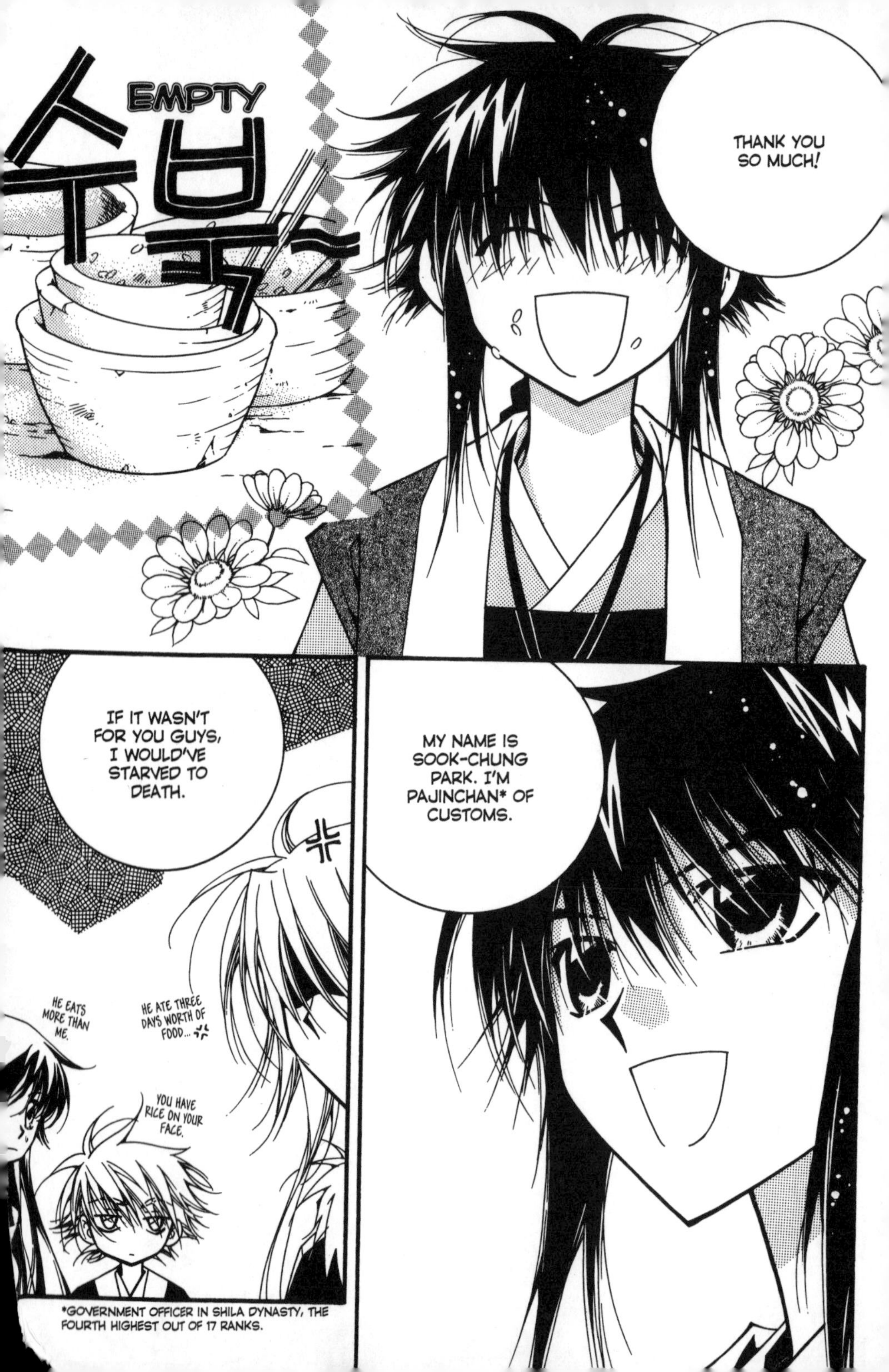
EMPTY
THANK YOU SO MUCH!
IF IT WASN'T FOR YOU GUYS, I WOULD'VE STARVED TO DEATH.
HE EATS MORE THAN ME.
HE ATE THREE DAYS WORTH OF FOOD...
YOU HAVE RICE ON YOUR FACE.
MY NAME IS SOOK-CHUNG PARK. I'M PAJINCHAN* OF CUSTOMS.

*GOVERNMENT OFFICER IN SHILA DYNASTY, THE FOURTH HIGHEST OUT OF 17 RANKS.

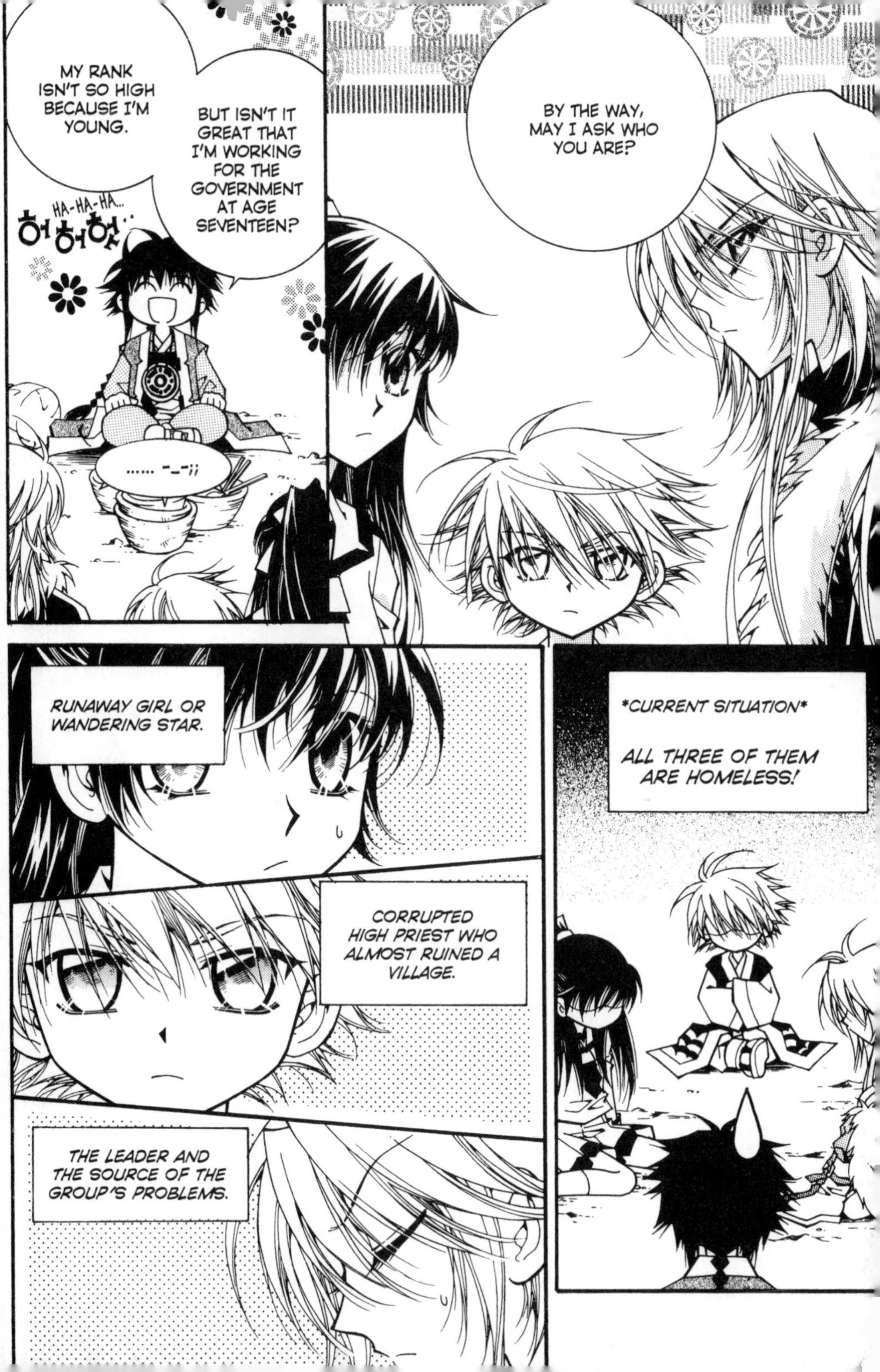

MY RANK ISN'T SO HIGH BECAUSE I'M YOUNG.
BUT ISN'T IT GREAT THAT I'M WORKING FOR THE GOVERNMENT AT AGE SEVENTEEN?
HA-HA-HA...
허허헛..
...... -_-;;
BY THE WAY, MAY I ASK WHO YOU ARE?
RUNAWAY GIRL OR WANDERING STAR.
CORRUPTED HIGH PRIEST WHO ALMOST RUINED A VILLAGE.
THE LEADER AND THE SOURCE OF THE GROUP'S PROBLEMS.
CURRENT SITUATION
ALL THREE OF THEM ARE HOMELESS!

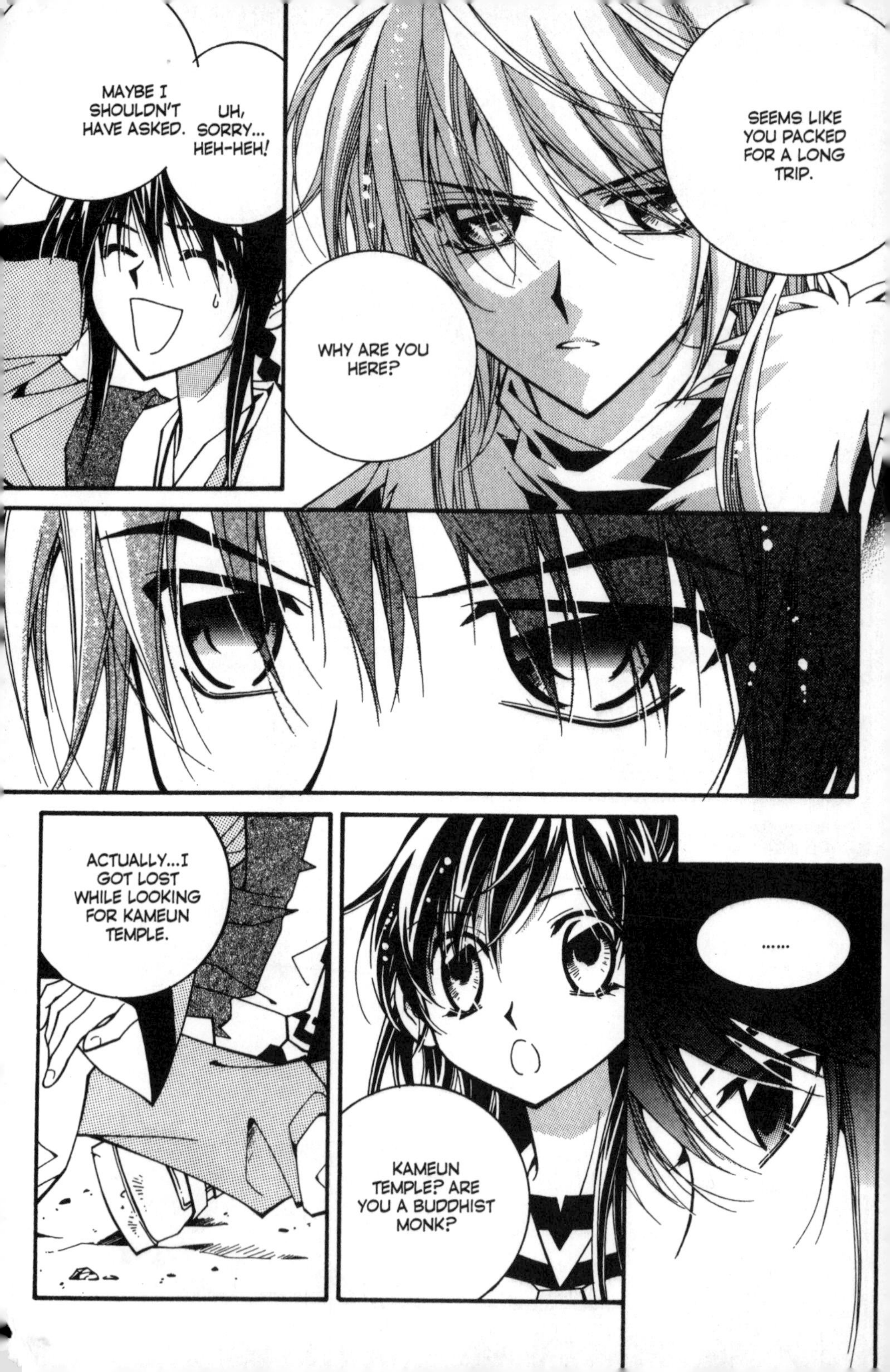
MAYBE I SHOULDN'T HAVE ASKED.
UH, SORRY... HEH-HEH!
SEEMS LIKE YOU PACKED FOR A LONG TRIP.
WHY ARE YOU HERE?
ACTUALLY...I GOT LOST WHILE LOOKING FOR KAMEUN TEMPLE.
KAMEUN TEMPLE? ARE YOU A BUDDHIST MONK?
......

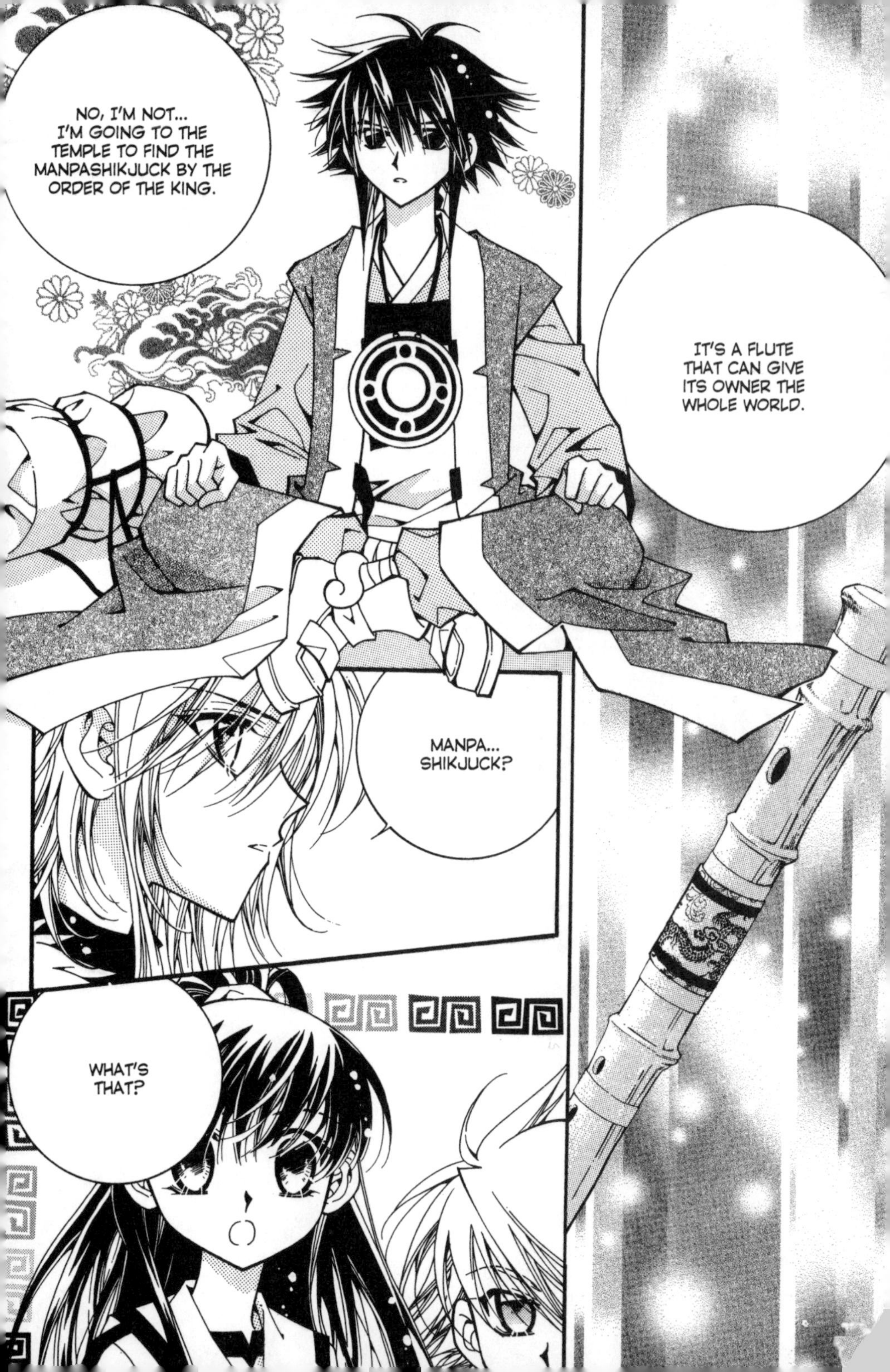
NO, I'M NOT... I'M GOING TO THE TEMPLE TO FIND THE MANPASHIKJUCK BY THE ORDER OF THE KING.
MANPA... SHIKJUCK?
WHAT'S THAT?
IT'S A FLUTE THAT CAN GIVE ITS OWNER THE WHOLE WORLD.

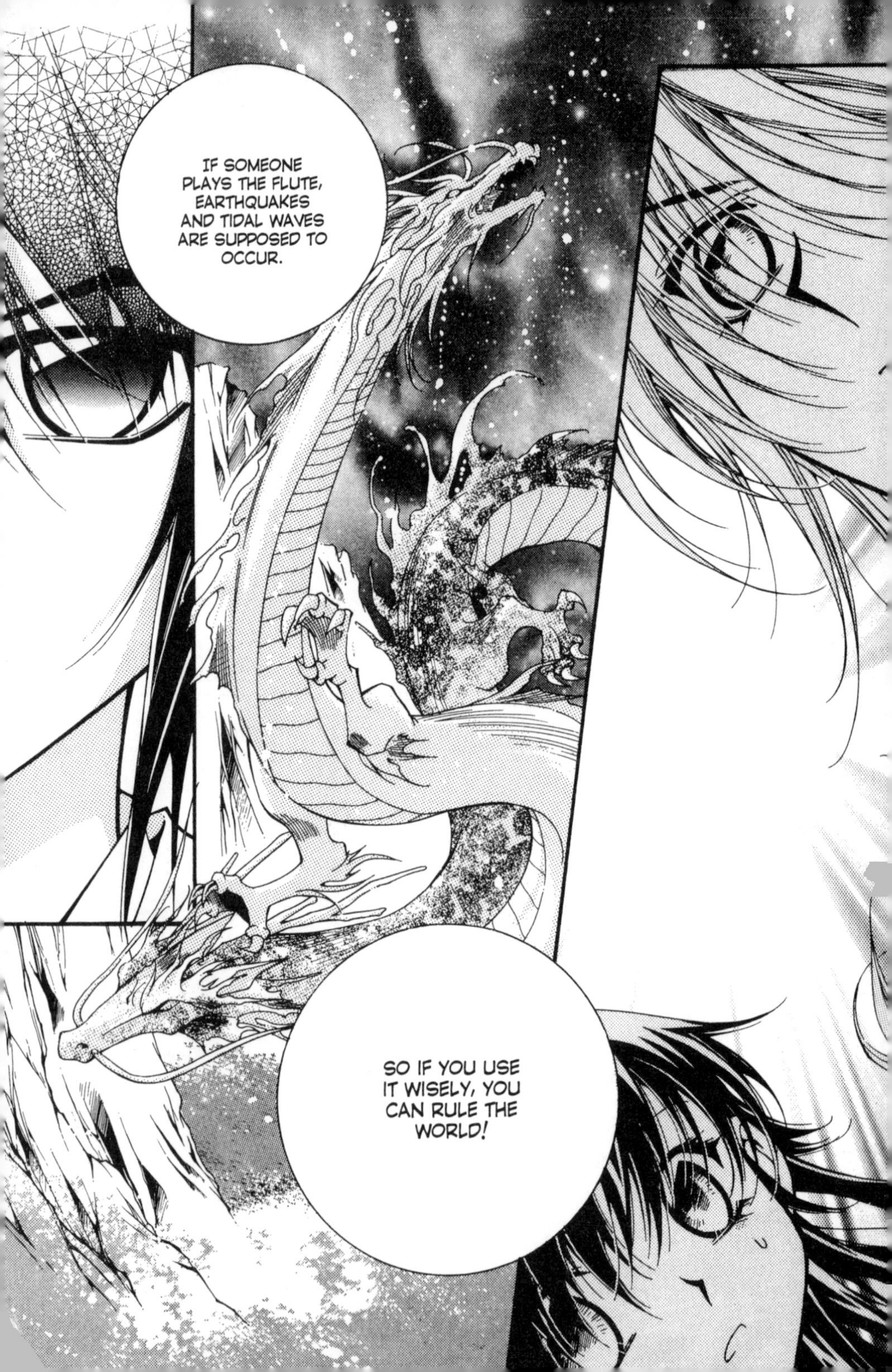
IF SOMEONE PLAYS THE FLUTE, EARTHQUAKES AND TIDAL WAVES ARE SUPPOSED TO OCCUR.
SO IF YOU USE IT WISELY, YOU CAN RULE THE WORLD!

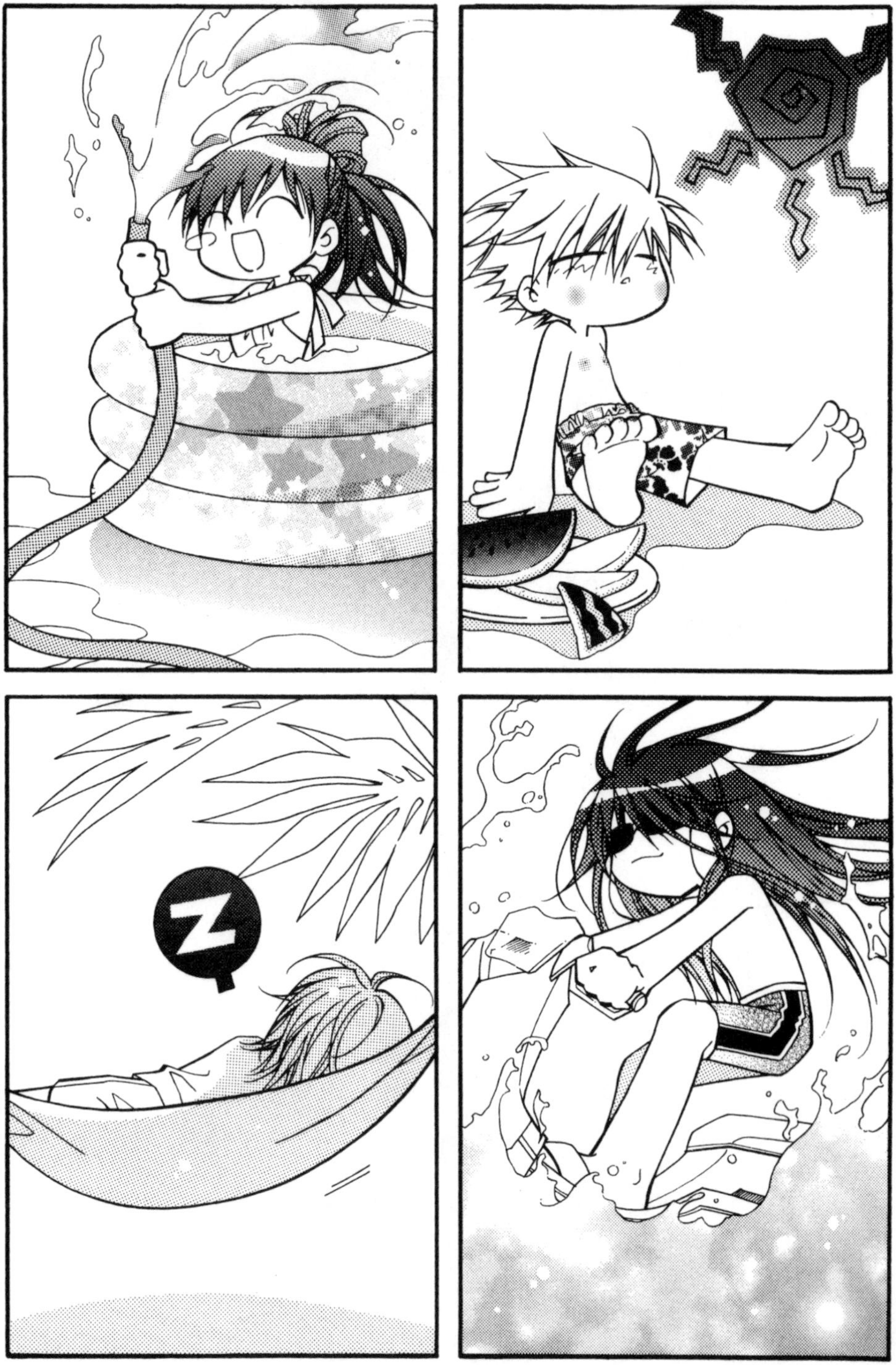
Z

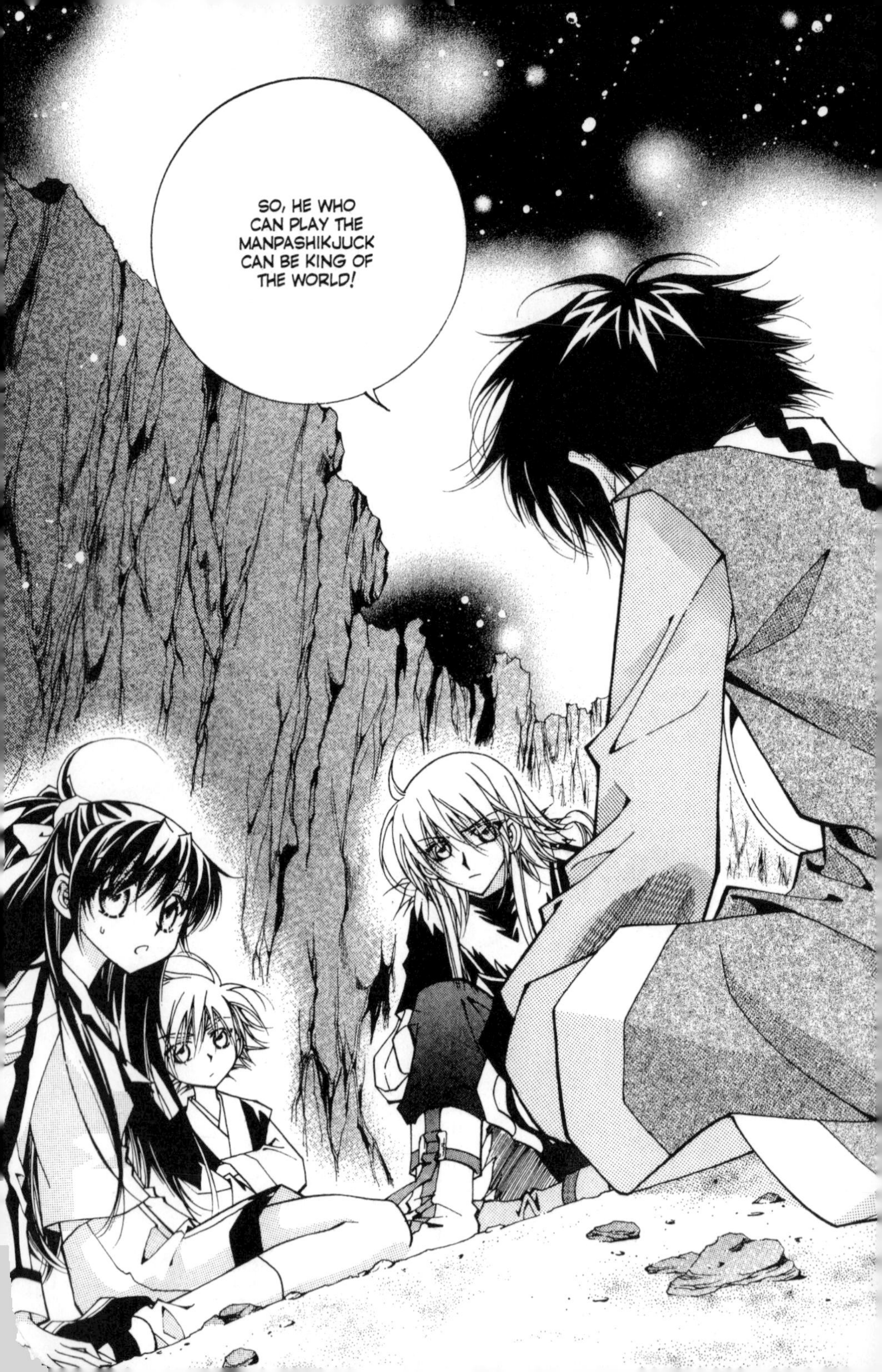
SO, HE WHO CAN PLAY THE MANPASHIKJUCK CAN BE KING OF THE WORLD!

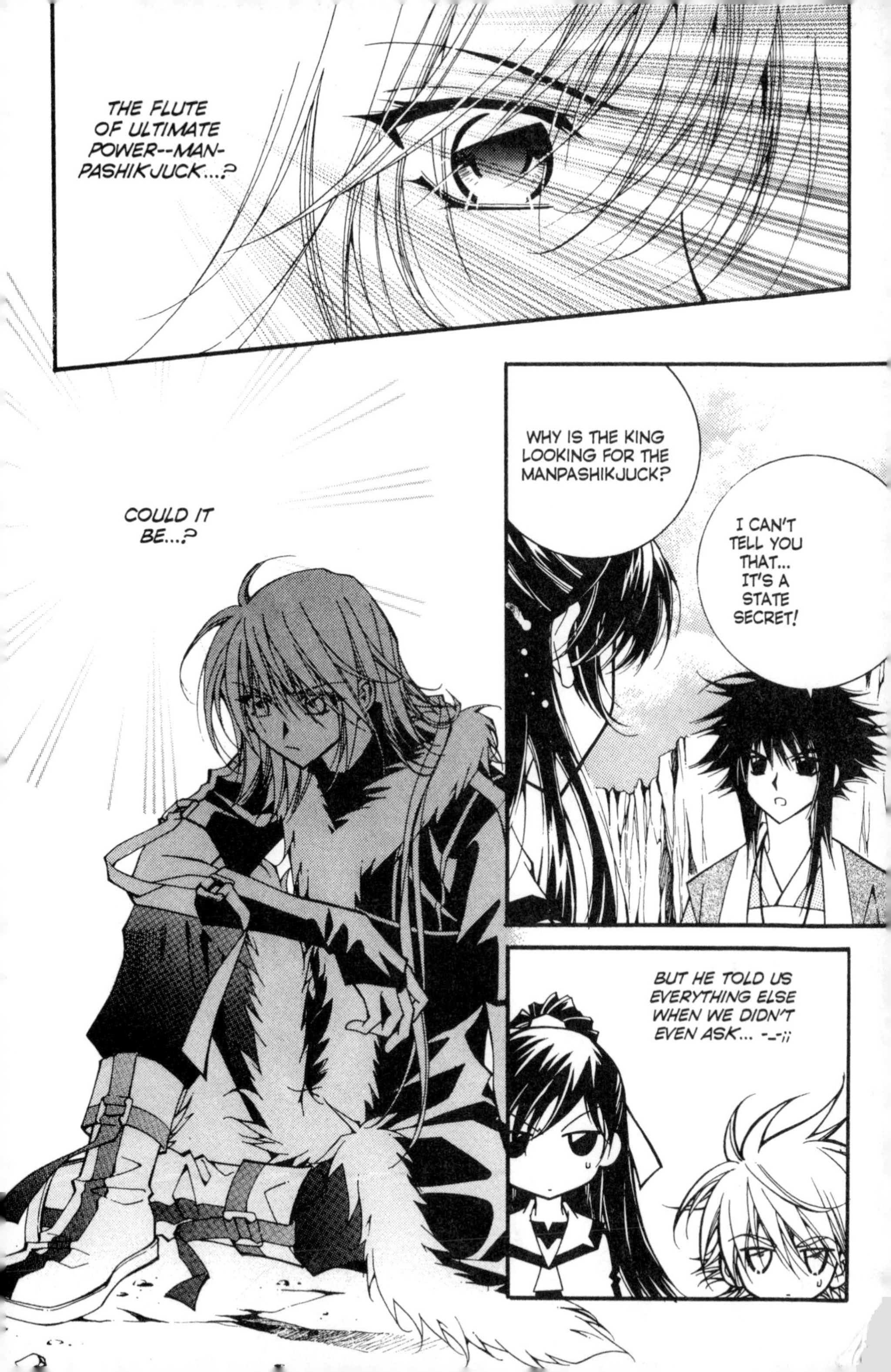
THE FLUTE OF ULTIMATE POWER--MAN-PASHIKJUCK...?
COULD IT BE...?
WHY IS THE KING LOOKING FOR THE MANPASHIKJUCK?
I CAN'T TELL YOU THAT... IT'S A STATE SECRET!
BUT HE TOLD US EVERYTHING ELSE WHEN WE DIDN'T EVEN ASK... -_-;;

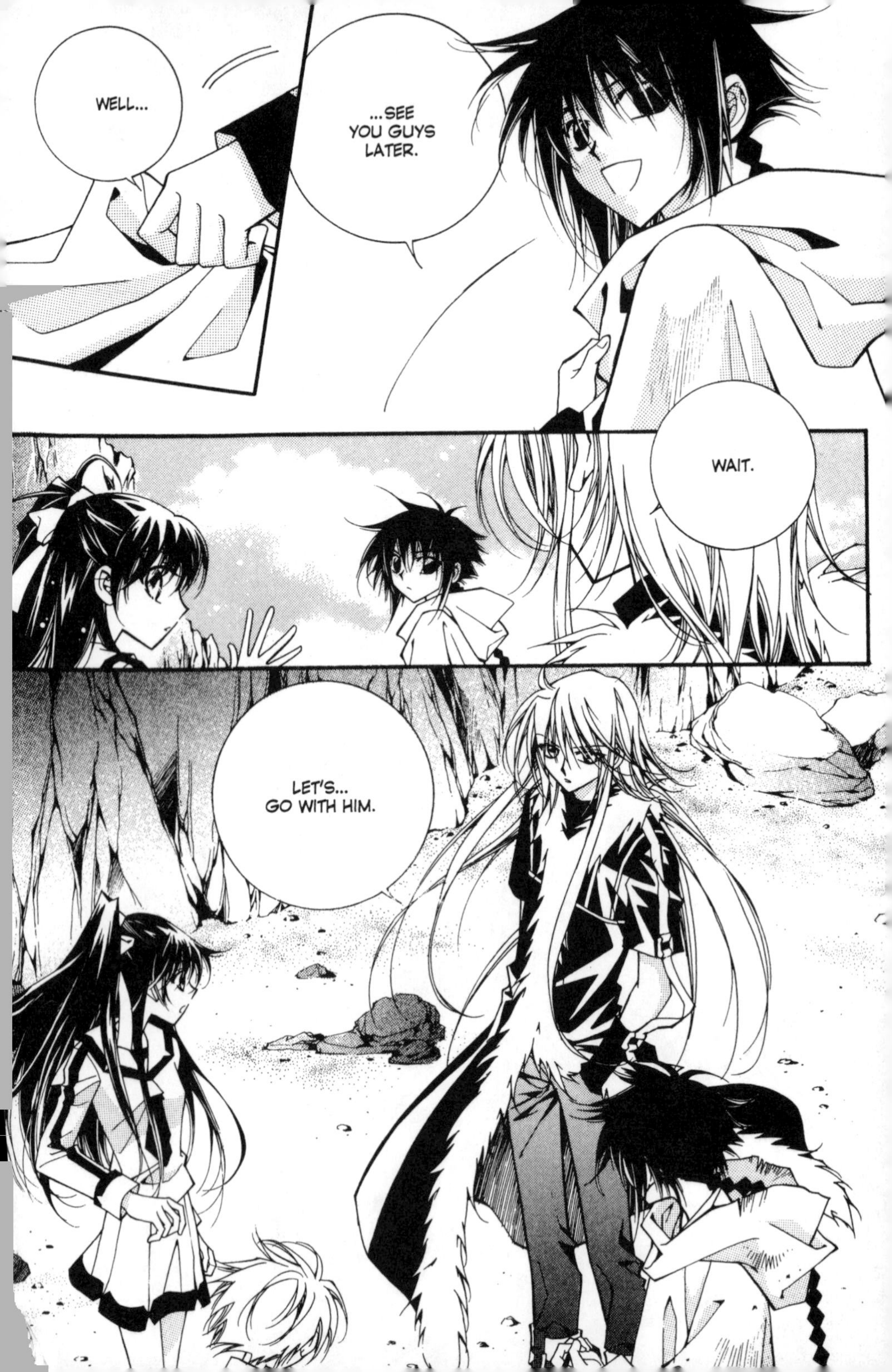

WELL...
...SEE YOU GUYS LATER.
WAIT.
LET'S... GO WITH HIM.

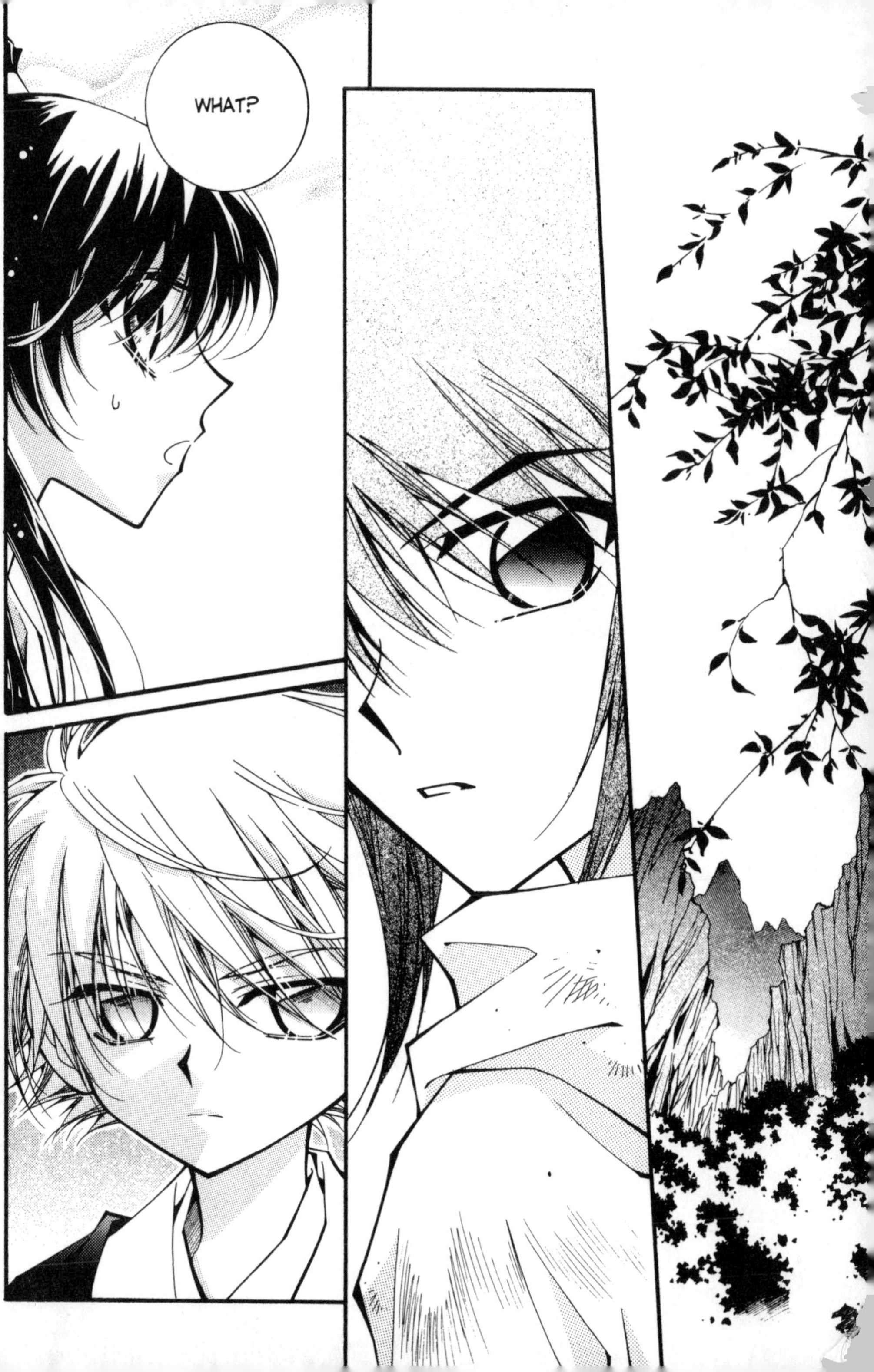
WHAT?

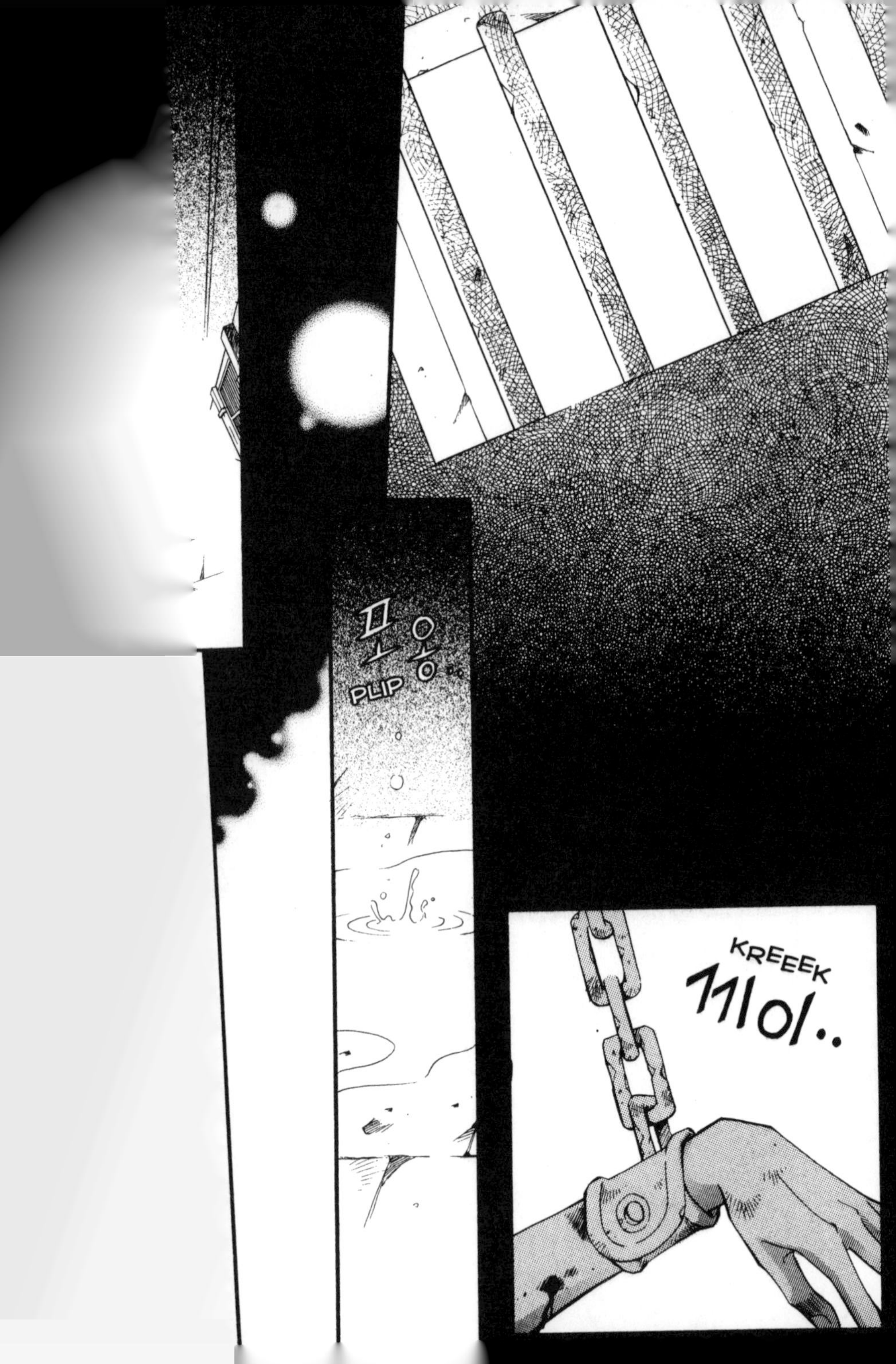
포옹..
PLIP
KREEEK
끼이..

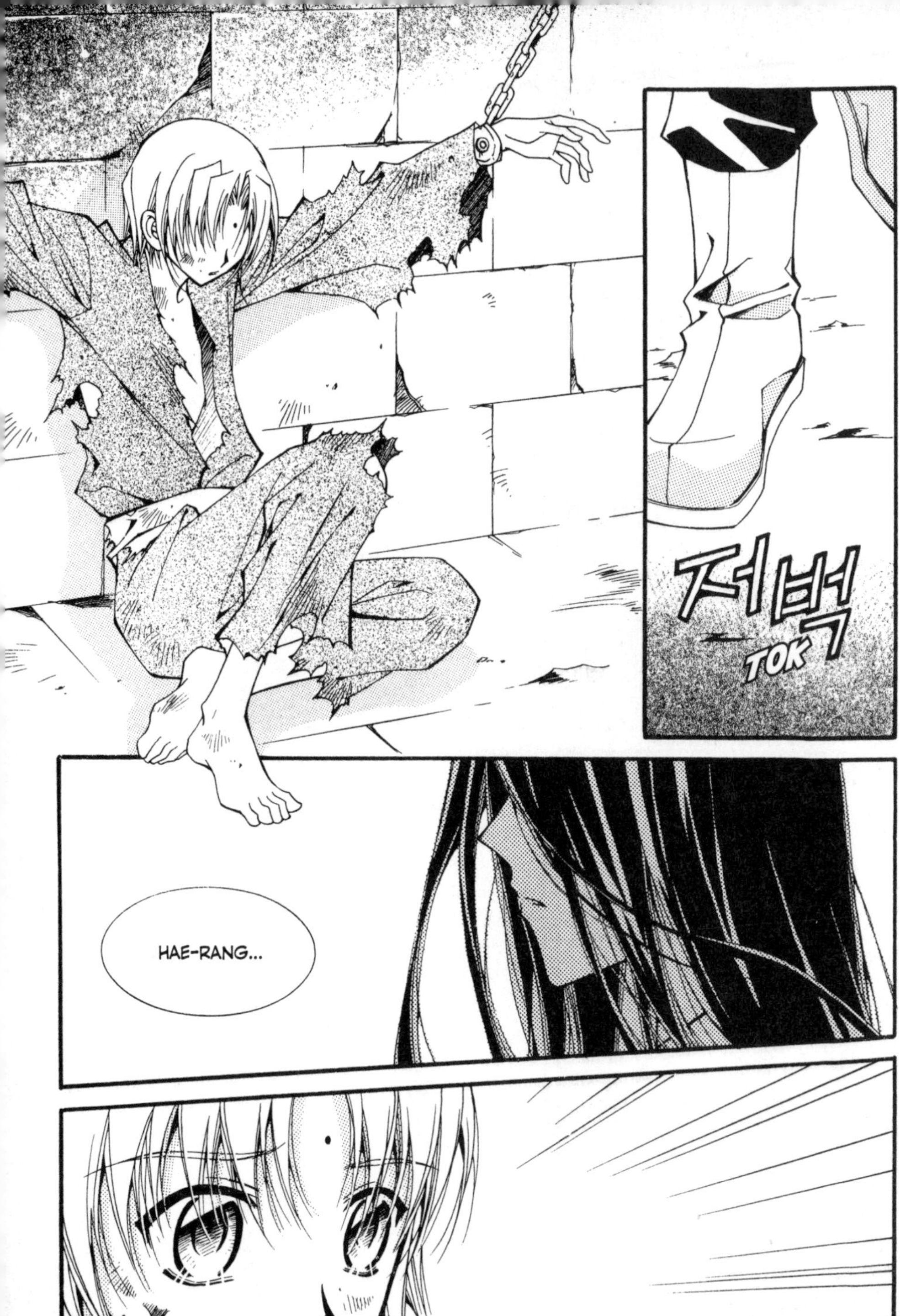
저벅
TOK
HAE-RANG...

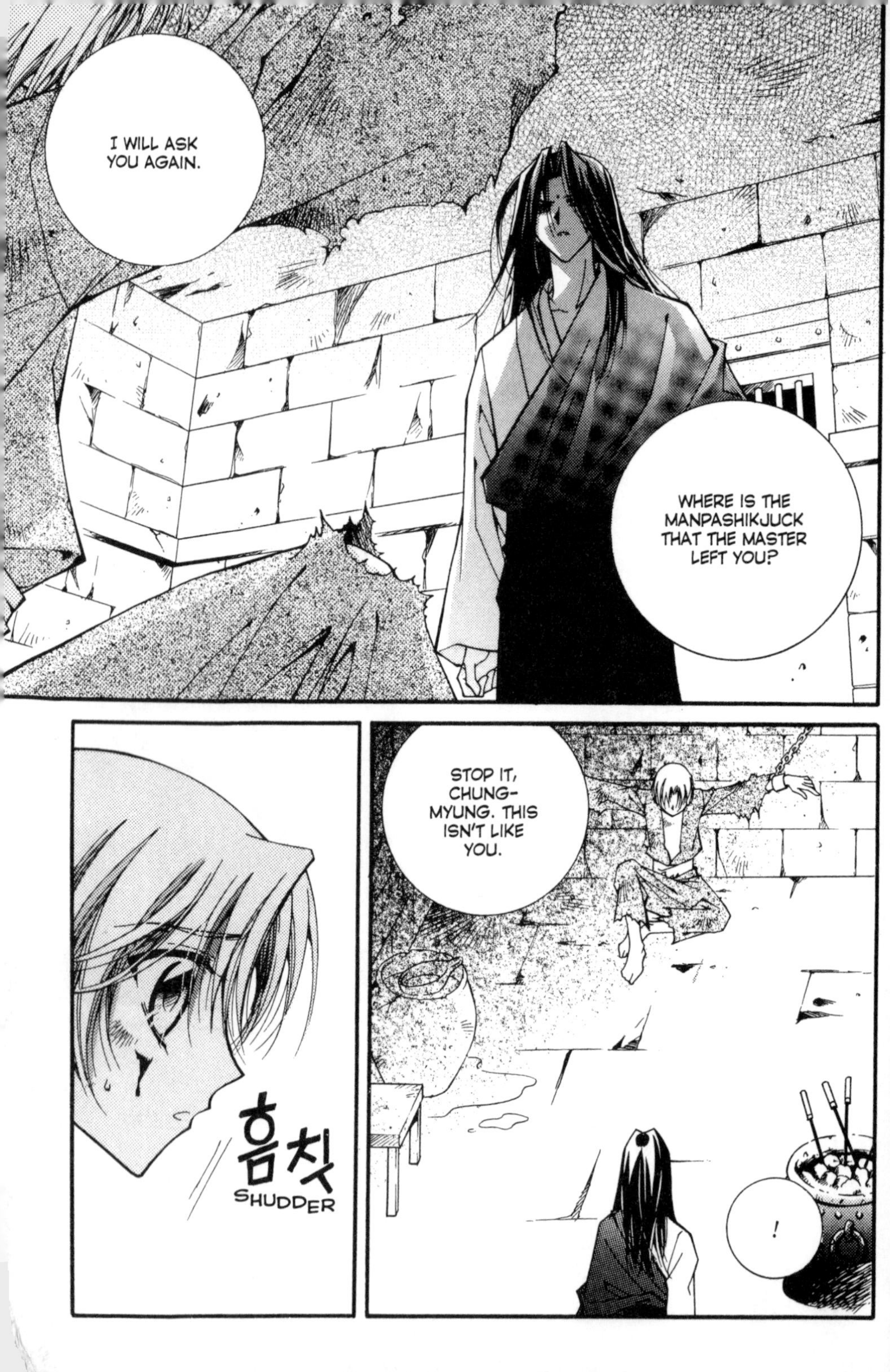
I WILL ASK YOU AGAIN.
WHERE IS THE MANPASHIKJUCK THAT THE MASTER LEFT YOU?
흠칫
SHUDDER
STOP IT, CHUNG-MYUNG. THIS ISN'T LIKE YOU.
!

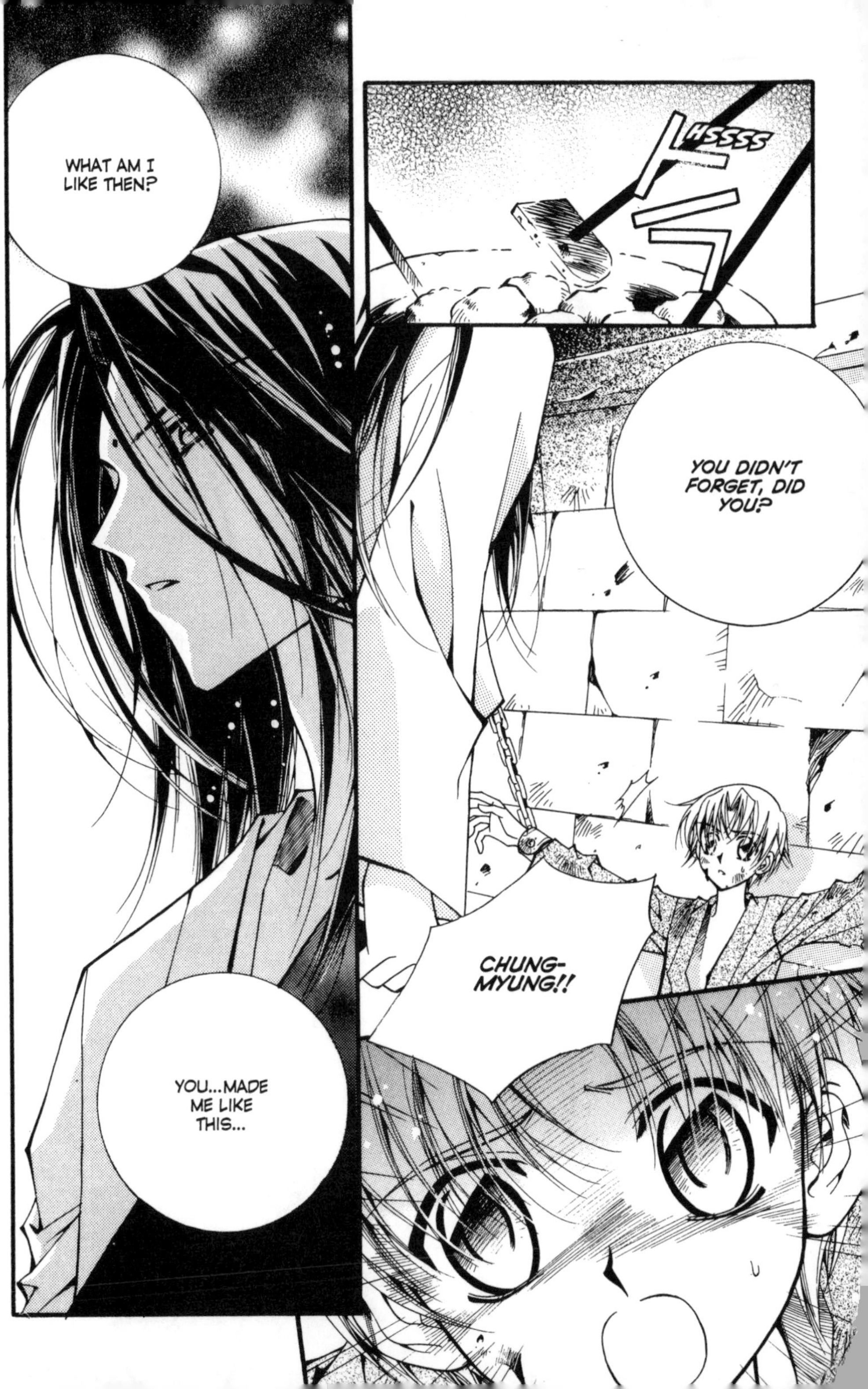
WHAT AM I LIKE THEN?
YOU...MADE ME LIKE THIS...
HSSSS
YOU DIDN'T FORGET, DID YOU?
CHUNG-MYUNG!!

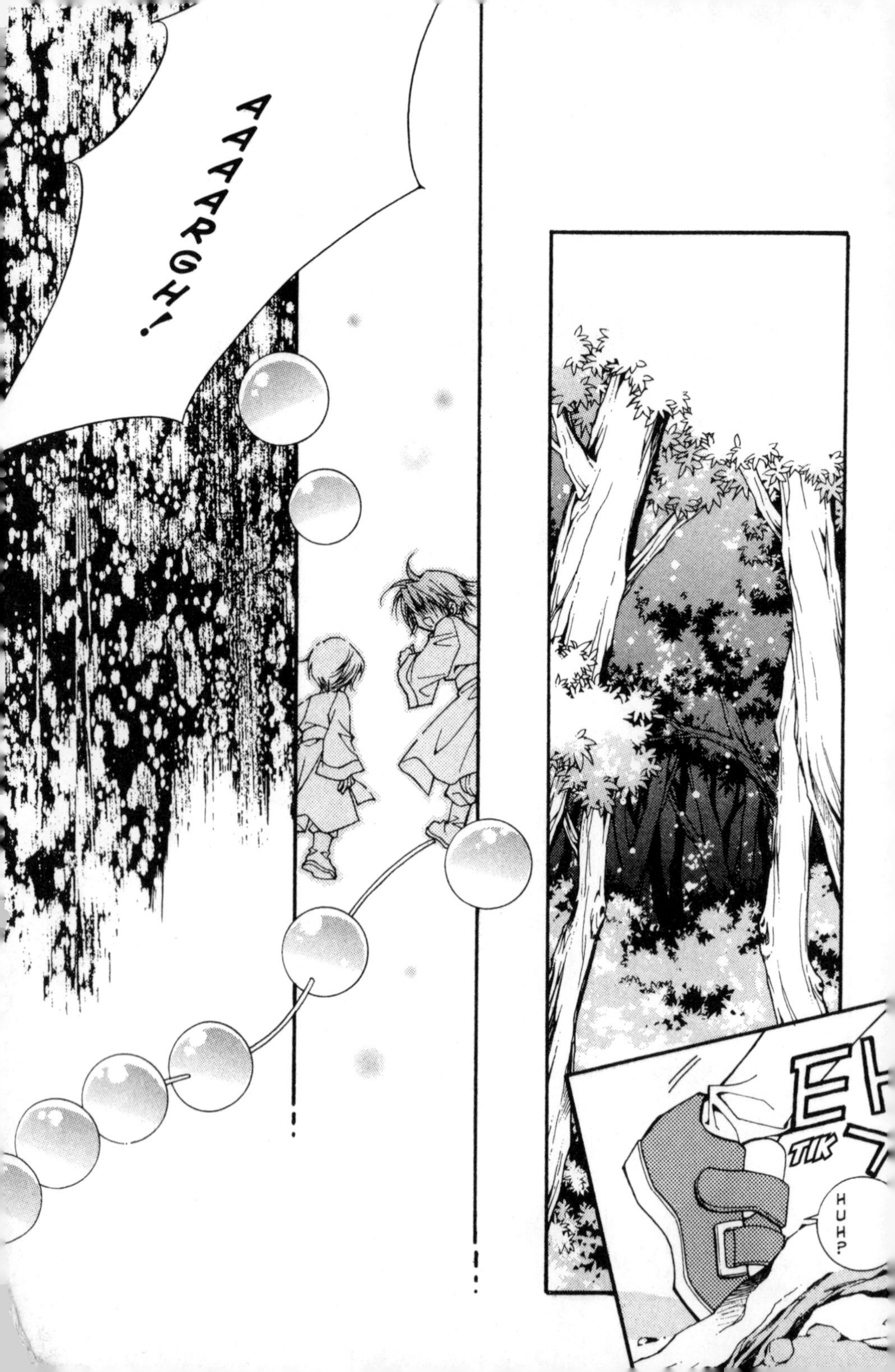

AAAARGH!
EH
TIK
HUH?

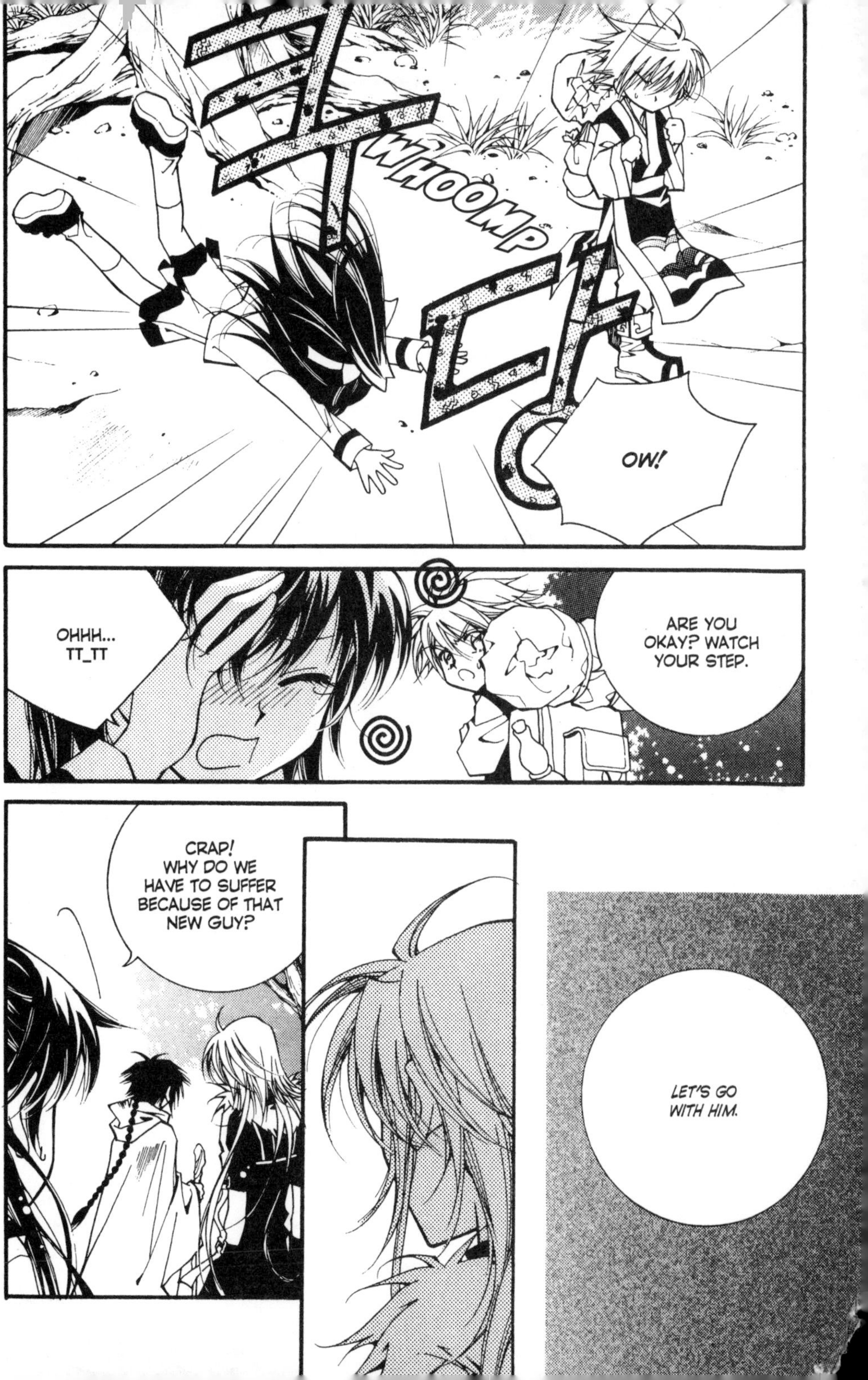
WHOOMP
OW!
OHHH... TT_TT
ARE YOU OKAY? WATCH YOUR STEP.
CRAP! WHY DO WE HAVE TO SUFFER BECAUSE OF THAT NEW GUY?
LET'S GO WITH HIM.

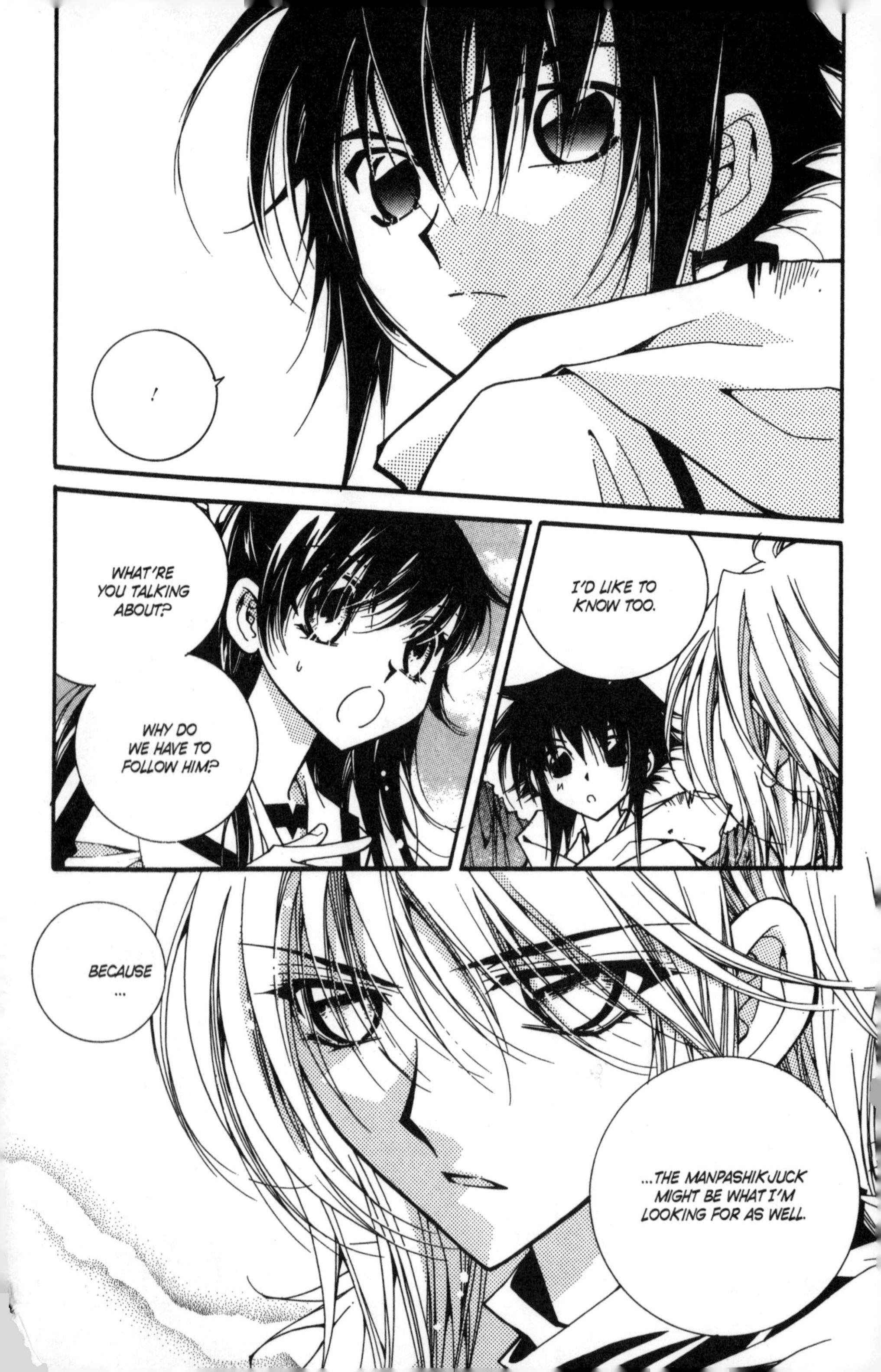
!
WHAT'RE YOU TALKING ABOUT?
WHY DO WE HAVE TO FOLLOW HIM?
I'D LIKE TO KNOW TOO.
BECAUSE ...
...THE MANPASHIKJUCK MIGHT BE WHAT I'M LOOKING FOR AS WELL.

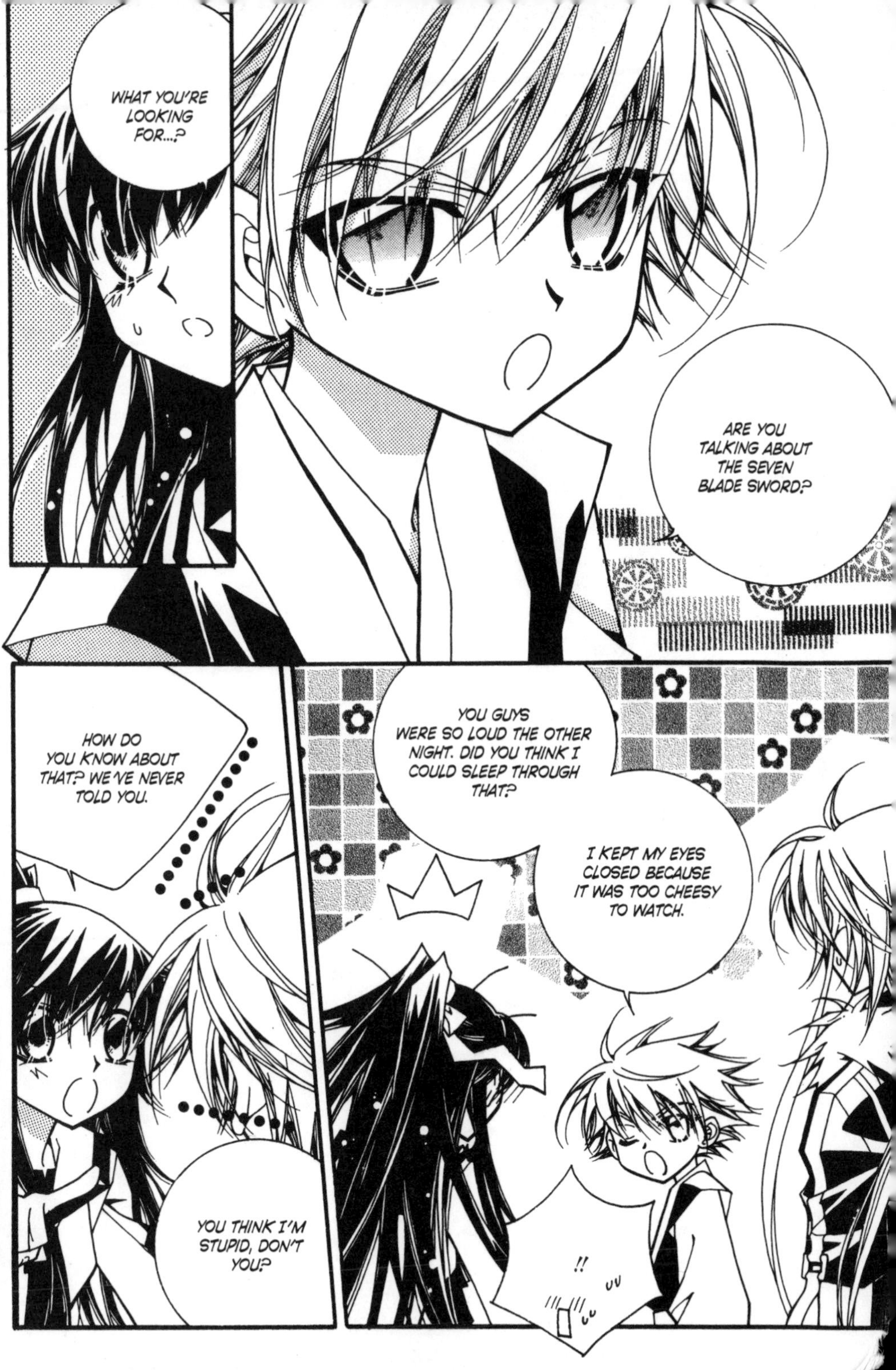
WHAT YOU'RE LOOKING FOR...?
ARE YOU TALKING ABOUT THE SEVEN BLADE SWORD?
HOW DO YOU KNOW ABOUT THAT? WE'VE NEVER TOLD YOU.
YOU THINK I'M STUPID, DON'T YOU?
YOU GUYS WERE SO LOUD THE OTHER NIGHT. DID YOU THINK I COULD SLEEP THROUGH THAT?
I KEPT MY EYES CLOSED BECAUSE IT WAS TOO CHEESY TO WATCH.
!!

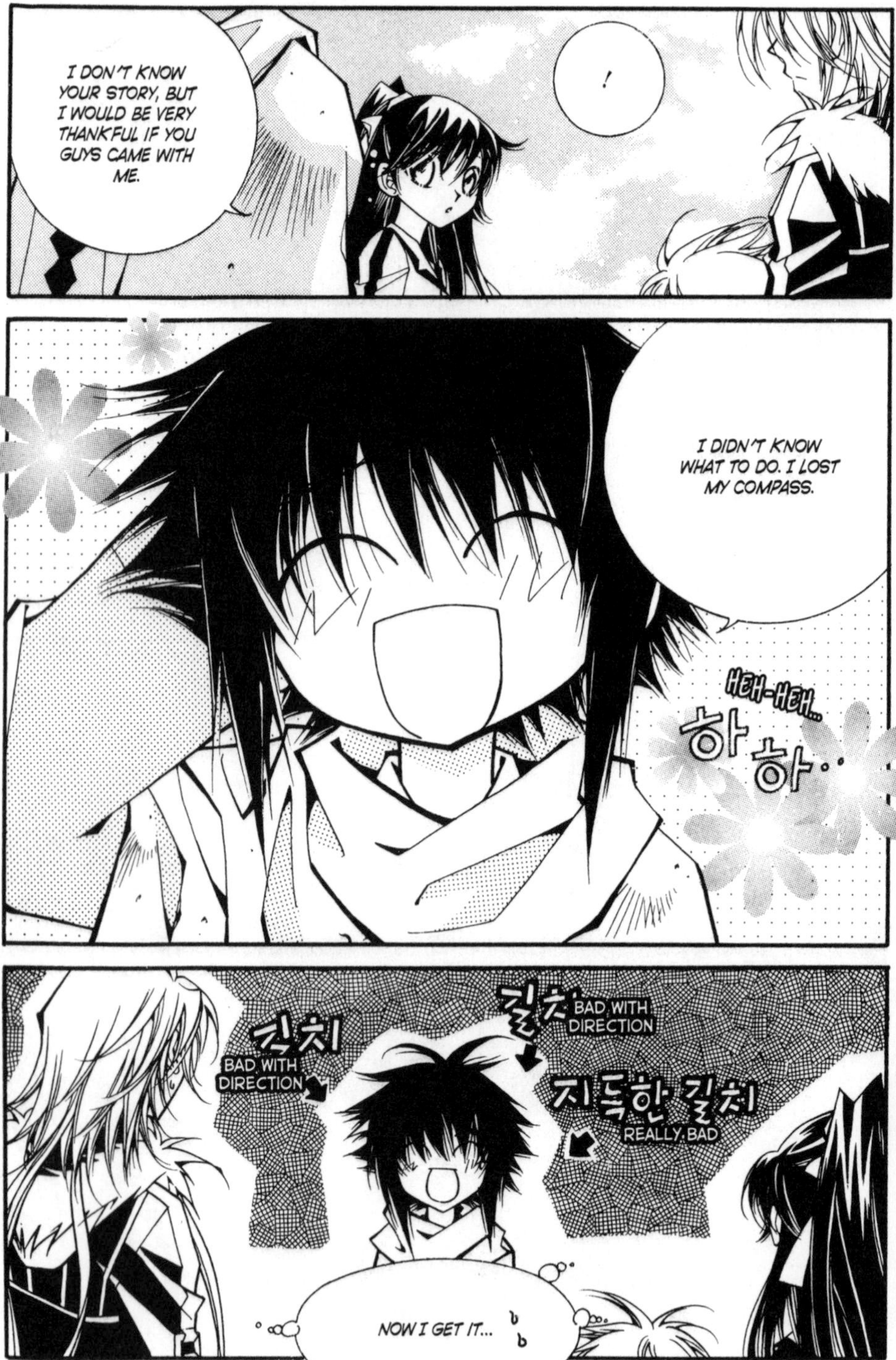
I DON'T KNOW YOUR STORY, BUT I WOULD BE VERY THANKFUL IF YOU GUYS CAME WITH ME.
!
I DIDN'T KNOW WHAT TO DO. I LOST MY COMPASS.
HEH-HEH...
하하..
길치
BAD WITH DIRECTION
길치
BAD WITH DIRECTION
지독한 길치
REALLY BAD
NOW I GET IT...

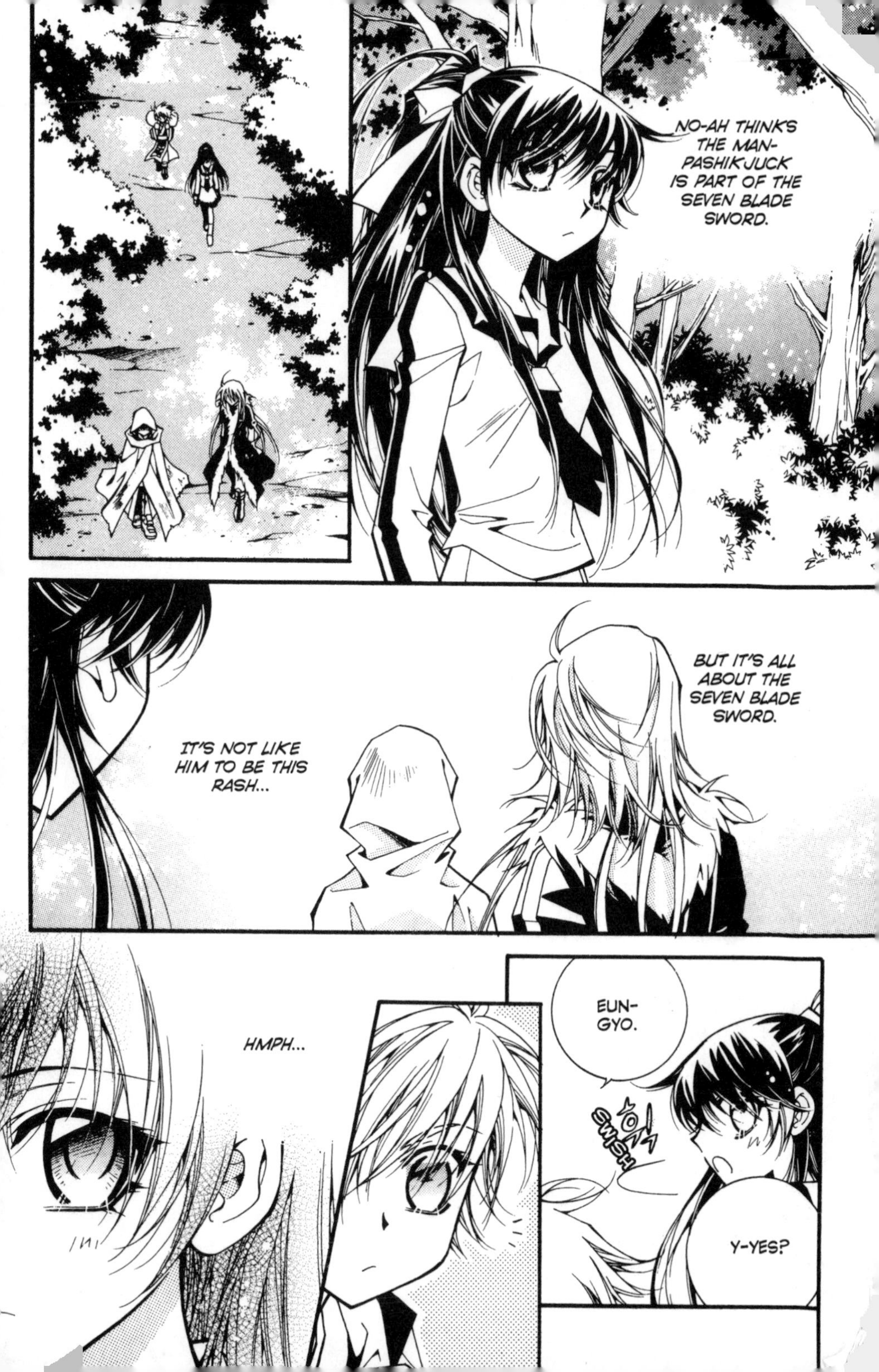
NO-AH THINKS THE MAN-PASHIKJUCK IS PART OF THE SEVEN BLADE SWORD.
IT'S NOT LIKE HIM TO BE THIS RASH...
BUT IT'S ALL ABOUT THE SEVEN BLADE SWORD.
HMPH...
EUN-GYO.
SWISH
Y-YES?

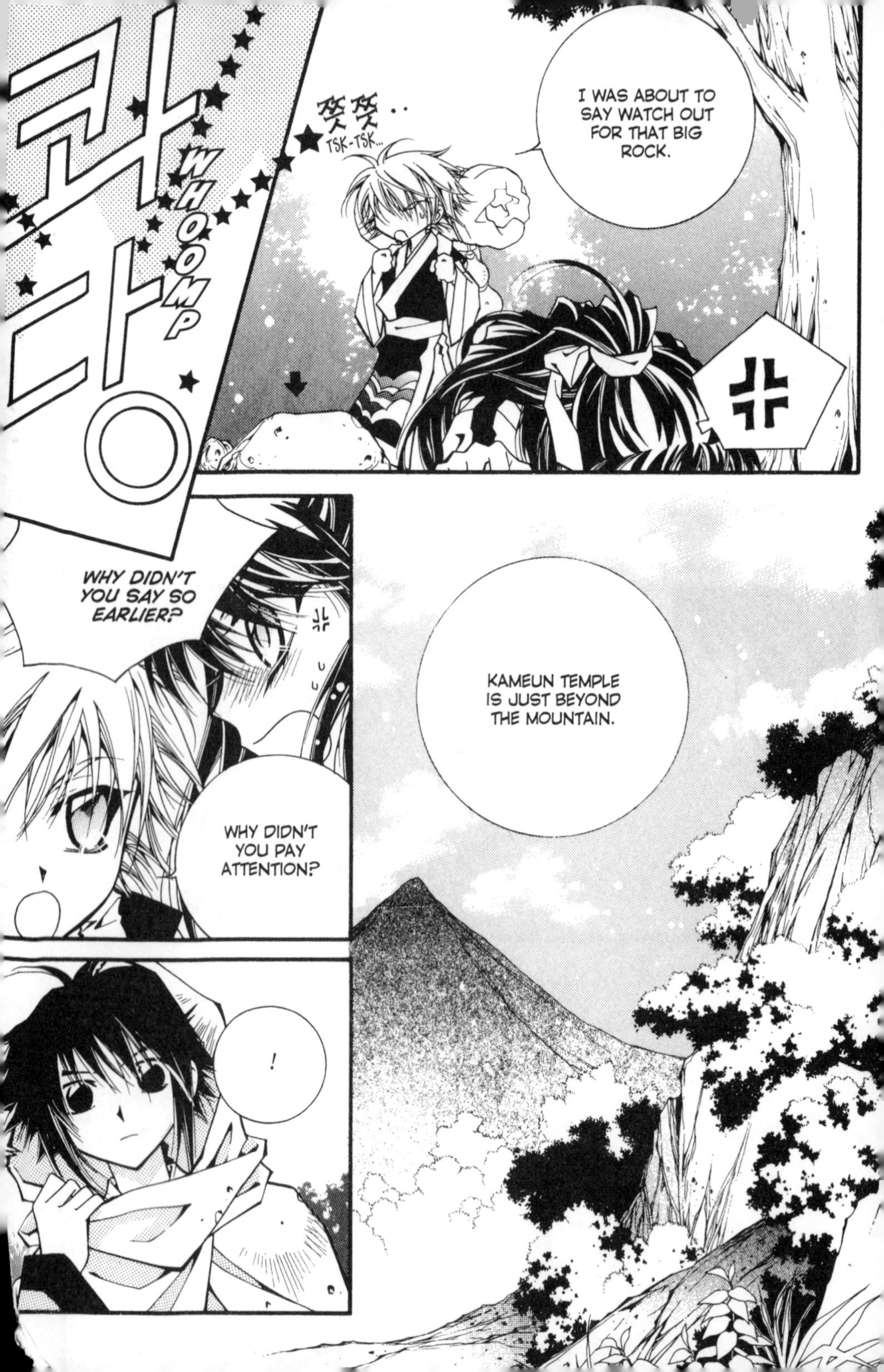

쿠당
WHOOMP
쯧쯧..
TSK-TSK...
I WAS ABOUT TO SAY WATCH OUT FOR THAT BIG ROCK.
WHY DIDN'T YOU SAY SO EARLIER?
WHY DIDN'T YOU PAY ATTENTION?
!
KAMEUN TEMPLE IS JUST BEYOND THE MOUNTAIN.

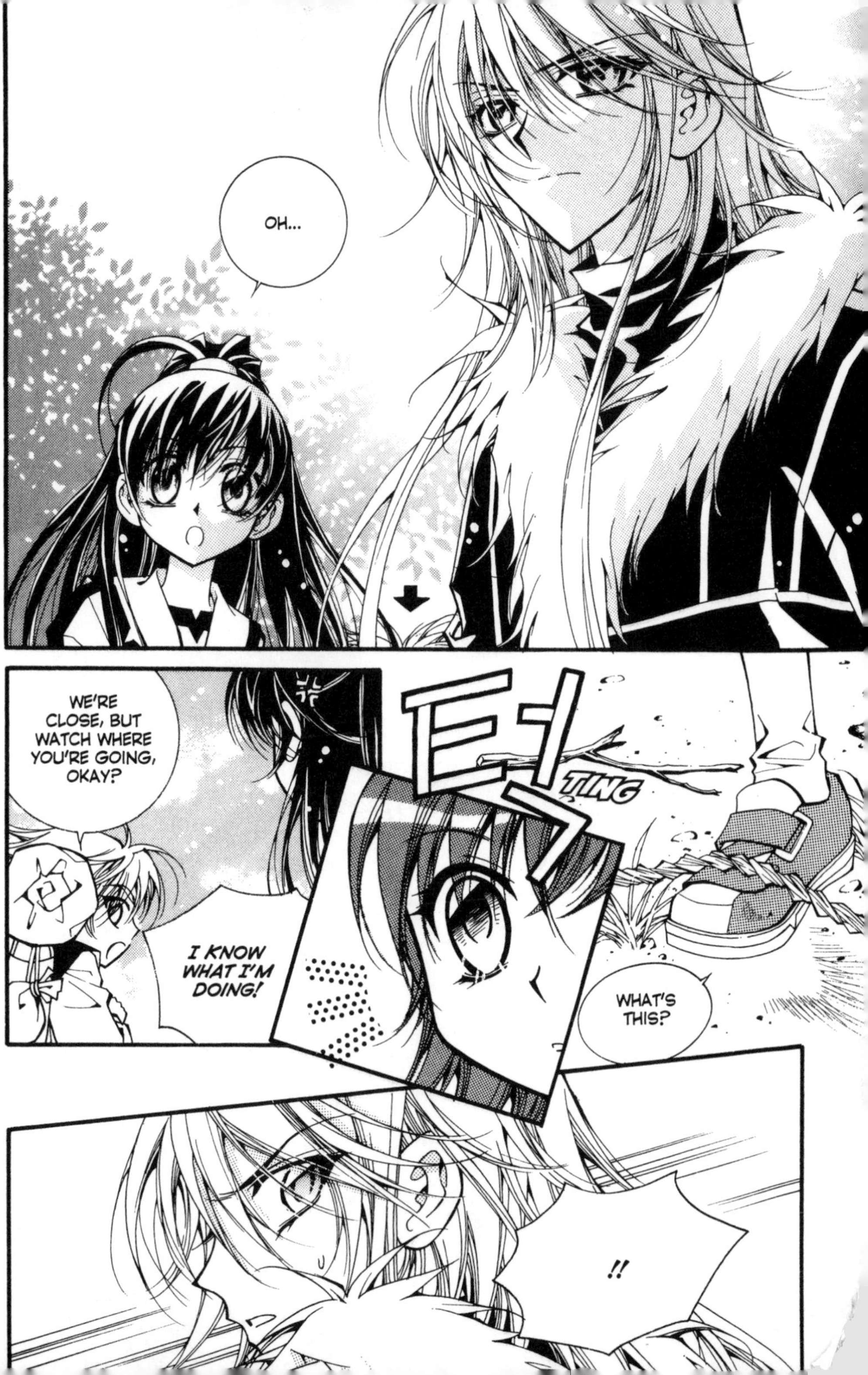
OH...
WE'RE CLOSE, BUT WATCH WHERE YOU'RE GOING, OKAY?
I KNOW WHAT I'M DOING!
TING
WHAT'S THIS?
!!

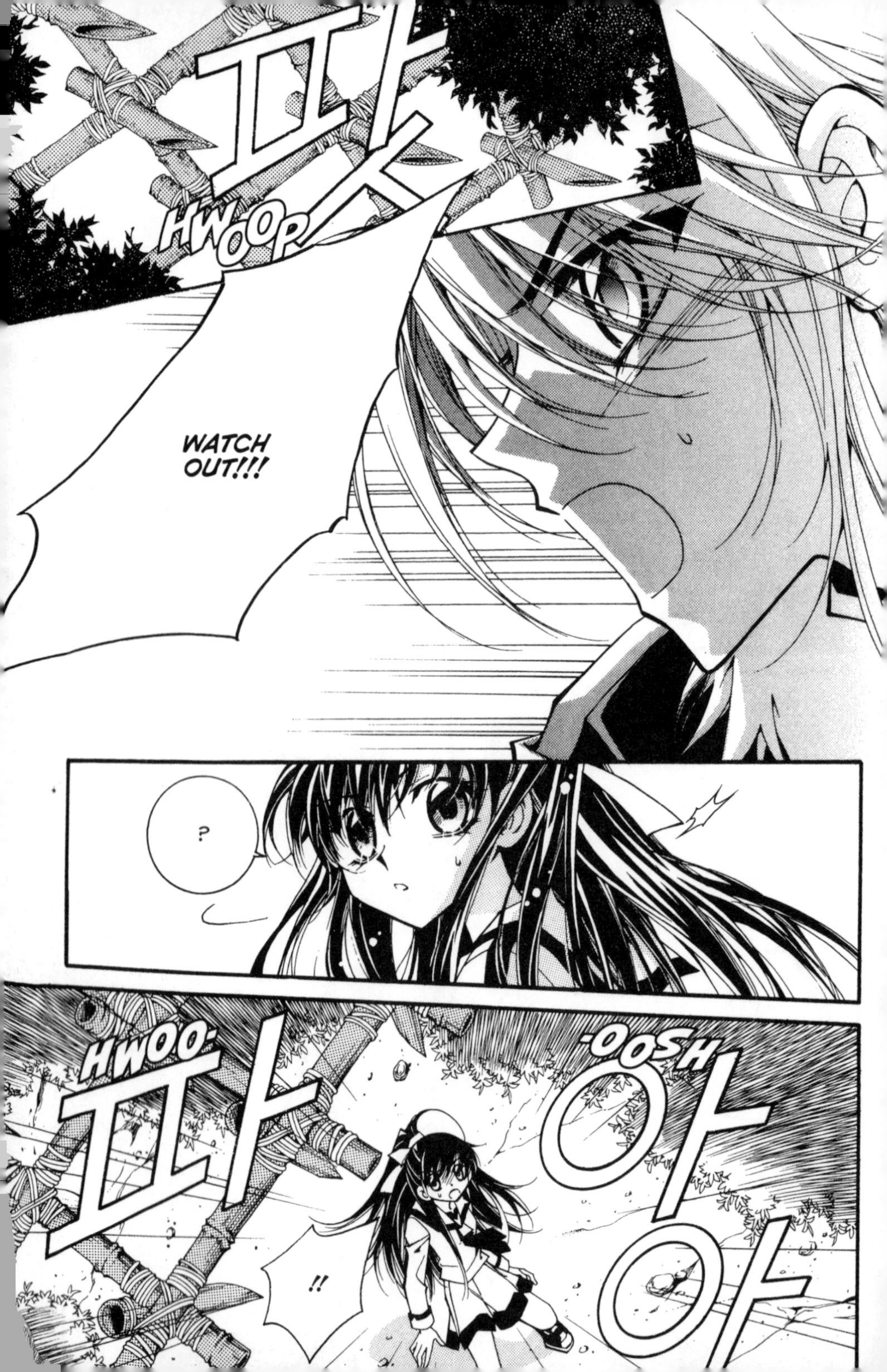
HWOOP
WATCH OUT!!!
?
HWOO-
-OOSH
!!

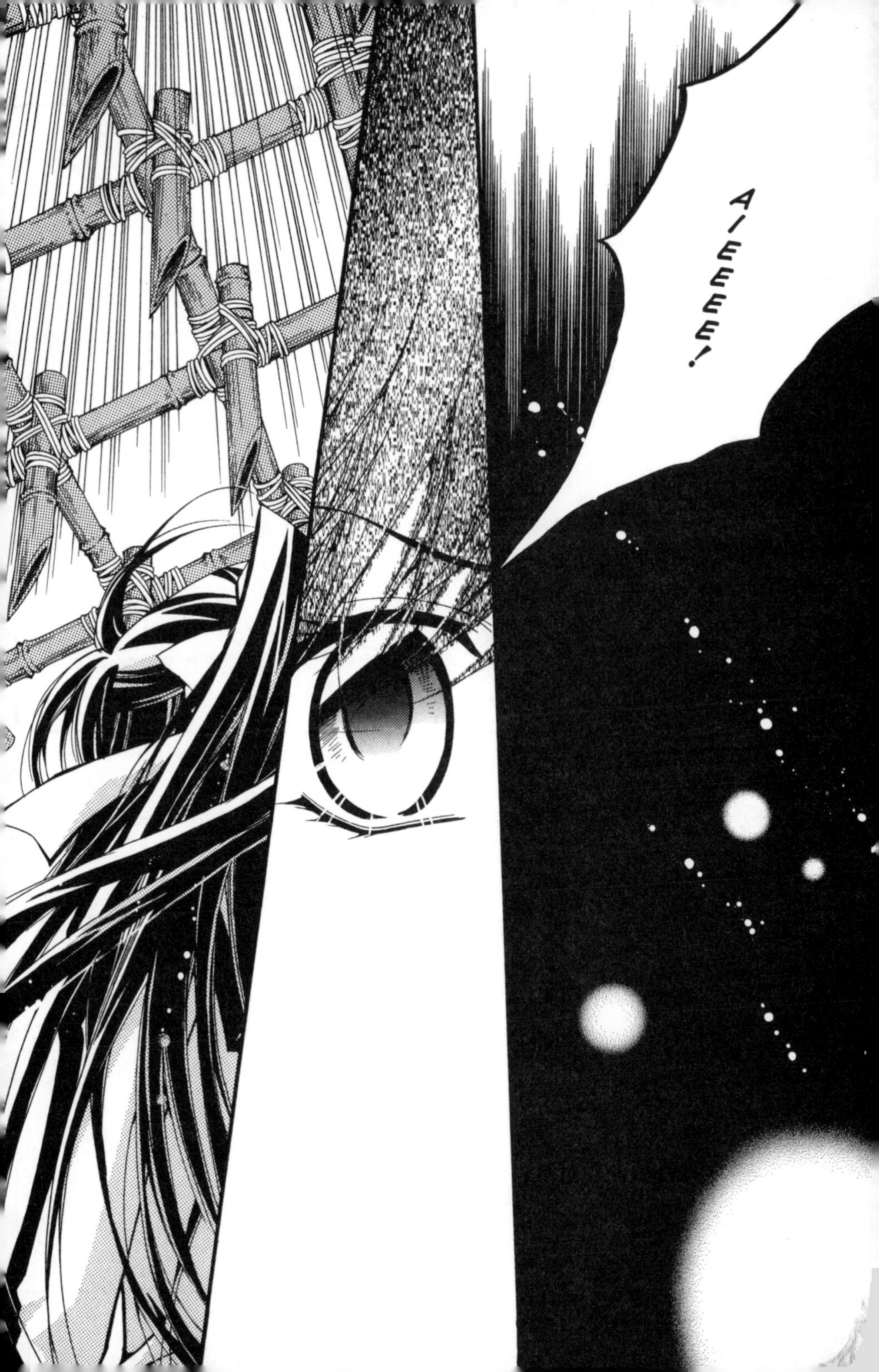
AIEEEE!

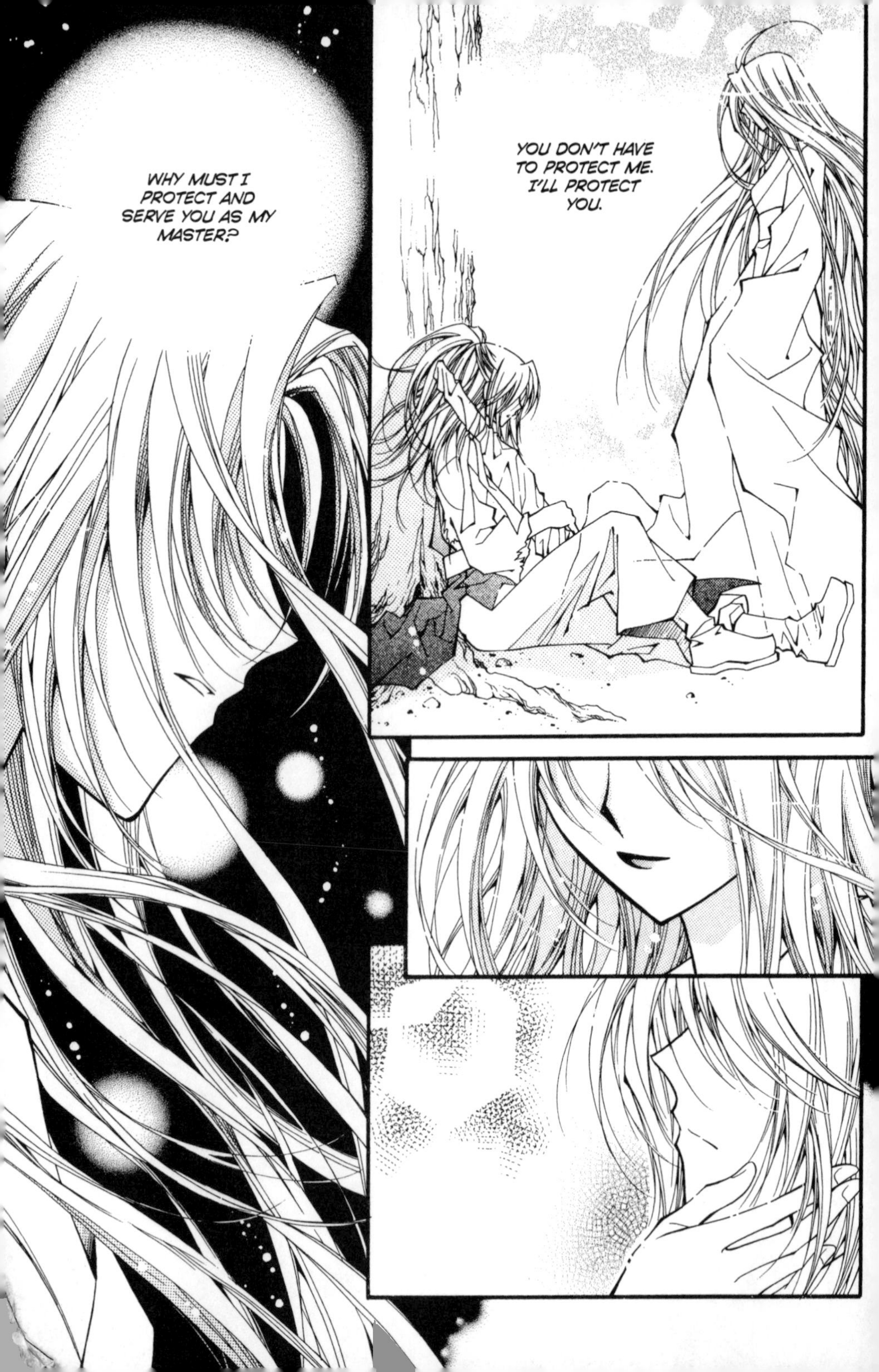
WHY MUST I PROTECT AND SERVE YOU AS MY MASTER?
YOU DON'T HAVE TO PROTECT ME. I'LL PROTECT YOU.

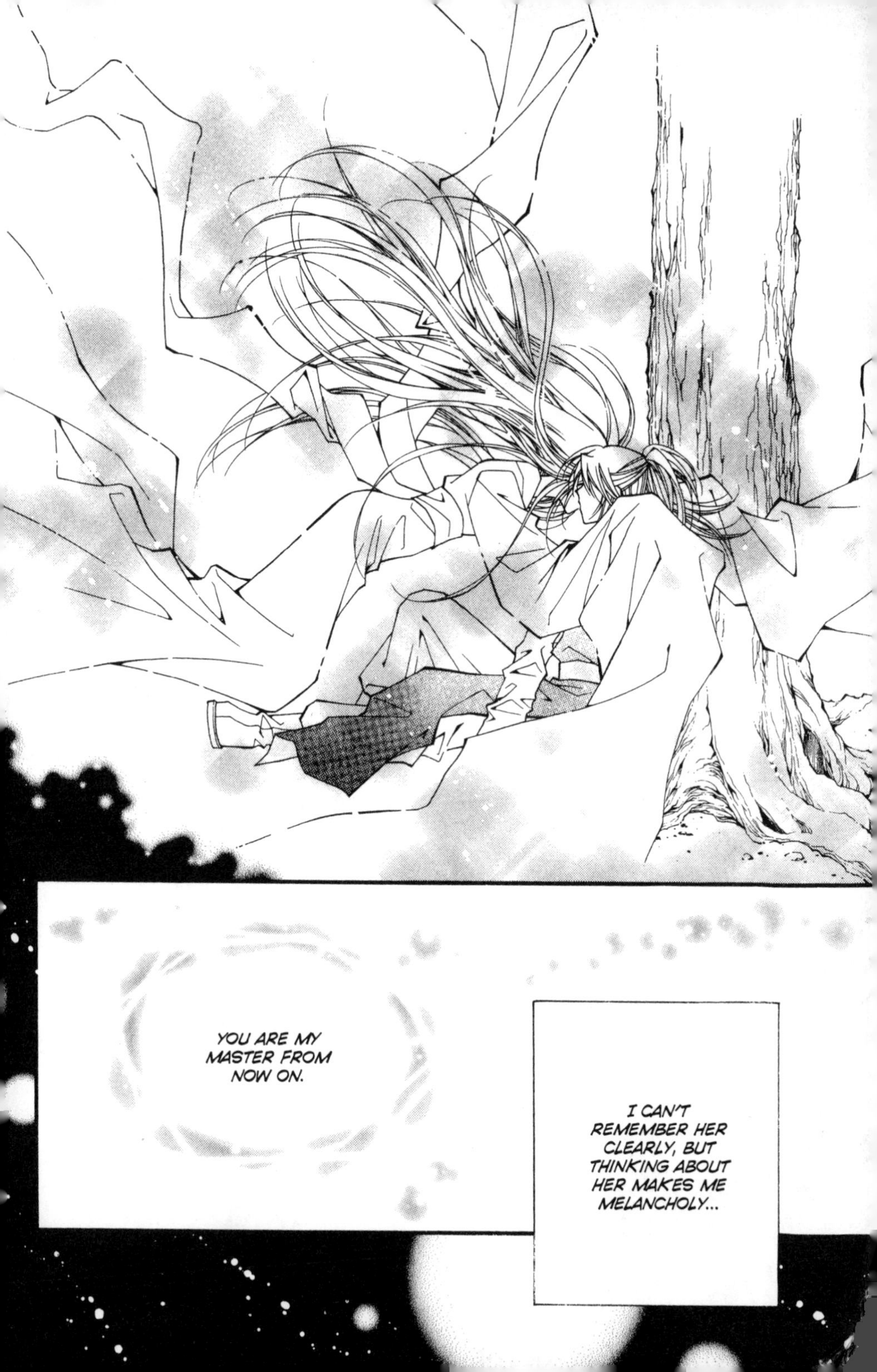
YOU ARE MY MASTER FROM NOW ON.
I CAN'T REMEMBER HER CLEARLY, BUT THINKING ABOUT HER MAKES ME MELANCHOLY...

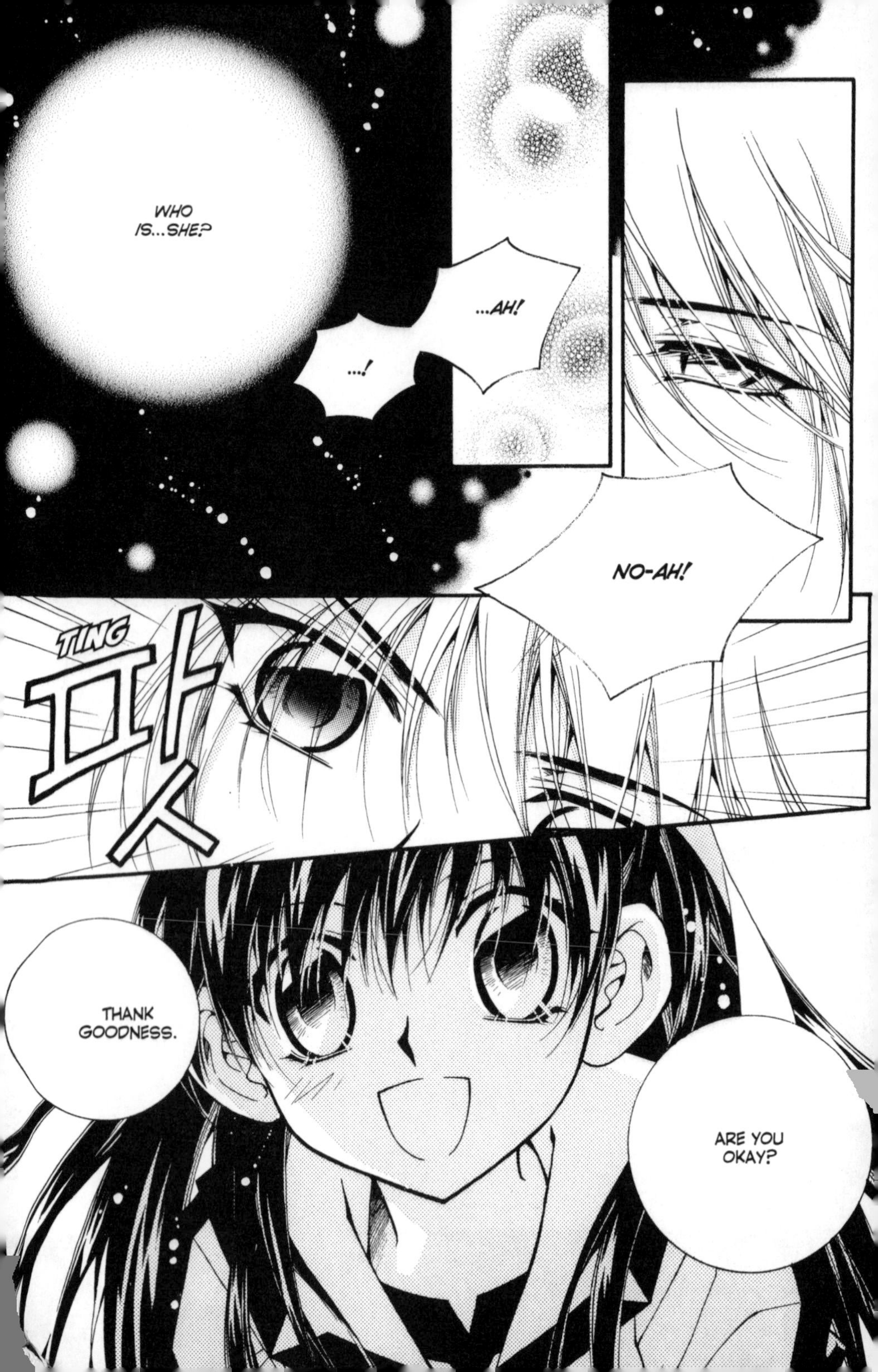
WHO IS...SHE?
...!
...AH!
NO-AH!
TING
THANK GOODNESS.
ARE YOU OKAY?

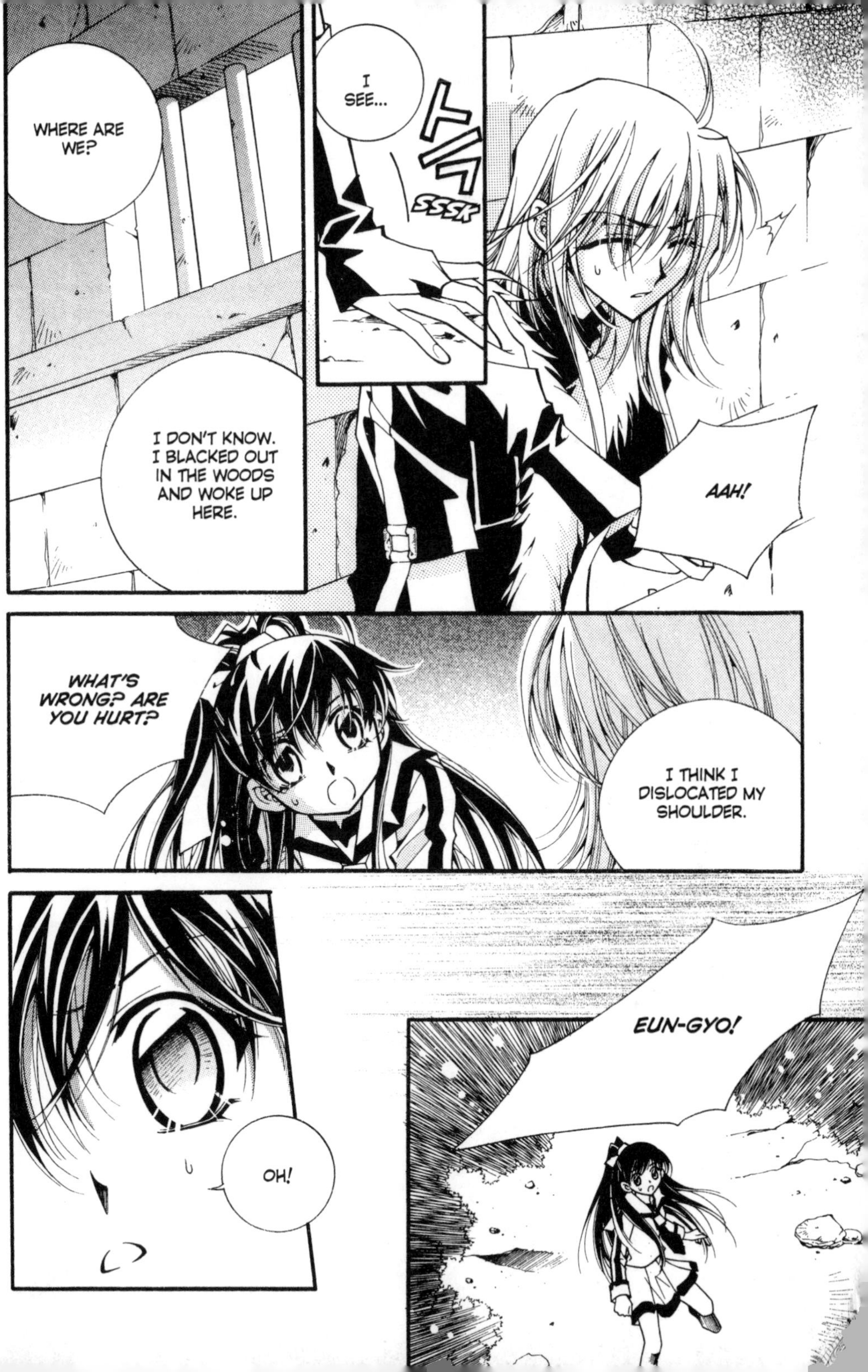
WHERE ARE WE?
I DON'T KNOW. I BLACKED OUT IN THE WOODS AND WOKE UP HERE.
I SEE...
SSSK
AAH!
WHAT'S WRONG? ARE YOU HURT?
I THINK I DISLOCATED MY SHOULDER.
OH!
EUN-GYO!

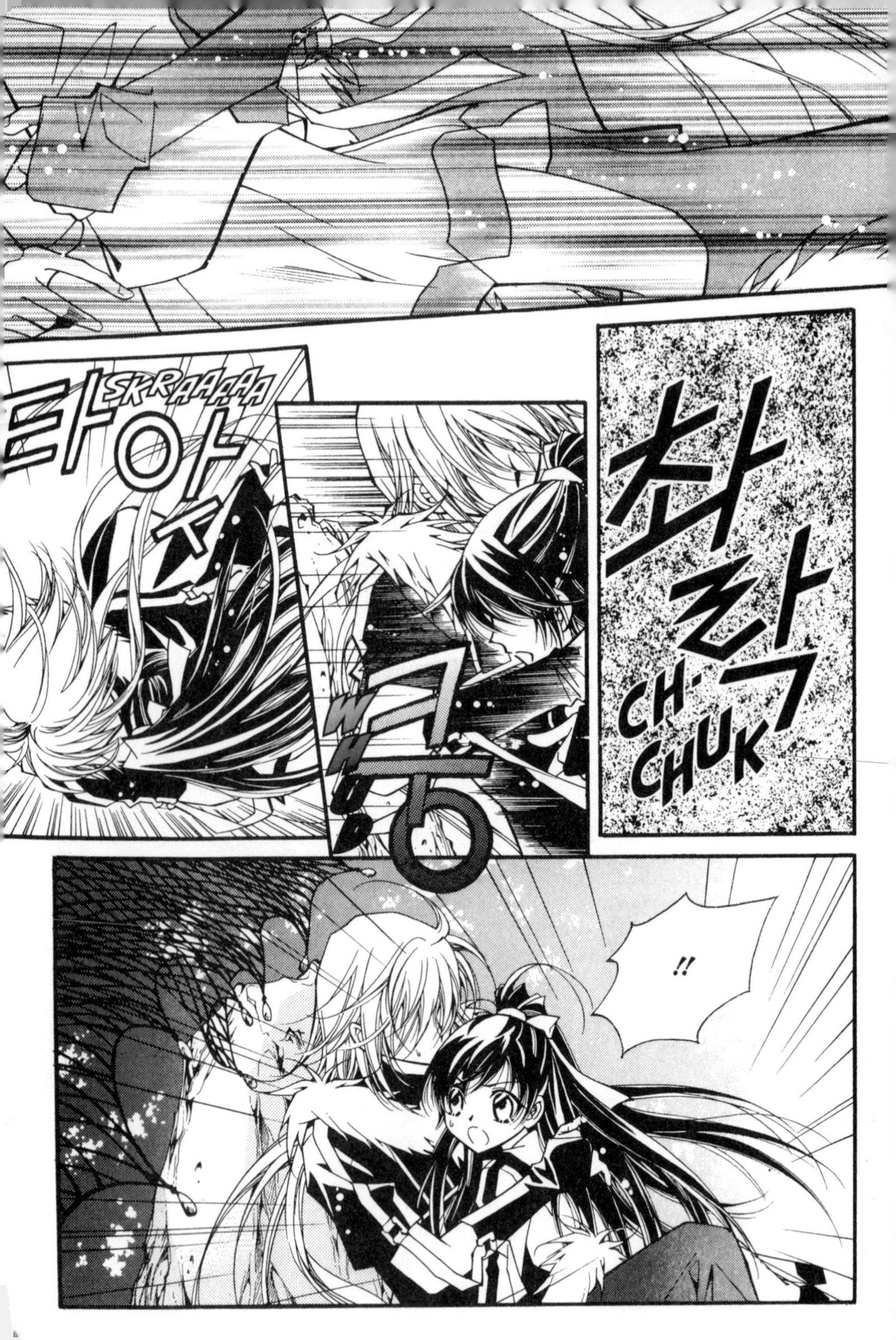
SKRAAAAA
WHUD
CH-CHUK
!!

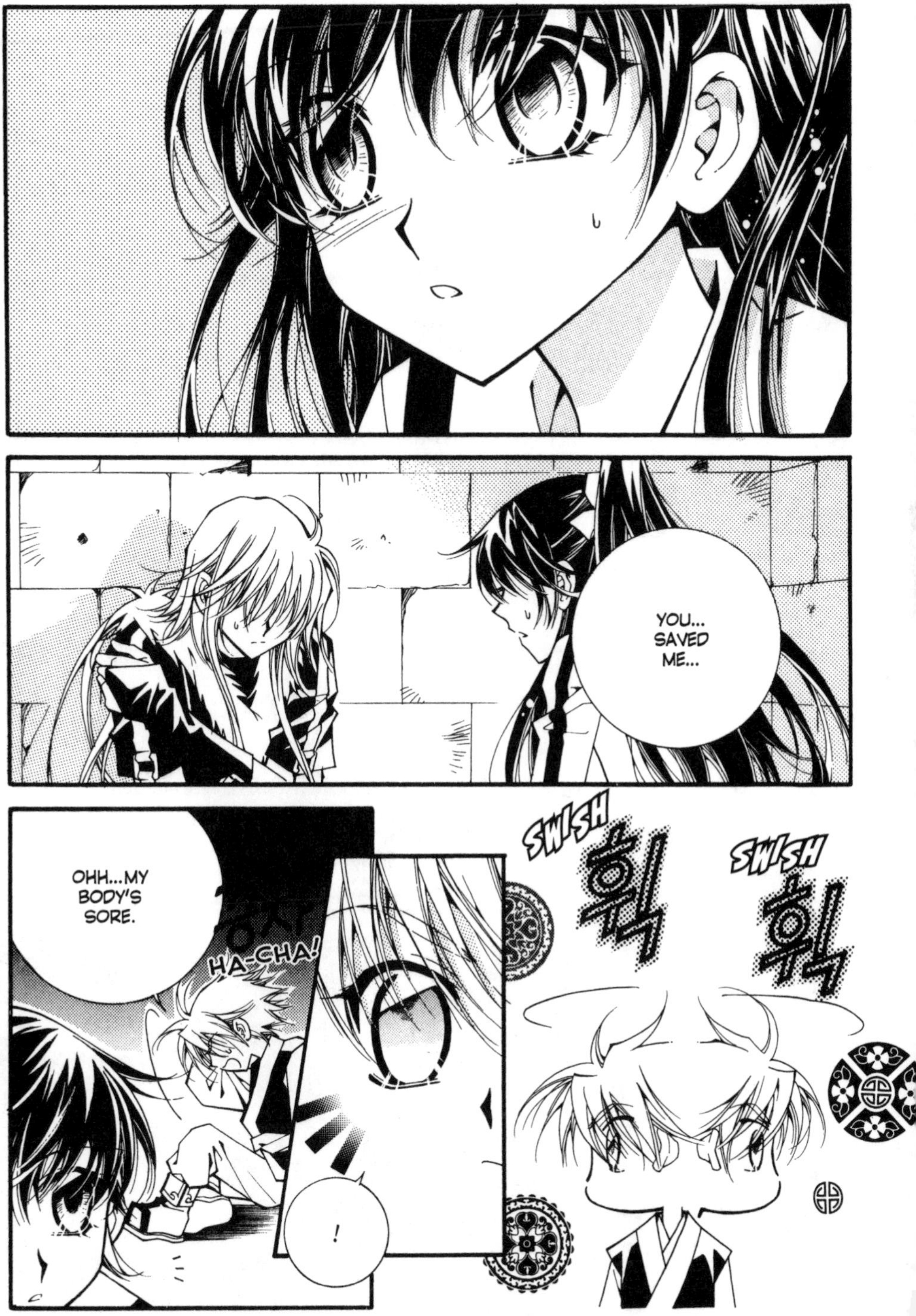
YOU...
SAVED
ME...
OHH...MY
BODY'S
SORE.
HA-CHA!
!
SWISH
휙
SWISH
휙

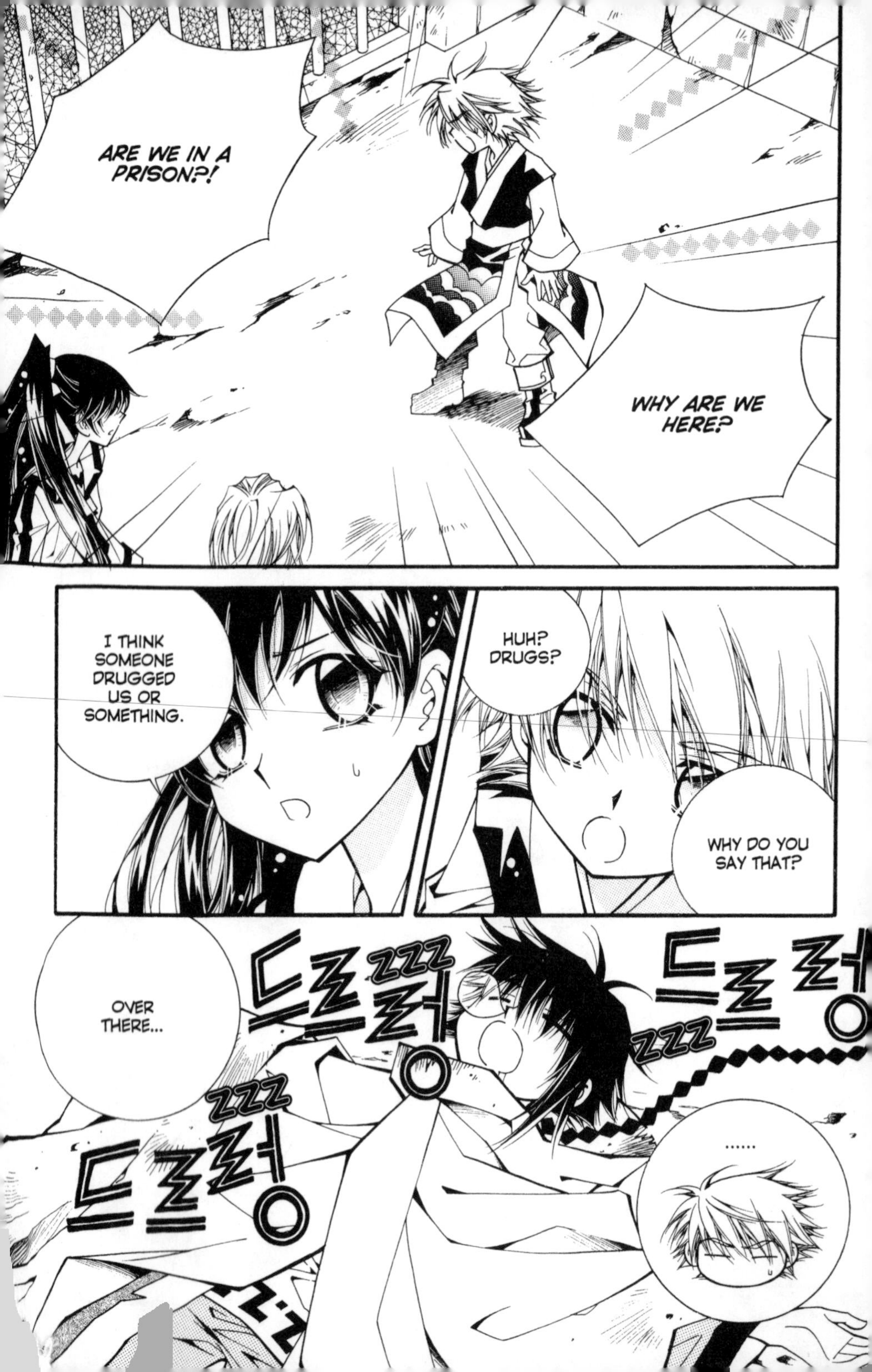
ARE WE IN A PRISON?!
WHY ARE WE HERE?
HUH? DRUGS?
WHY DO YOU SAY THAT?
I THINK SOMEONE DRUGGED US OR SOMETHING.
ZZZ
ZZZ
OVER THERE...
ZZZ
......

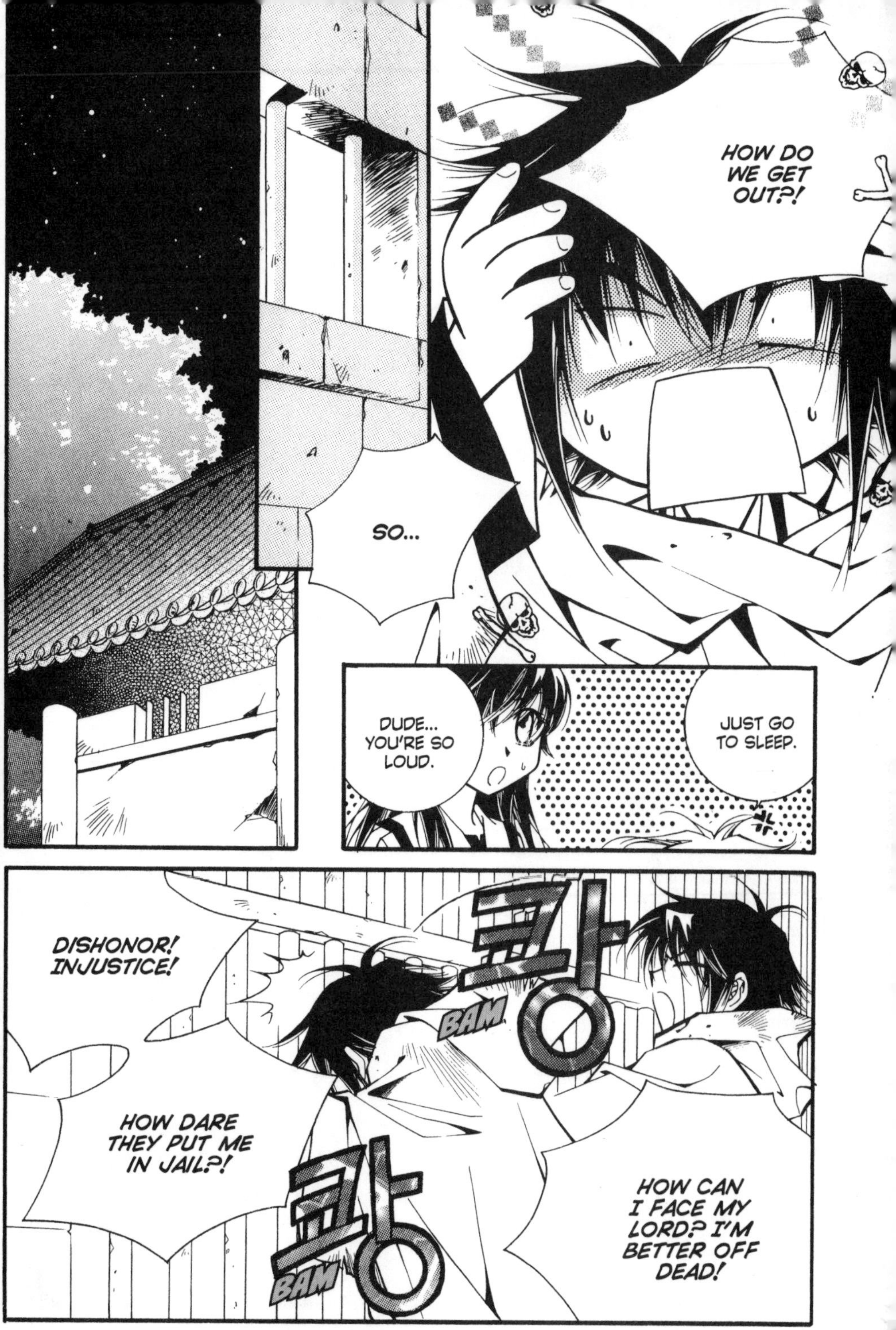
SO...
HOW DO WE GET OUT?!
DUDE... YOU'RE SO LOUD.
JUST GO TO SLEEP.
DISHONOR! INJUSTICE!
쾅
BAM
HOW DARE THEY PUT ME IN JAIL?!
쾅
BAM
HOW CAN I FACE MY LORD? I'M BETTER OFF DEAD!

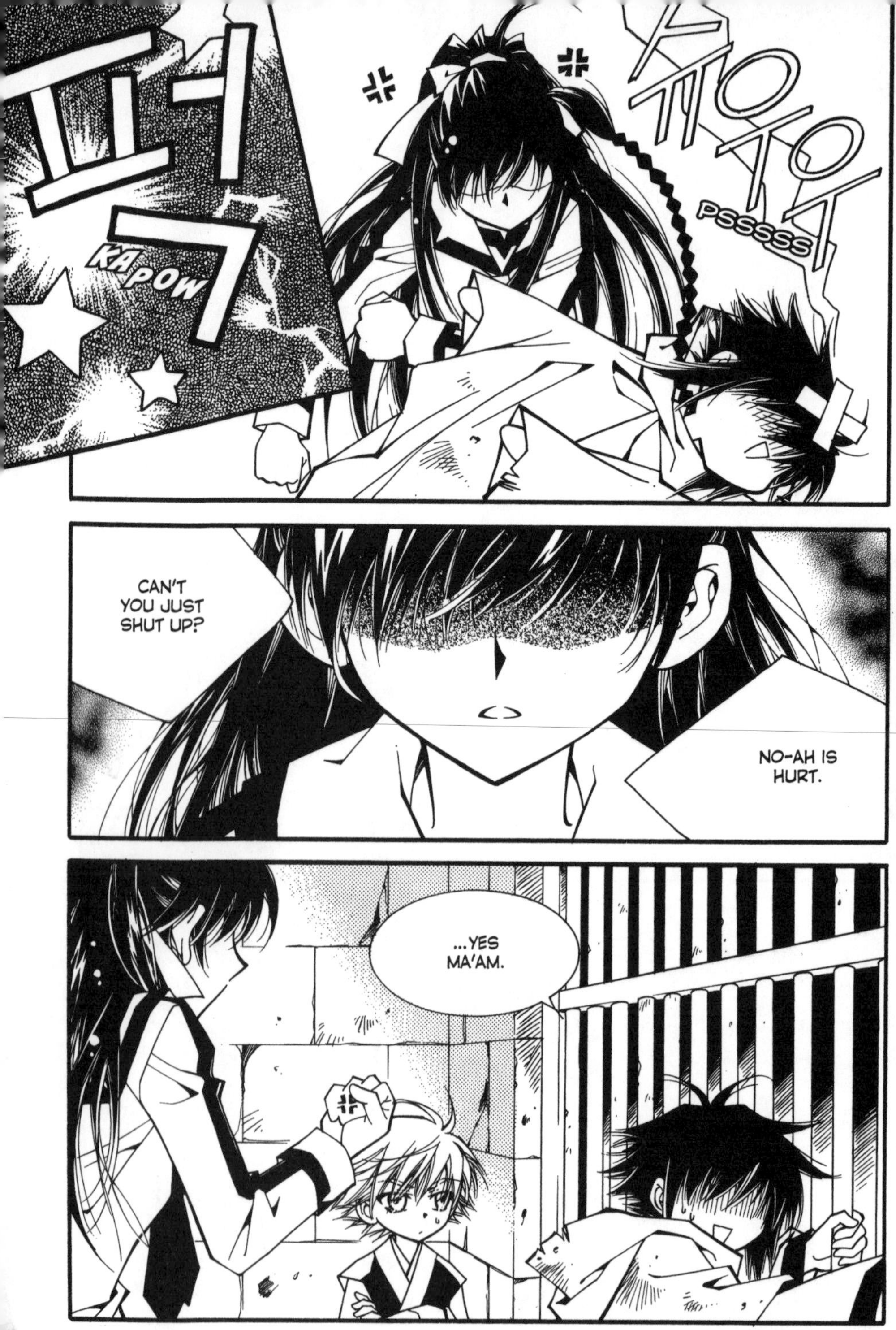
KAPOW
PSSSSS
CAN'T YOU JUST SHUT UP?
NO-AH IS HURT.
...YES MA'AM.

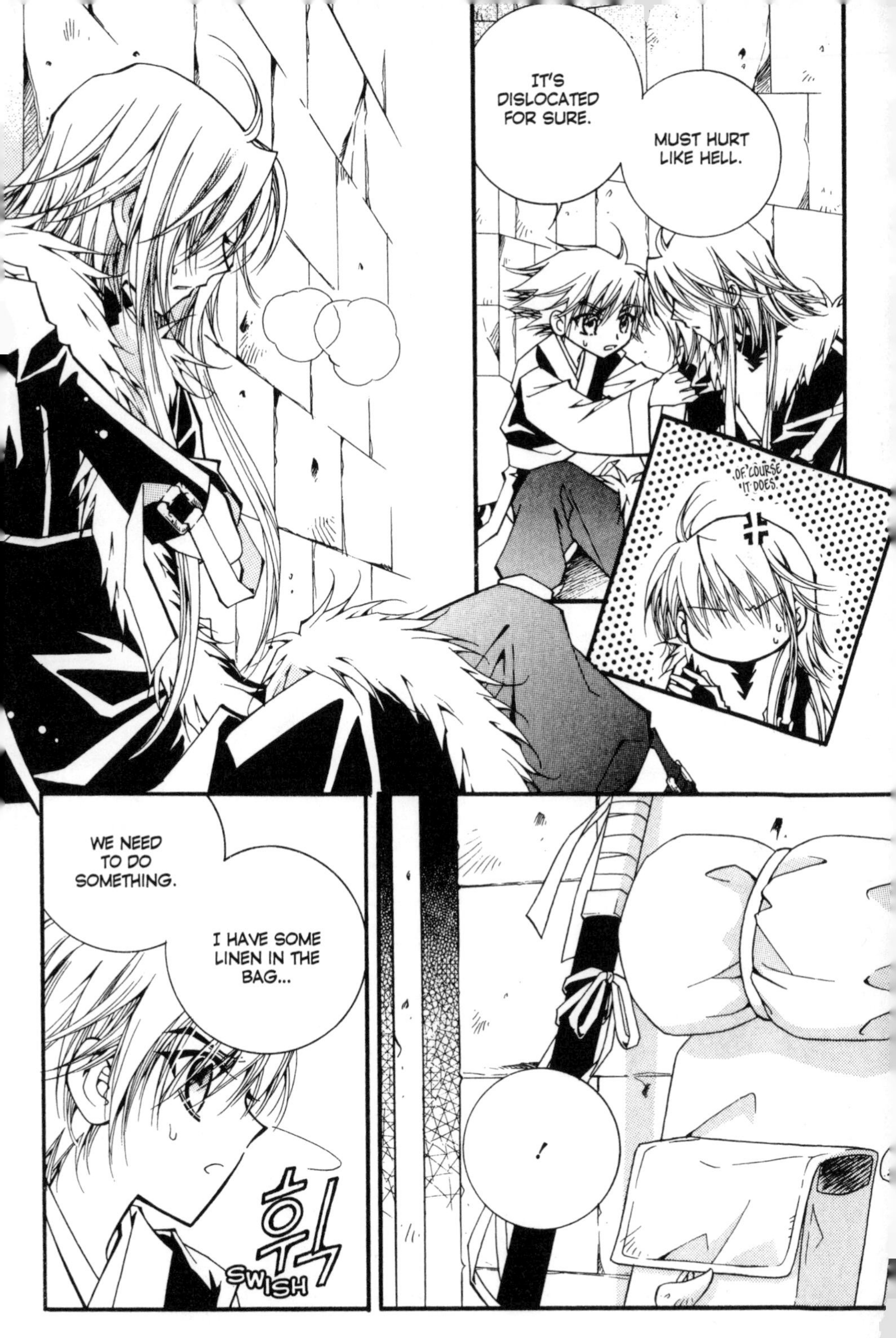
IT'S DISLOCATED FOR SURE.
MUST HURT LIKE HELL.
OF COURSE IT DOES.
WE NEED TO DO SOMETHING.
I HAVE SOME LINEN IN THE BAG...
훅
SWISH
!

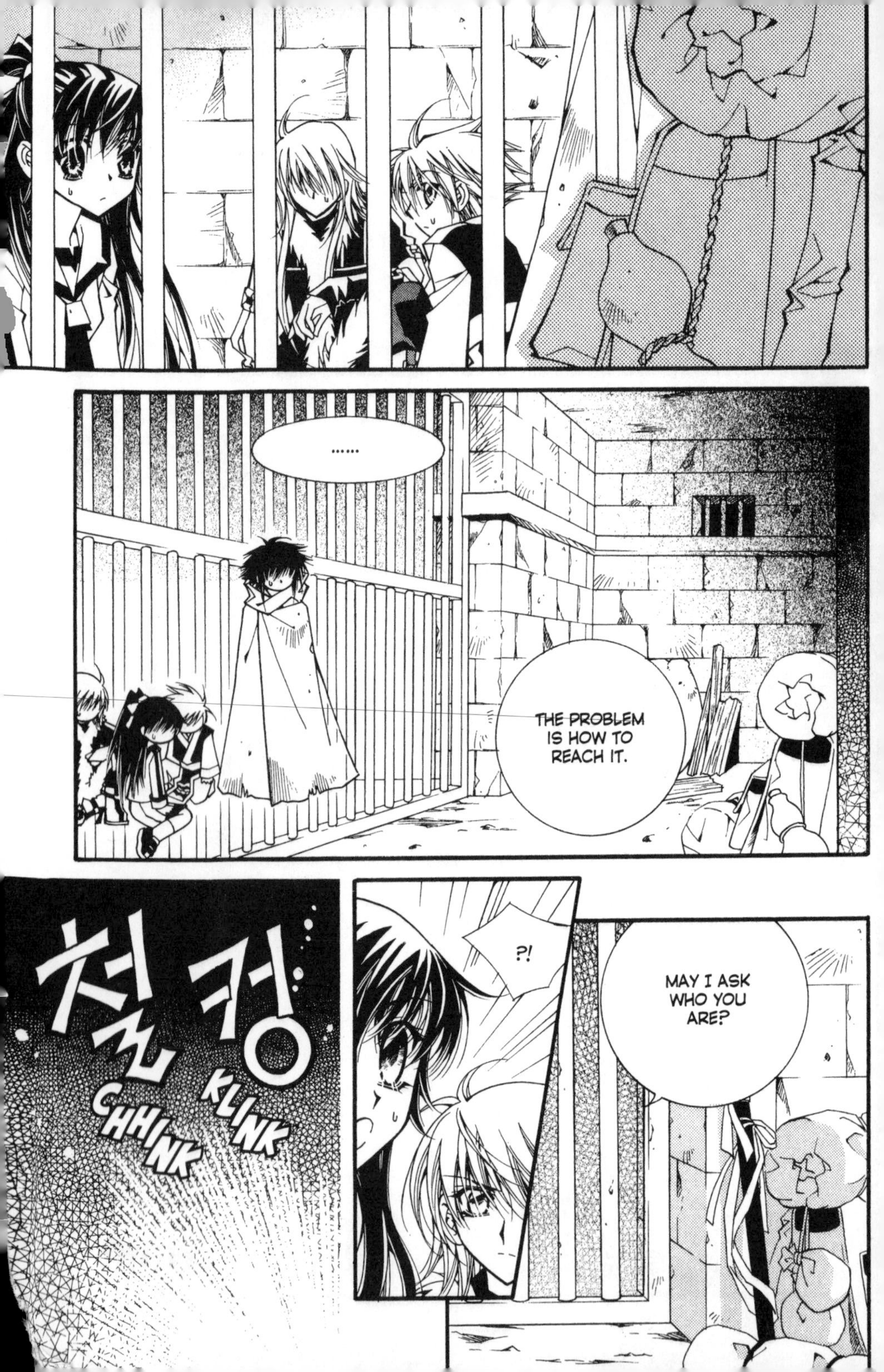
......
THE PROBLEM IS HOW TO REACH IT.
철컹
CHHINK KLINK
?!
MAY I ASK WHO YOU ARE?

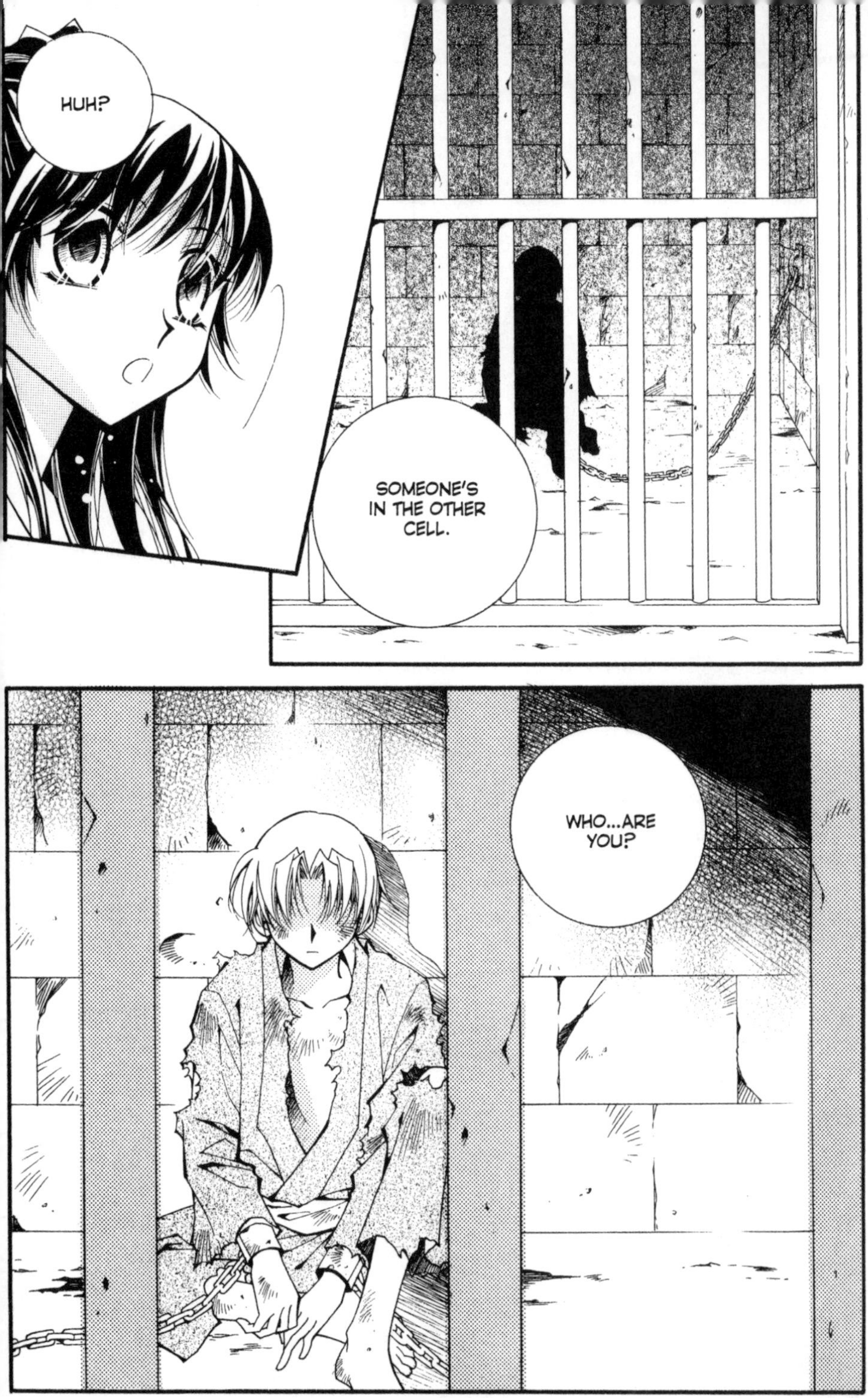
HUH?
SOMEONE'S IN THE OTHER CELL.
WHO...ARE YOU?

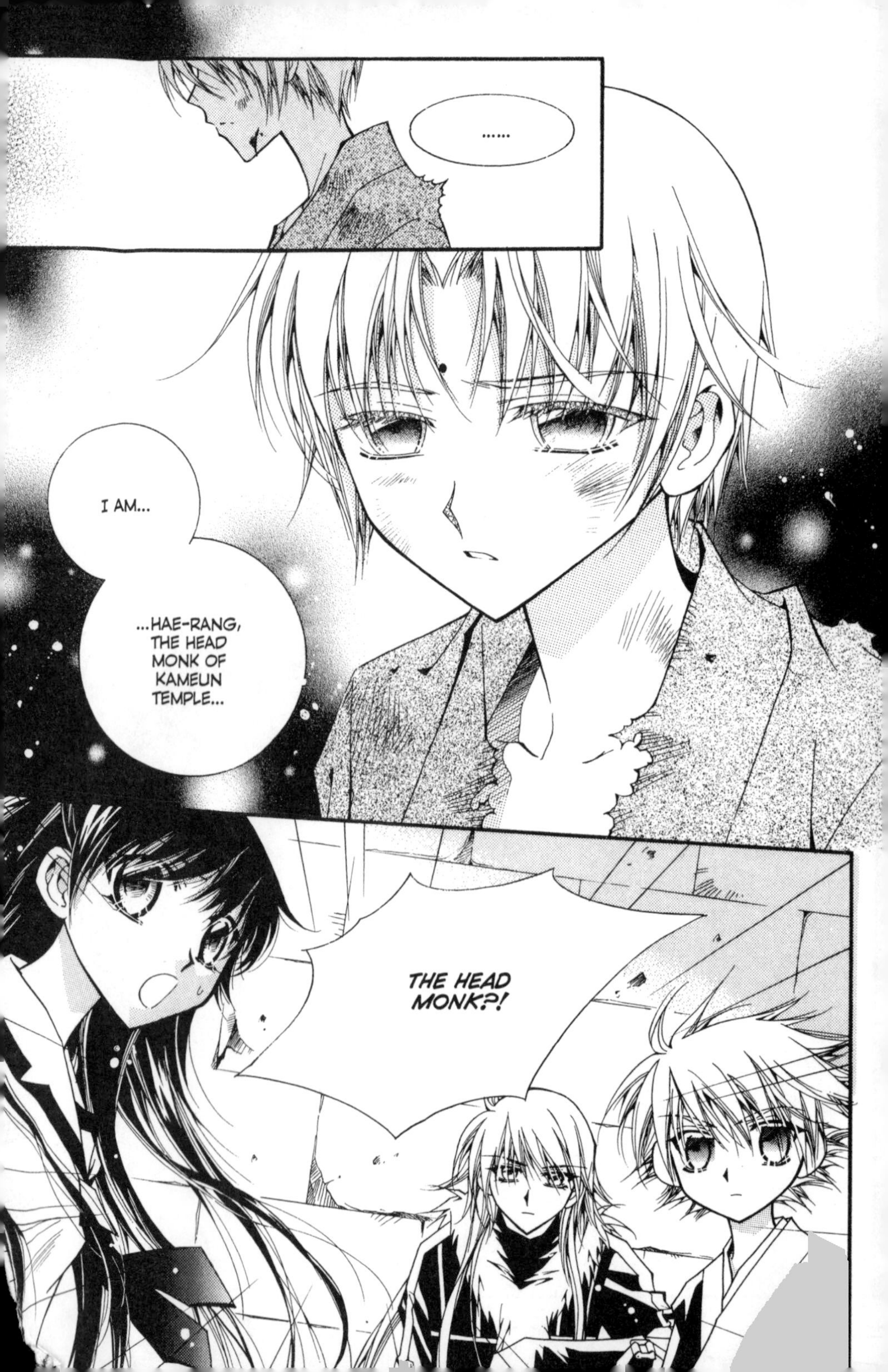
......
I AM...
...HAE-RANG, THE HEAD MONK OF KAMEUN TEMPLE...
THE HEAD MONK?!

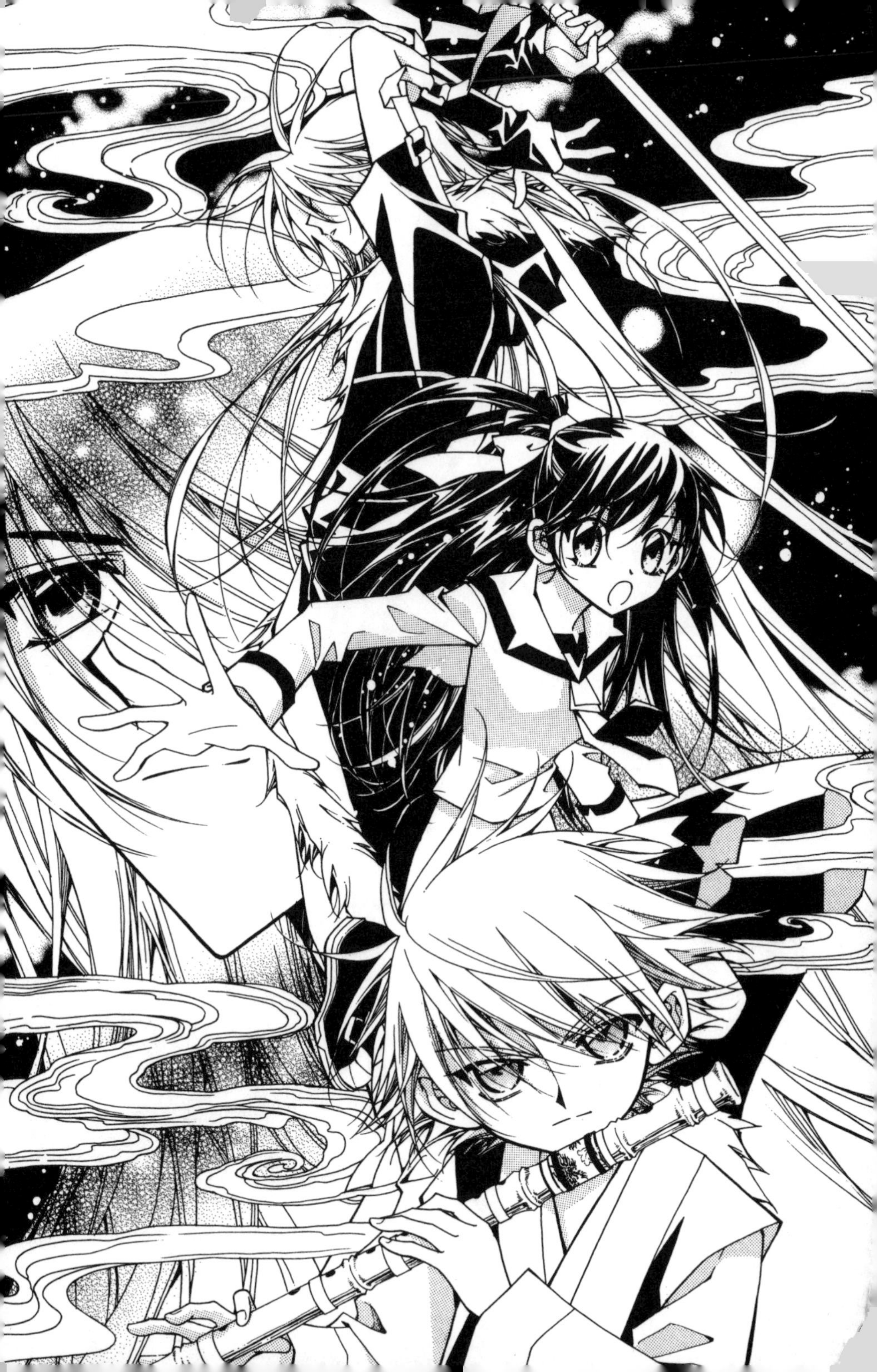

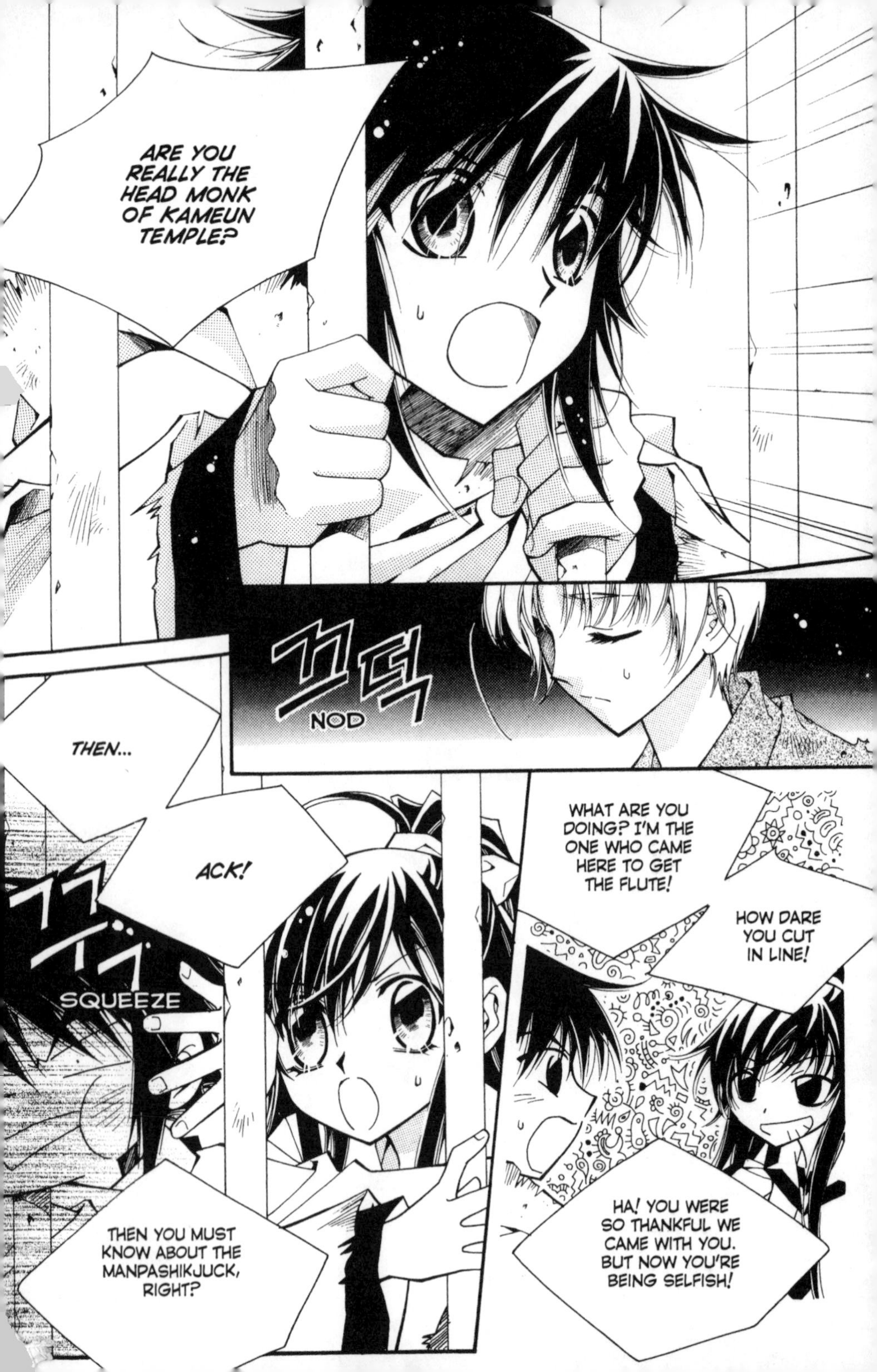
ARE YOU REALLY THE HEAD MONK OF KAMEUN TEMPLE?
끄덕
NOD
THEN...
ACK!
SQUEEZE
THEN YOU MUST KNOW ABOUT THE MANPASHIKJUCK, RIGHT?
WHAT ARE YOU DOING? I'M THE ONE WHO CAME HERE TO GET THE FLUTE!
HOW DARE YOU CUT IN LINE!
HA! YOU WERE SO THANKFUL WE CAME WITH YOU. BUT NOW YOU'RE BEING SELFISH!

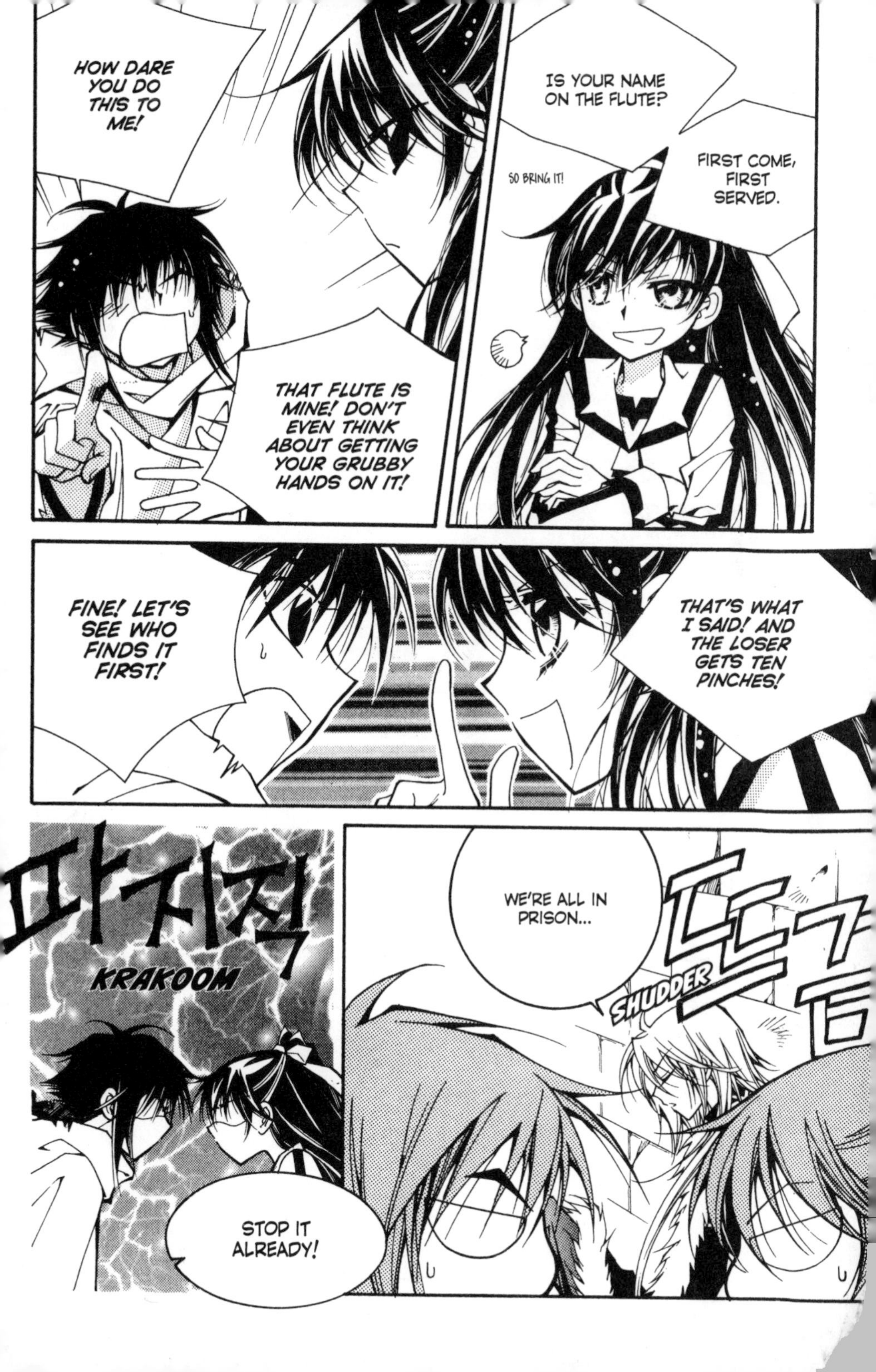
HOW DARE YOU DO THIS TO ME!
THAT FLUTE IS MINE! DON'T EVEN THINK ABOUT GETTING YOUR GRUBBY HANDS ON IT!
IS YOUR NAME ON THE FLUTE?
SO BRING IT!
FIRST COME, FIRST SERVED.
FINE! LET'S SEE WHO FINDS IT FIRST!
THAT'S WHAT I SAID! AND THE LOSER GETS TEN PINCHES!
KRAKOOM
STOP IT ALREADY!
WE'RE ALL IN PRISON...
SHUDDER

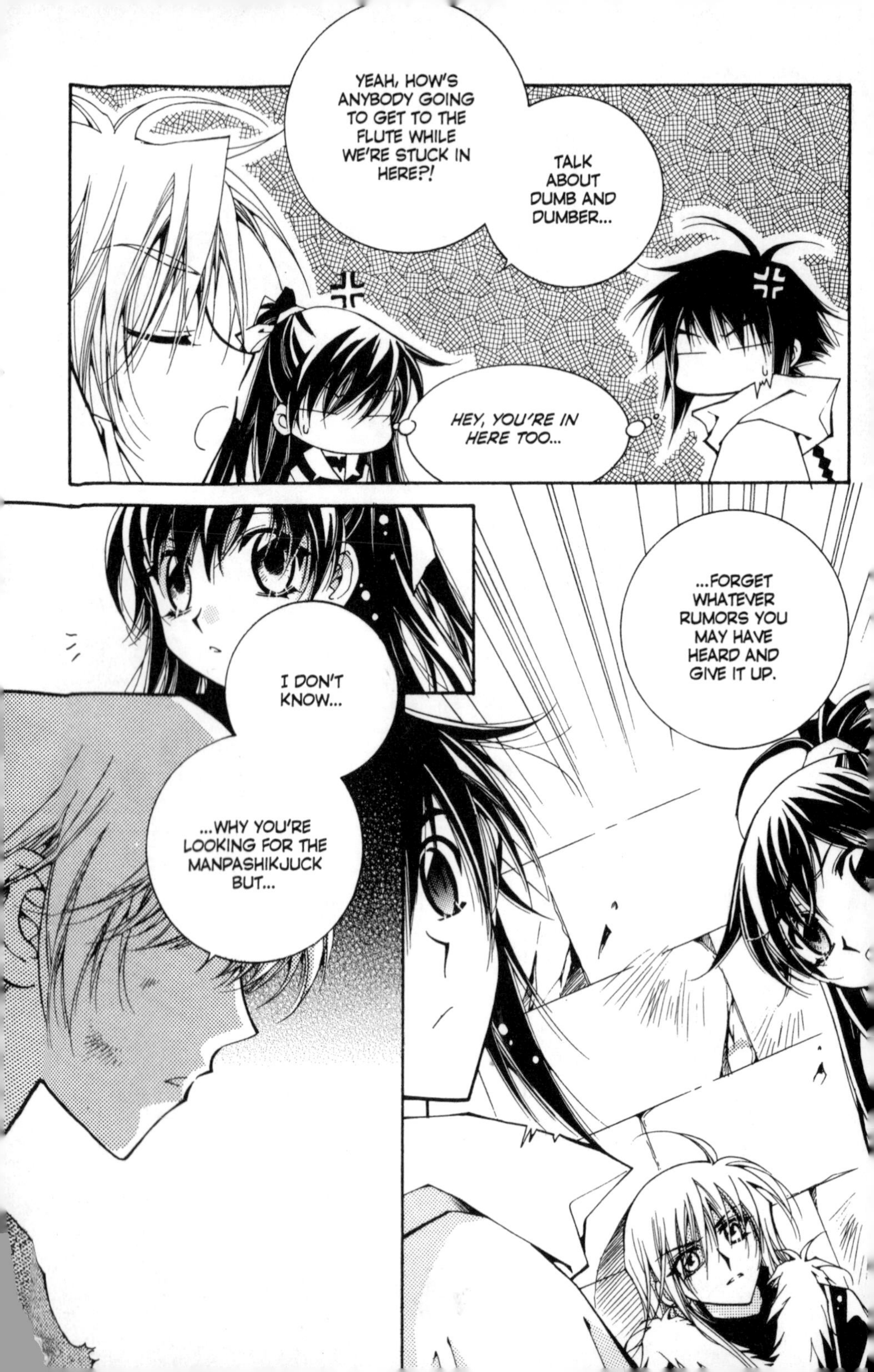
YEAH, HOW'S ANYBODY GOING TO GET TO THE FLUTE WHILE WE'RE STUCK IN HERE?!
TALK ABOUT DUMB AND DUMBER...
HEY, YOU'RE IN HERE TOO...
I DON'T KNOW...
...WHY YOU'RE LOOKING FOR THE MANPASHIKJUCK BUT...
...FORGET WHATEVER RUMORS YOU MAY HAVE HEARD AND GIVE IT UP.

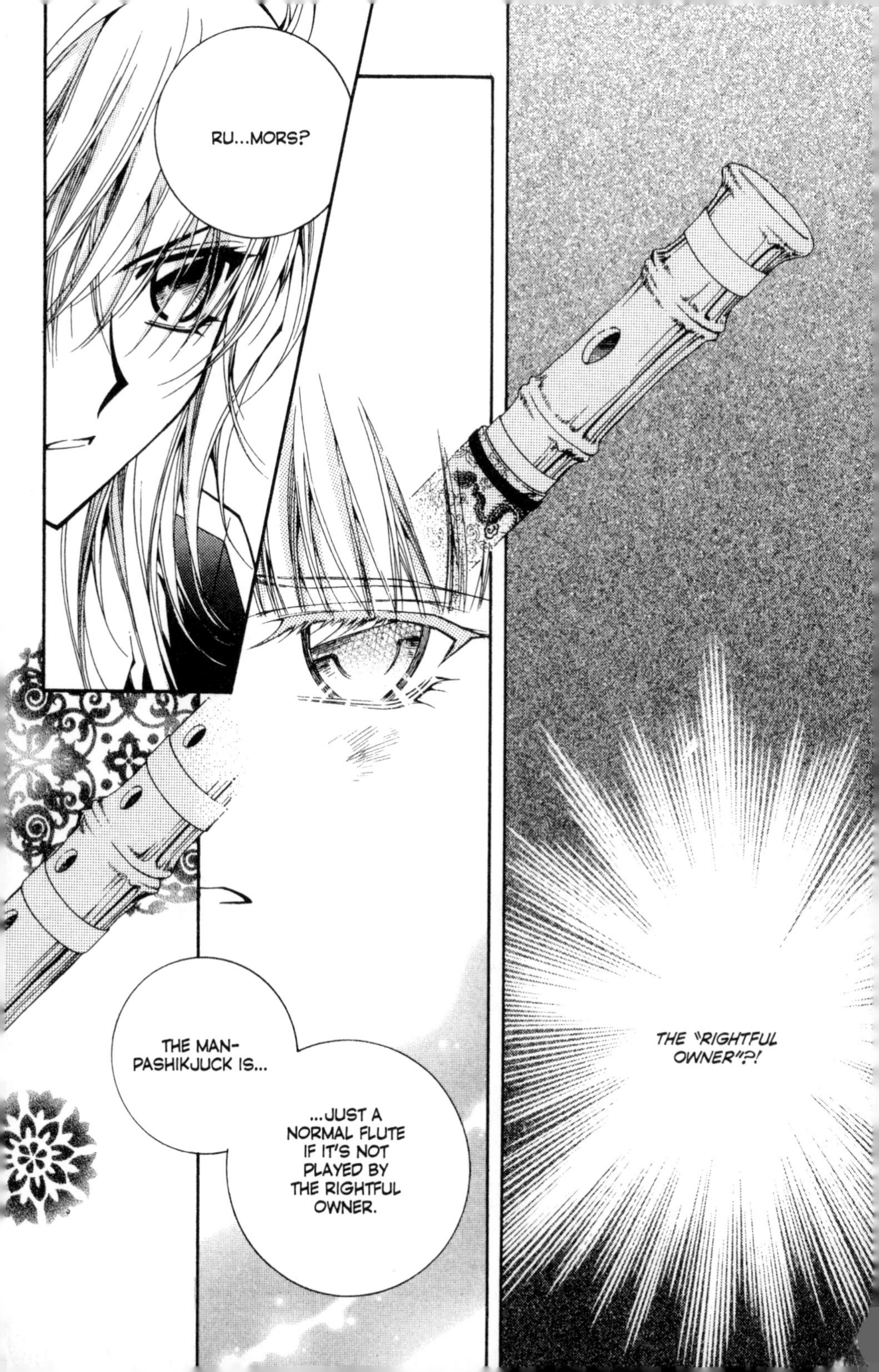
RU...MORS?
THE MAN-PASHIKJUCK IS...
...JUST A NORMAL FLUTE IF IT'S NOT PLAYED BY THE RIGHTFUL OWNER.
THE "RIGHTFUL OWNER"?!

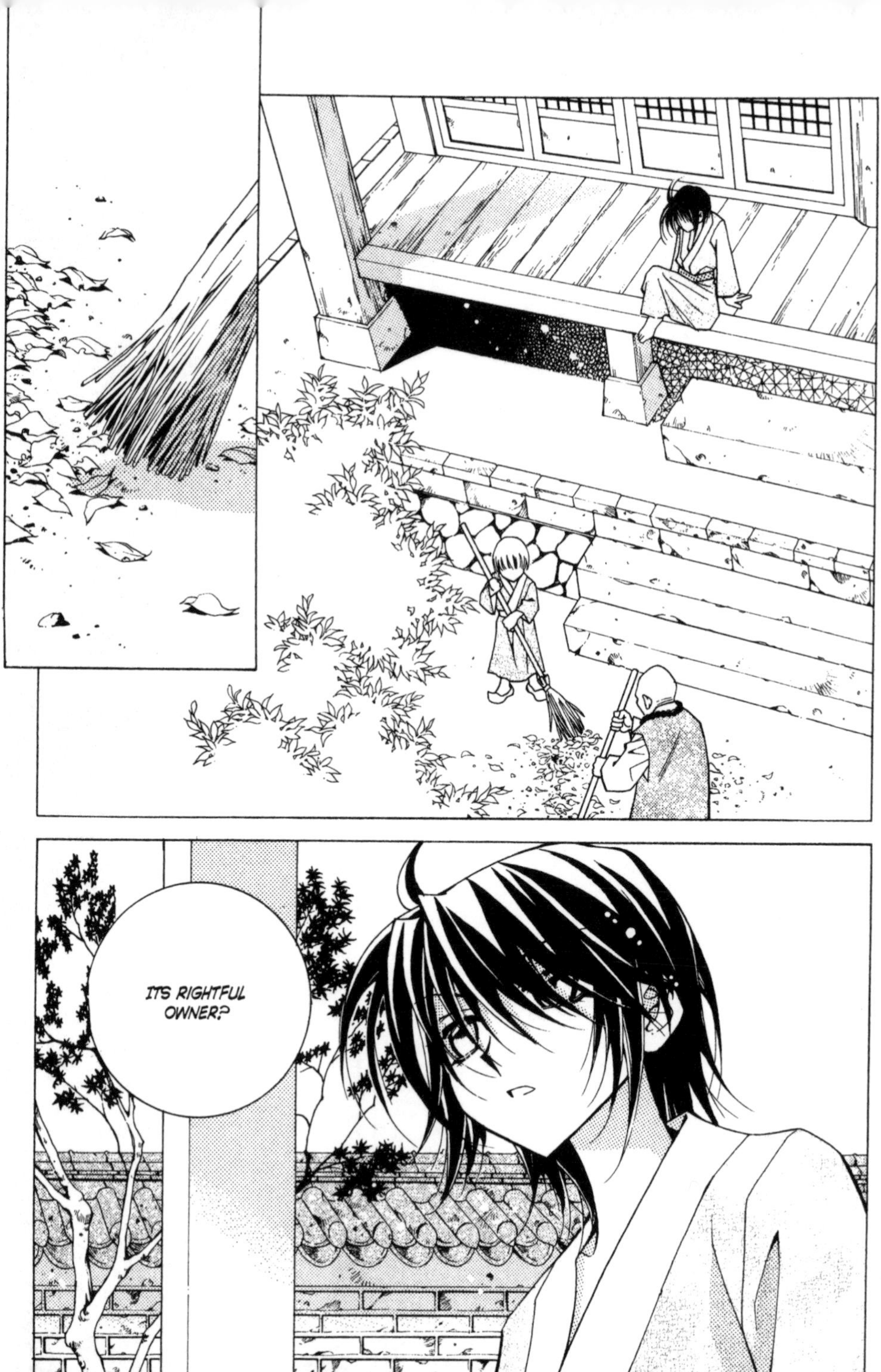
ITS RIGHTFUL OWNER?

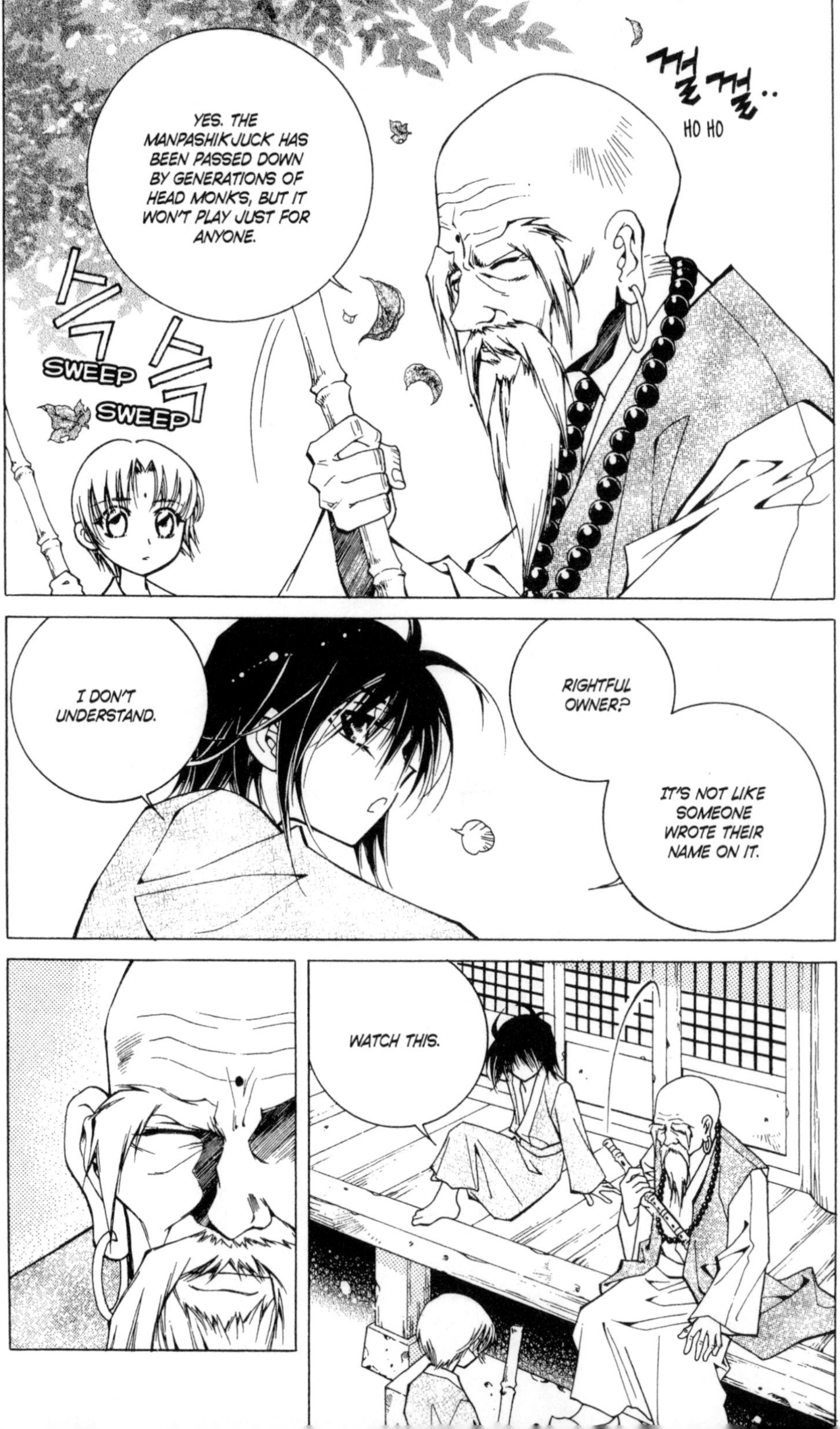
YES. THE MANPASHIKJUCK HAS BEEN PASSED DOWN BY GENERATIONS OF HEAD MONKS, BUT IT WON'T PLAY JUST FOR ANYONE.
껄껄..
HO HO
SWEEP
SWEEP
I DON'T UNDERSTAND.
RIGHTFUL OWNER?
IT'S NOT LIKE SOMEONE WROTE THEIR NAME ON IT.
WATCH THIS.

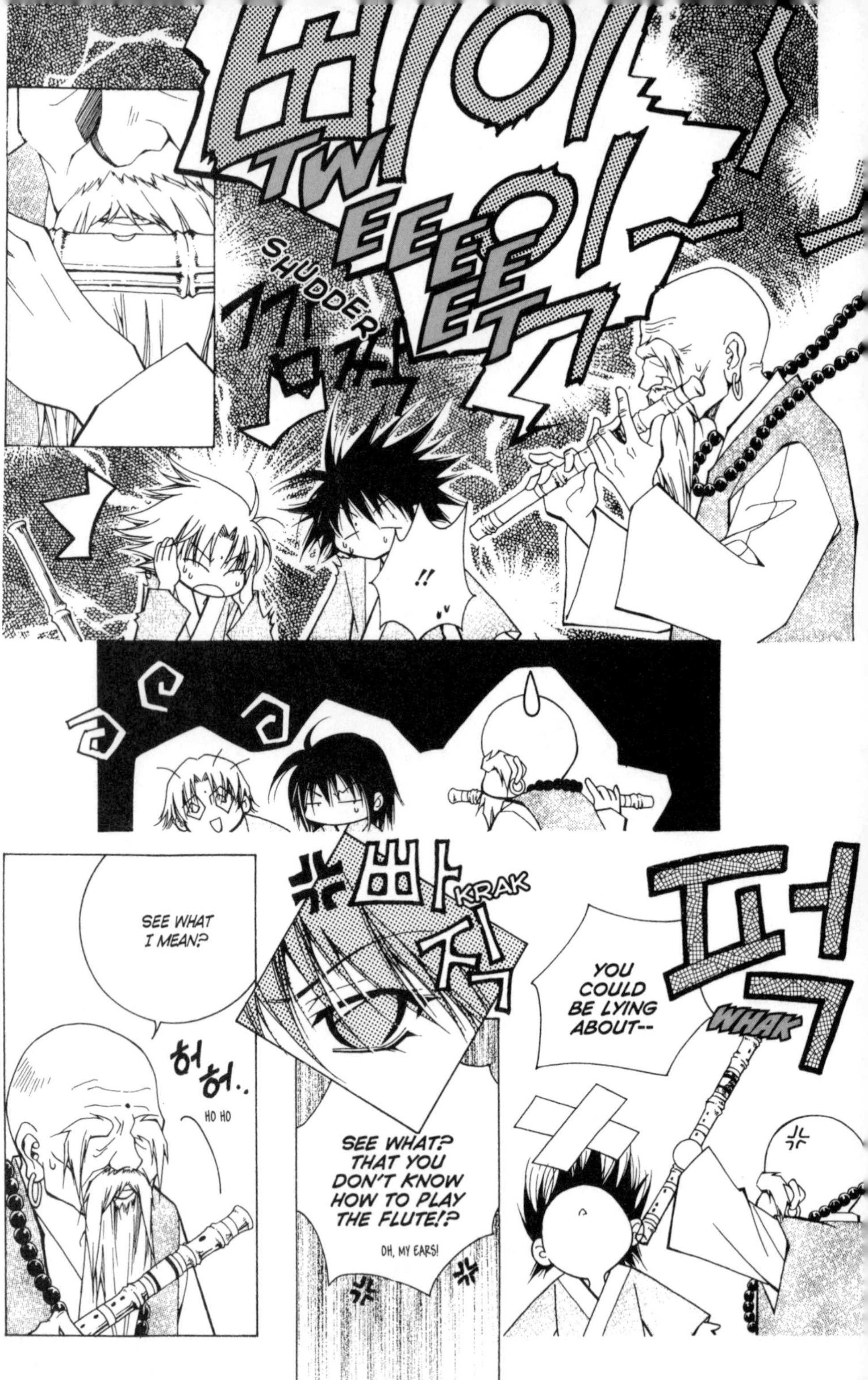
TWEEEEEEET
SHUDDER
!!
SEE WHAT I MEAN?
허허..
HO HO
빠직
KRAK
SEE WHAT? THAT YOU DON'T KNOW HOW TO PLAY THE FLUTE!?
OH, MY EARS!
YOU COULD BE LYING ABOUT--
퍽
WHAK

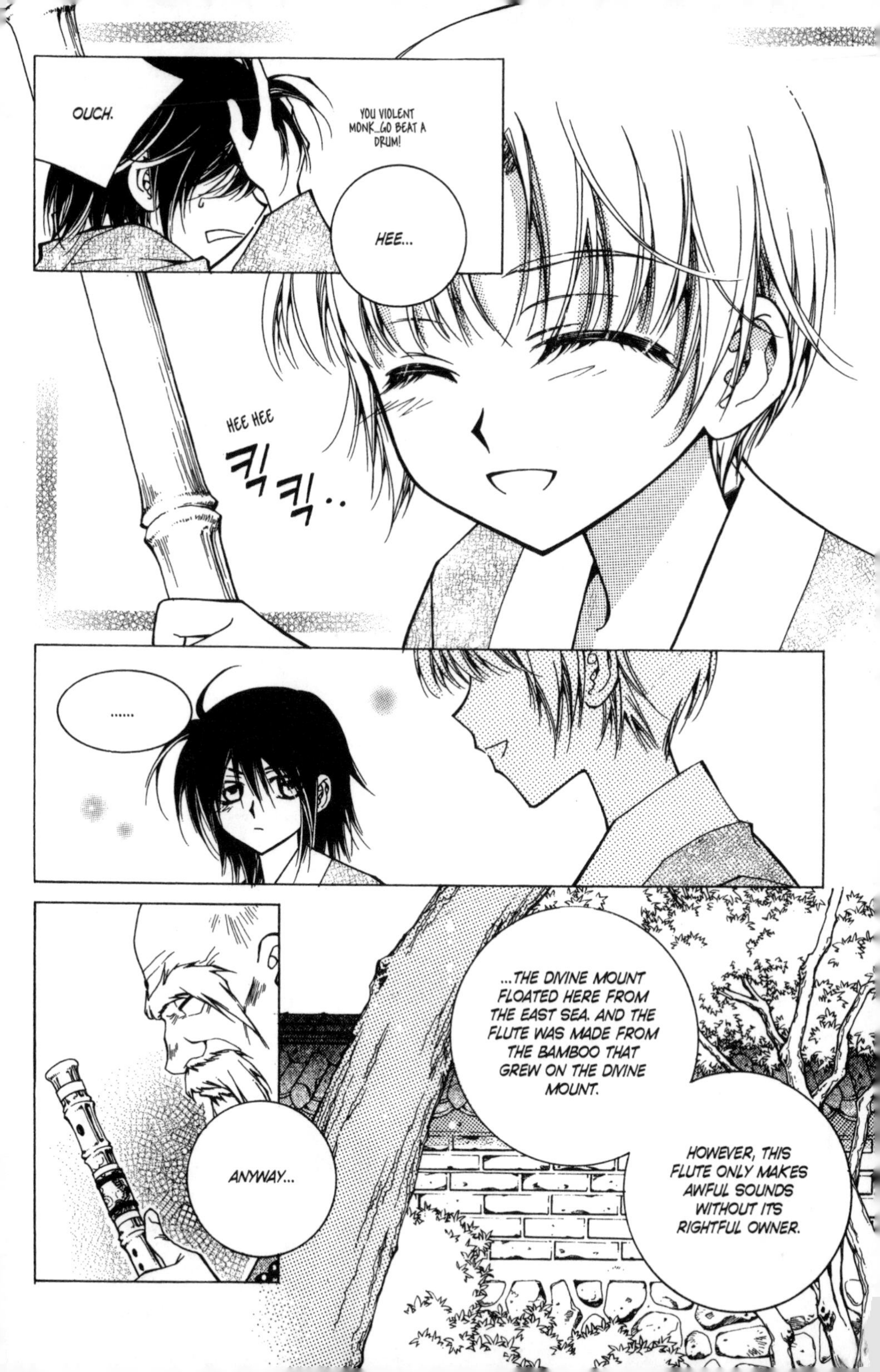
OUCH.
YOU VIOLENT MONK...GO BEAT A DRUM!
HEE...
HEE HEE
킥 킥..
......
ANYWAY...
...THE DIVINE MOUNT FLOATED HERE FROM THE EAST SEA. AND THE FLUTE WAS MADE FROM THE BAMBOO THAT GREW ON THE DIVINE MOUNT.
HOWEVER, THIS FLUTE ONLY MAKES AWFUL SOUNDS WITHOUT ITS RIGHTFUL OWNER.

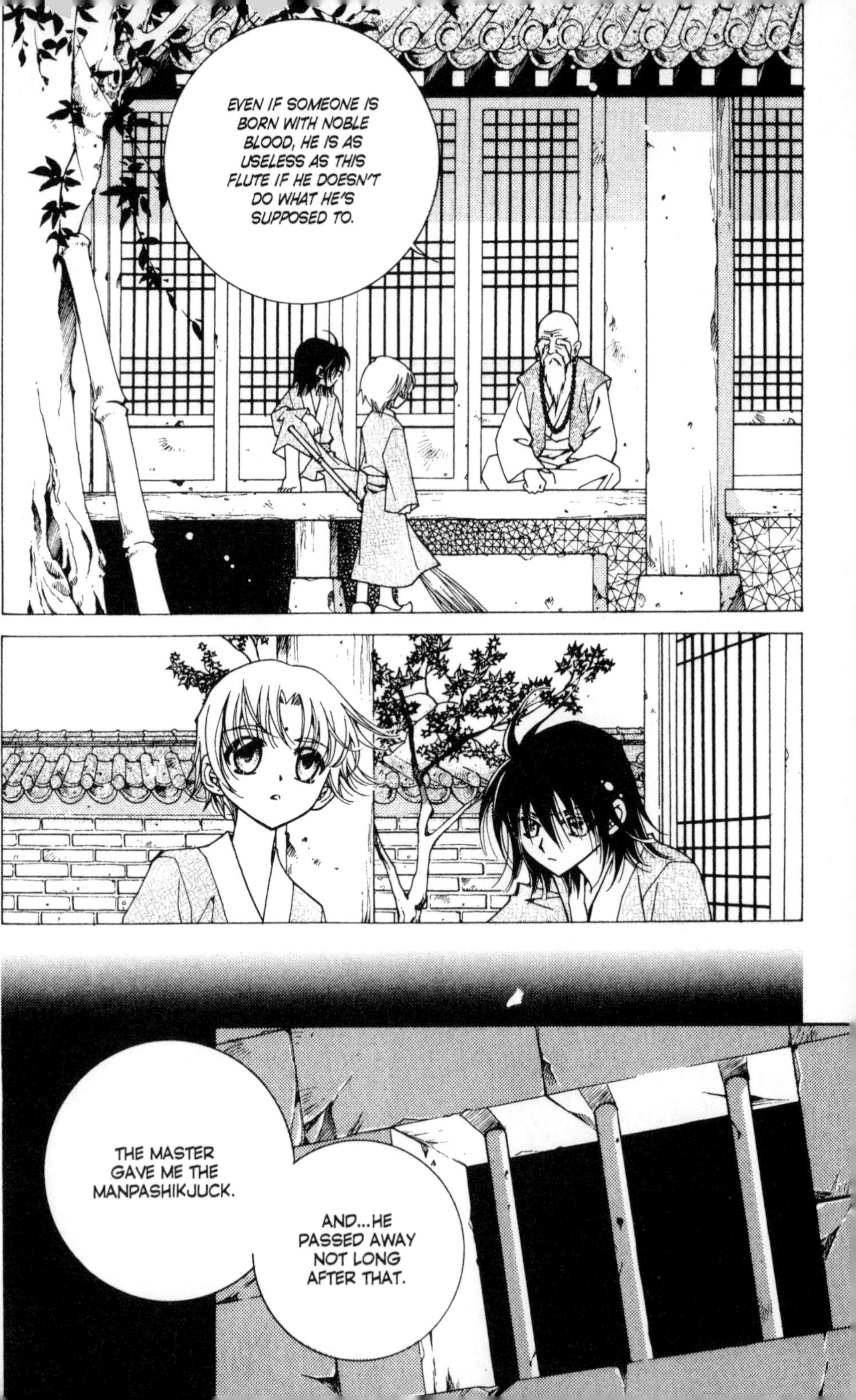
EVEN IF SOMEONE IS BORN WITH NOBLE BLOOD, HE IS AS USELESS AS THIS FLUTE IF HE DOESN'T DO WHAT HE'S SUPPOSED TO.
THE MASTER GAVE ME THE MANPASHIKJUCK.
AND...HE PASSED AWAY NOT LONG AFTER THAT.

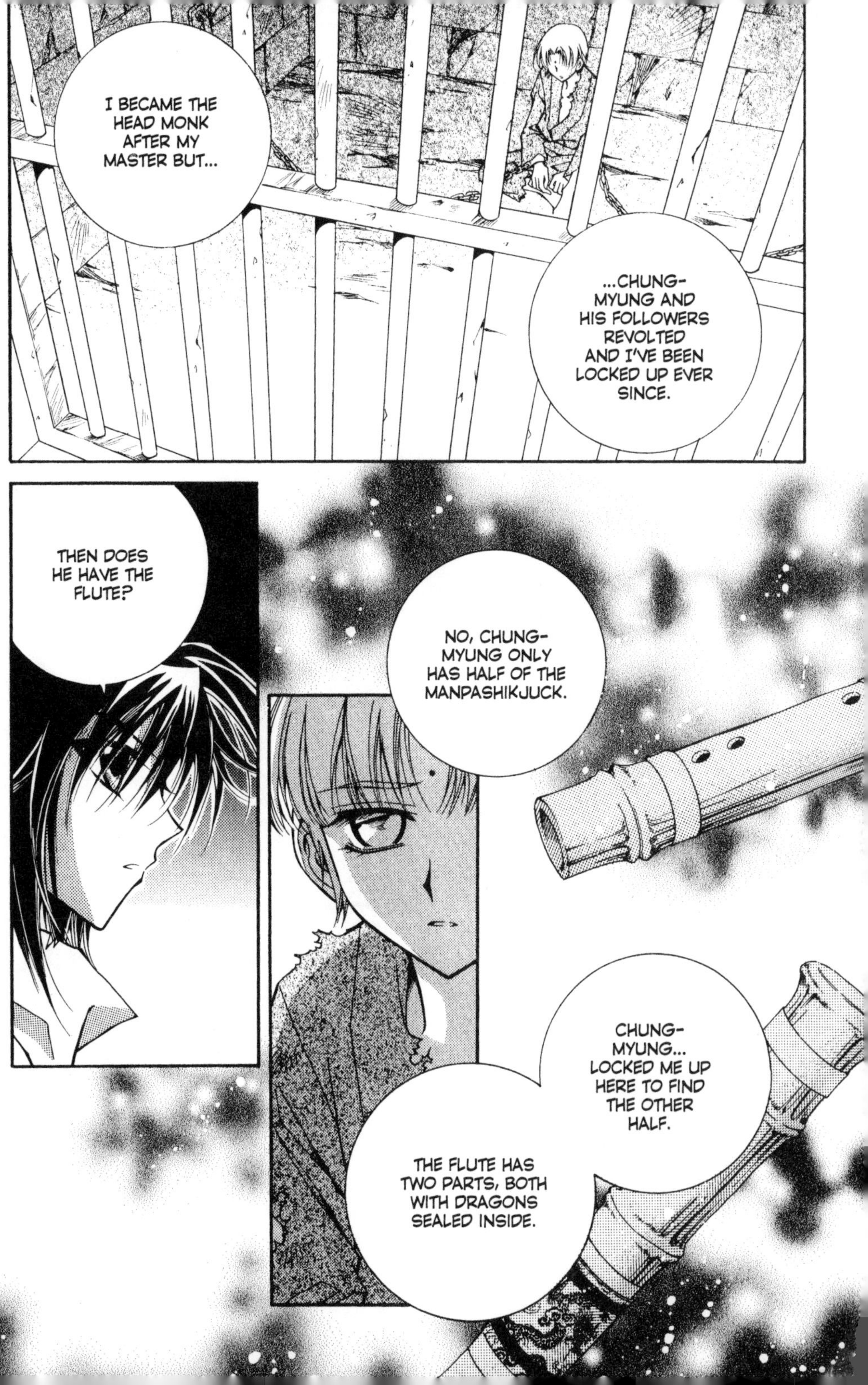
I BECAME THE HEAD MONK AFTER MY MASTER BUT...
...CHUNG-MYUNG AND HIS FOLLOWERS REVOLTED AND I'VE BEEN LOCKED UP EVER SINCE.
THEN DOES HE HAVE THE FLUTE?
NO, CHUNG-MYUNG ONLY HAS HALF OF THE MANPASHIKJUCK.
CHUNG-MYUNG... LOCKED ME UP HERE TO FIND THE OTHER HALF.
THE FLUTE HAS TWO PARTS, BOTH WITH DRAGONS SEALED INSIDE.

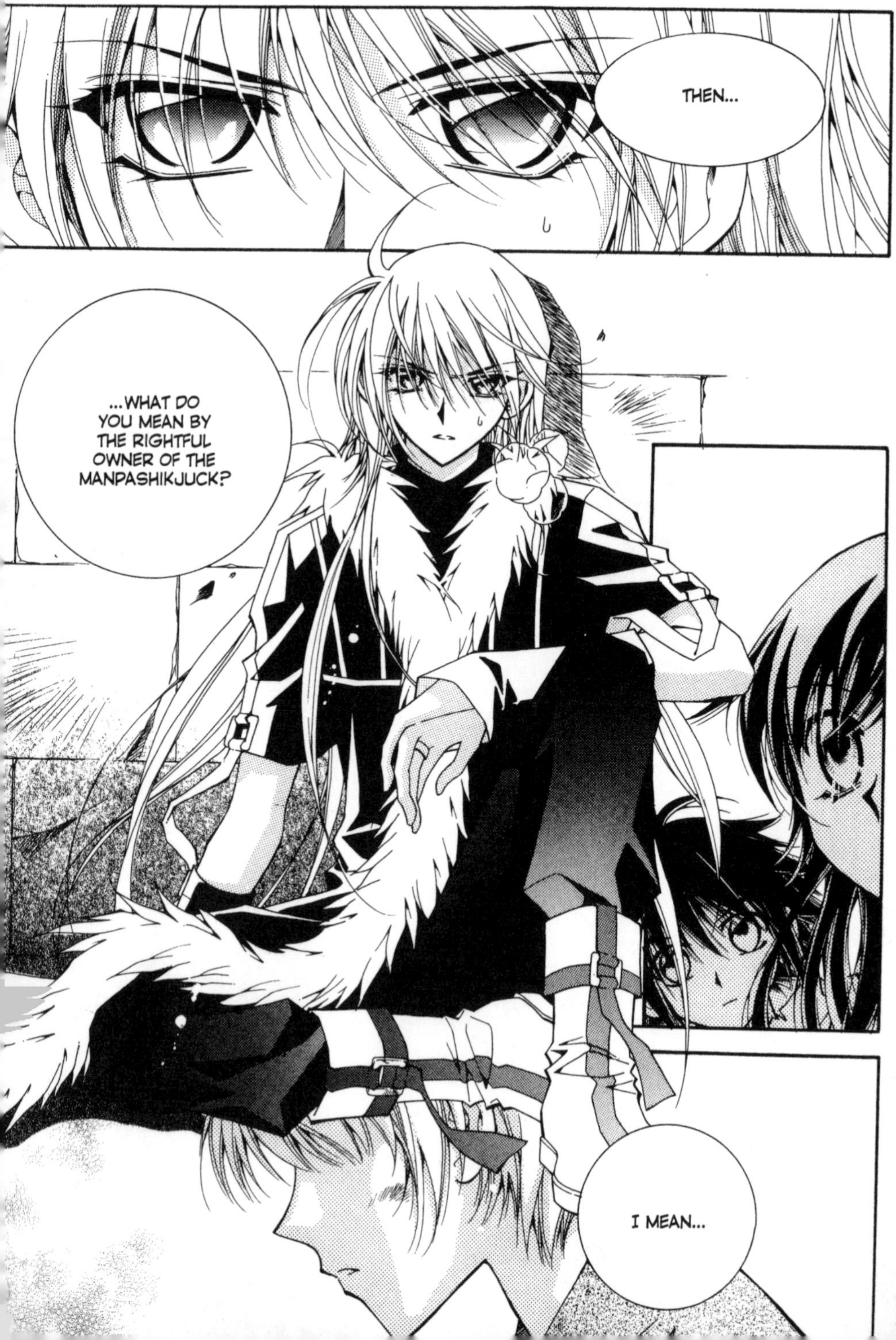
THEN...
...WHAT DO YOU MEAN BY THE RIGHTFUL OWNER OF THE MANPASHIKJUCK?
I MEAN...

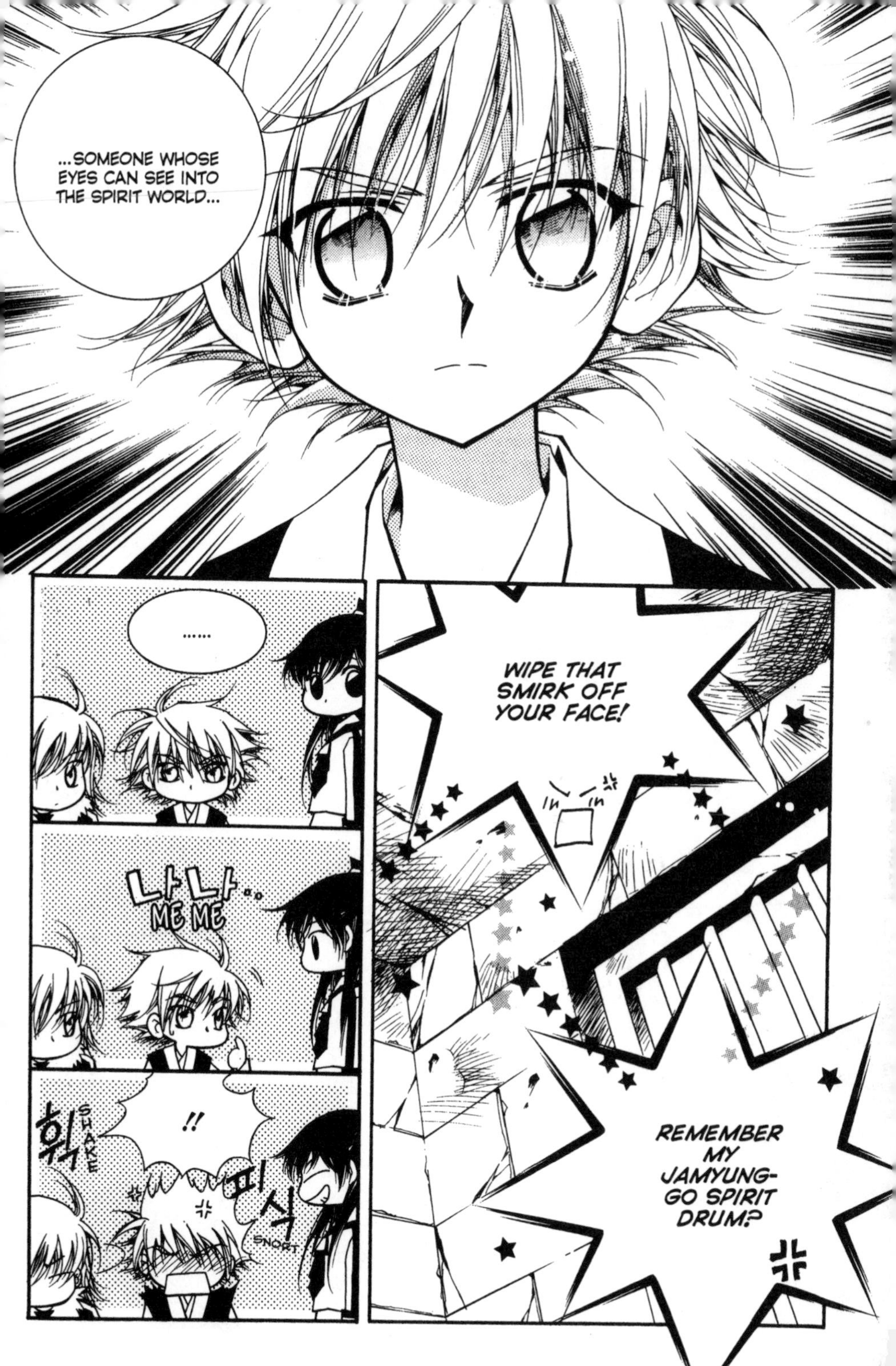
...SOMEONE WHOSE EYES CAN SEE INTO THE SPIRIT WORLD...
......
나나나..
ME ME
휙
SHAKE
!!
피식
SNORT
WIPE THAT SMIRK OFF YOUR FACE!
REMEMBER MY JAMYUNG-GO SPIRIT DRUM?

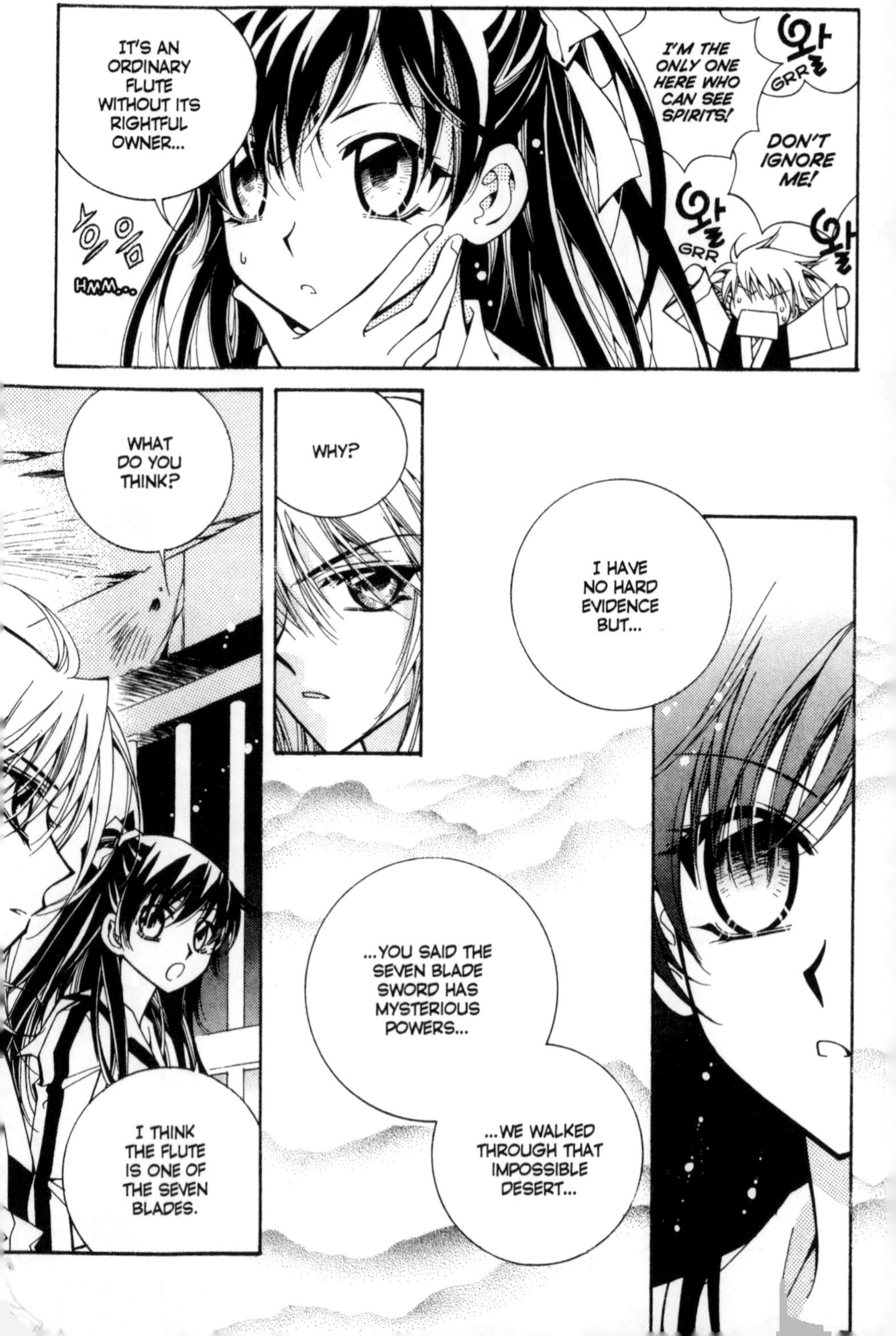
IT'S AN ORDINARY FLUTE WITHOUT ITS RIGHTFUL OWNER...
HMM...
I'M THE ONLY ONE HERE WHO CAN SEE SPIRITS!
GRR
DON'T IGNORE ME!
GRR
WHAT DO YOU THINK?
I THINK THE FLUTE IS ONE OF THE SEVEN BLADES.
WHY?
I HAVE NO HARD EVIDENCE BUT...
...YOU SAID THE SEVEN BLADE SWORD HAS MYSTERIOUS POWERS...
...WE WALKED THROUGH THAT IMPOSSIBLE DESERT...

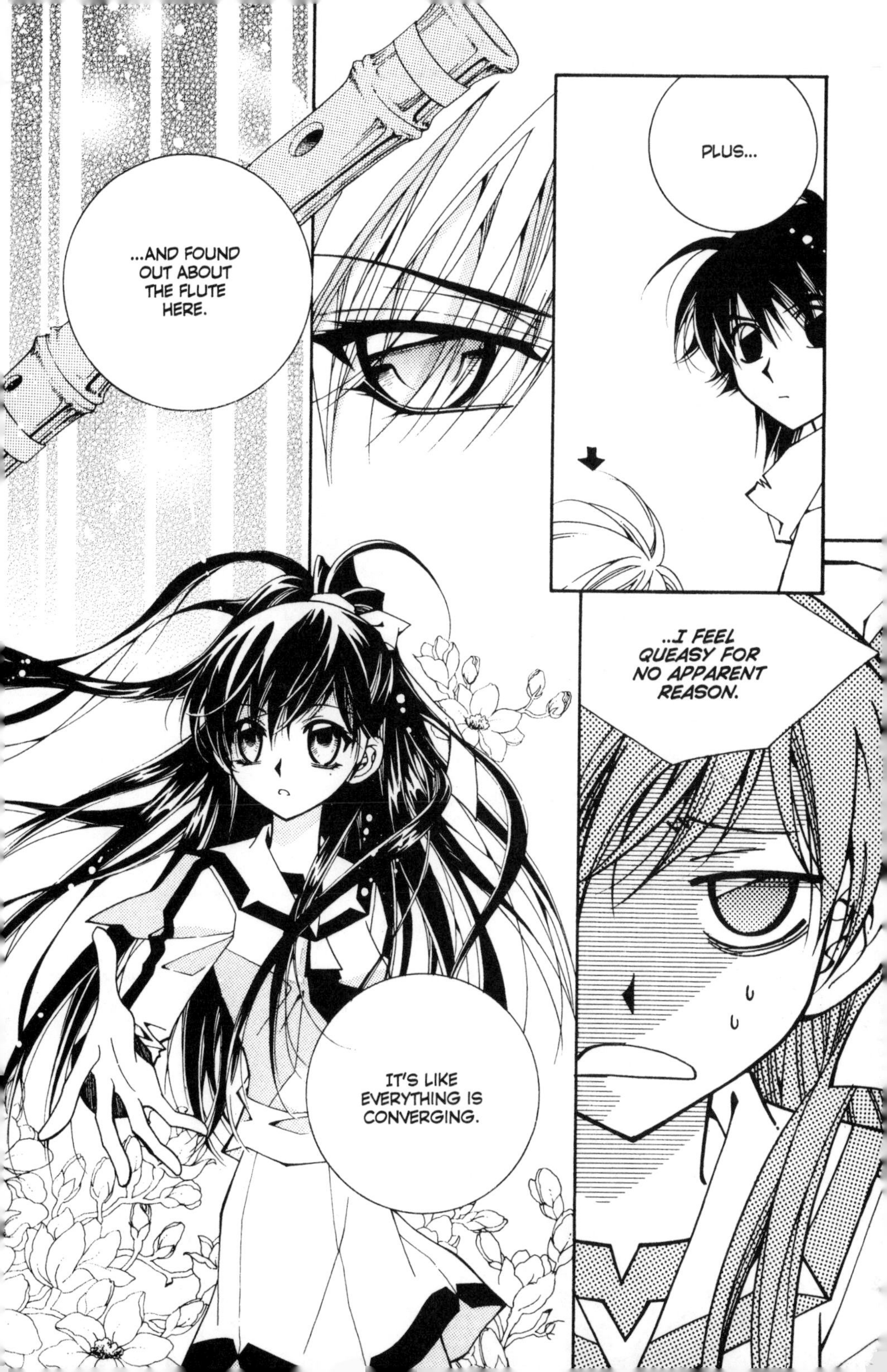
...AND FOUND OUT ABOUT THE FLUTE HERE.
PLUS...
IT'S LIKE EVERYTHING IS CONVERGING.
...I FEEL QUEASY FOR NO APPARENT REASON.

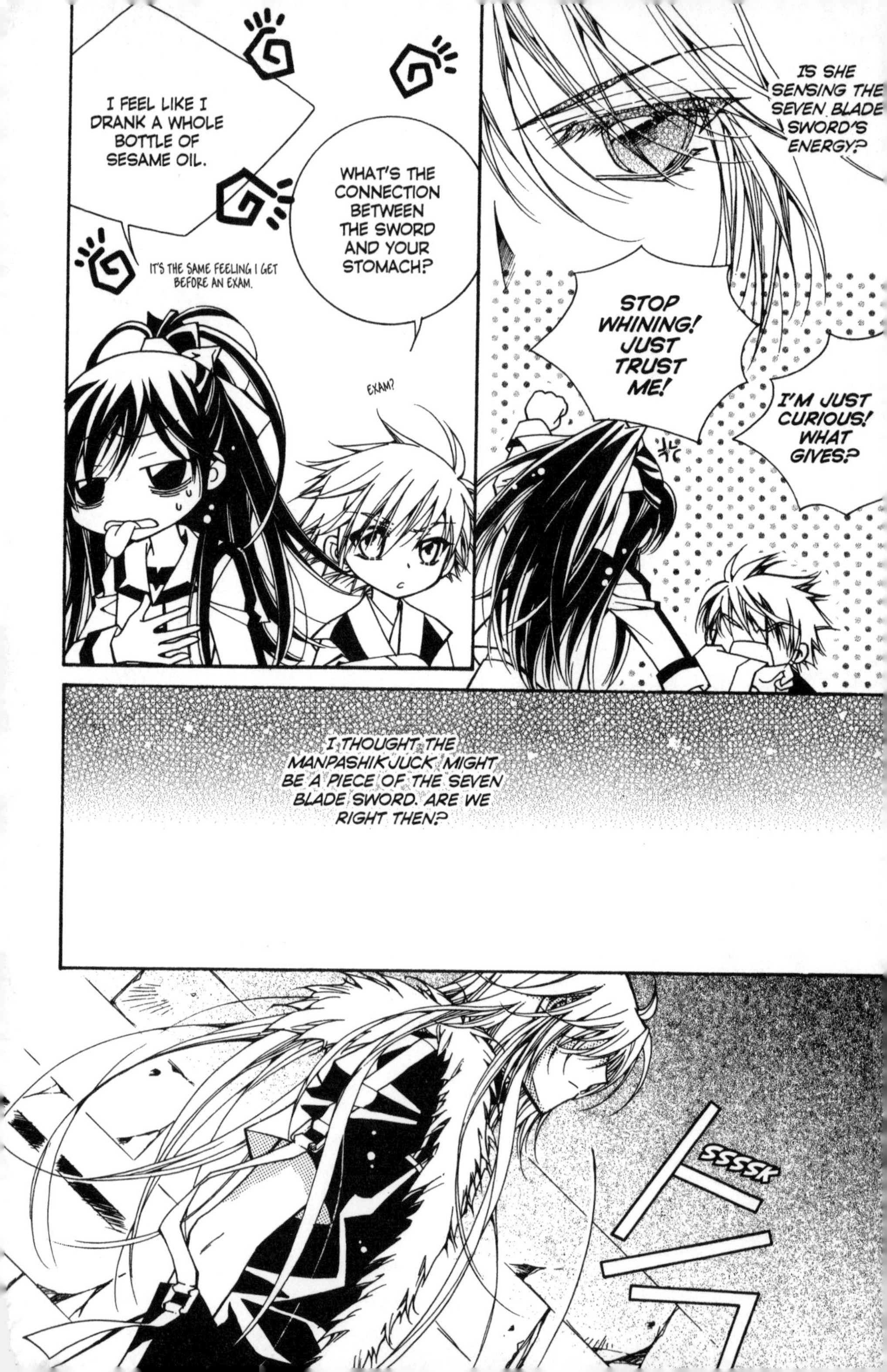
I FEEL LIKE I DRANK A WHOLE BOTTLE OF SESAME OIL.
IT'S THE SAME FEELING I GET BEFORE AN EXAM.
WHAT'S THE CONNECTION BETWEEN THE SWORD AND YOUR STOMACH?
EXAM?
IS SHE SENSING THE SEVEN BLADE SWORD'S ENERGY?
STOP WHINING! JUST TRUST ME!
I'M JUST CURIOUS! WHAT GIVES?
I THOUGHT THE MANPASHIKJUCK MIGHT BE A PIECE OF THE SEVEN BLADE SWORD. ARE WE RIGHT THEN?
SSSSK

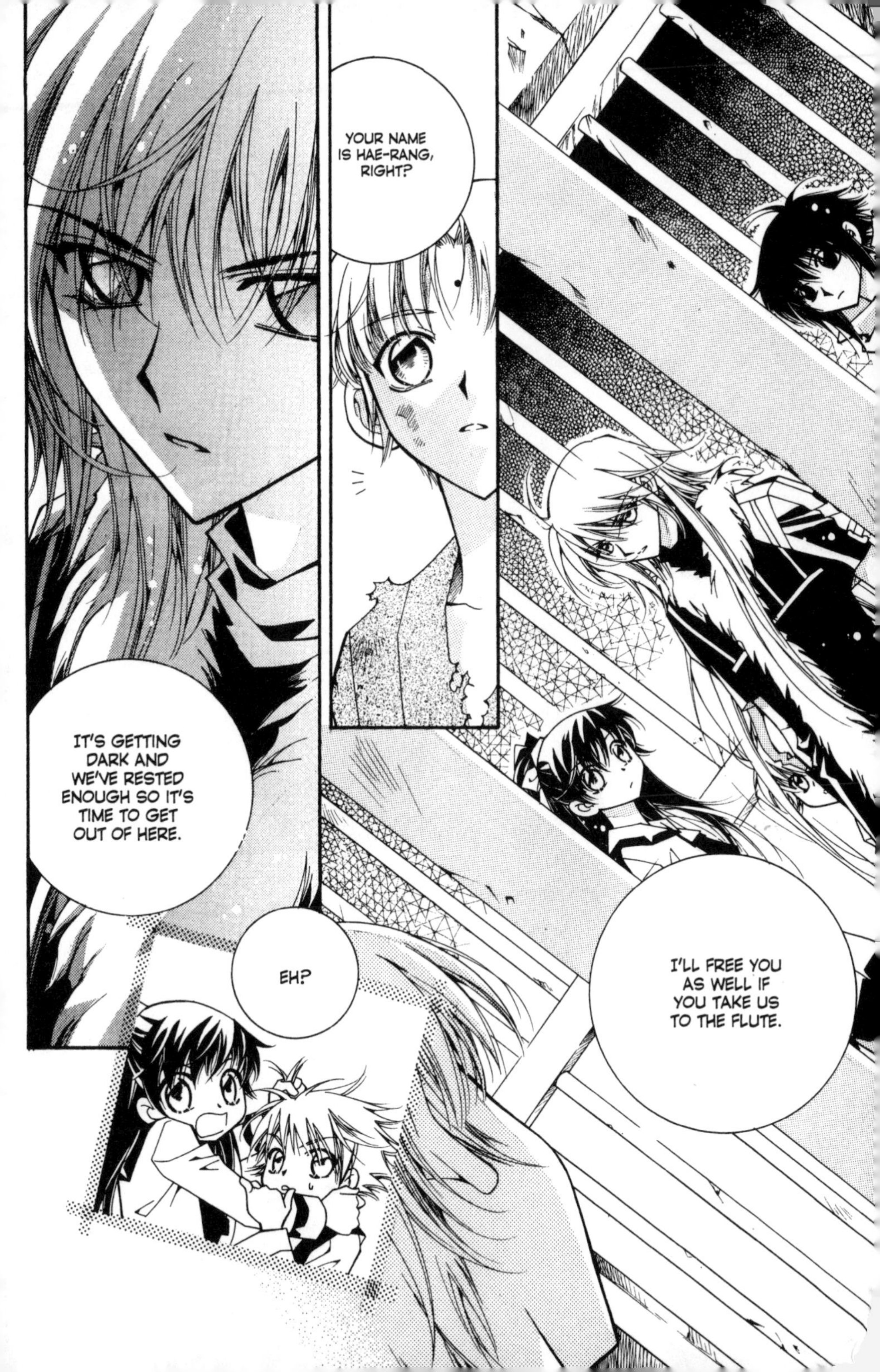
YOUR NAME IS HAE-RANG, RIGHT?
IT'S GETTING DARK AND WE'VE RESTED ENOUGH SO IT'S TIME TO GET OUT OF HERE.
I'LL FREE YOU AS WELL IF YOU TAKE US TO THE FLUTE.
EH?

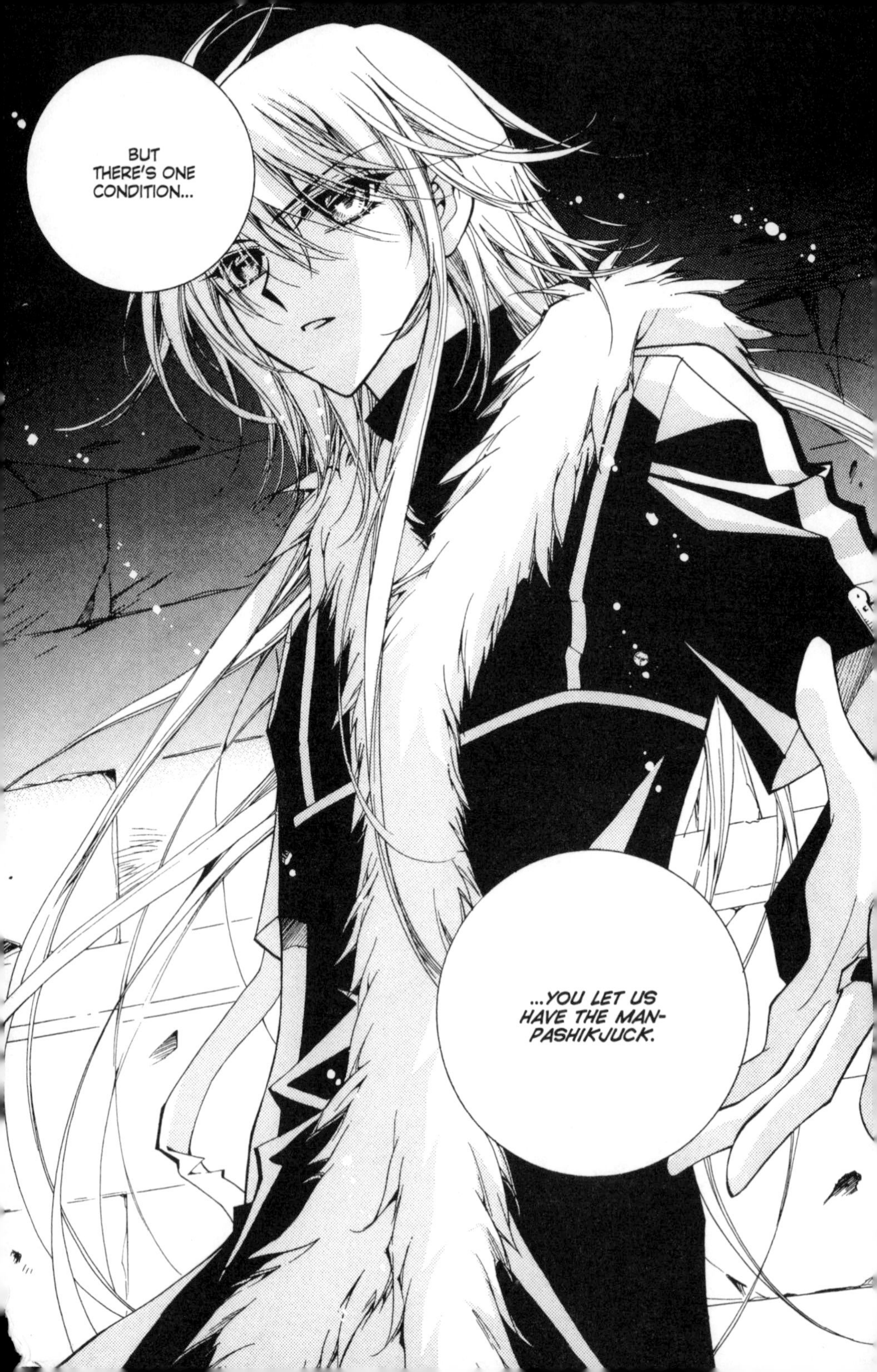
BUT THERE'S ONE CONDITION...
...YOU LET US HAVE THE MAN-PASHIKJUCK.

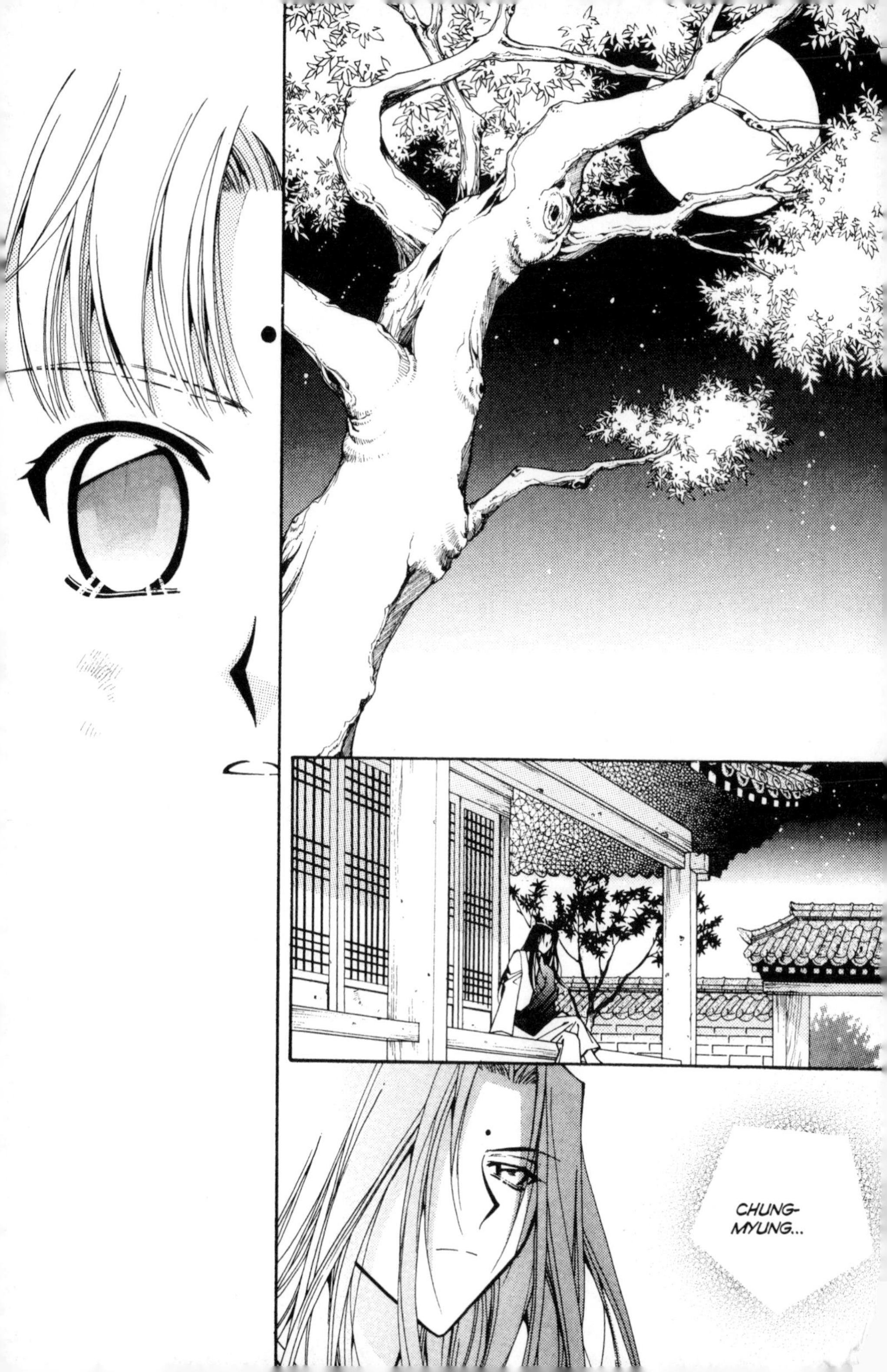
CHUNG-
MYUNG...

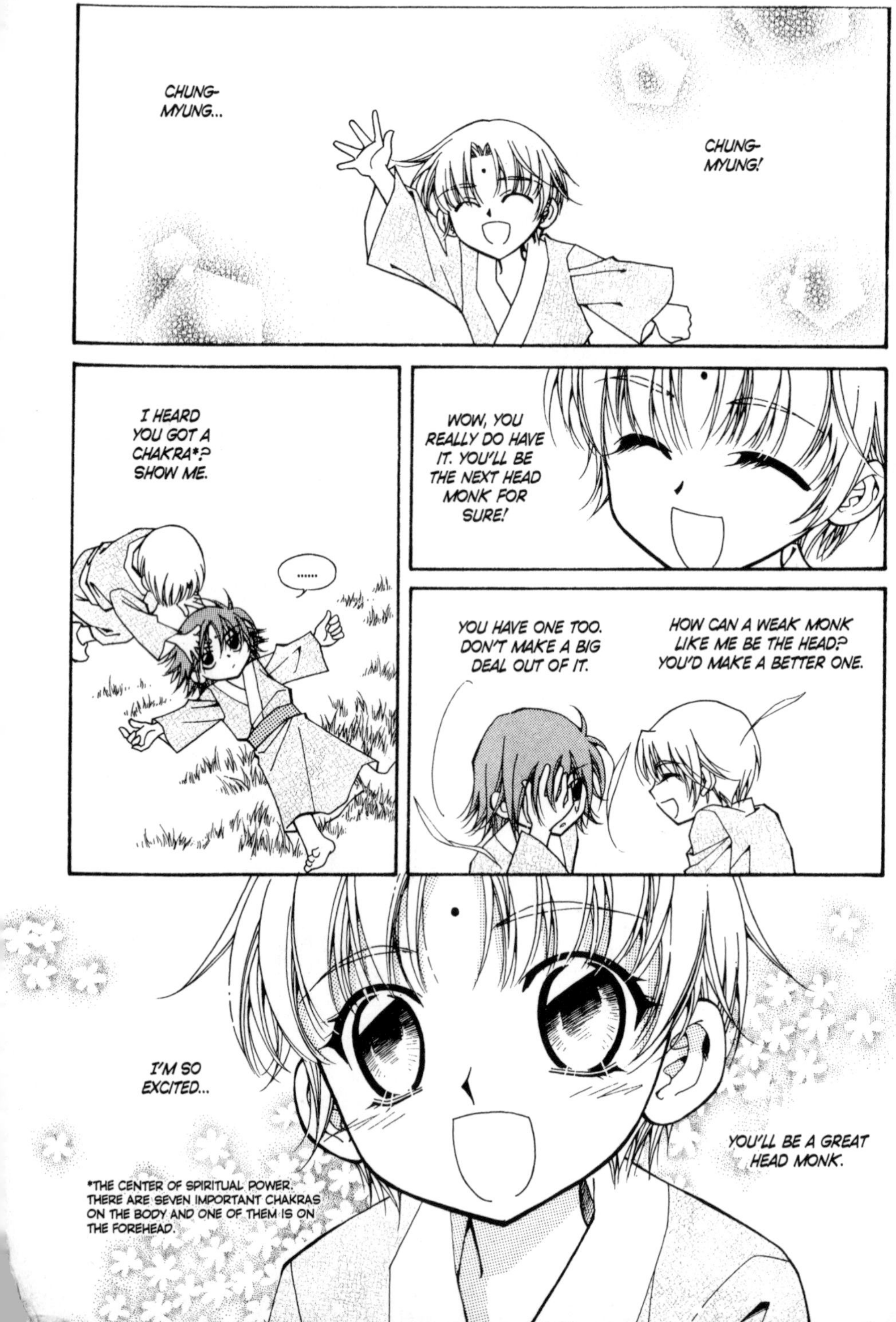
CHUNG-MYUNG...
CHUNG-MYUNG!
I HEARD YOU GOT A CHAKRA*? SHOW ME.
......
WOW, YOU REALLY DO HAVE IT. YOU'LL BE THE NEXT HEAD MONK FOR SURE!
YOU HAVE ONE TOO. DON'T MAKE A BIG DEAL OUT OF IT.
HOW CAN A WEAK MONK LIKE ME BE THE HEAD? YOU'D MAKE A BETTER ONE.
I'M SO EXCITED...
YOU'LL BE A GREAT HEAD MONK.

*THE CENTER OF SPIRITUAL POWER. THERE ARE SEVEN IMPORTANT CHAKRAS ON THE BODY AND ONE OF THEM IS ON THE FOREHEAD.

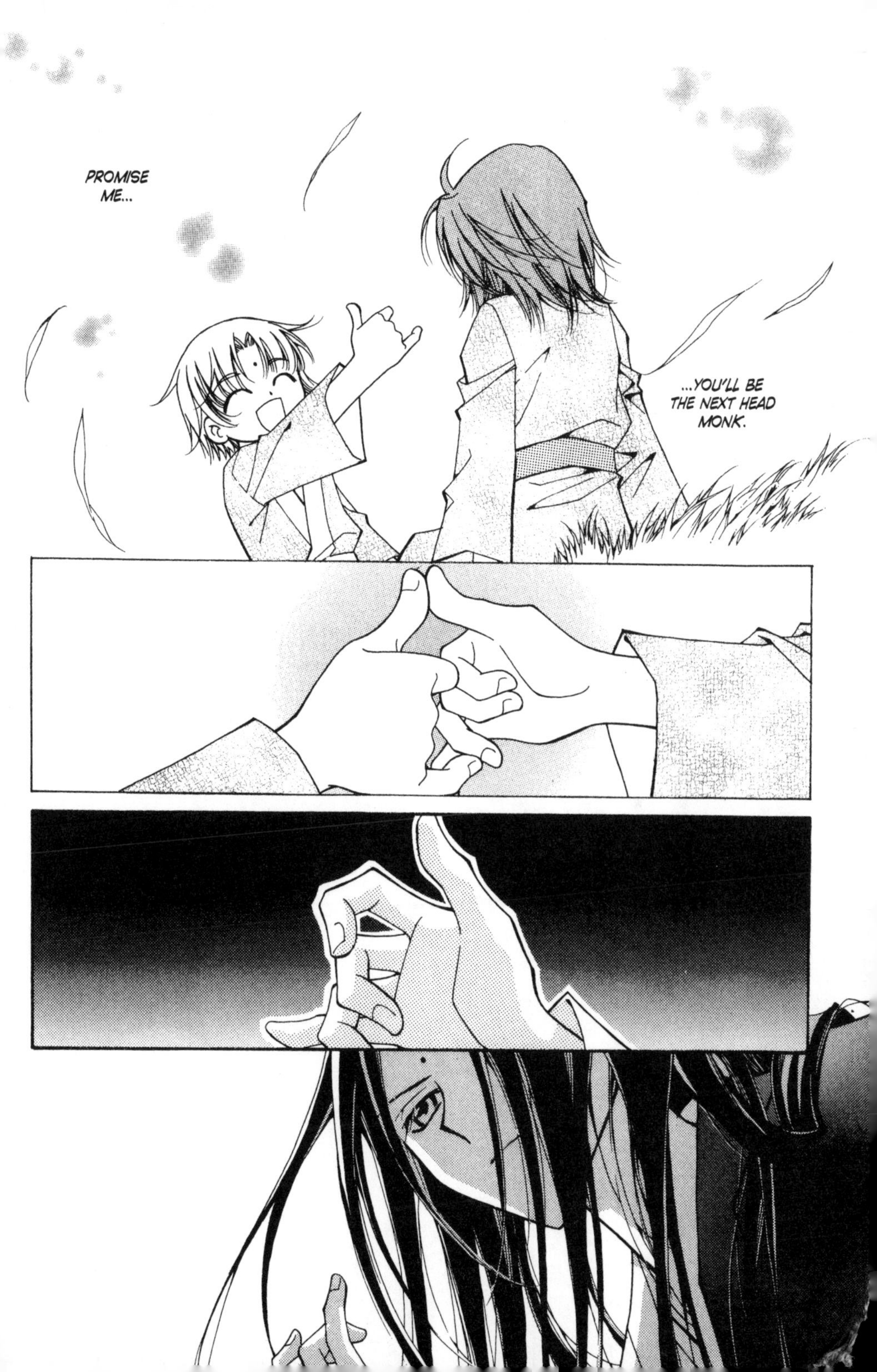
PROMISE ME...
...YOU'LL BE THE NEXT HEAD MONK.

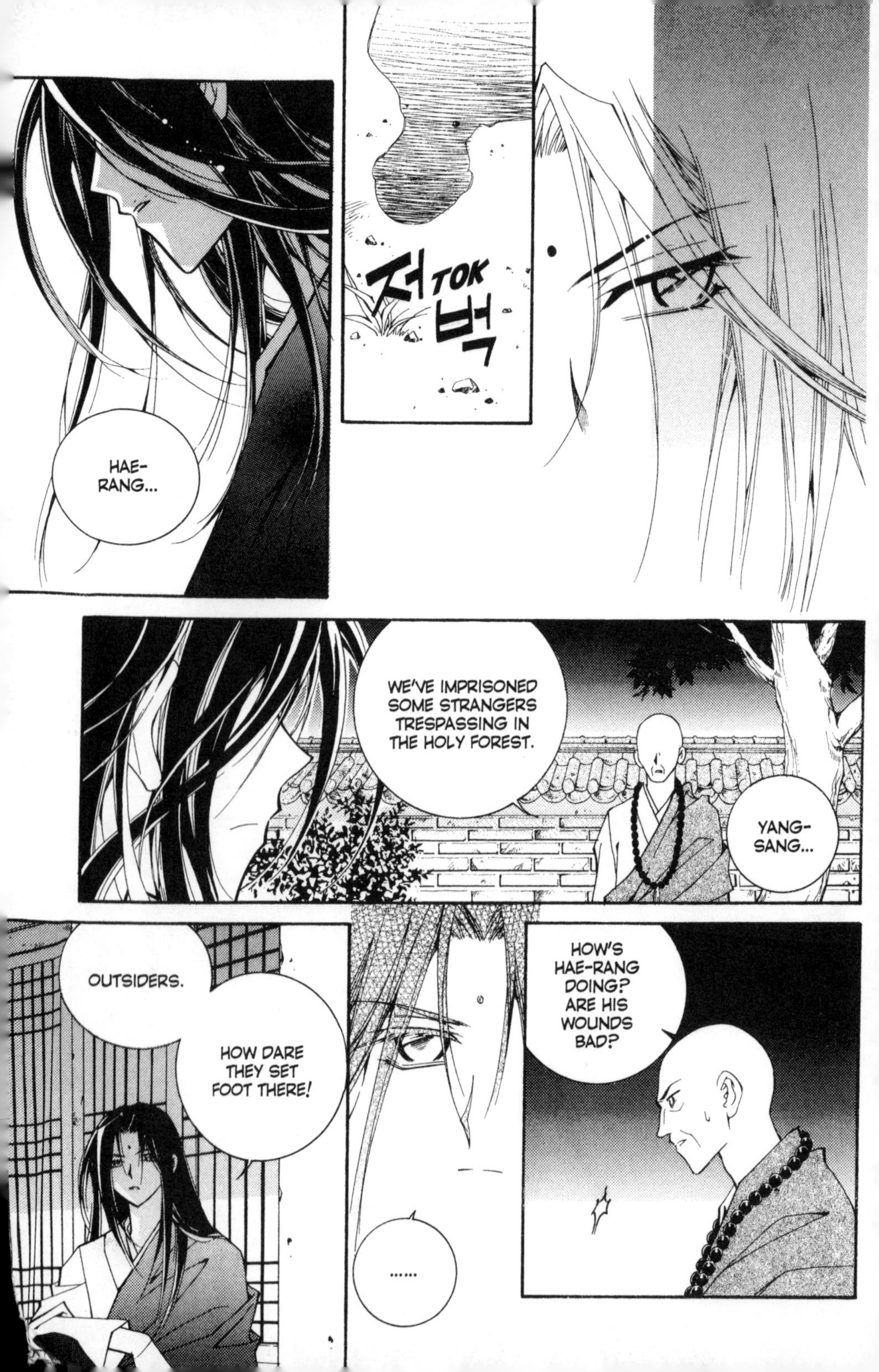
HAE-RANG...
저벅
TOK
WE'VE IMPRISONED SOME STRANGERS TRESPASSING IN THE HOLY FOREST.
YANG-SANG...
OUTSIDERS.
HOW DARE THEY SET FOOT THERE!
......
HOW'S HAE-RANG DOING? ARE HIS WOUNDS BAD?

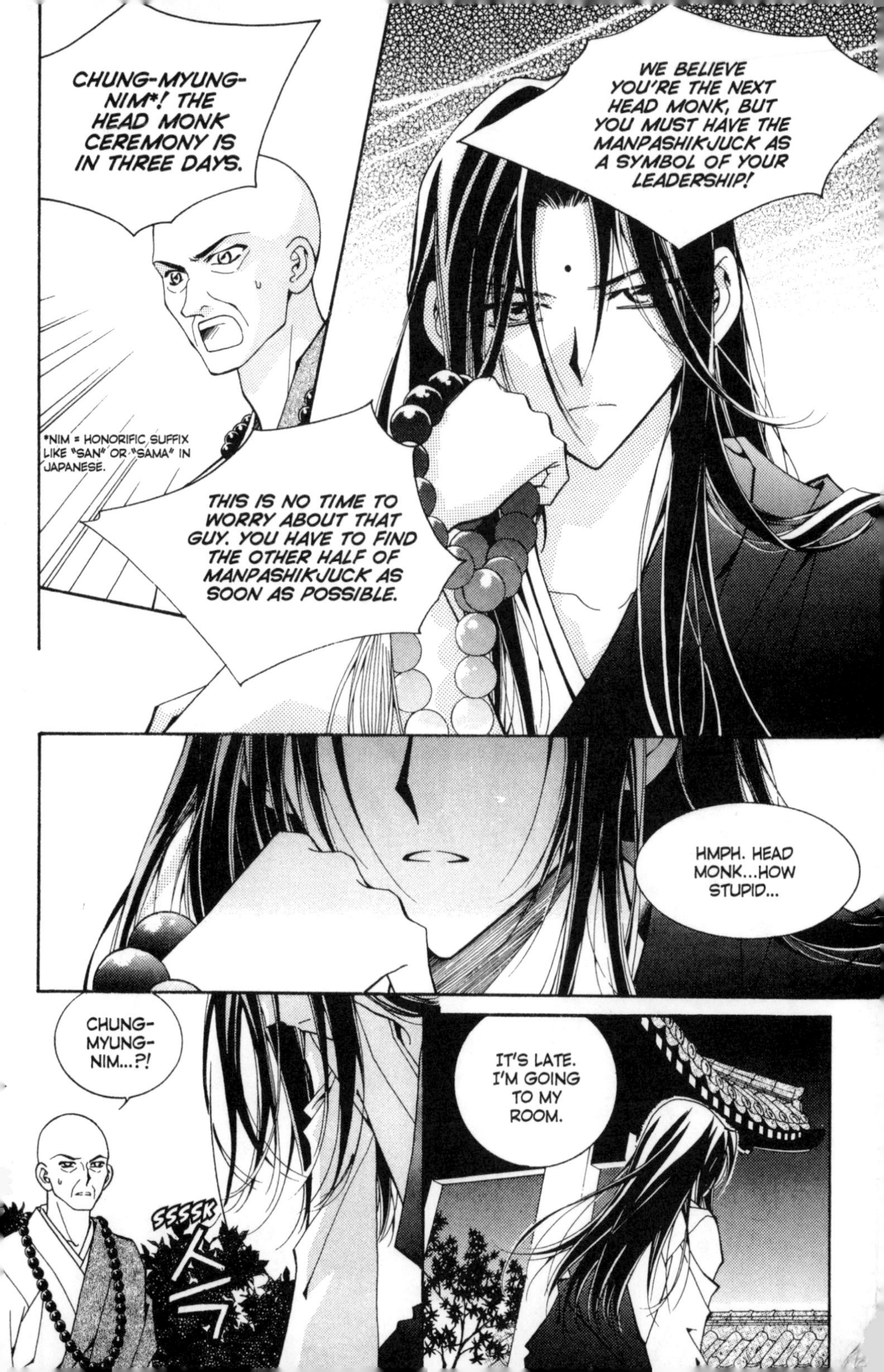
CHUNG-MYUNG-NIM*! THE HEAD MONK CEREMONY IS IN THREE DAYS.
WE BELIEVE YOU'RE THE NEXT HEAD MONK, BUT YOU MUST HAVE THE MANPASHIKJUCK AS A SYMBOL OF YOUR LEADERSHIP!
*NIM = HONORIFIC SUFFIX LIKE "SAN" OR "SAMA" IN JAPANESE.
THIS IS NO TIME TO WORRY ABOUT THAT GUY. YOU HAVE TO FIND THE OTHER HALF OF MANPASHIKJUCK AS SOON AS POSSIBLE.
HMPH. HEAD MONK...HOW STUPID...
CHUNG-MYUNG-NIM...?!
SSSSK
IT'S LATE. I'M GOING TO MY ROOM.

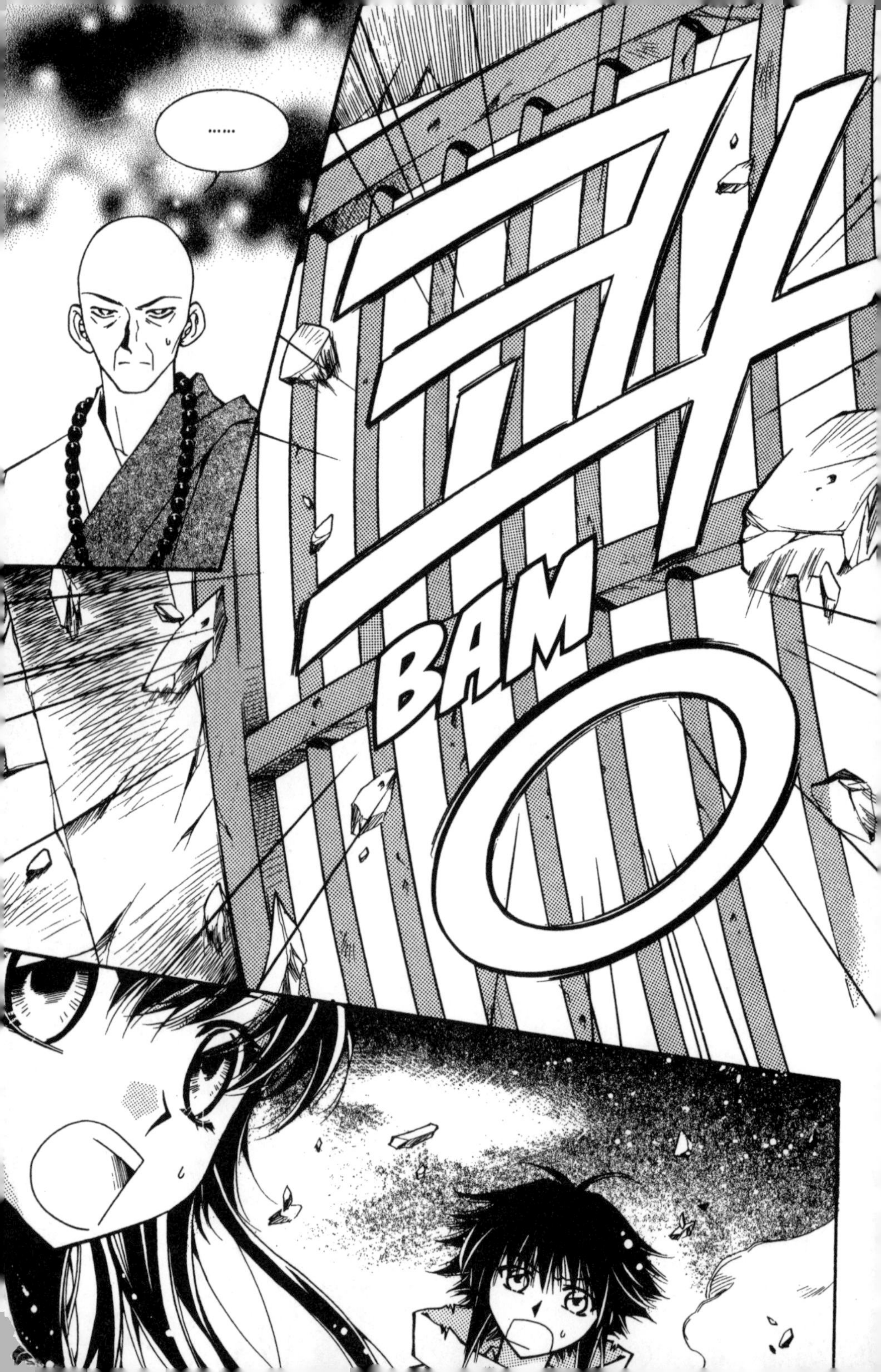......
BAM

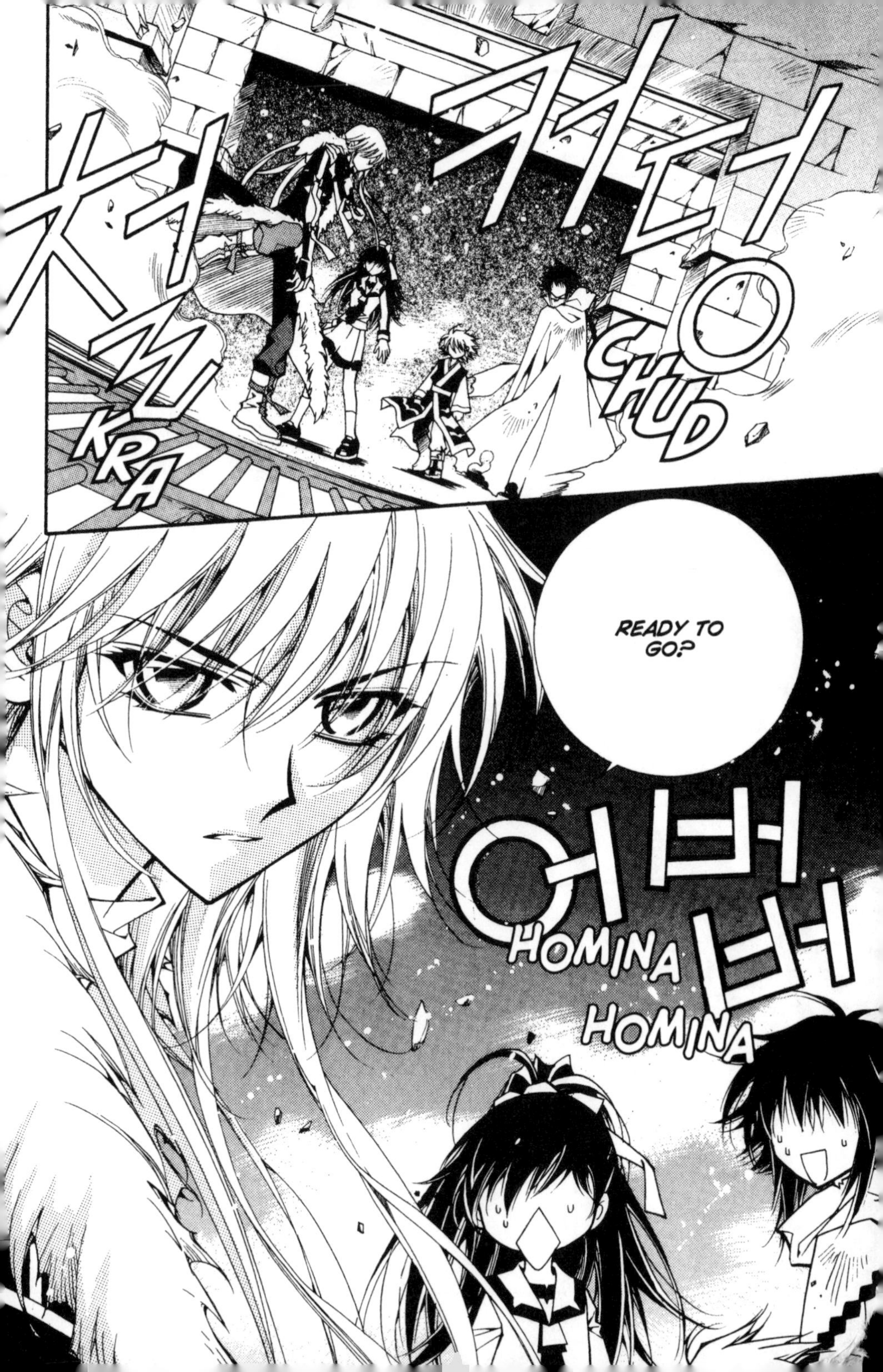
KRA
CHUD
READY TO GO?
HOMINA
HOMINA

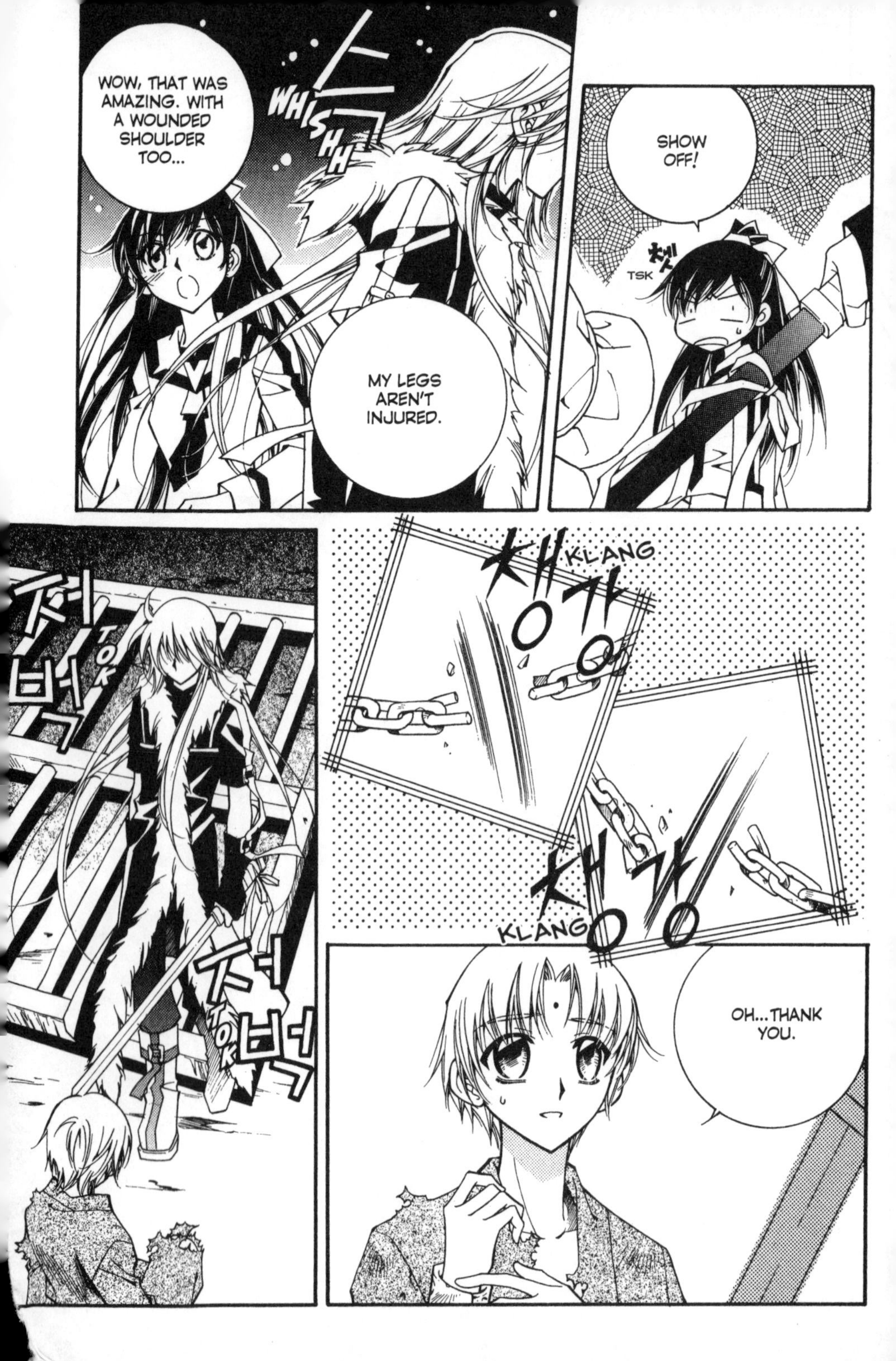
WOW, THAT WAS AMAZING. WITH A WOUNDED SHOULDER TOO...
WHISHH
MY LEGS AREN'T INJURED.
SHOW OFF!
TSK
TOK
TOK
KLANG
KLANG
OH...THANK YOU.

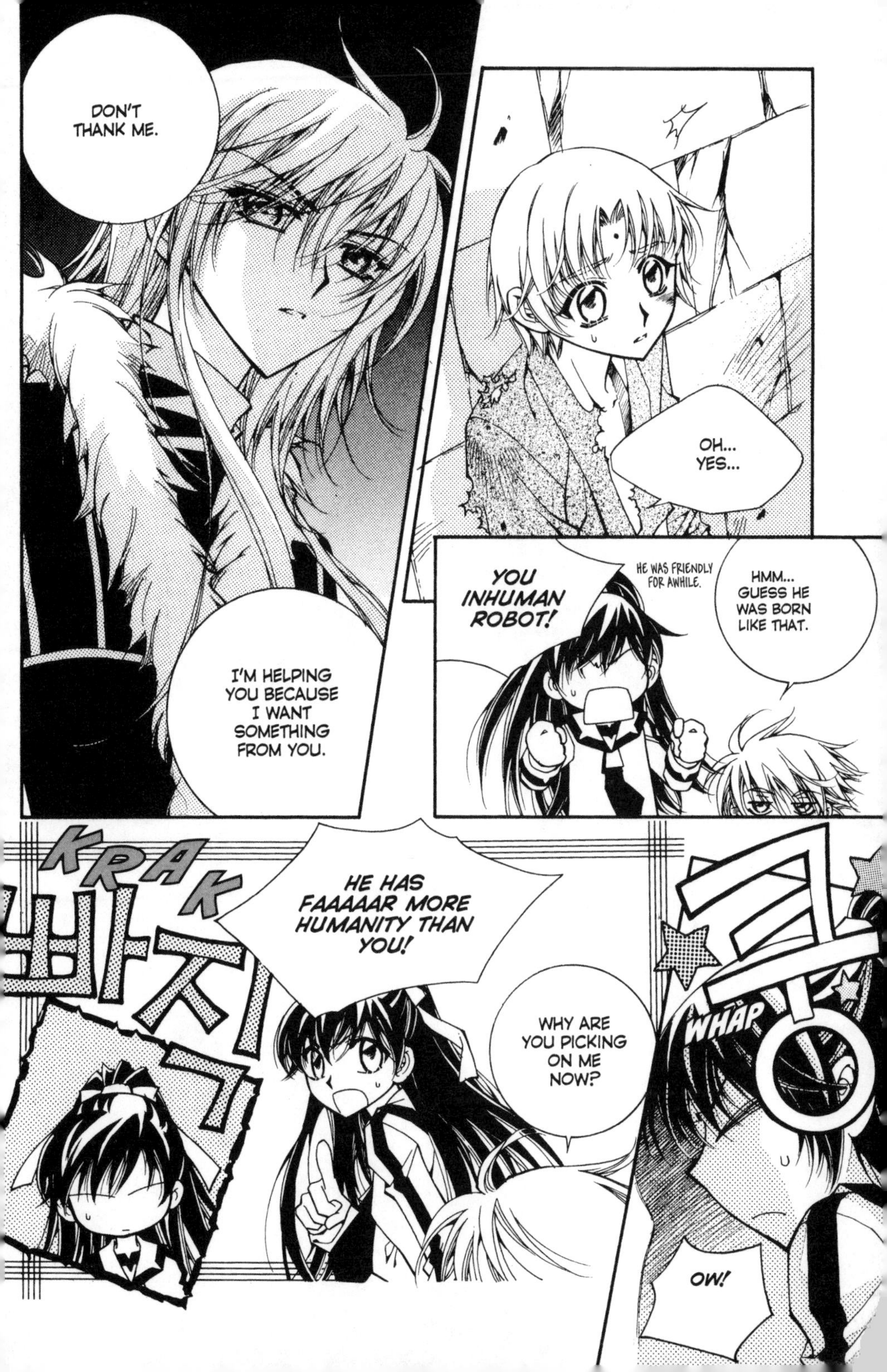
DON'T THANK ME.
I'M HELPING YOU BECAUSE I WANT SOMETHING FROM YOU.
OH... YES...
YOU INHUMAN ROBOT!
HE WAS FRIENDLY FOR AWHILE.
HMM... GUESS HE WAS BORN LIKE THAT.
KRAK
HE HAS FAAAAAR MORE HUMANITY THAN YOU!
WHY ARE YOU PICKING ON ME NOW?
WHAP
OW!

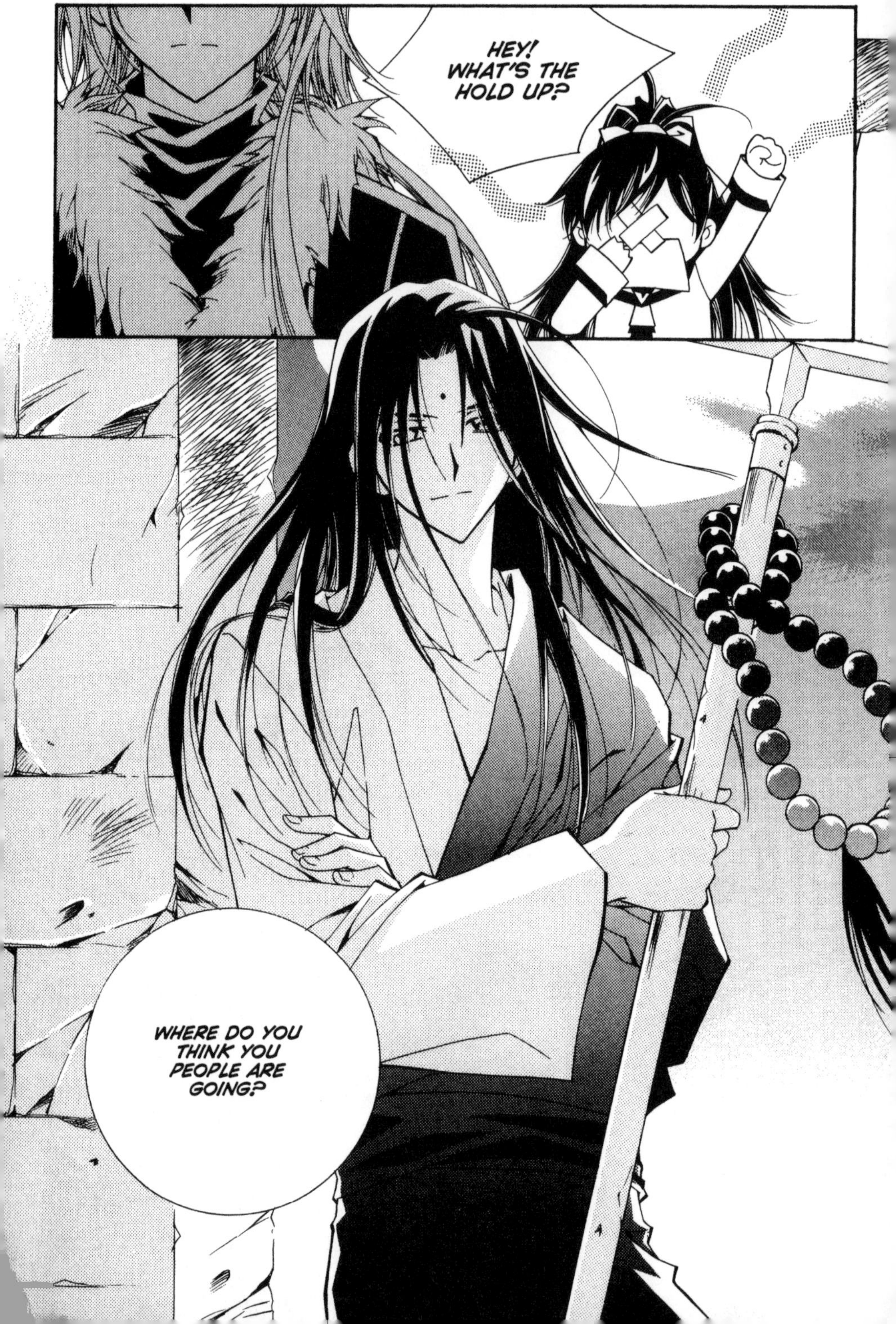
HEY! WHAT'S THE HOLD UP?
WHERE DO YOU THINK YOU PEOPLE ARE GOING?

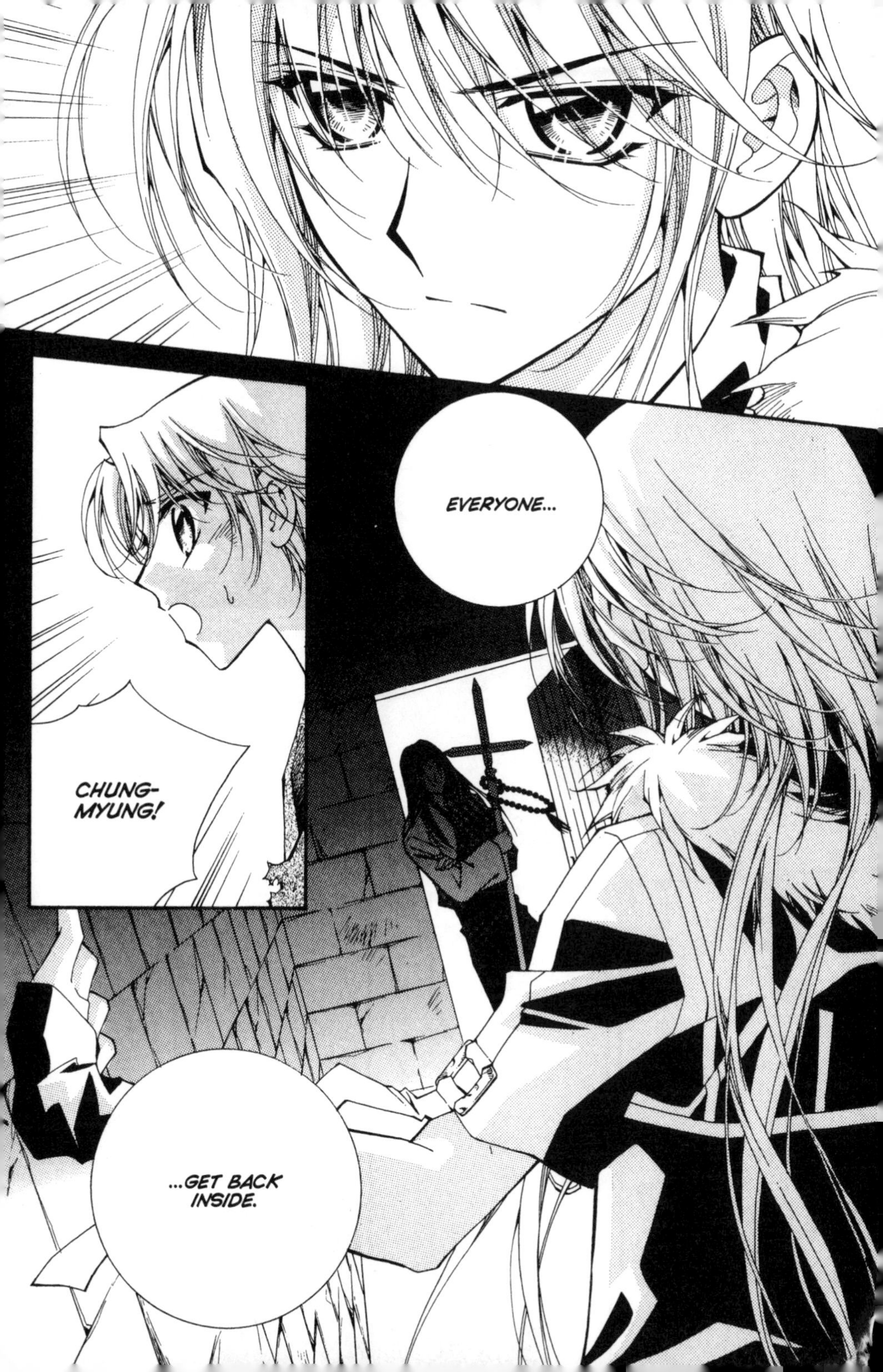
CHUNG-
MYUNG!
EVERYONE...
...GET BACK
INSIDE.

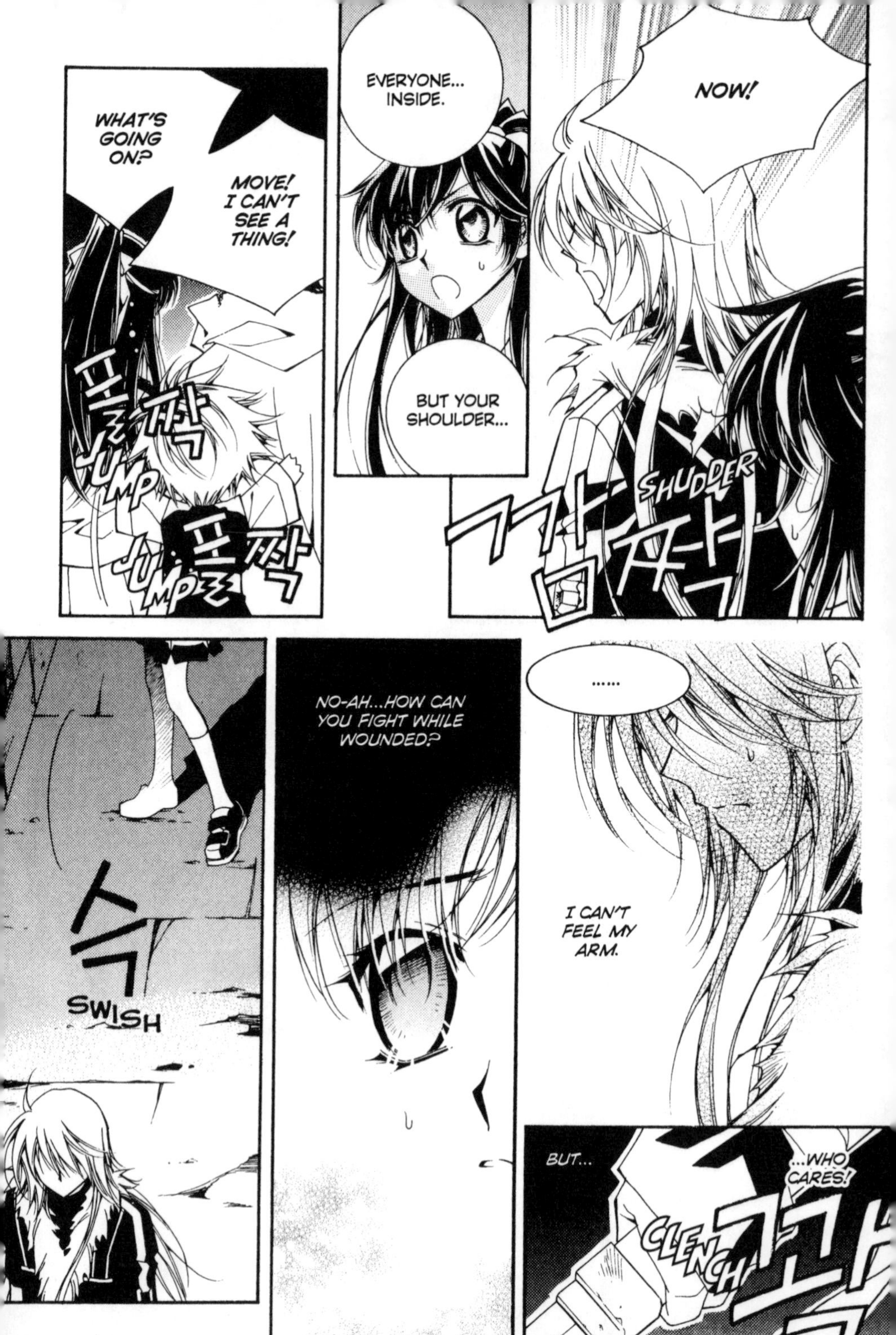
WHAT'S GOING ON?
MOVE! I CAN'T SEE A THING!
JUMP
JUMP
EVERYONE... INSIDE.
BUT YOUR SHOULDER...
NOW!
SHUDDER
SWISH
NO-AH...HOW CAN YOU FIGHT WHILE WOUNDED?
......
I CAN'T FEEL MY ARM.
BUT...
...WHO CARES!
CLENCH

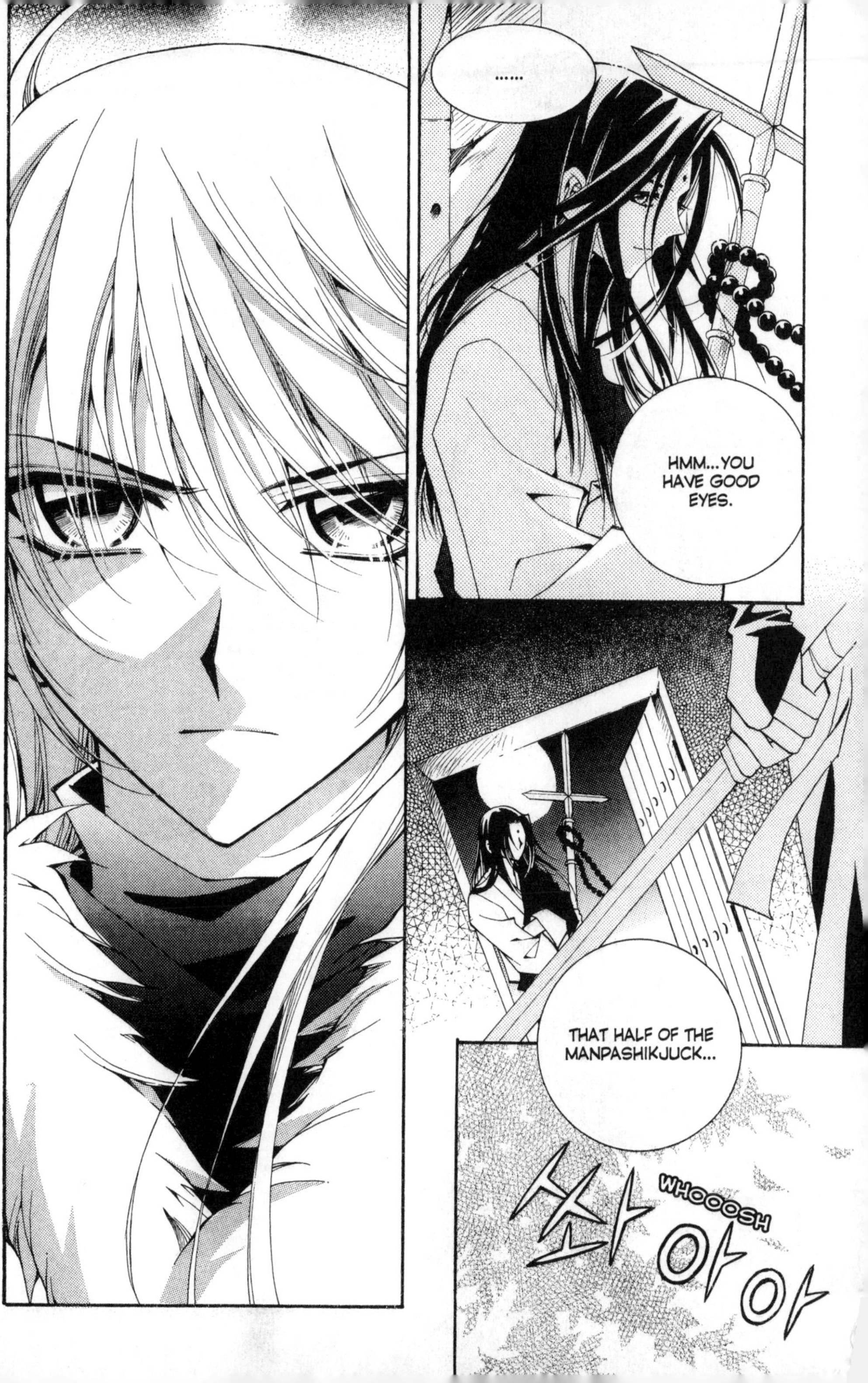
......
HMM...YOU HAVE GOOD EYES.
THAT HALF OF THE MANPASHIKJUCK...
WHOOOOSH

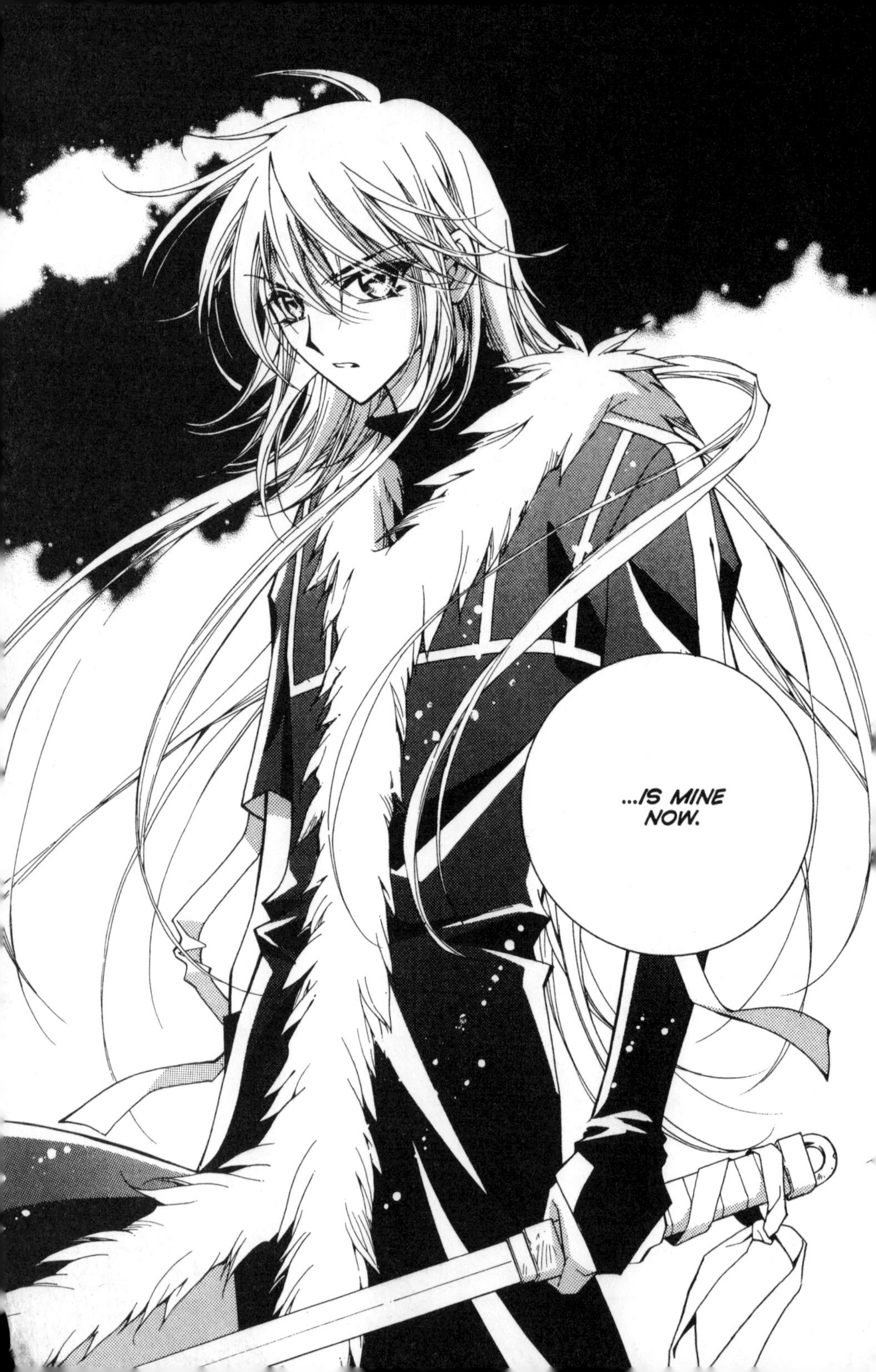
...IS MINE NOW.

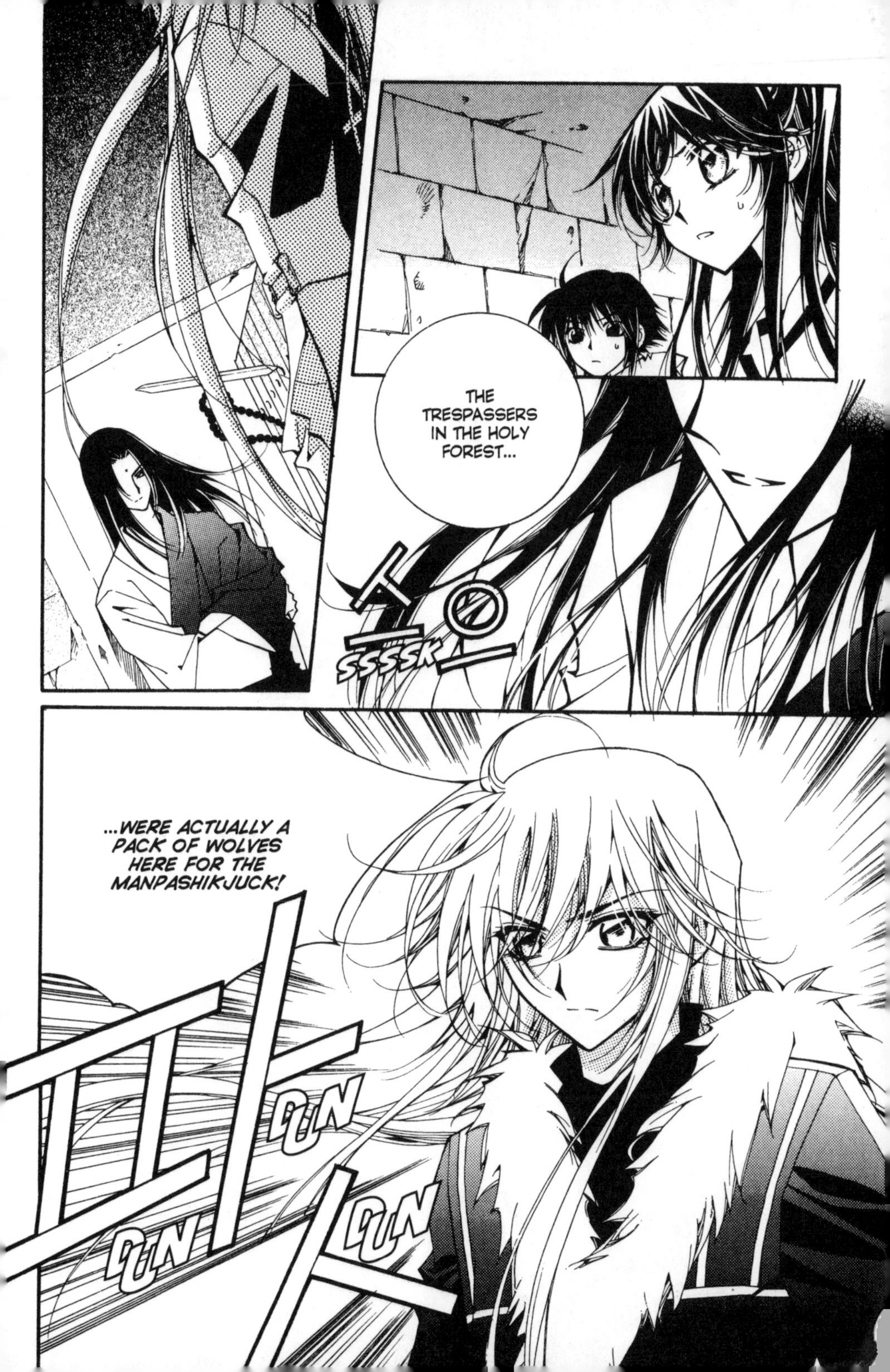
THE TRESPASSERS IN THE HOLY FOREST...
SSSSK
...WERE ACTUALLY A PACK OF WOLVES HERE FOR THE MANPASHIKJUCK!
DUN
DUN
DUN

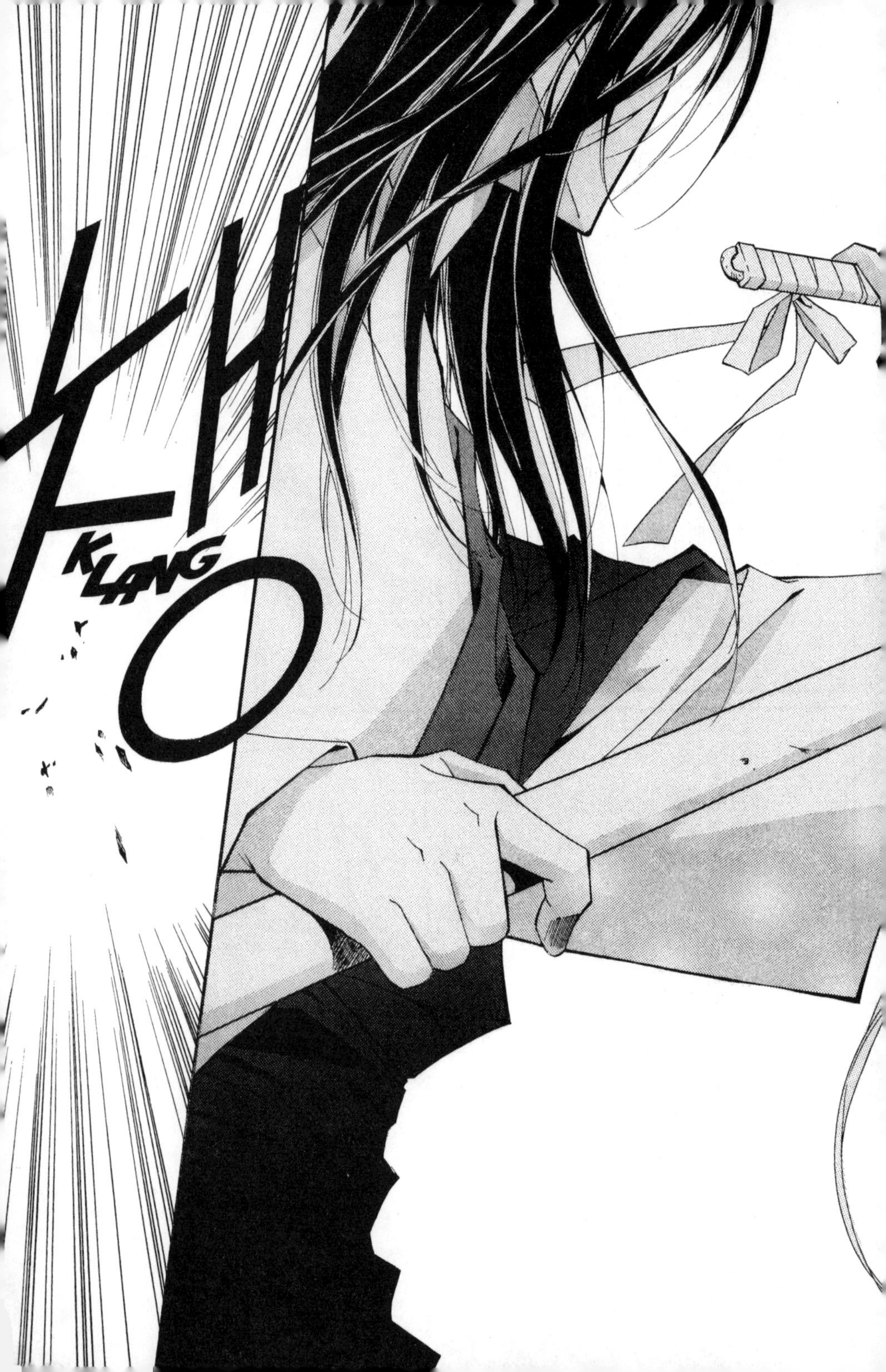
KLANG

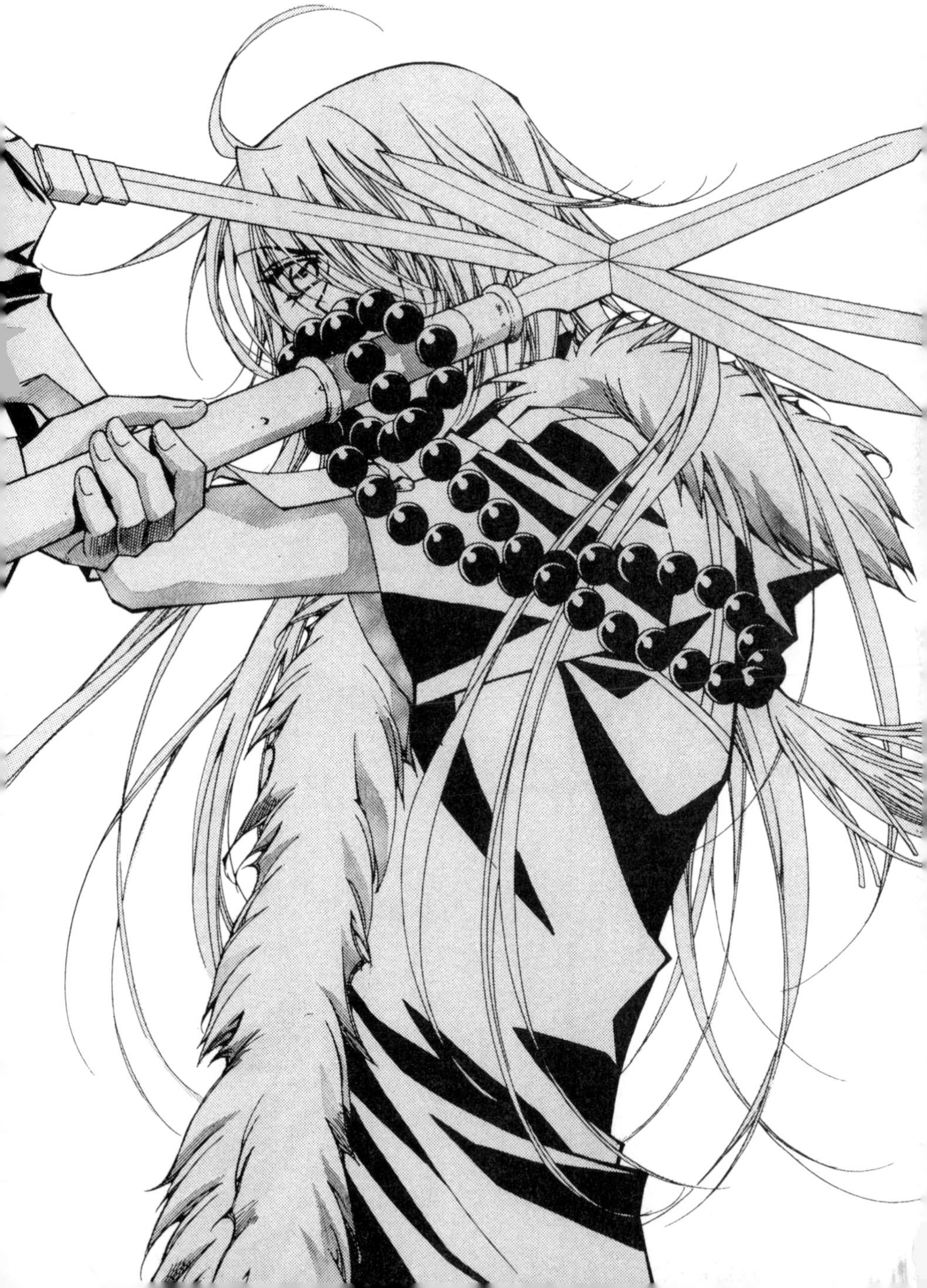

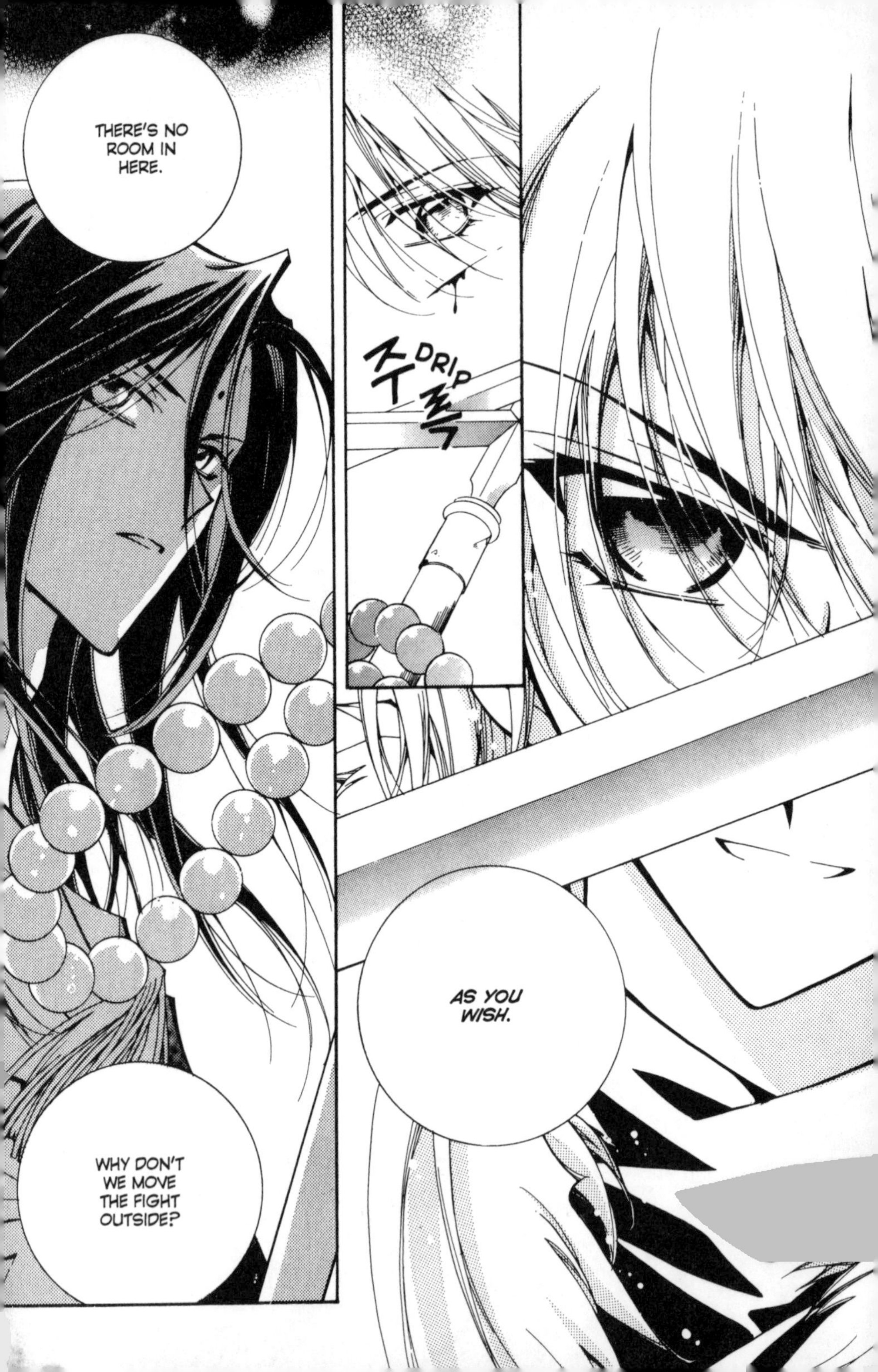
THERE'S NO ROOM IN HERE.
WHY DON'T WE MOVE THE FIGHT OUTSIDE?
DRIP
AS YOU WISH.

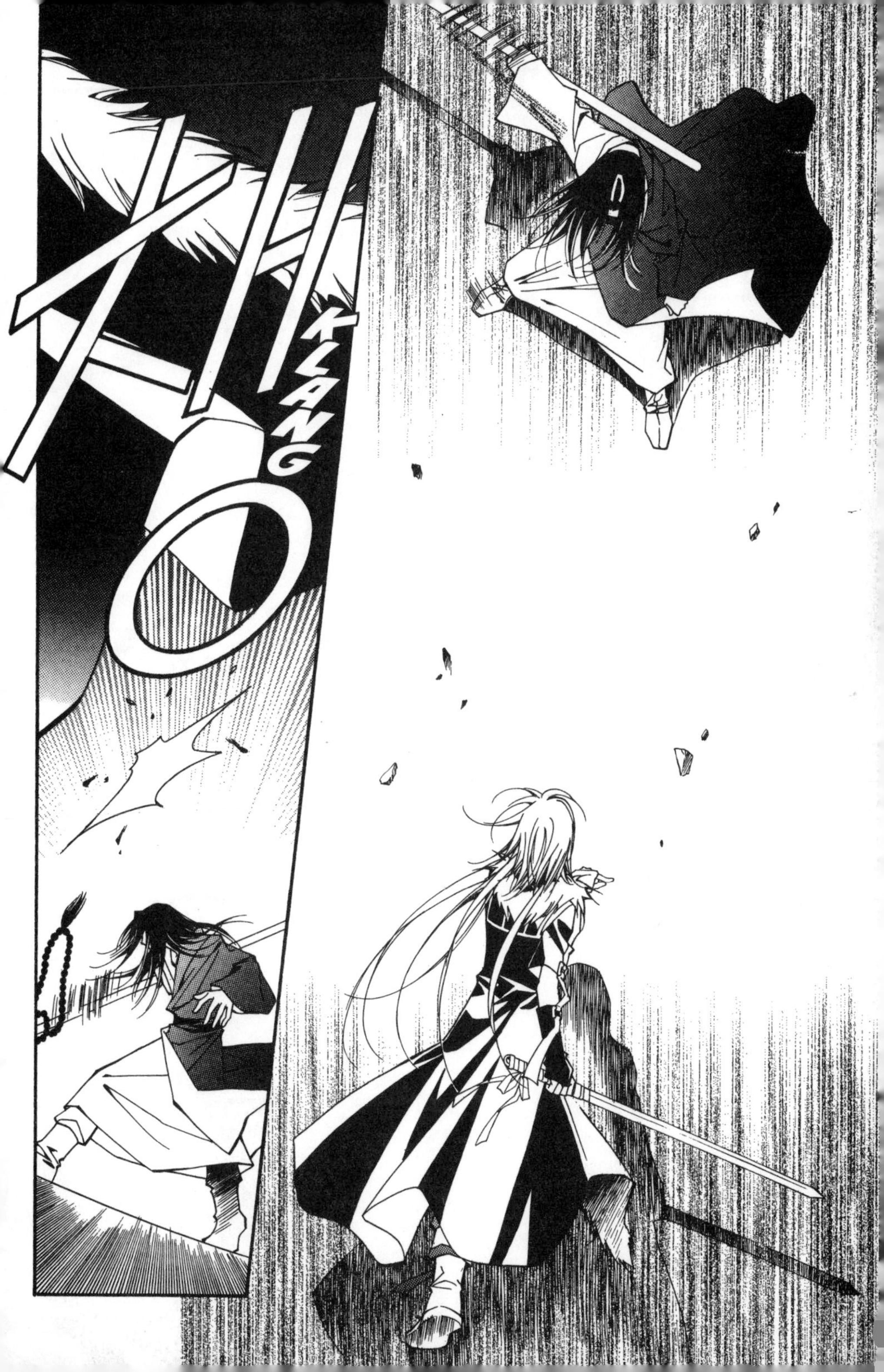
KLANG

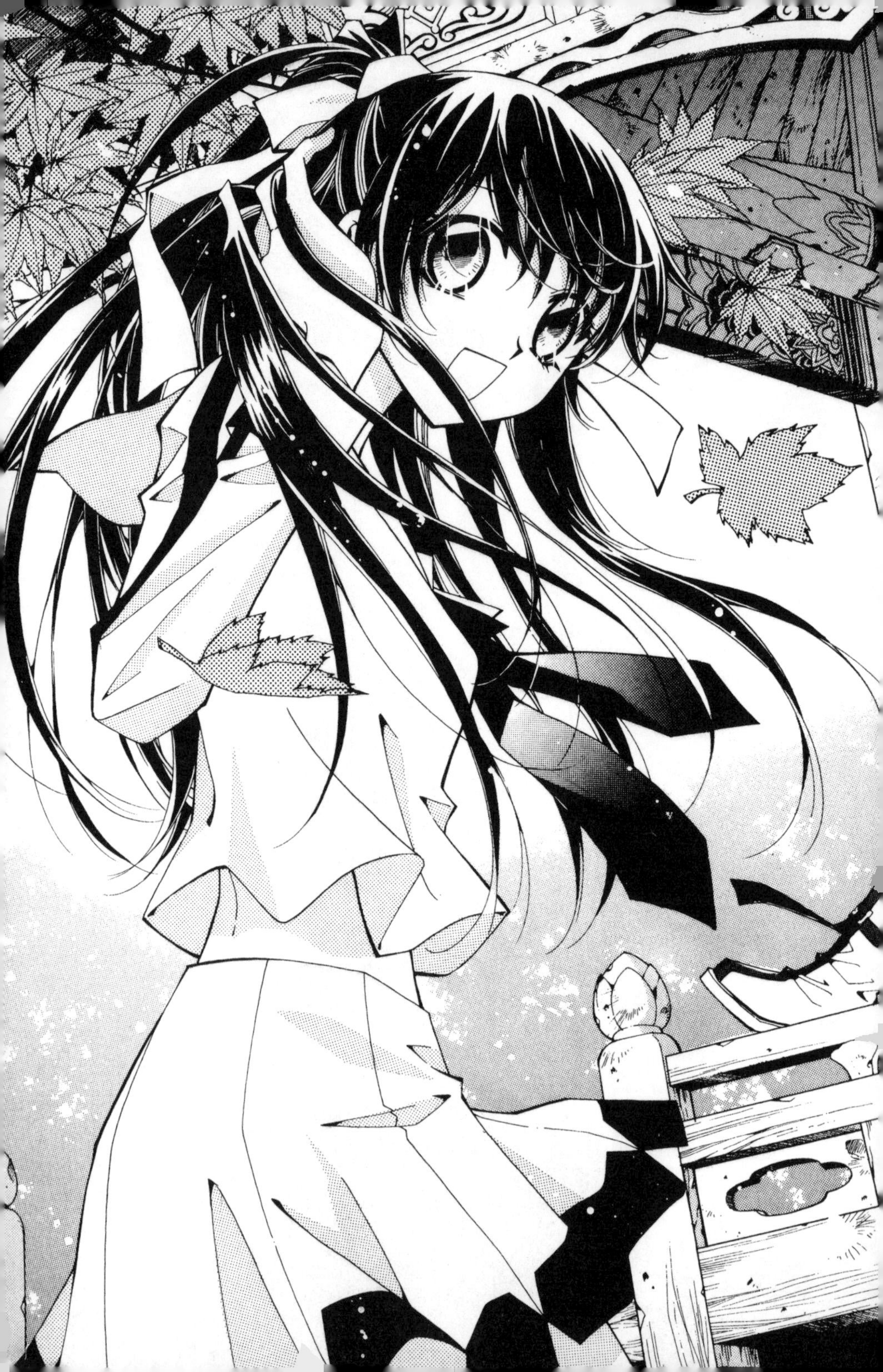

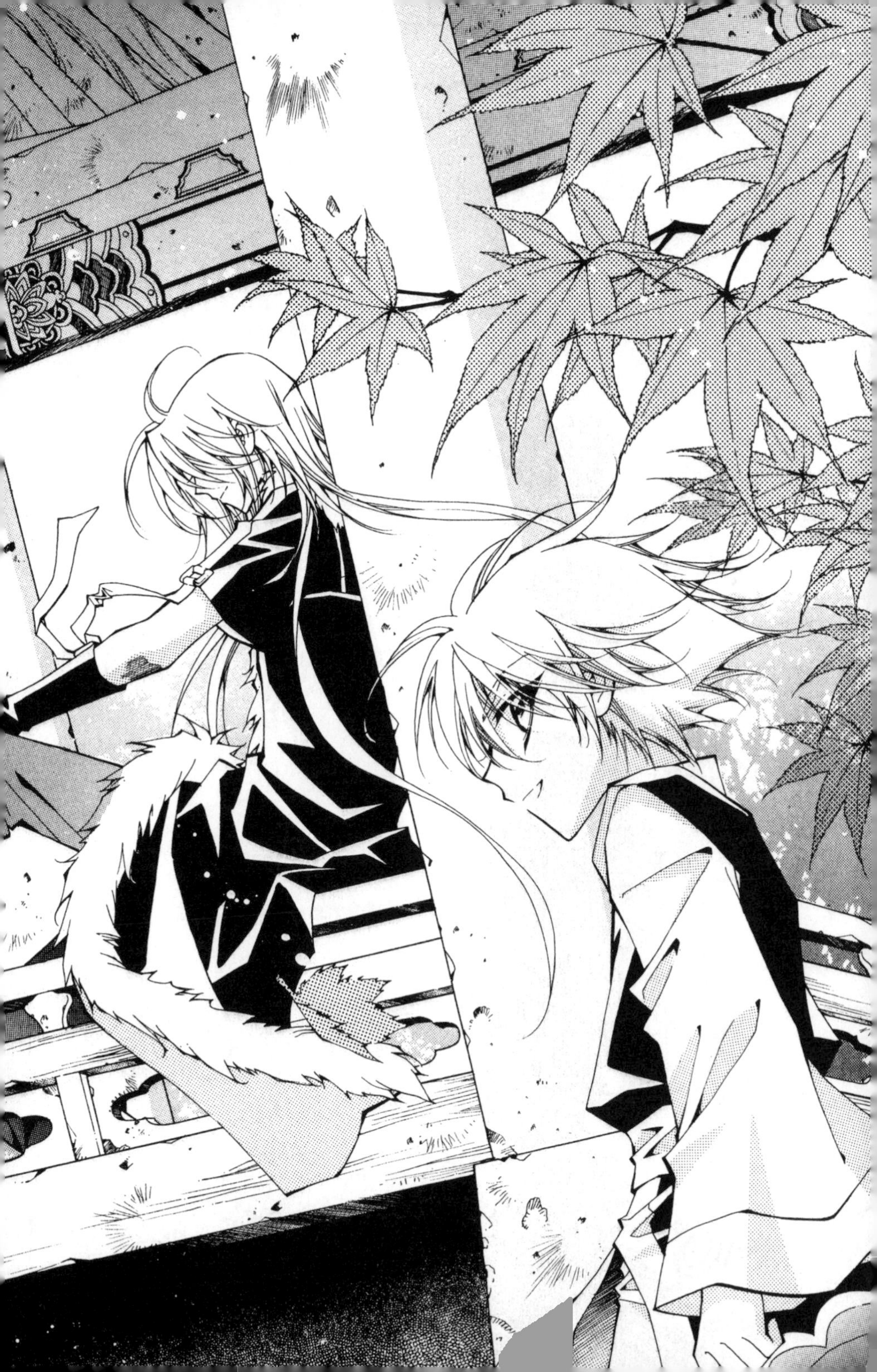

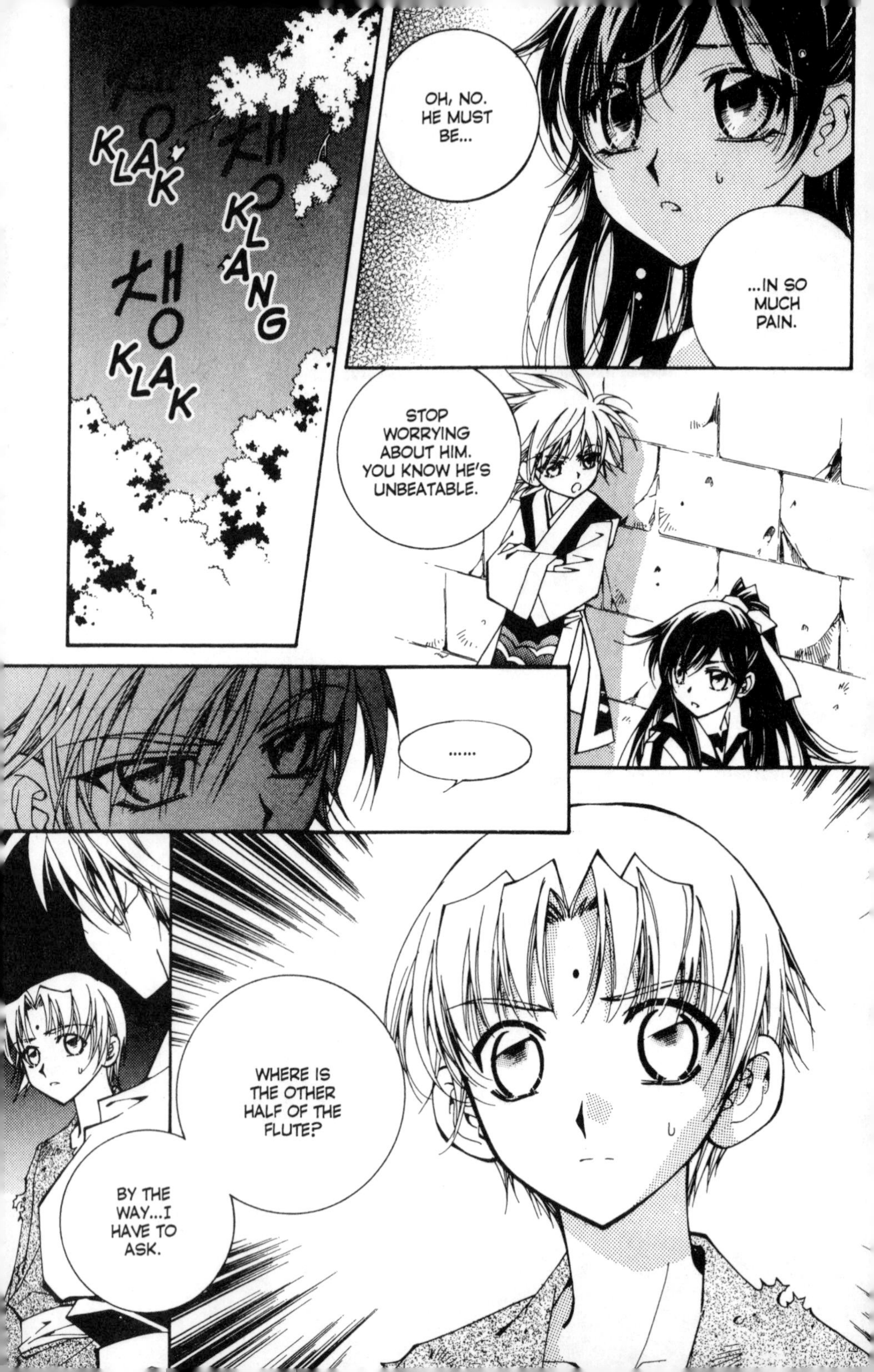
KLAK
KHO
KLANG
KHO
KLAK
OH, NO. HE MUST BE...
...IN SO MUCH PAIN.
STOP WORRYING ABOUT HIM. YOU KNOW HE'S UNBEATABLE.
......
BY THE WAY...I HAVE TO ASK.
WHERE IS THE OTHER HALF OF THE FLUTE?

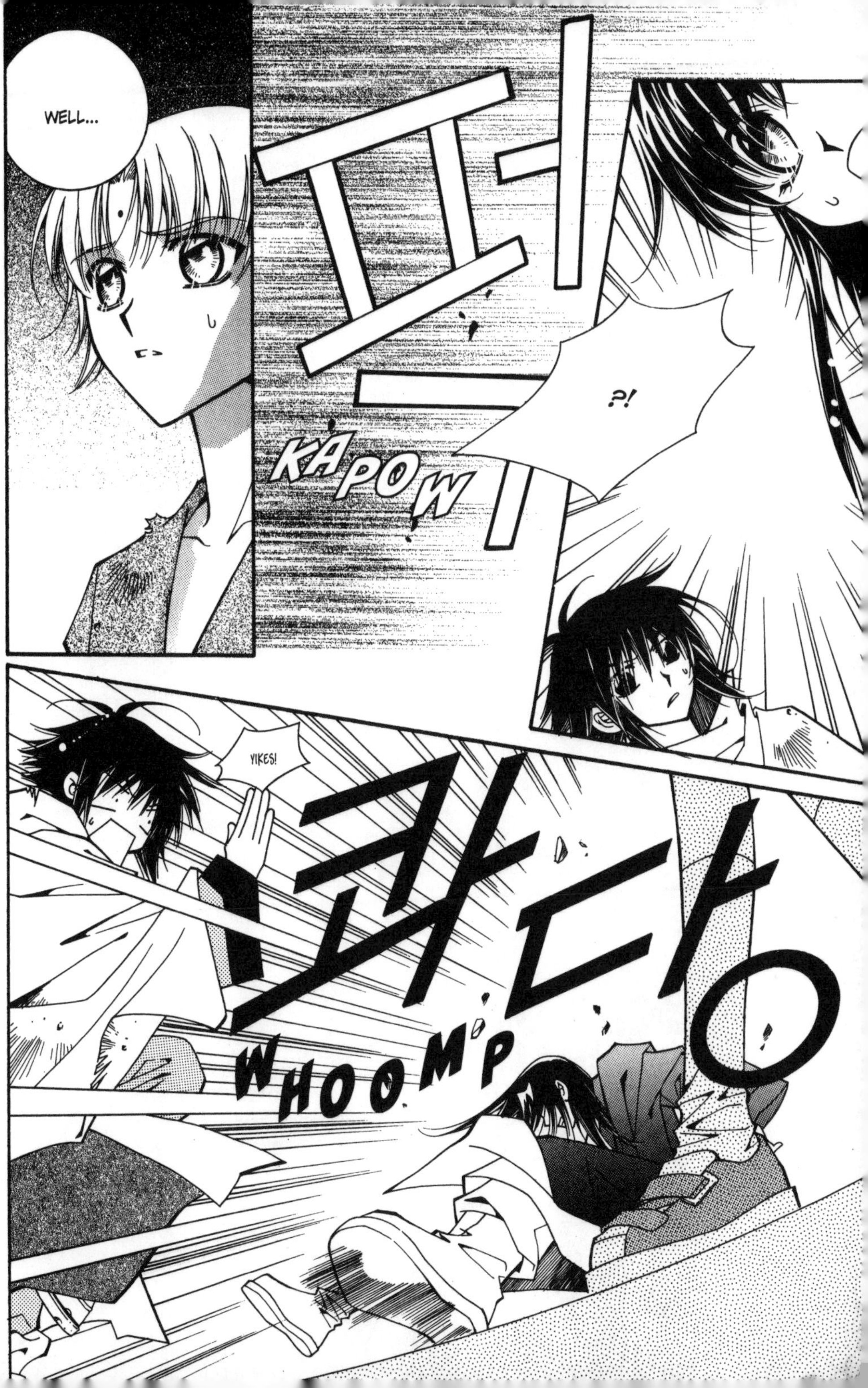
WELL...
KAPOW
?!
YIKES!
WHOOMP

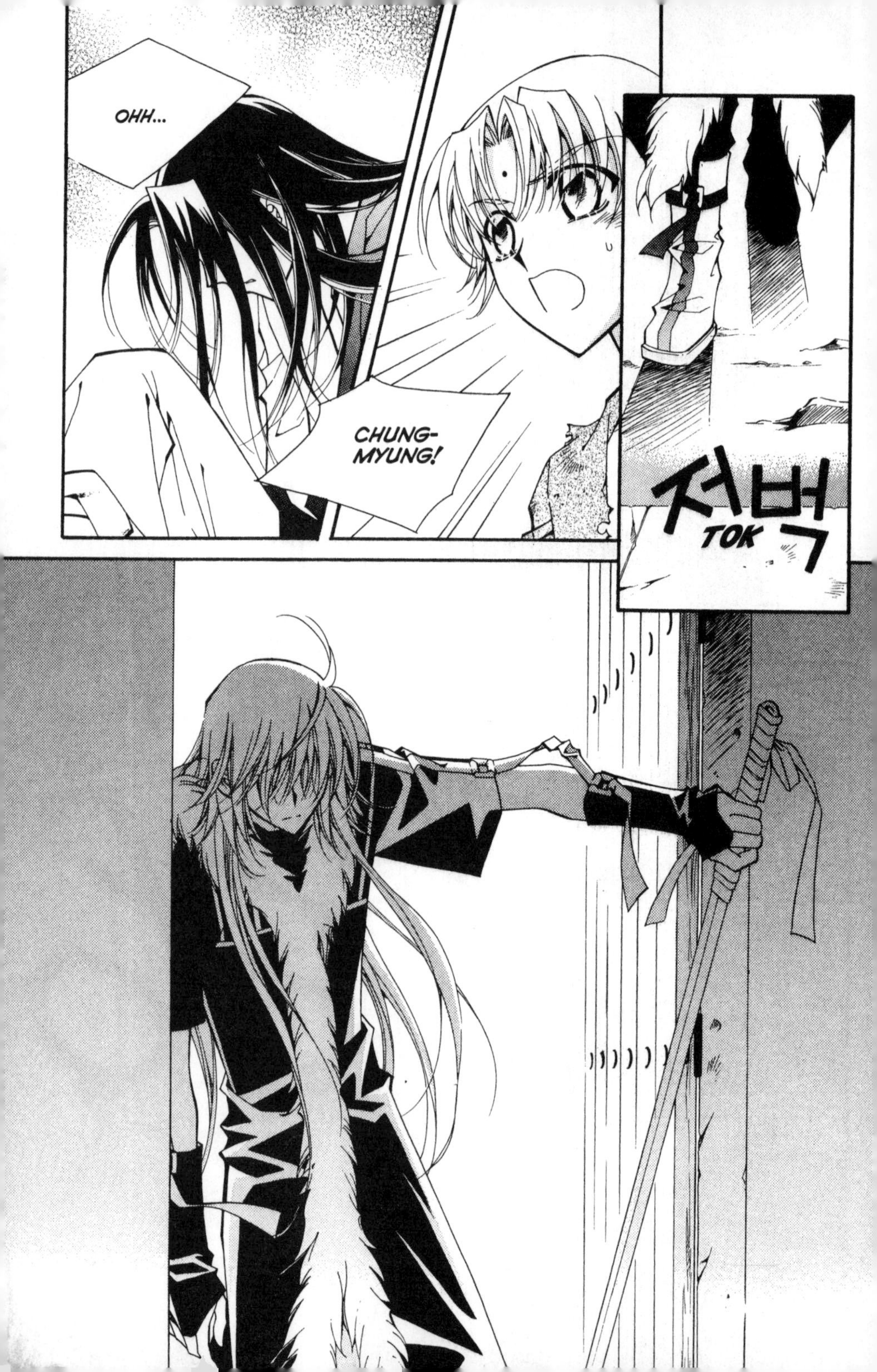
OHH...
CHUNG-MYUNG!
저벅
TOK

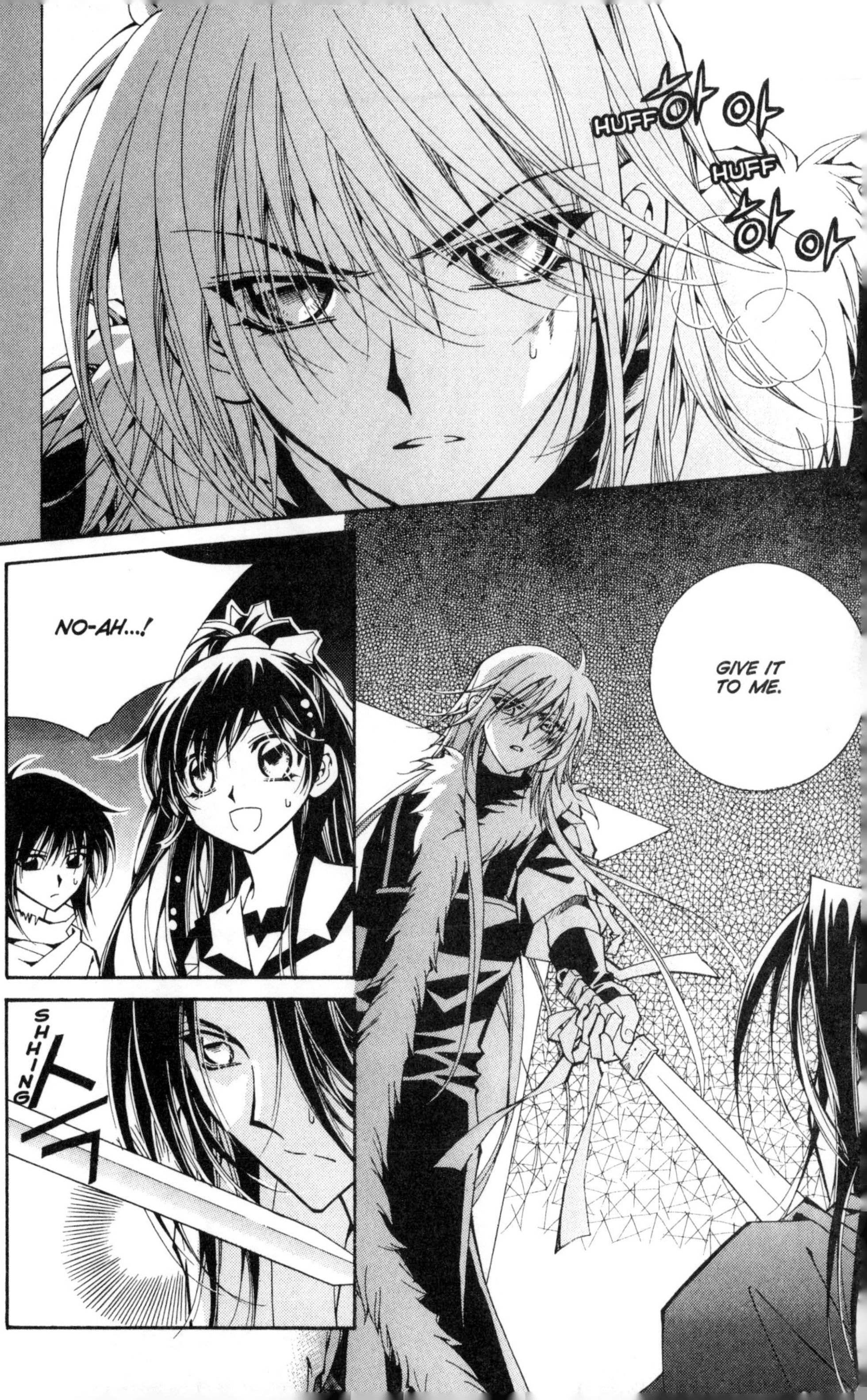
HUFF 하아
HUFF 하아
NO-AH...!
SHHING
GIVE IT TO ME.

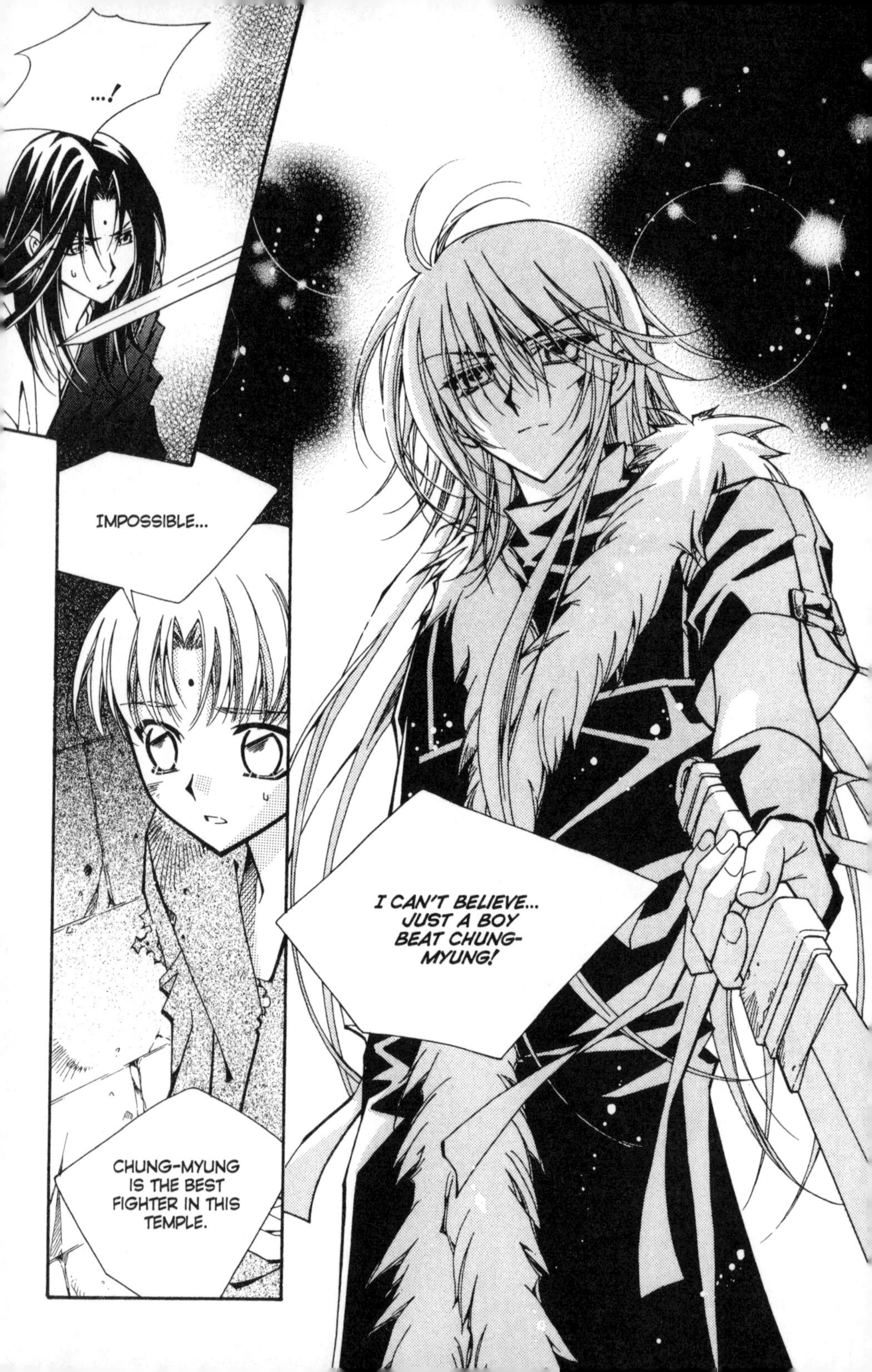
...!
IMPOSSIBLE...
CHUNG-MYUNG IS THE BEST FIGHTER IN THIS TEMPLE.
I CAN'T BELIEVE... JUST A BOY BEAT CHUNG-MYUNG!

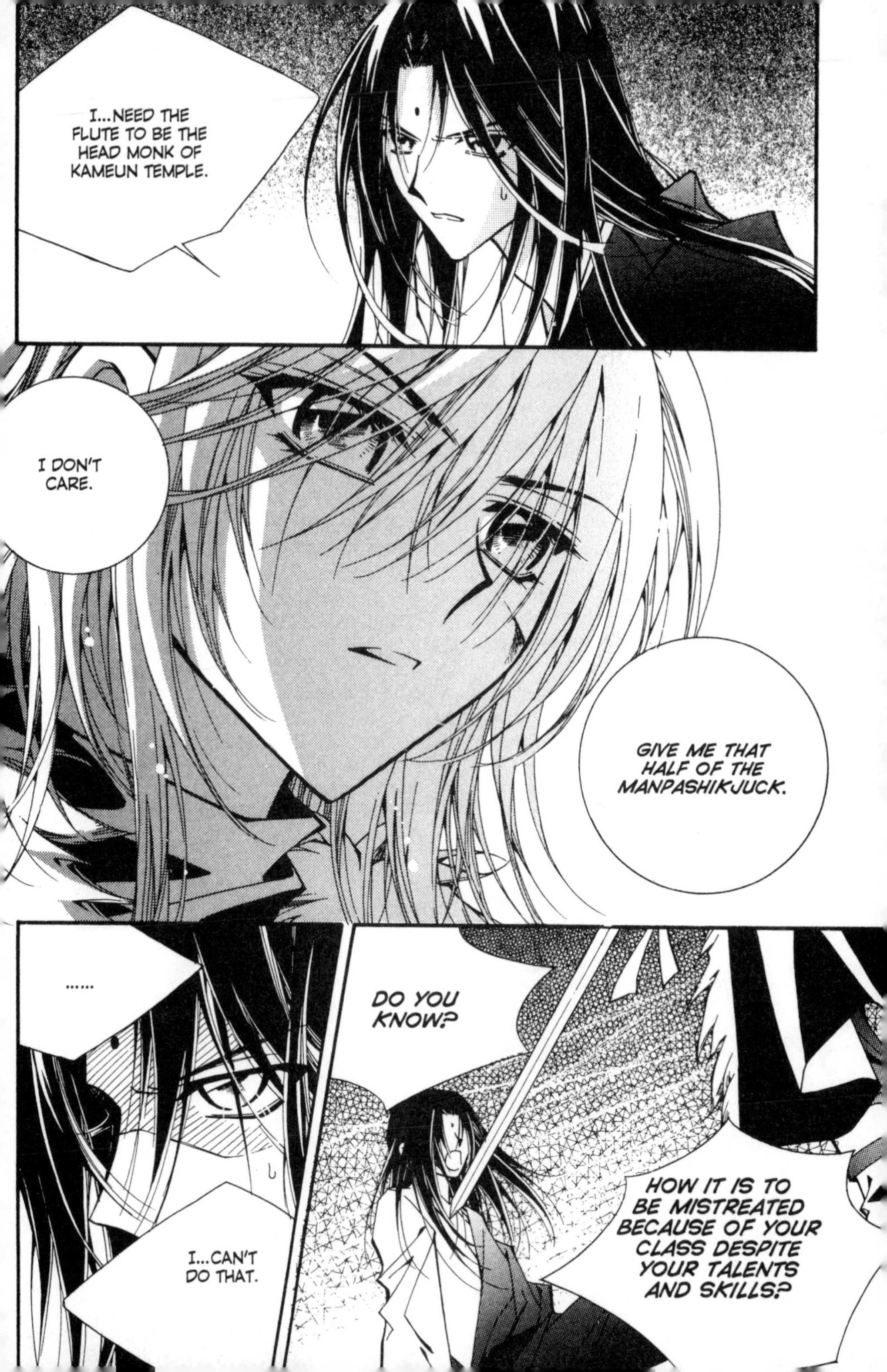
I...NEED THE FLUTE TO BE THE HEAD MONK OF KAMEUN TEMPLE.
I DON'T CARE.
GIVE ME THAT HALF OF THE MANPASHIKJUCK.
......
I...CAN'T DO THAT.
DO YOU KNOW?
HOW IT IS TO BE MISTREATED BECAUSE OF YOUR CLASS DESPITE YOUR TALENTS AND SKILLS?

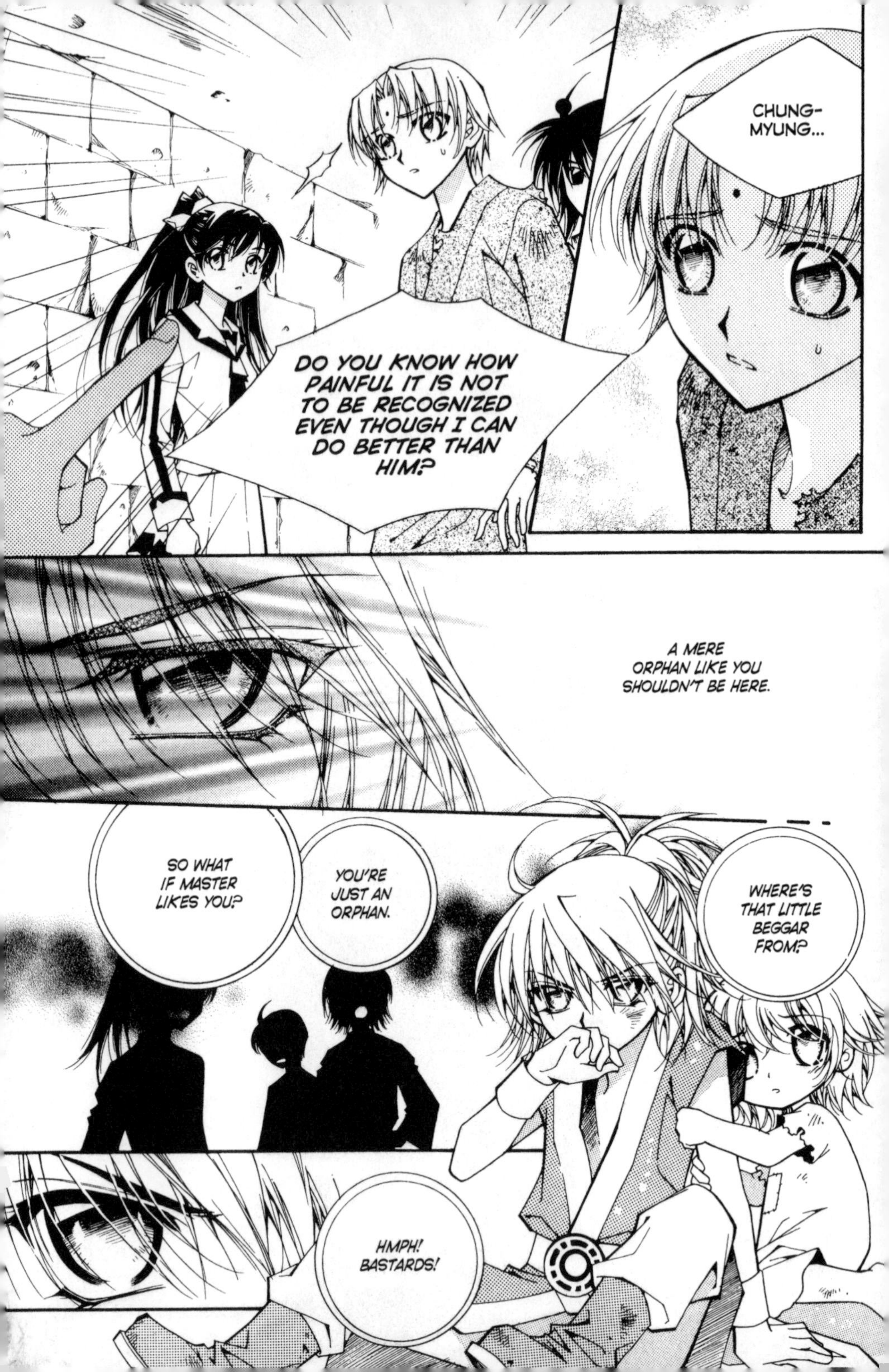
DO YOU KNOW HOW PAINFUL IT IS NOT TO BE RECOGNIZED EVEN THOUGH I CAN DO BETTER THAN HIM?
CHUNG-MYUNG...
A MERE ORPHAN LIKE YOU SHOULDN'T BE HERE.
SO WHAT IF MASTER LIKES YOU?
YOU'RE JUST AN ORPHAN.
WHERE'S THAT LITTLE BEGGAR FROM?
HMPH! BASTARDS!

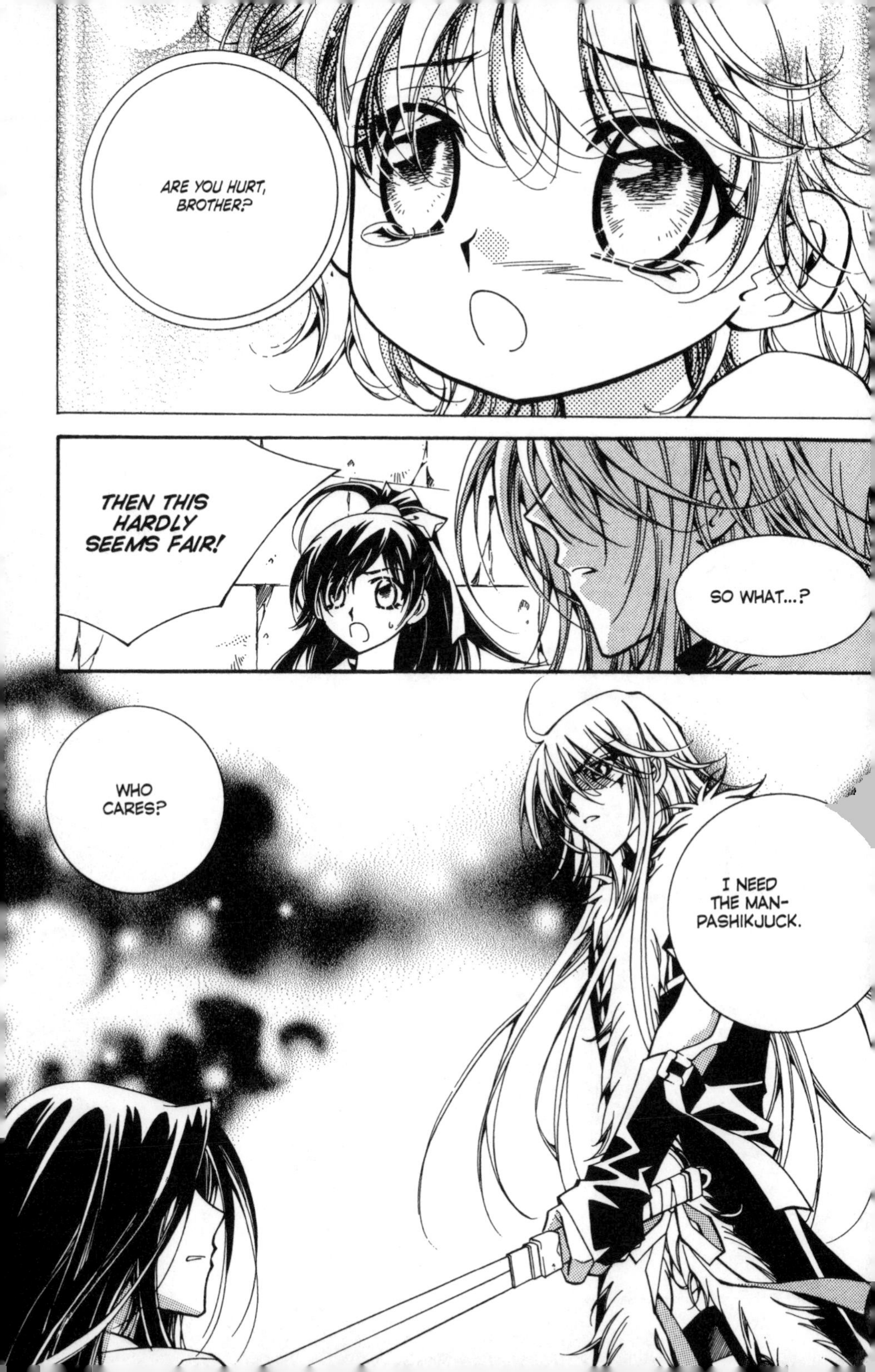
ARE YOU HURT, BROTHER?
THEN THIS HARDLY SEEMS FAIR!
SO WHAT...?
WHO CARES?
I NEED THE MAN-PASHIKJUCK.

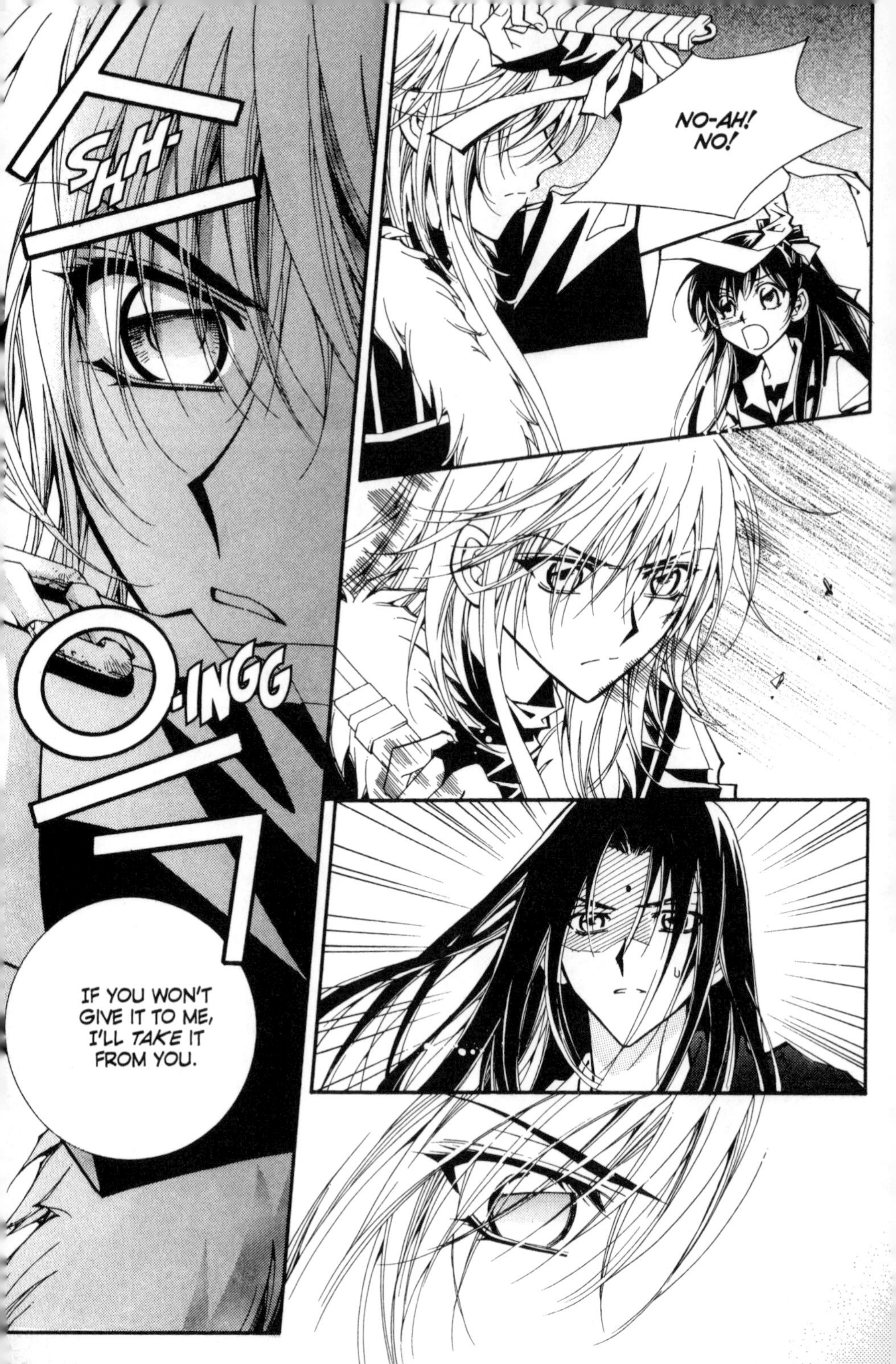
SHH-
O-INGG
IF YOU WON'T GIVE IT TO ME, I'LL *TAKE* IT FROM YOU.
NO-AH! NO!

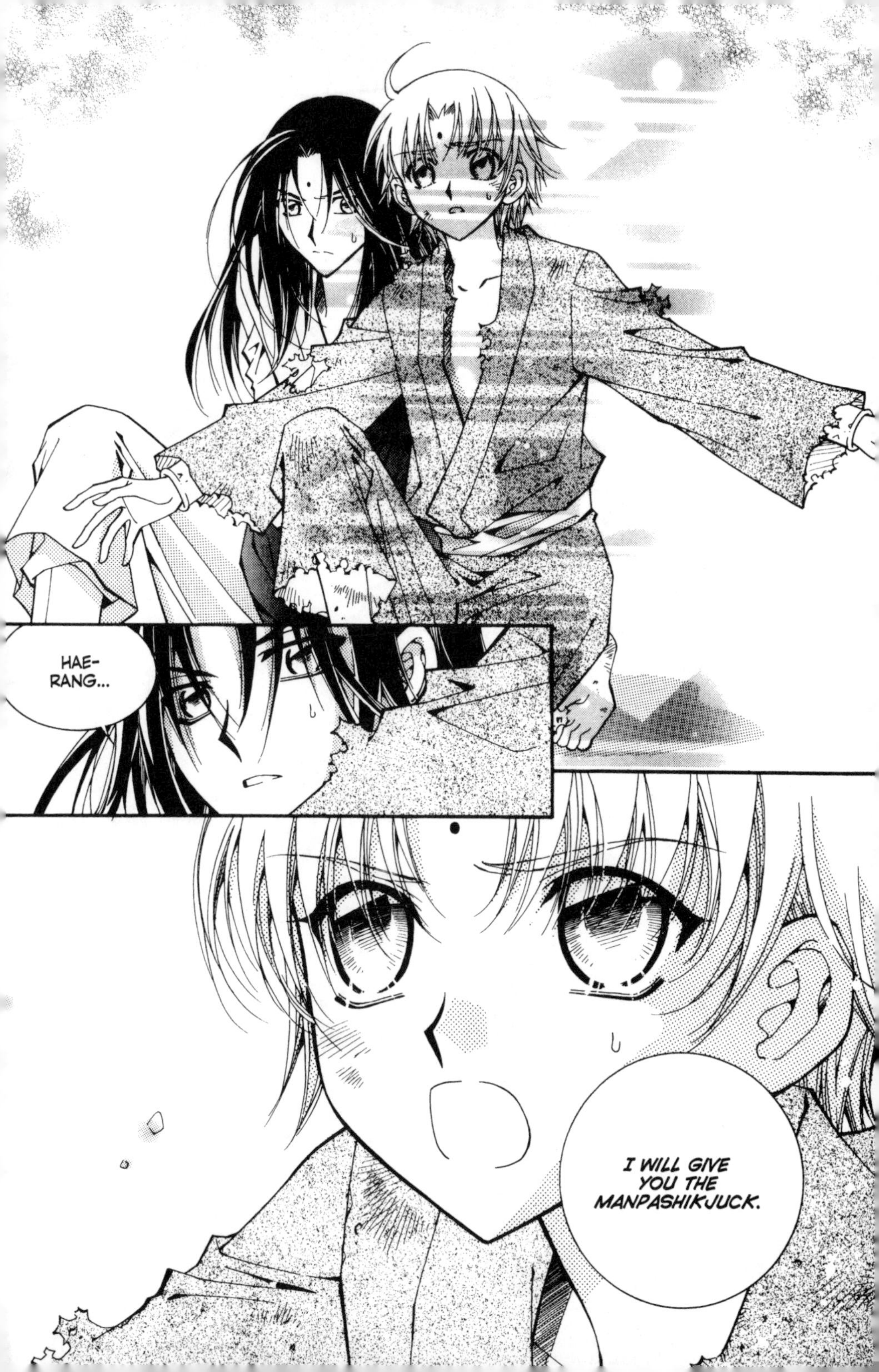
HAE-RANG...
I WILL GIVE YOU THE MANPASHIKJUCK.

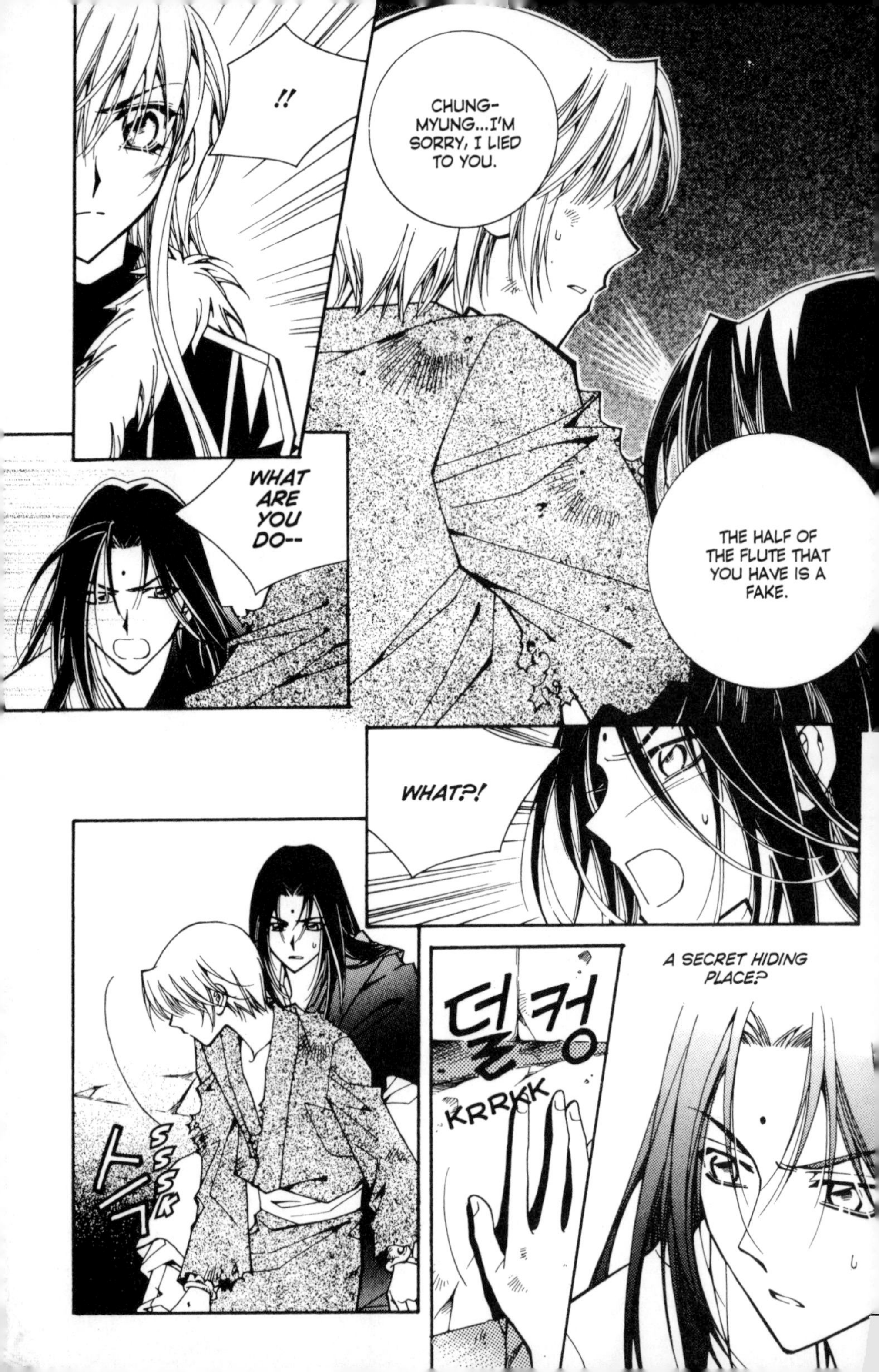
!!
CHUNG-MYUNG...I'M SORRY, I LIED TO YOU.
WHAT ARE YOU DO--
THE HALF OF THE FLUTE THAT YOU HAVE IS A FAKE.
WHAT?!
SSSK
덜컹
KRRKK
A SECRET HIDING PLACE?

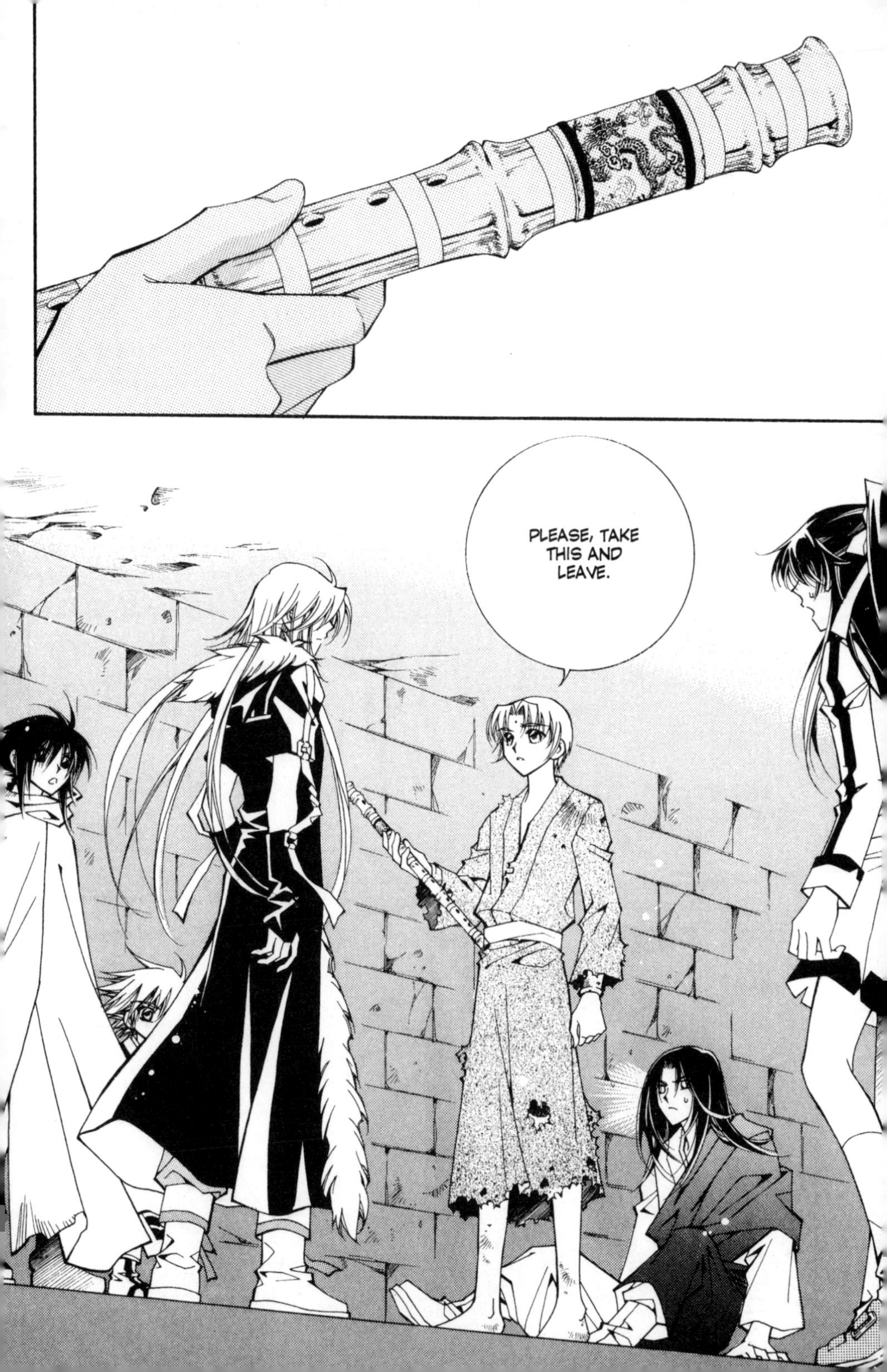
PLEASE, TAKE THIS AND LEAVE.

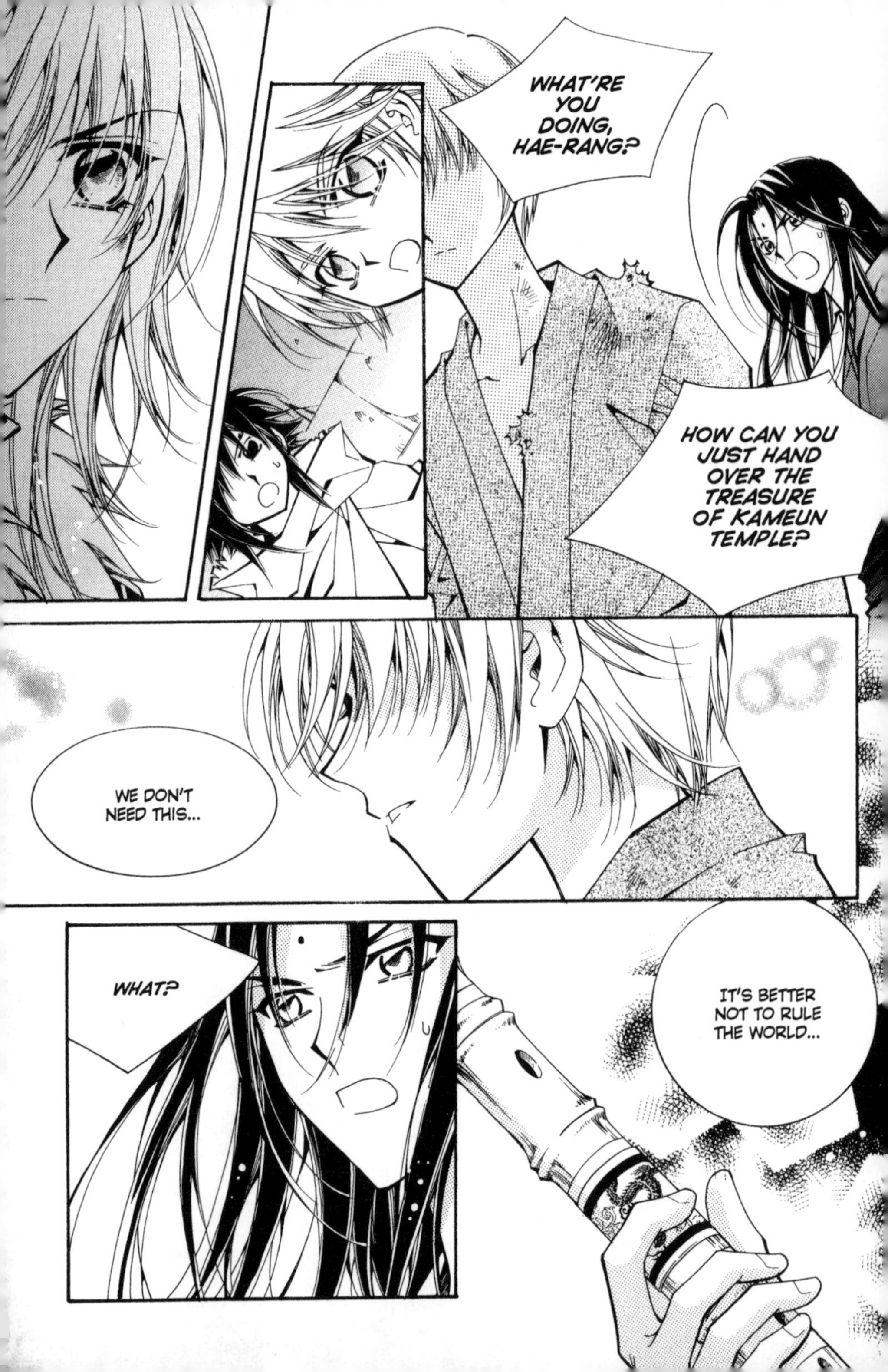
WHAT'RE YOU DOING, HAE-RANG?
HOW CAN YOU JUST HAND OVER THE TREASURE OF KAMEUN TEMPLE?
WE DON'T NEED THIS...
WHAT?
IT'S BETTER NOT TO RULE THE WORLD...

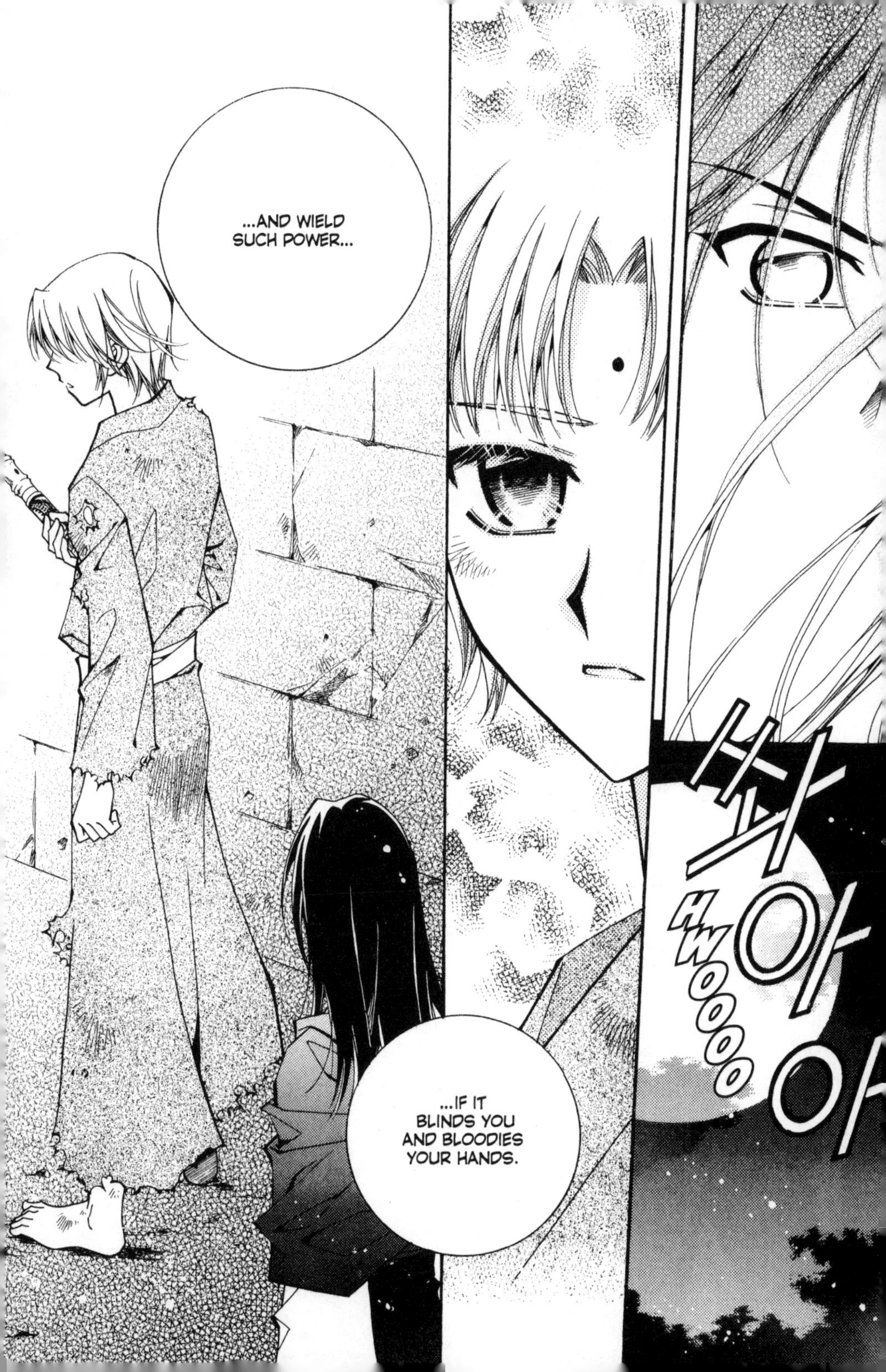
...AND WIELD SUCH POWER...
...IF IT BLINDS YOU AND BLOODIES YOUR HANDS.
화아아
HWOOOOO

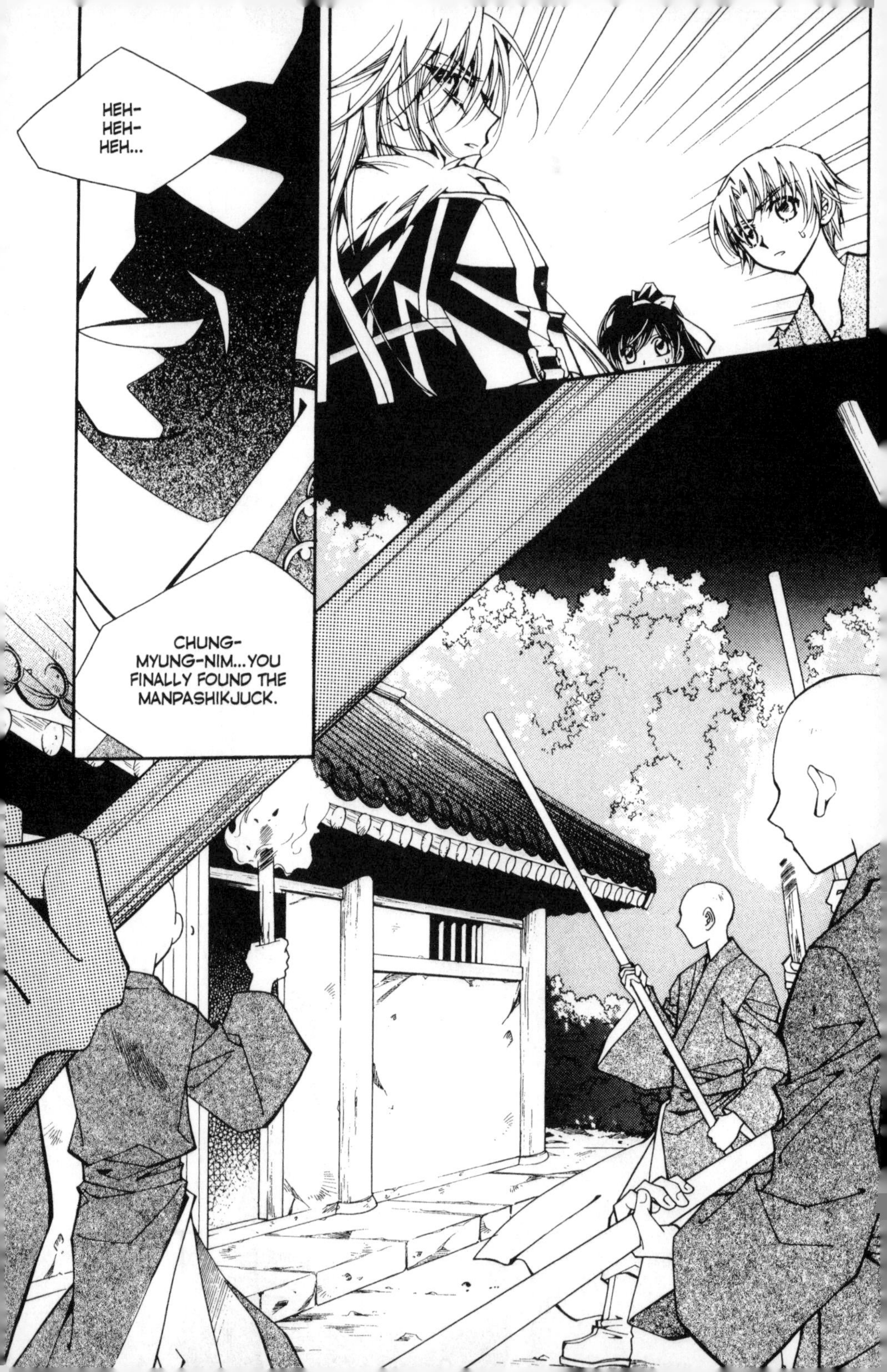
HEH-HEH-HEH...
CHUNG-MYUNG-NIM...YOU FINALLY FOUND THE MANPASHIKJUCK.

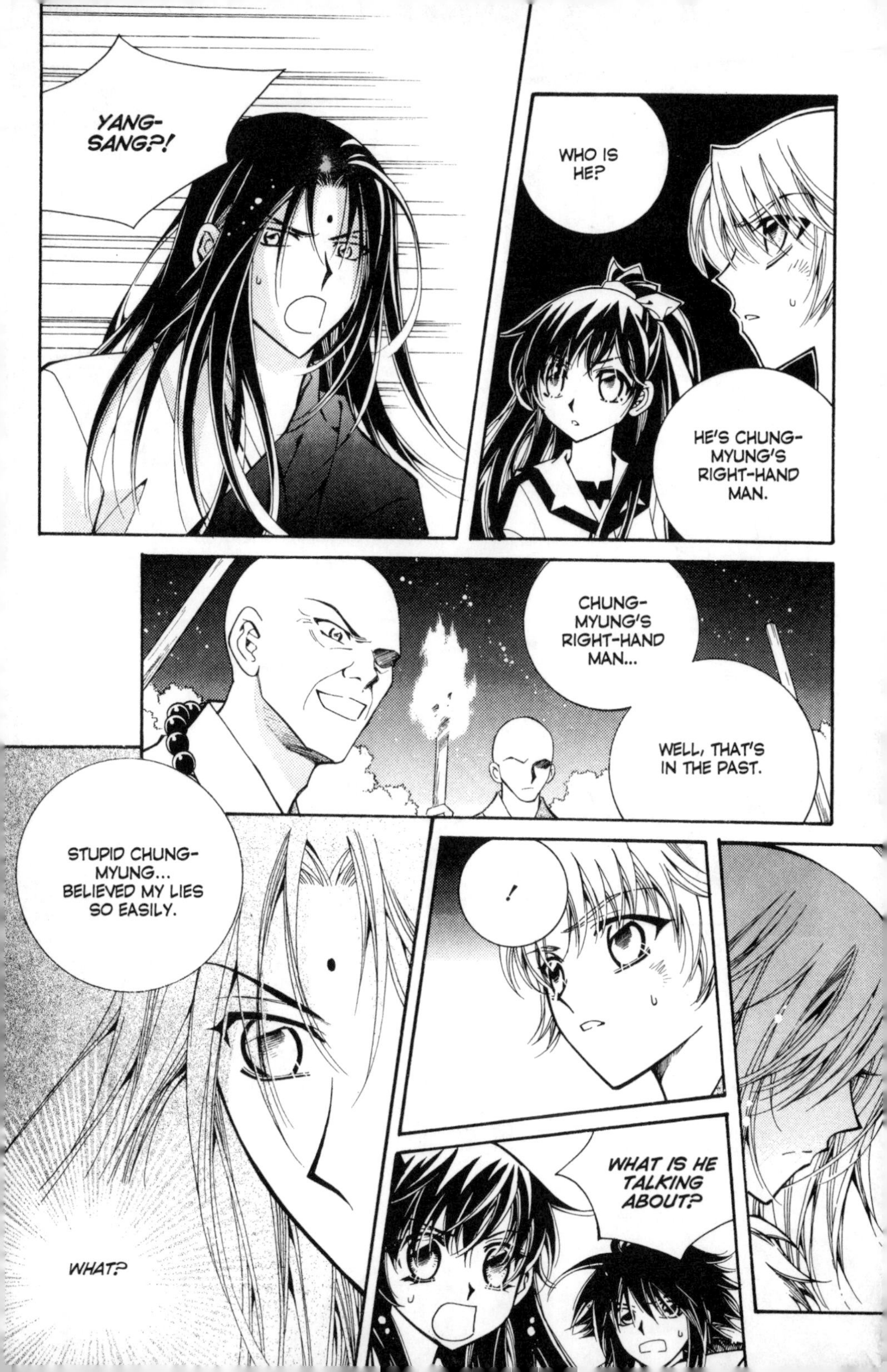
YANG-SANG?!
WHO IS HE?
HE'S CHUNG-MYUNG'S RIGHT-HAND MAN.
CHUNG-MYUNG'S RIGHT-HAND MAN...
WELL, THAT'S IN THE PAST.
STUPID CHUNG-MYUNG... BELIEVED MY LIES SO EASILY.
WHAT?
!
WHAT IS HE TALKING ABOUT?

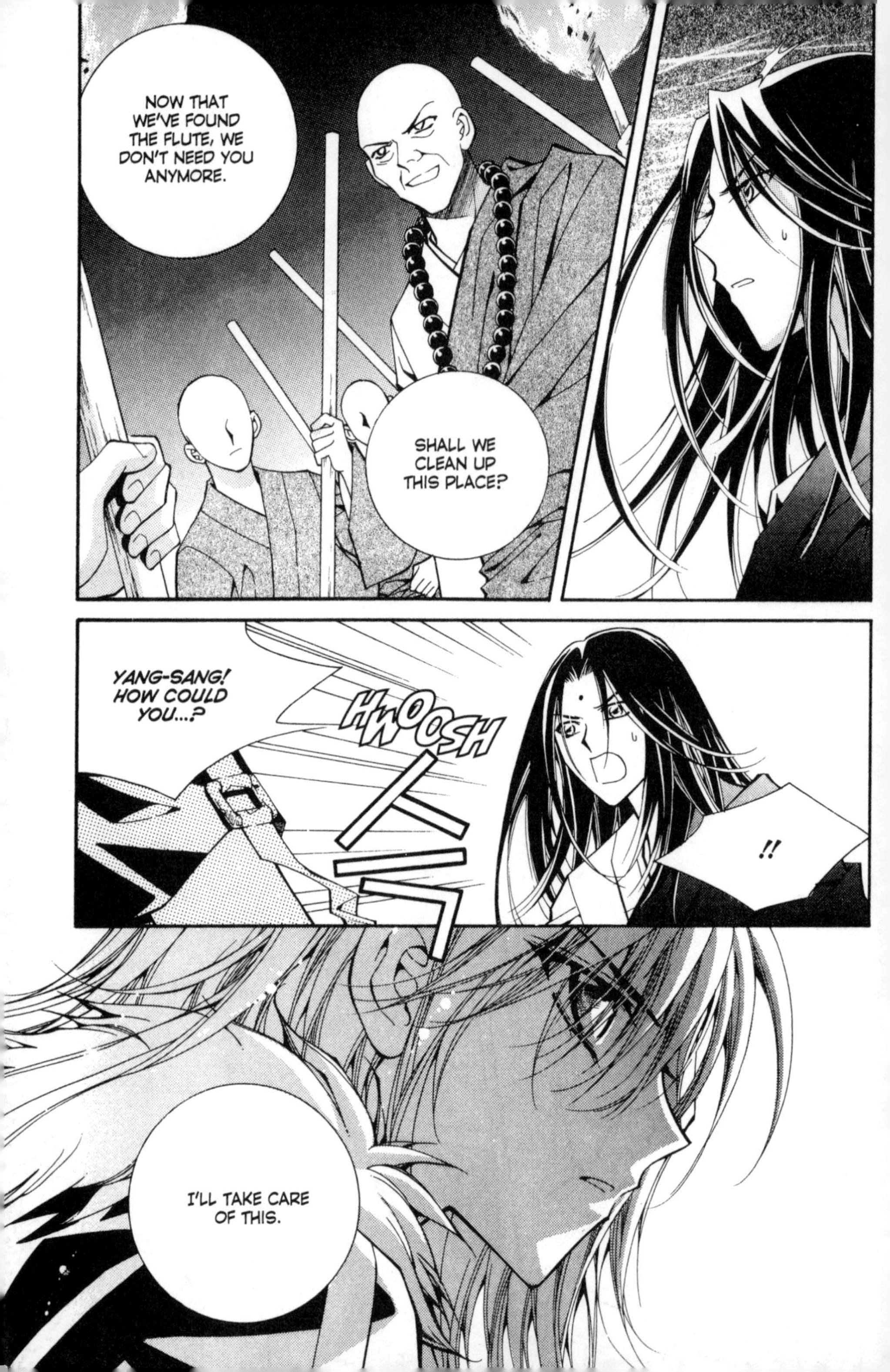
NOW THAT WE'VE FOUND THE FLUTE, WE DON'T NEED YOU ANYMORE.
SHALL WE CLEAN UP THIS PLACE?
YANG-SANG! HOW COULD YOU...?
HWOOSH
!!
I'LL TAKE CARE OF THIS.

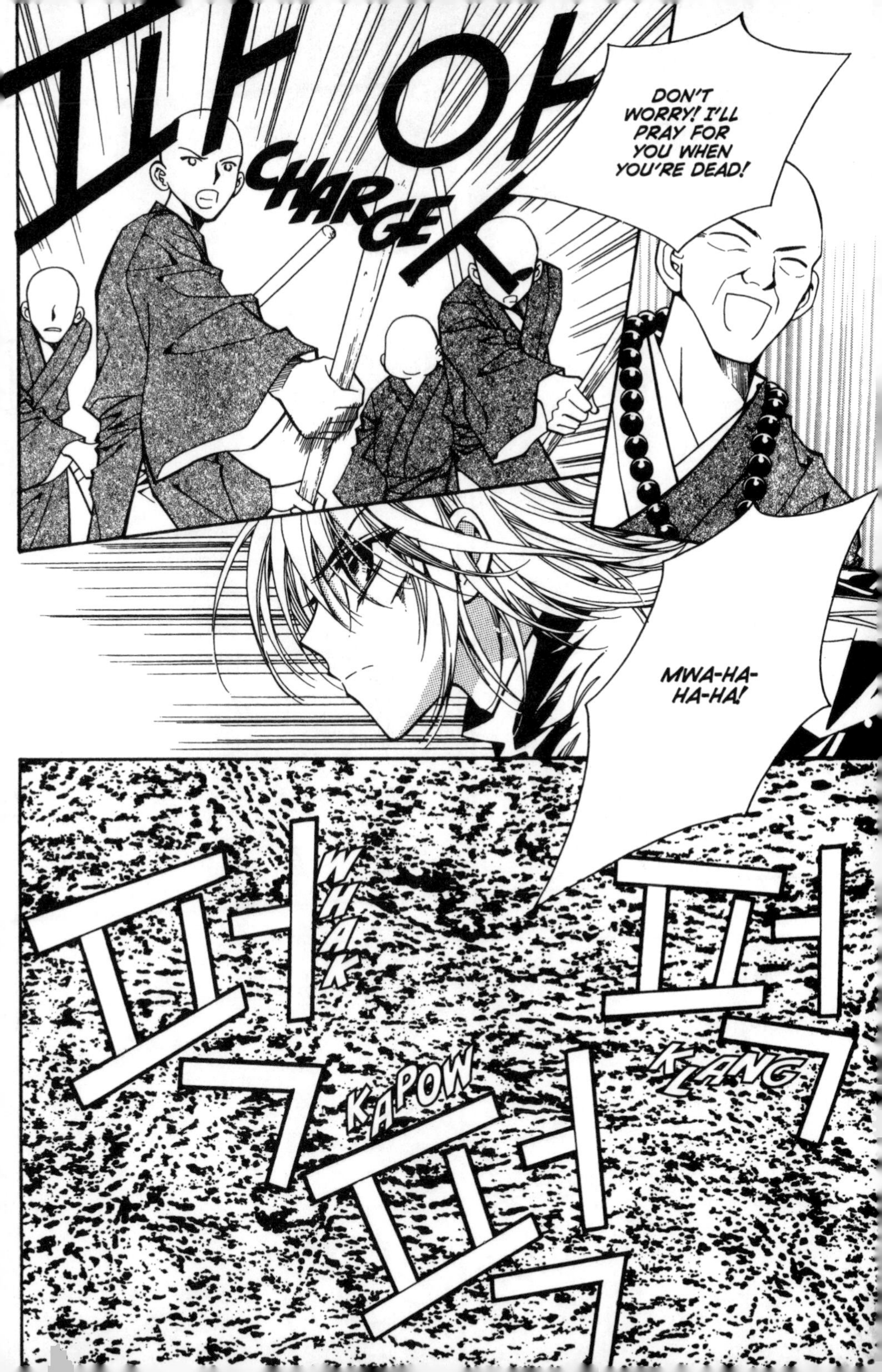
CHARGE
DON'T WORRY! I'LL PRAY FOR YOU WHEN YOU'RE DEAD!
MWA-HA-HA-HA!
WHAK
KAPOW
KLANG

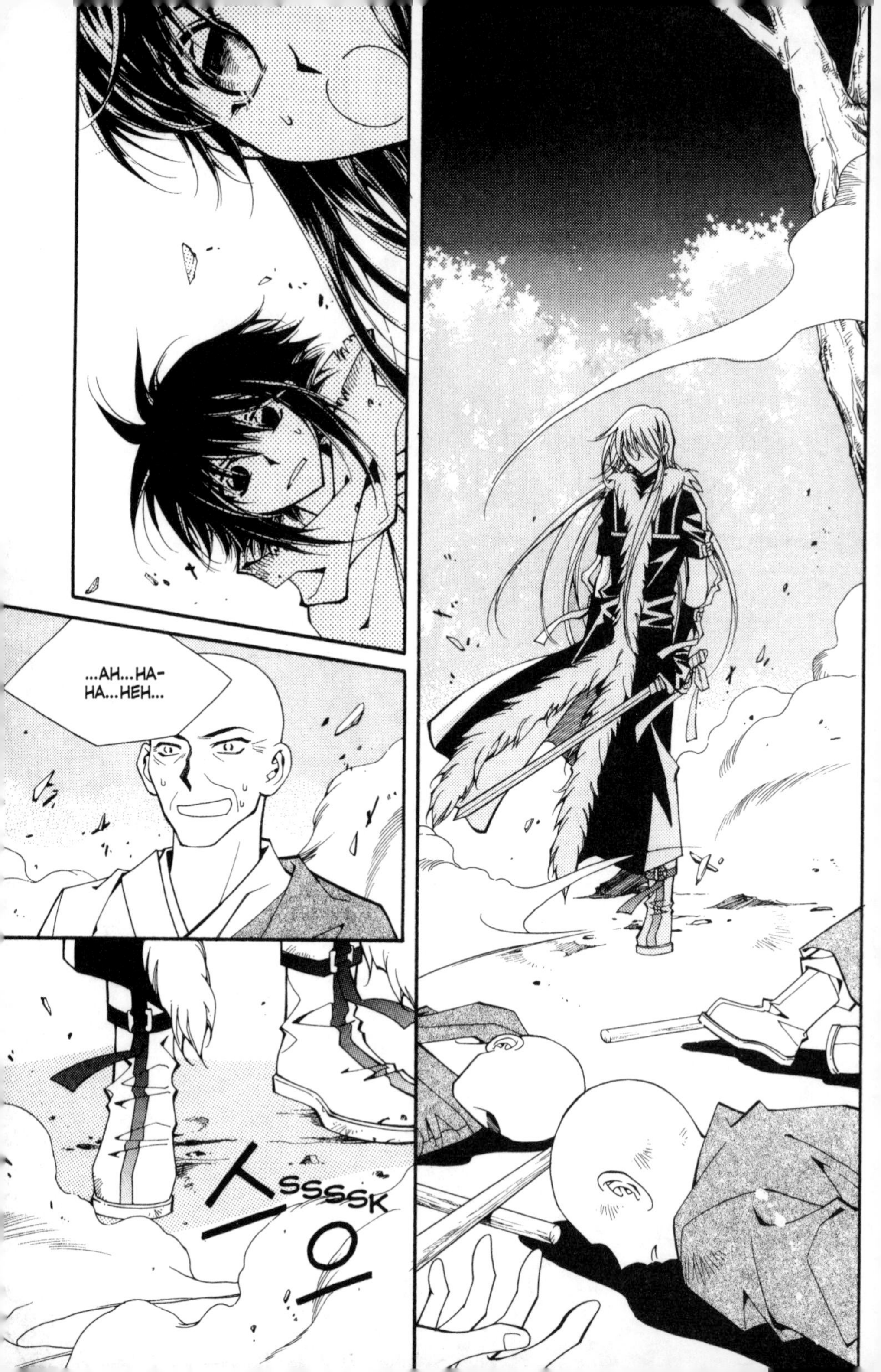
...AH...HA-HA...HEH...
SSSSK

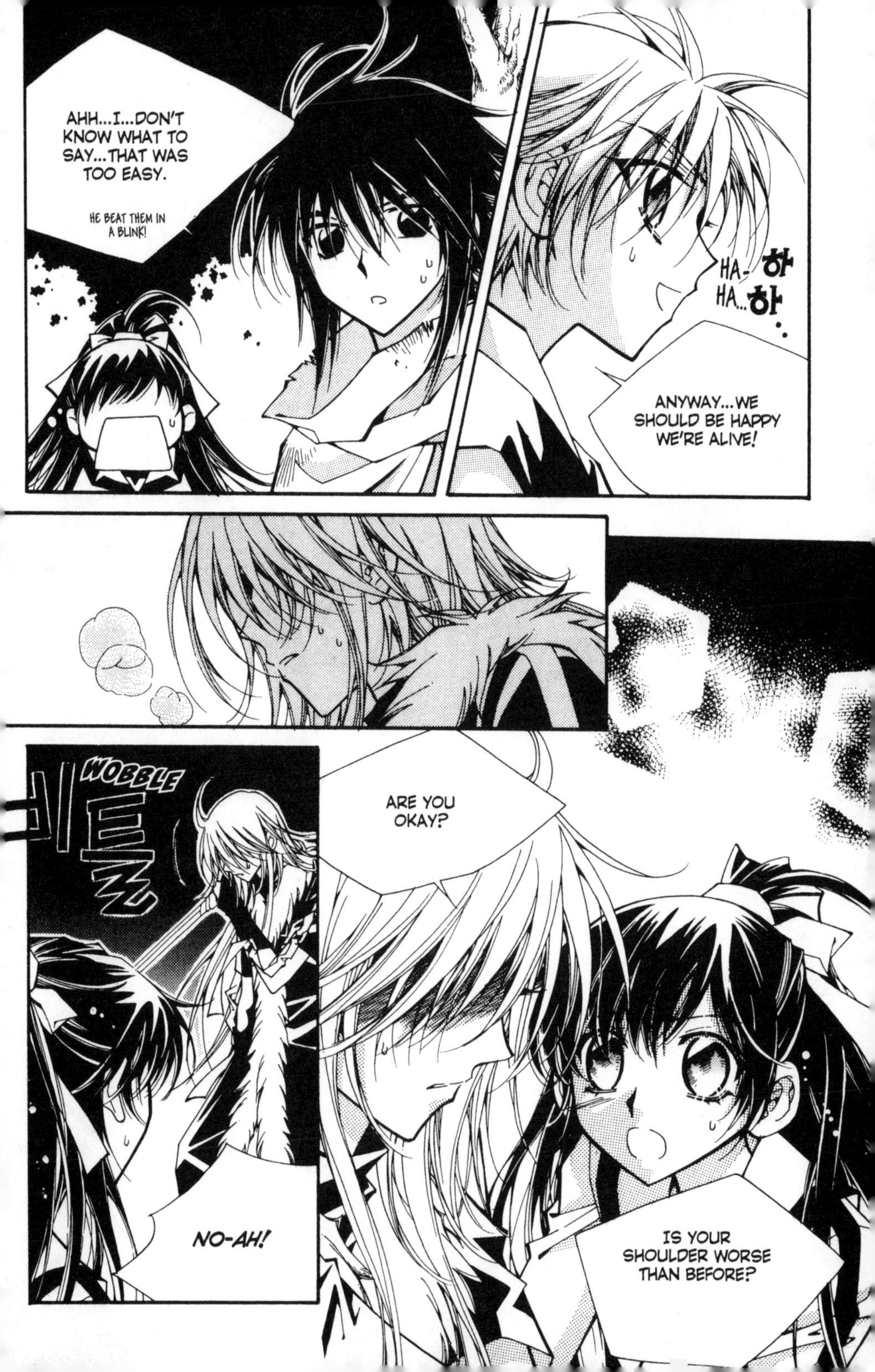
AHH...I...DON'T KNOW WHAT TO SAY...THAT WAS TOO EASY.
HE BEAT THEM IN A BLINK!
HA- 하
HA... 하
ANYWAY...WE SHOULD BE HAPPY WE'RE ALIVE!
WOBBLE
NO-AH!
ARE YOU OKAY?
IS YOUR SHOULDER WORSE THAN BEFORE?

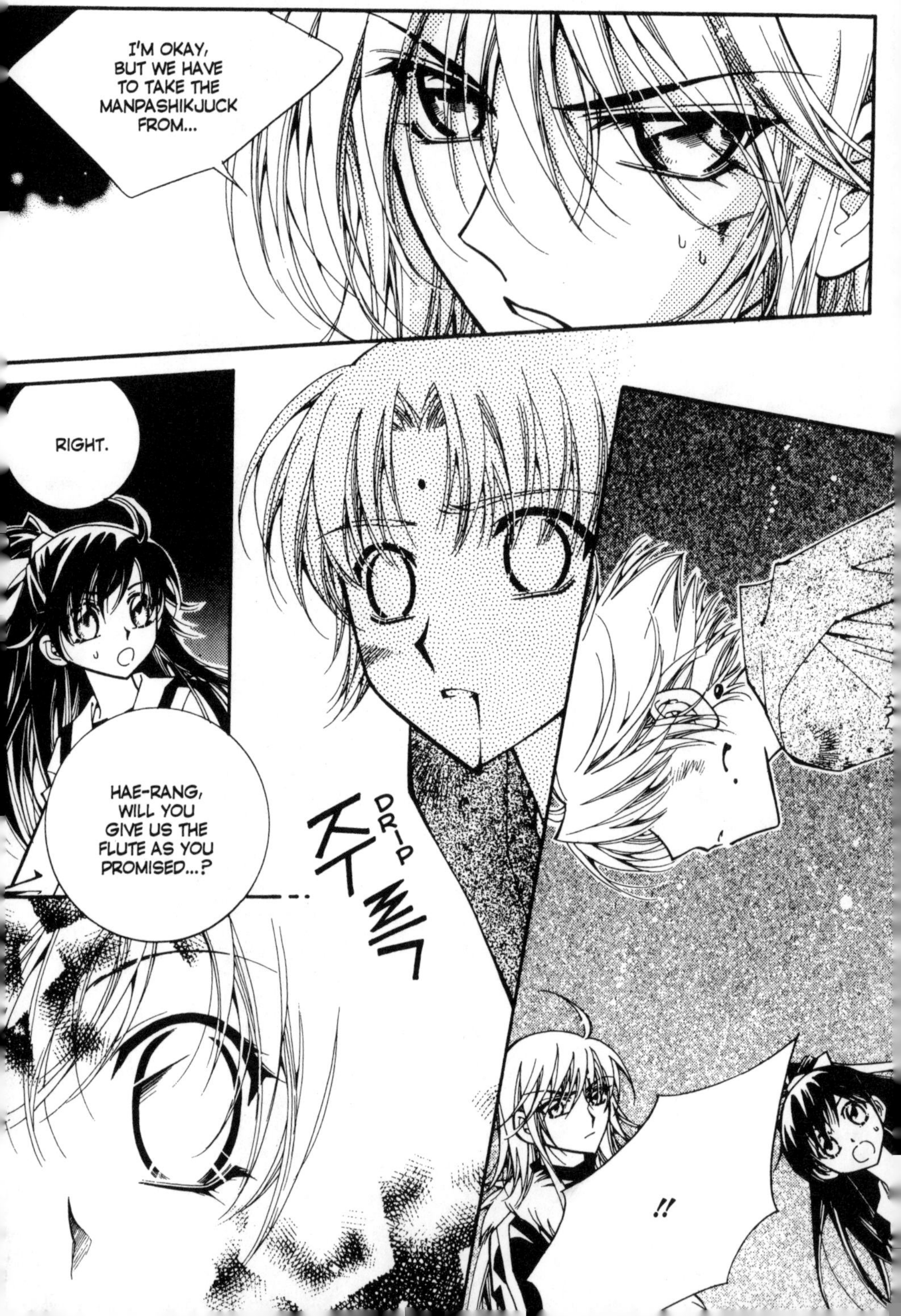
I'M OKAY, BUT WE HAVE TO TAKE THE MANPASHIKJUCK FROM...
RIGHT.
HAE-RANG, WILL YOU GIVE US THE FLUTE AS YOU PROMISED...?
DRIP
!!

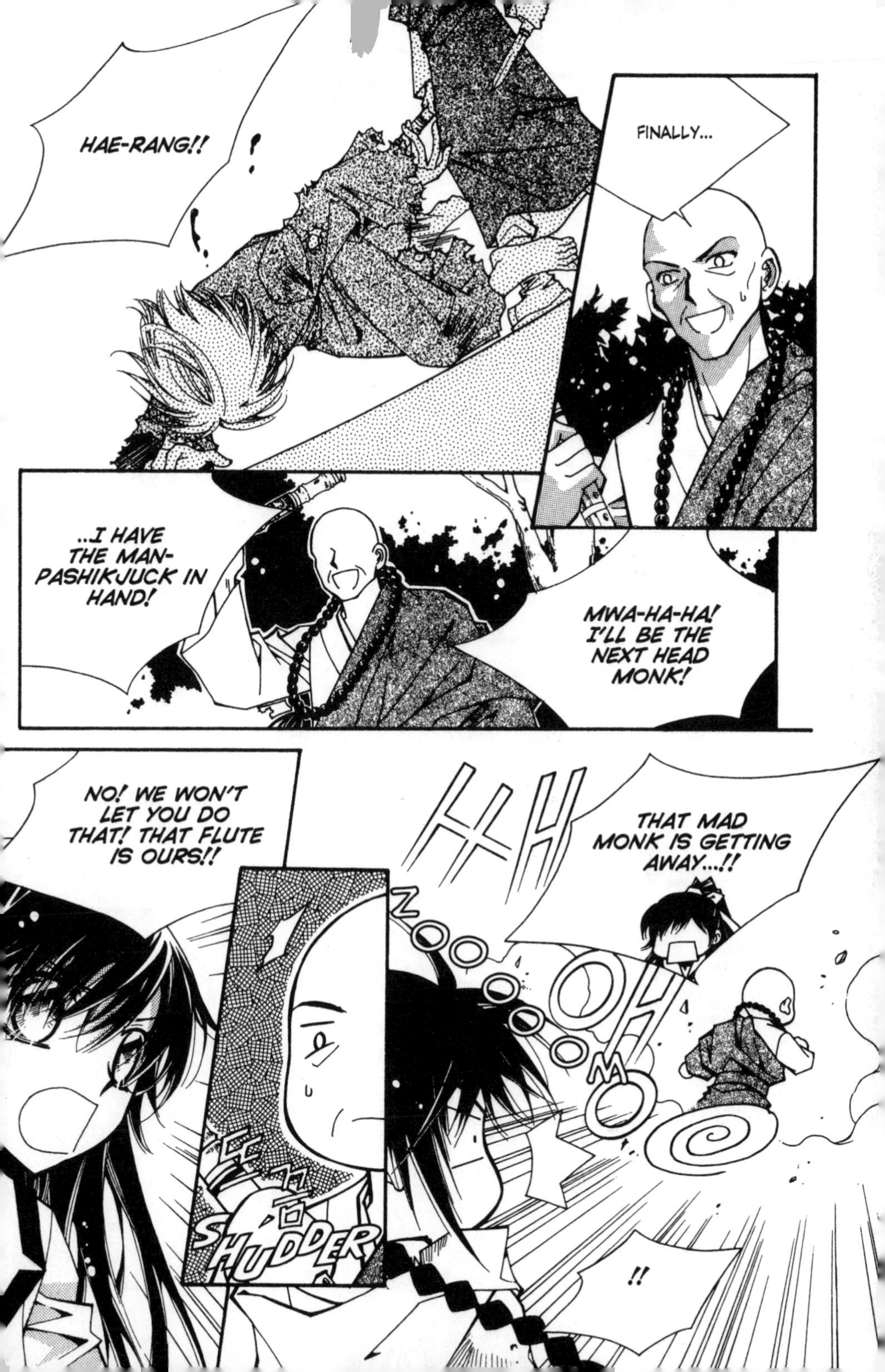
HAE-RANG!!
FINALLY...
...I HAVE THE MAN-PASHIKJUCK IN HAND!
MWA-HA-HA! I'LL BE THE NEXT HEAD MONK!
NO! WE WON'T LET YOU DO THAT! THAT FLUTE IS OURS!!
SHUDDER
HH
ZOOOOOOOM
THAT MAD MONK IS GETTING AWAY...!!
!!

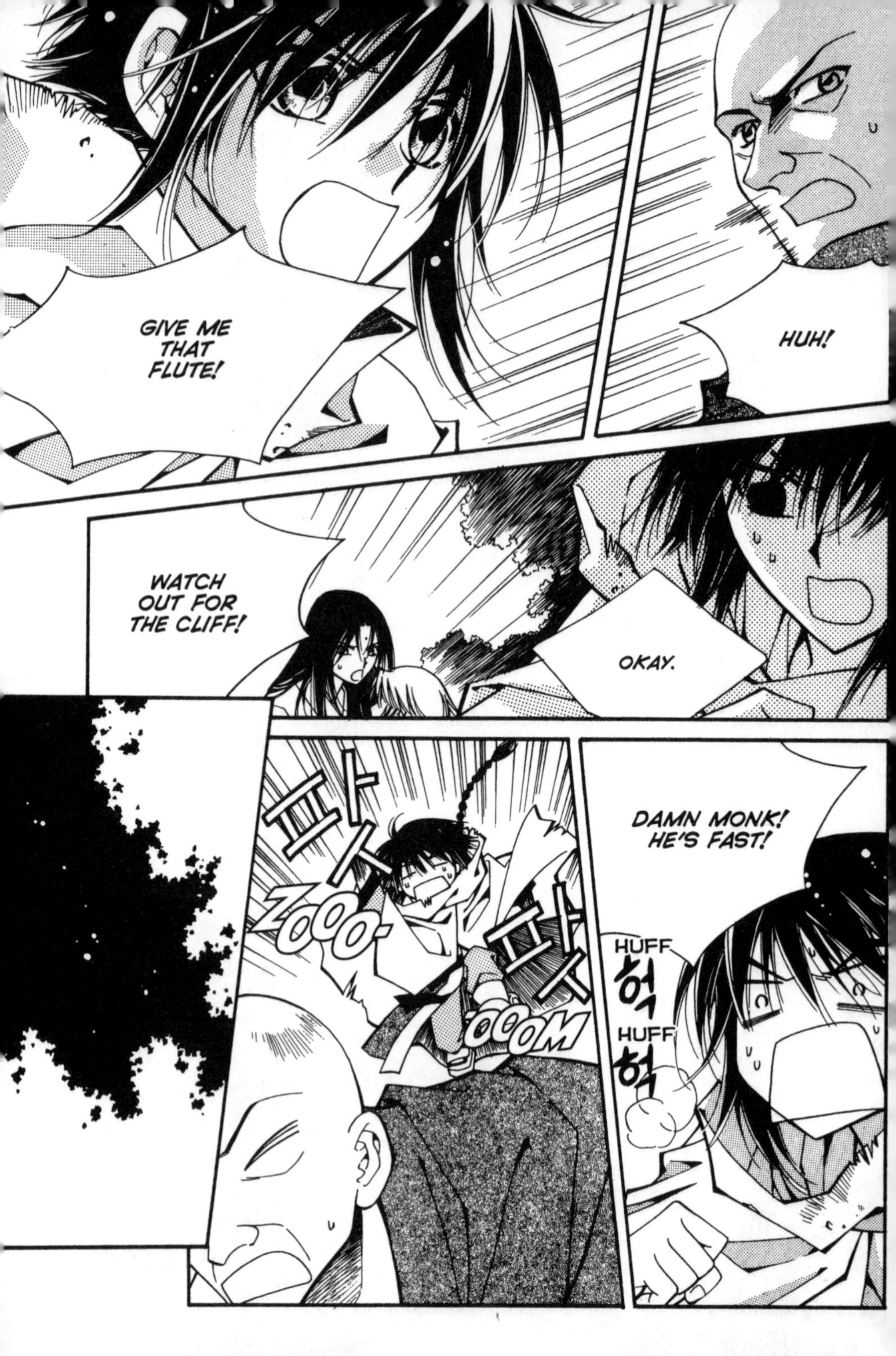
GIVE ME THAT FLUTE!
HUH!
WATCH OUT FOR THE CLIFF!
OKAY.
ZOOO-
-OOOM
DAMN MONK! HE'S FAST!
HUFF 헉
HUFF 헉

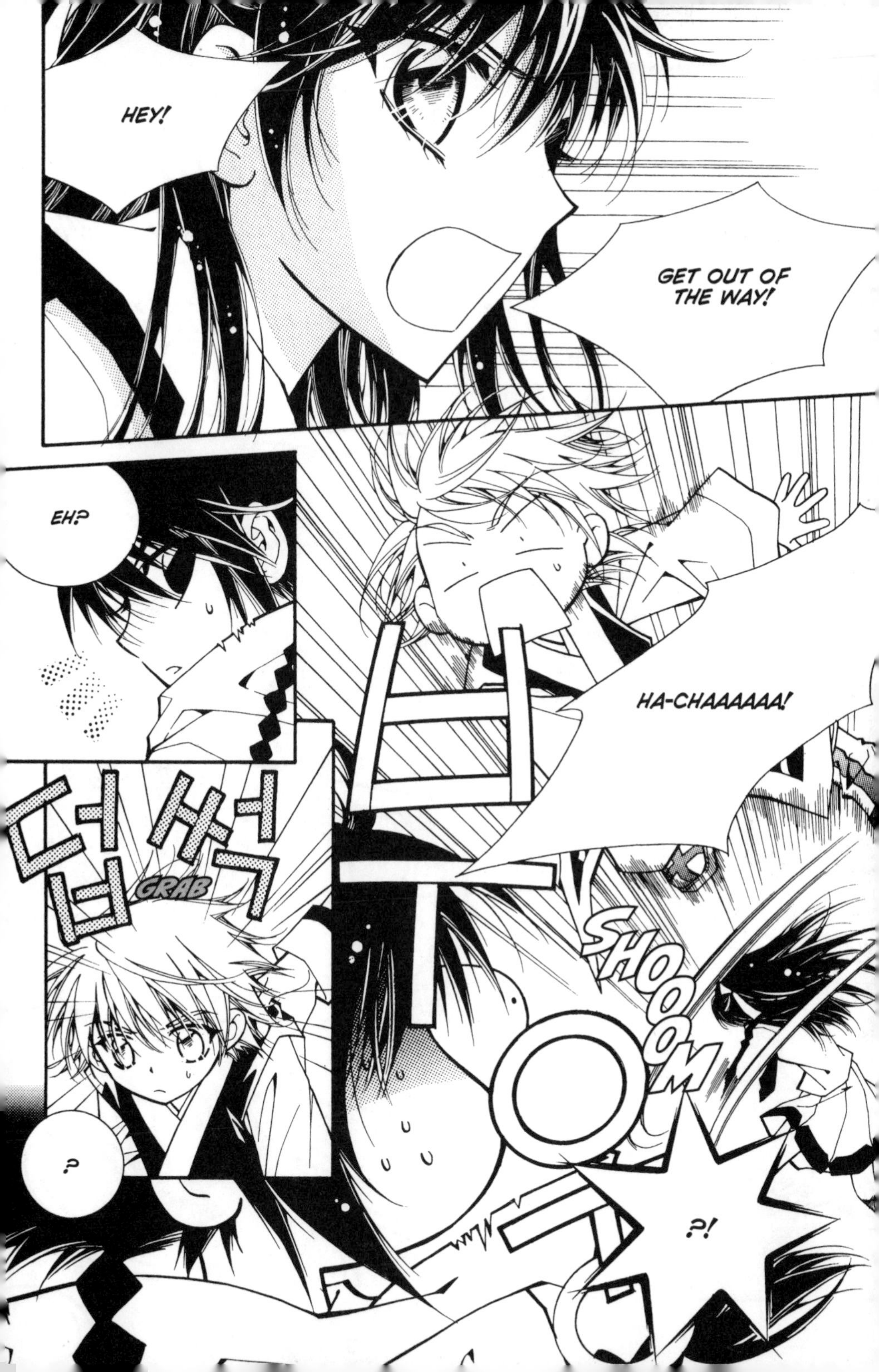
HEY!
GET OUT OF THE WAY!
EH?
덥석
GRAB
?
HA-CHAAAAAA!
SHOOOOM
?!

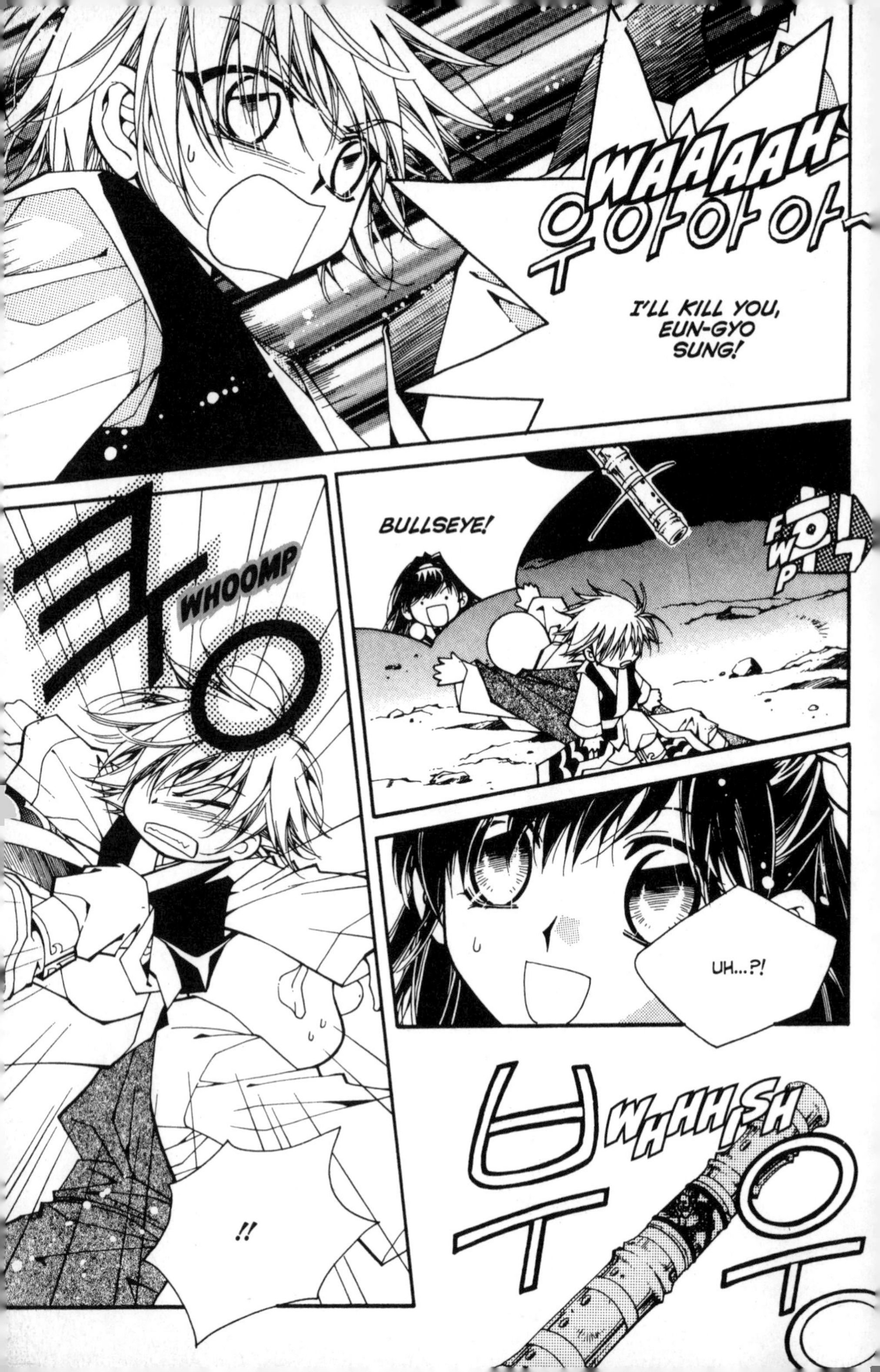
WAAAAH
우아아아아~
I'LL KILL YOU, EUN-GYO SUNG!
쿵
WHOOMP
!!
BULLSEYE!
FWP
UH...?!
부웅
WHHHISH

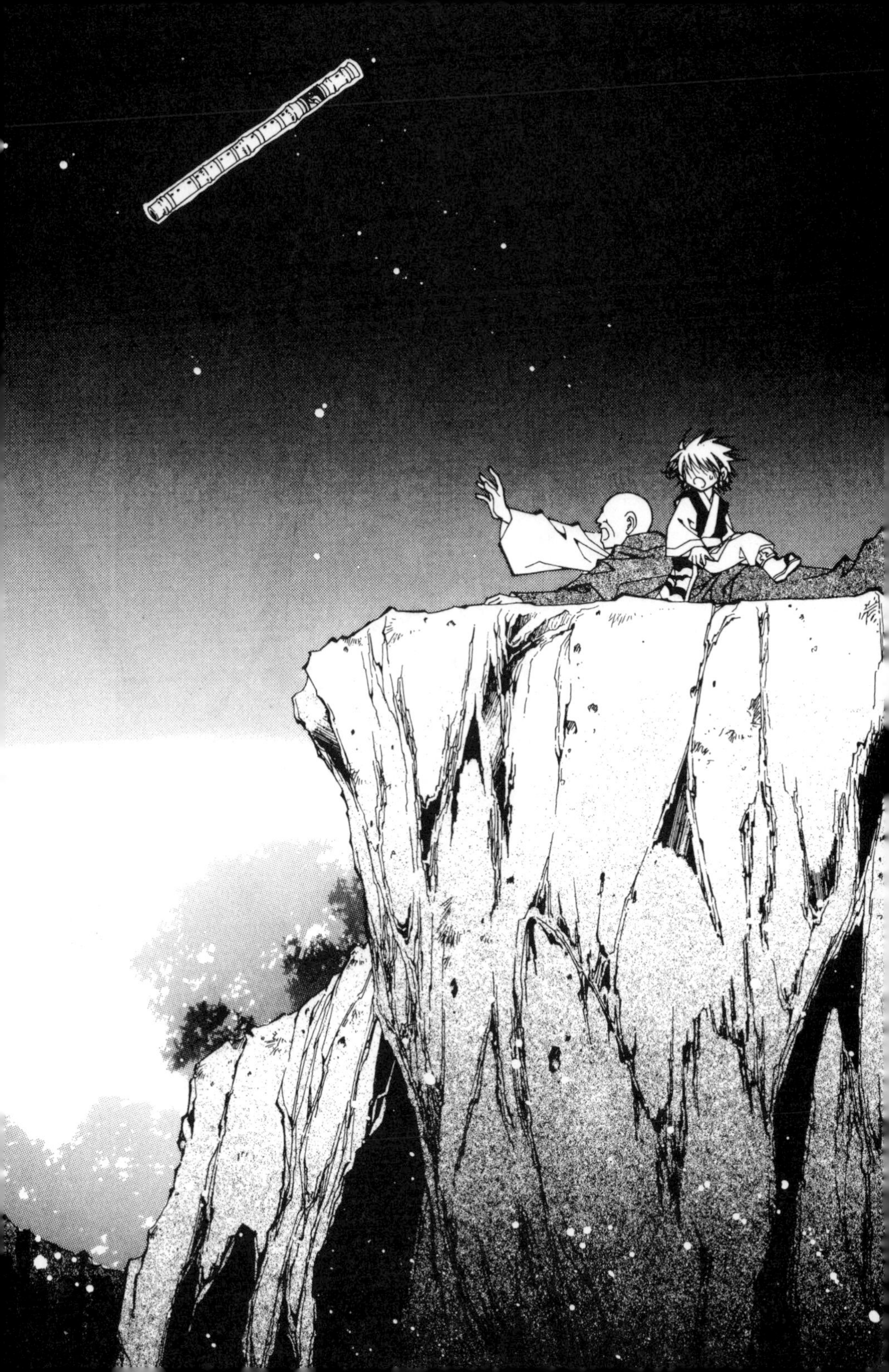

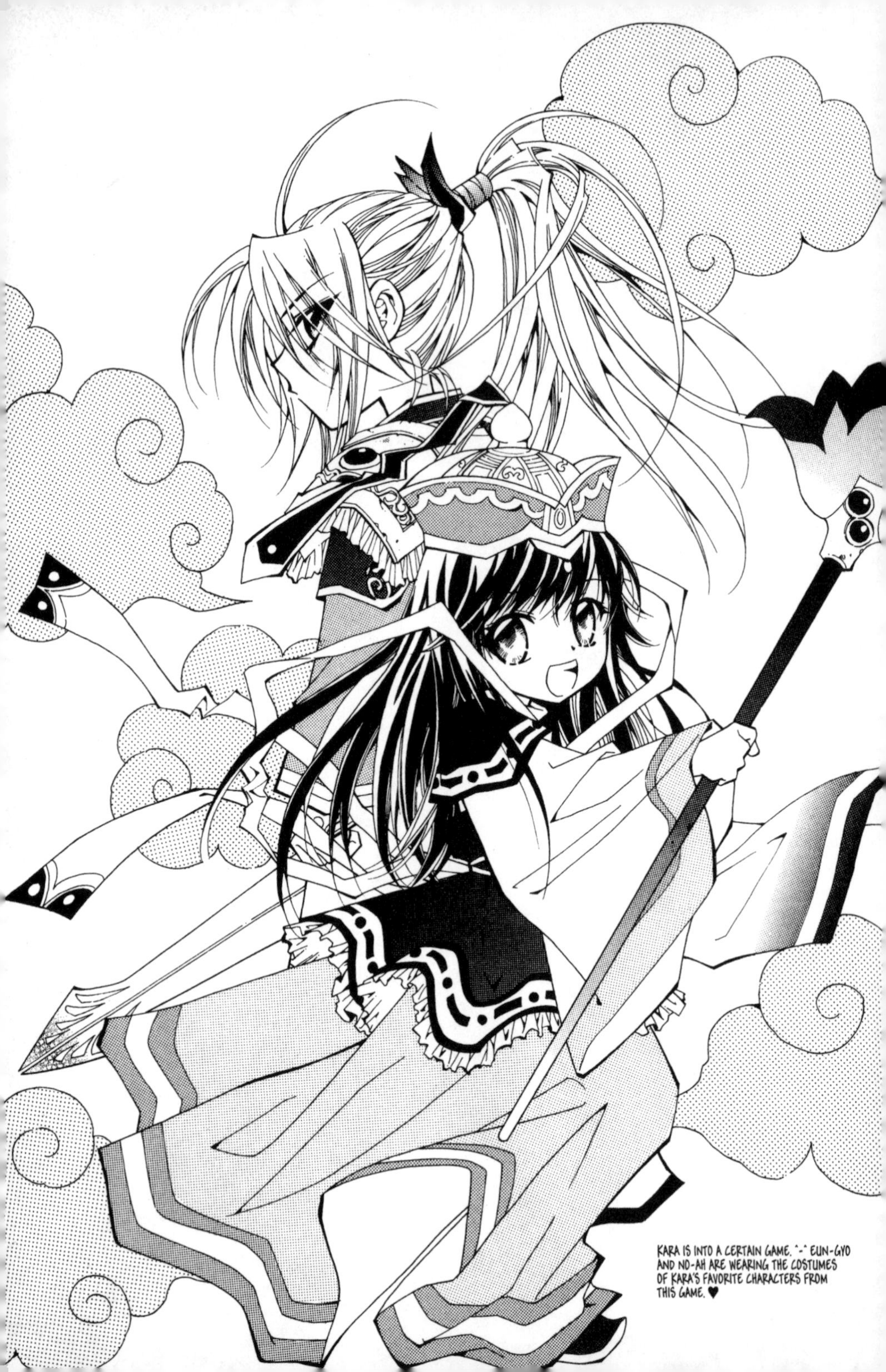

KARA IS INTO A CERTAIN GAME. ^-^ EUN-GYO AND NO-AH ARE WEARING THE COSTUMES OF KARA'S FAVORITE CHARACTERS FROM THIS GAME. ♥

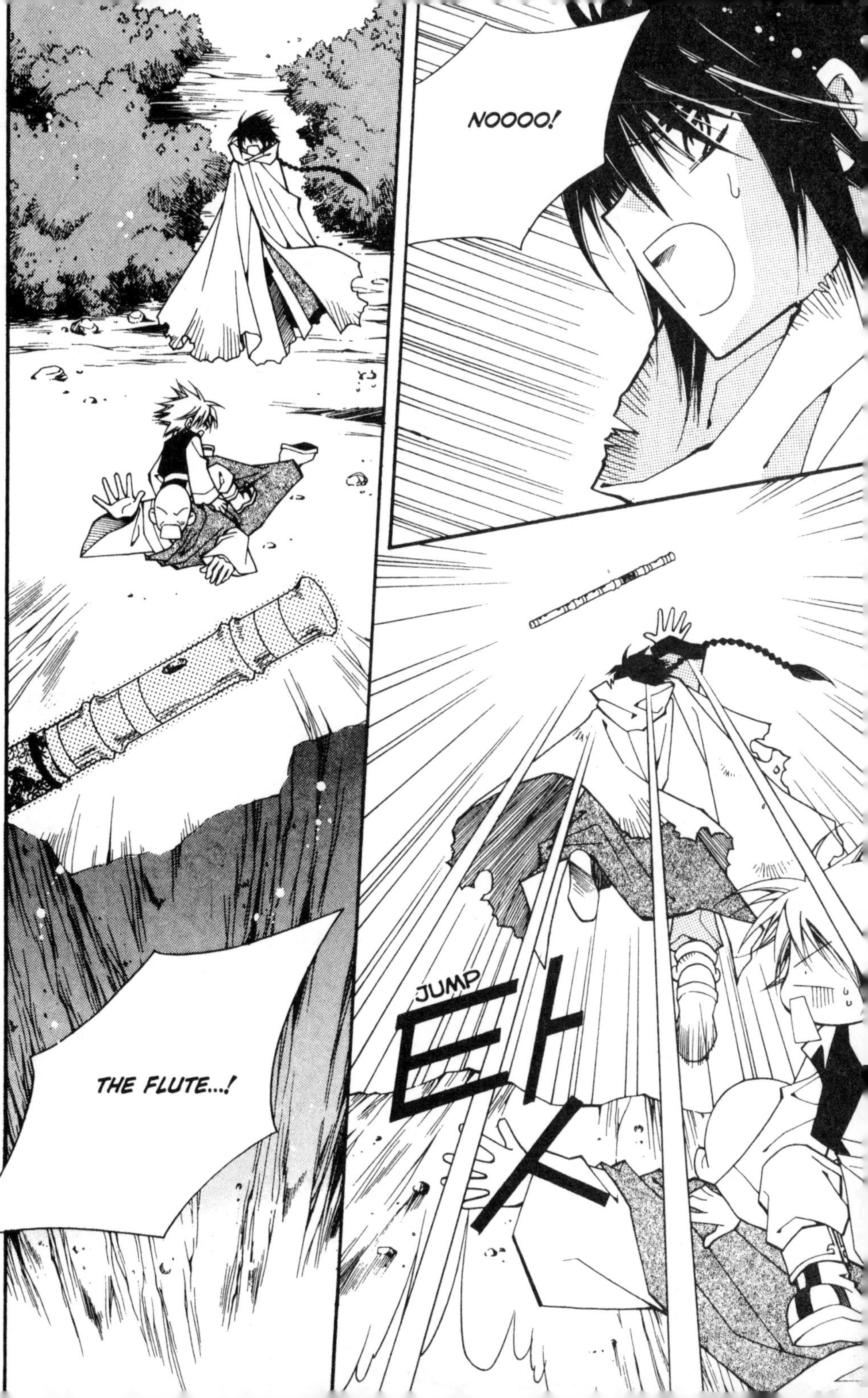
THE FLUTE...!
NOOOO!
JUMP

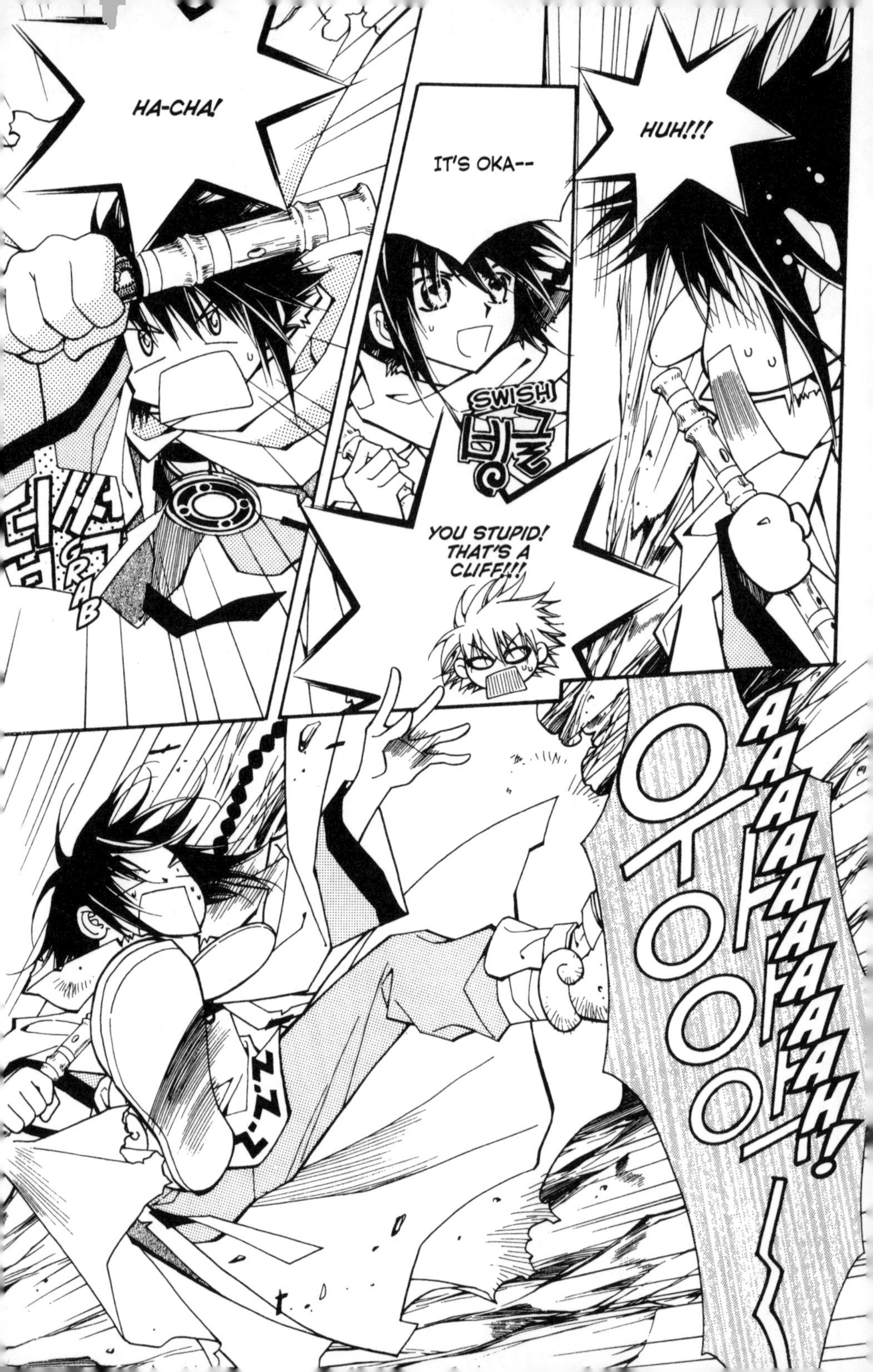
HA-CHA!
GRAB
IT'S OKA--
SWISH
HUH!!!
YOU STUPID! THAT'S A CLIFF!!!
AAAAAAAAAAH!!

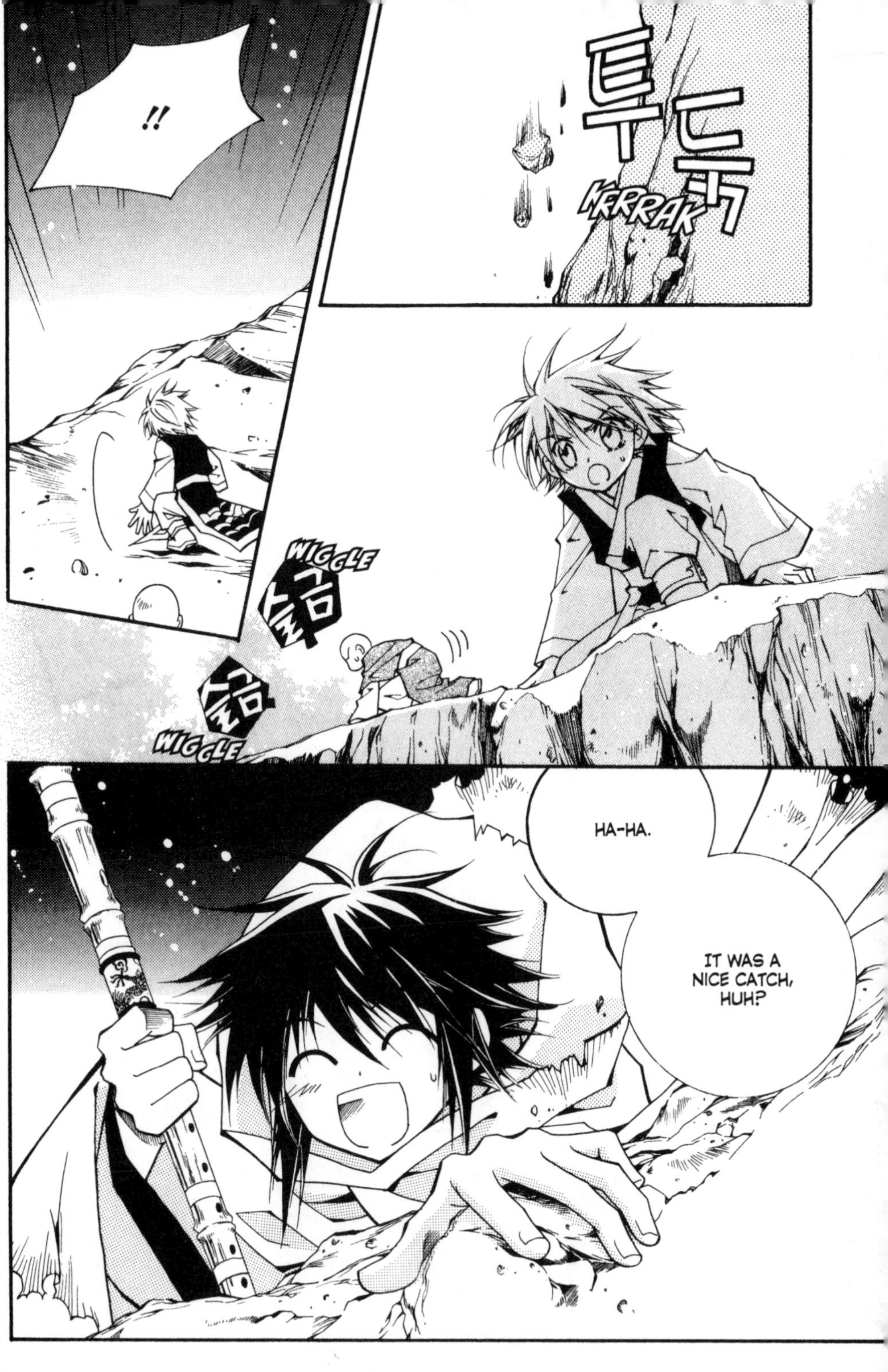
!!
투둑
KRRRAK
WIGGLE
WIGGLE
HA-HA.
IT WAS A NICE CATCH, HUH?

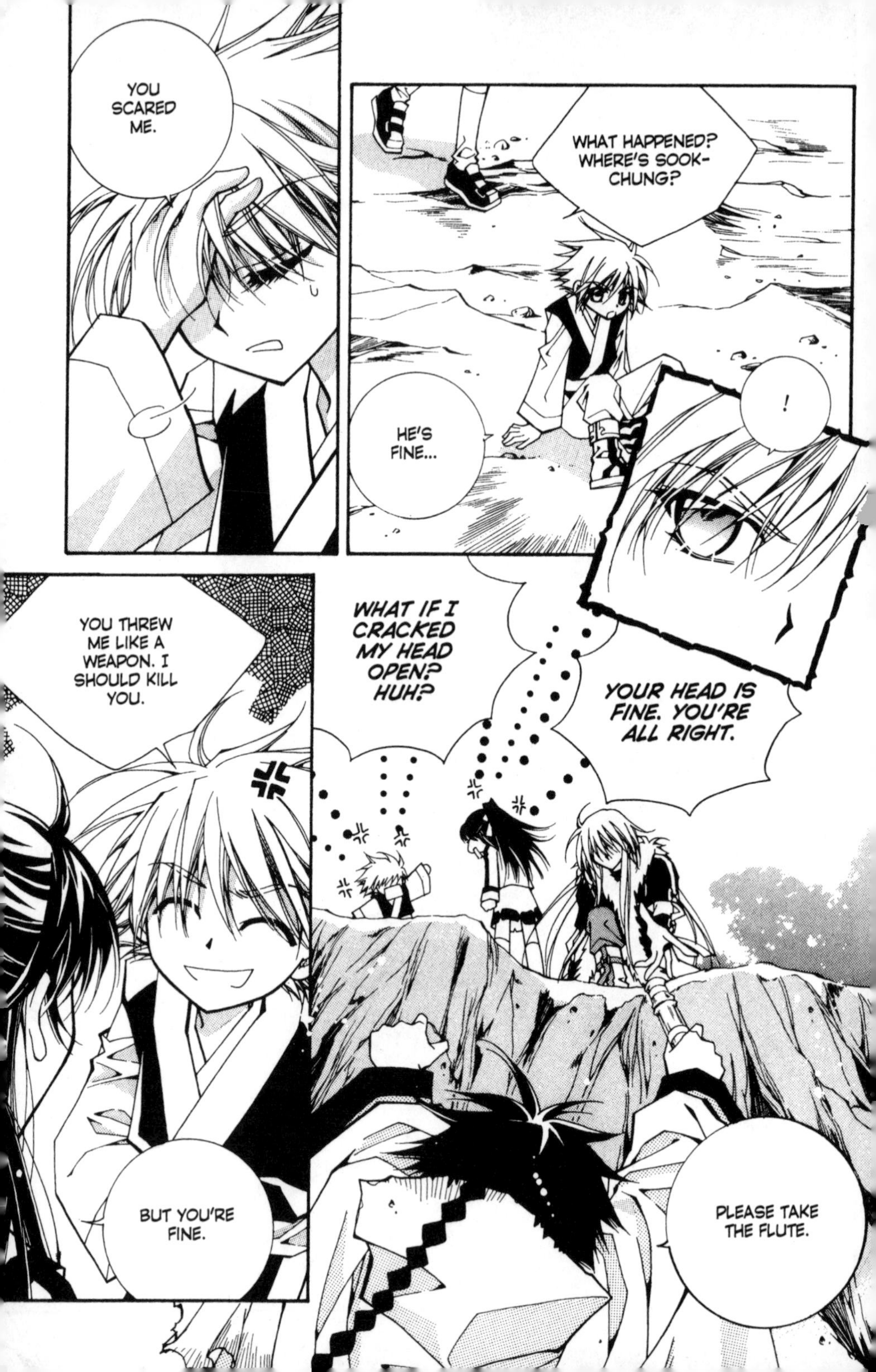
YOU SCARED ME.
WHAT HAPPENED? WHERE'S SOOK-CHUNG?
HE'S FINE...
!
YOU THREW ME LIKE A WEAPON. I SHOULD KILL YOU.
BUT YOU'RE FINE.
WHAT IF I CRACKED MY HEAD OPEN? HUH?
YOUR HEAD IS FINE. YOU'RE ALL RIGHT.
PLEASE TAKE THE FLUTE.

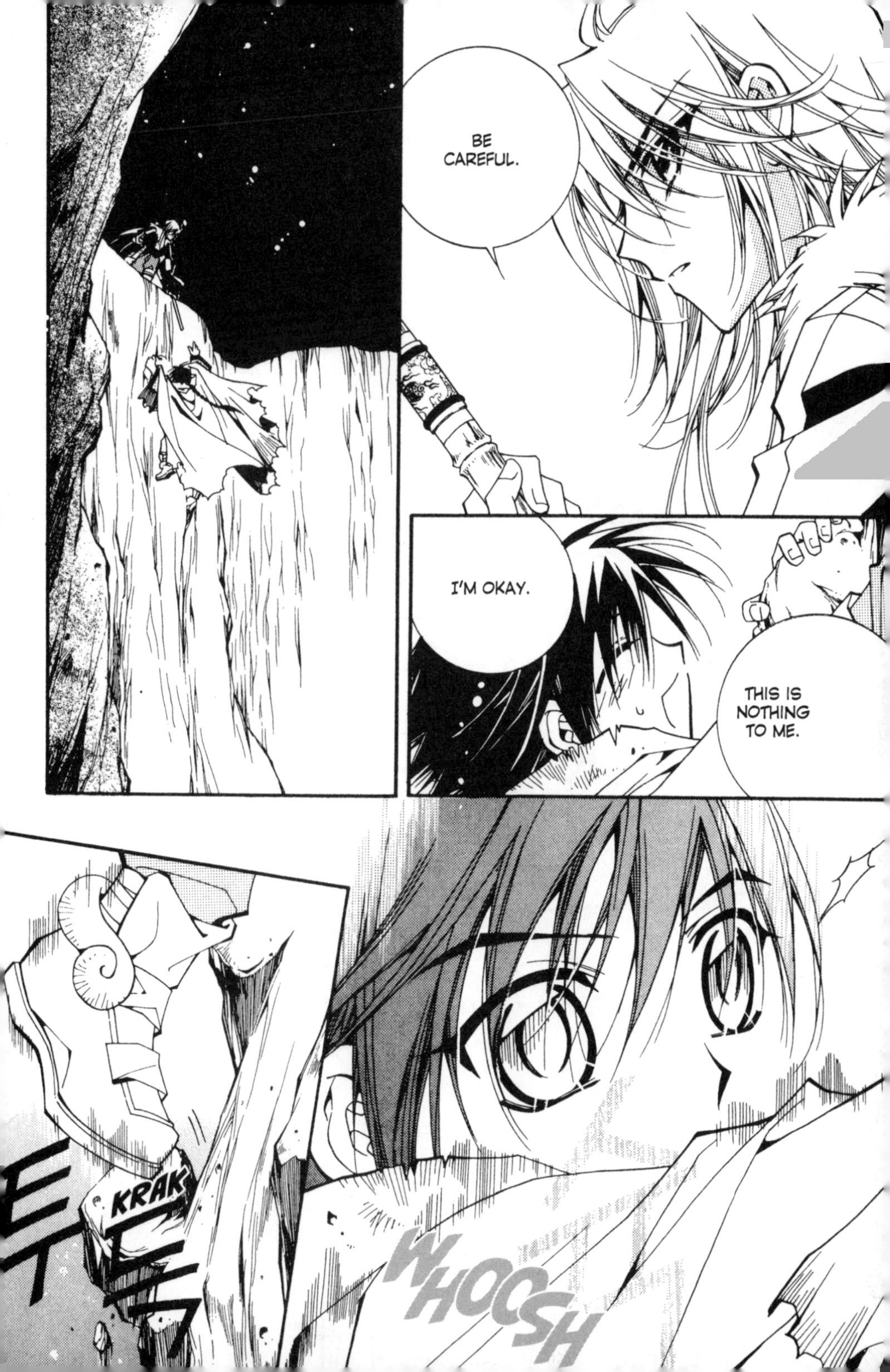
BE CAREFUL.
I'M OKAY.
THIS IS NOTHING TO ME.
KRAK
WHOOSH

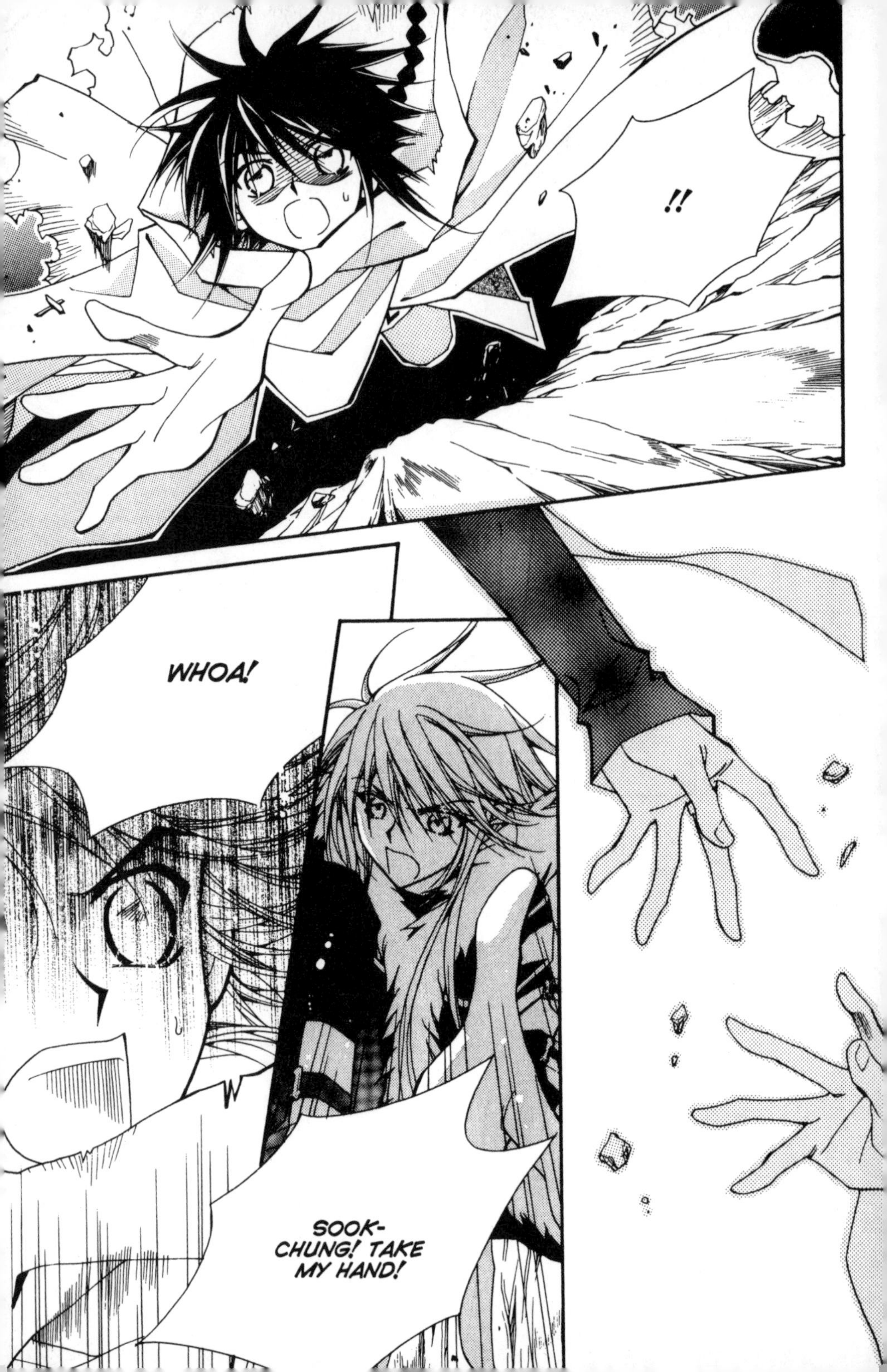
!!
WHOA!
SOOK-CHUNG! TAKE MY HAND!

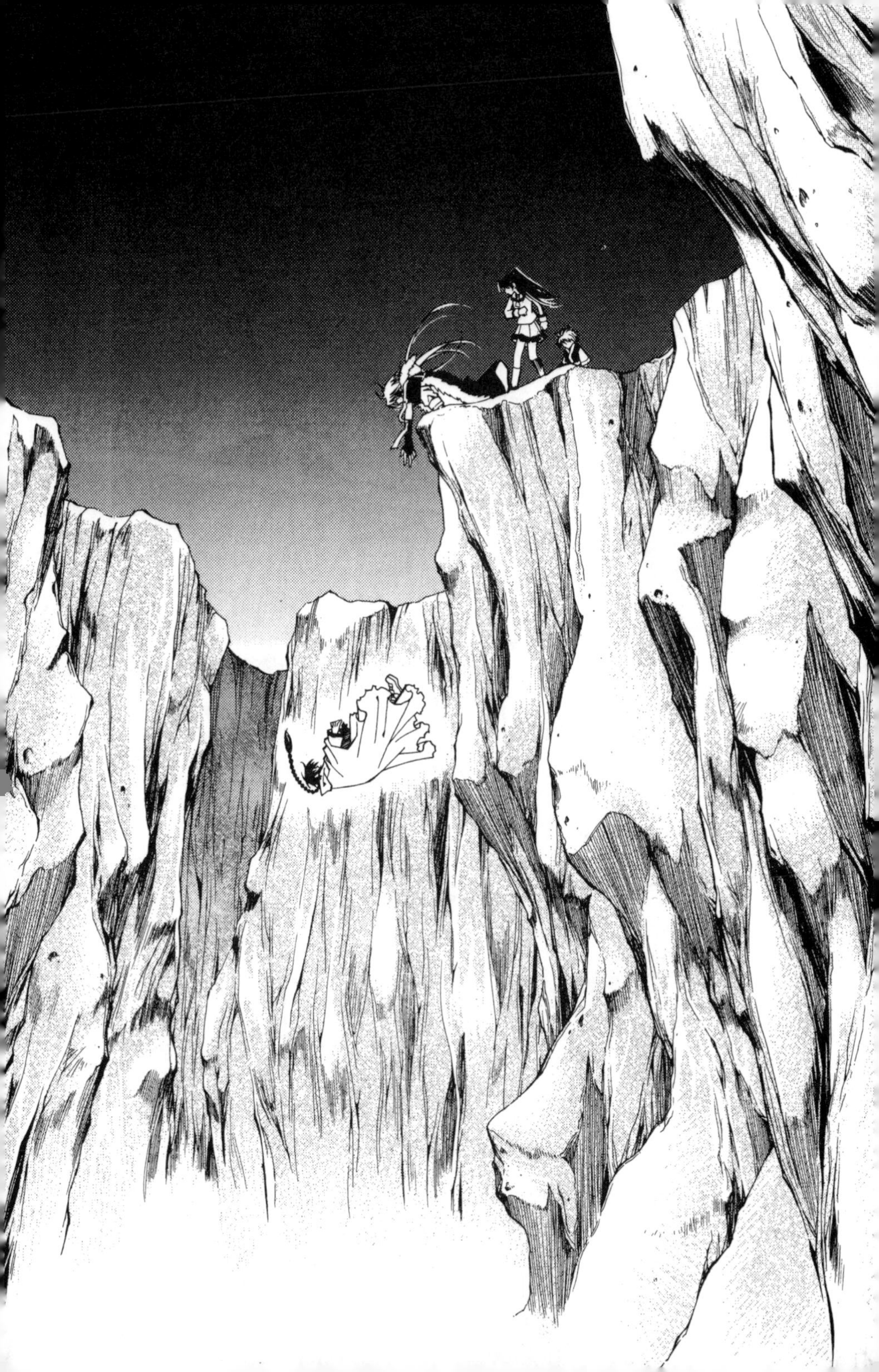

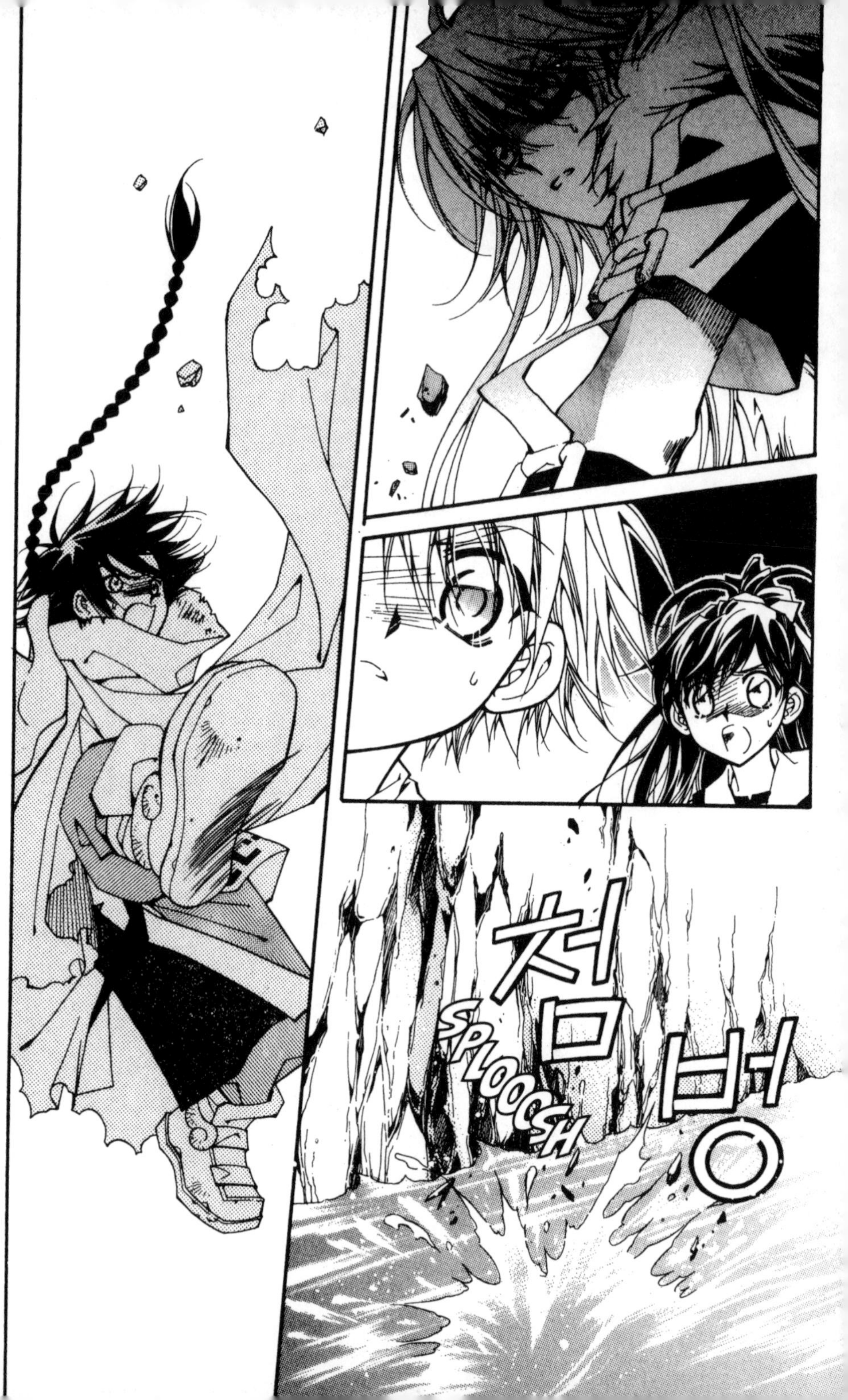

첨벙
SPLOOOSH

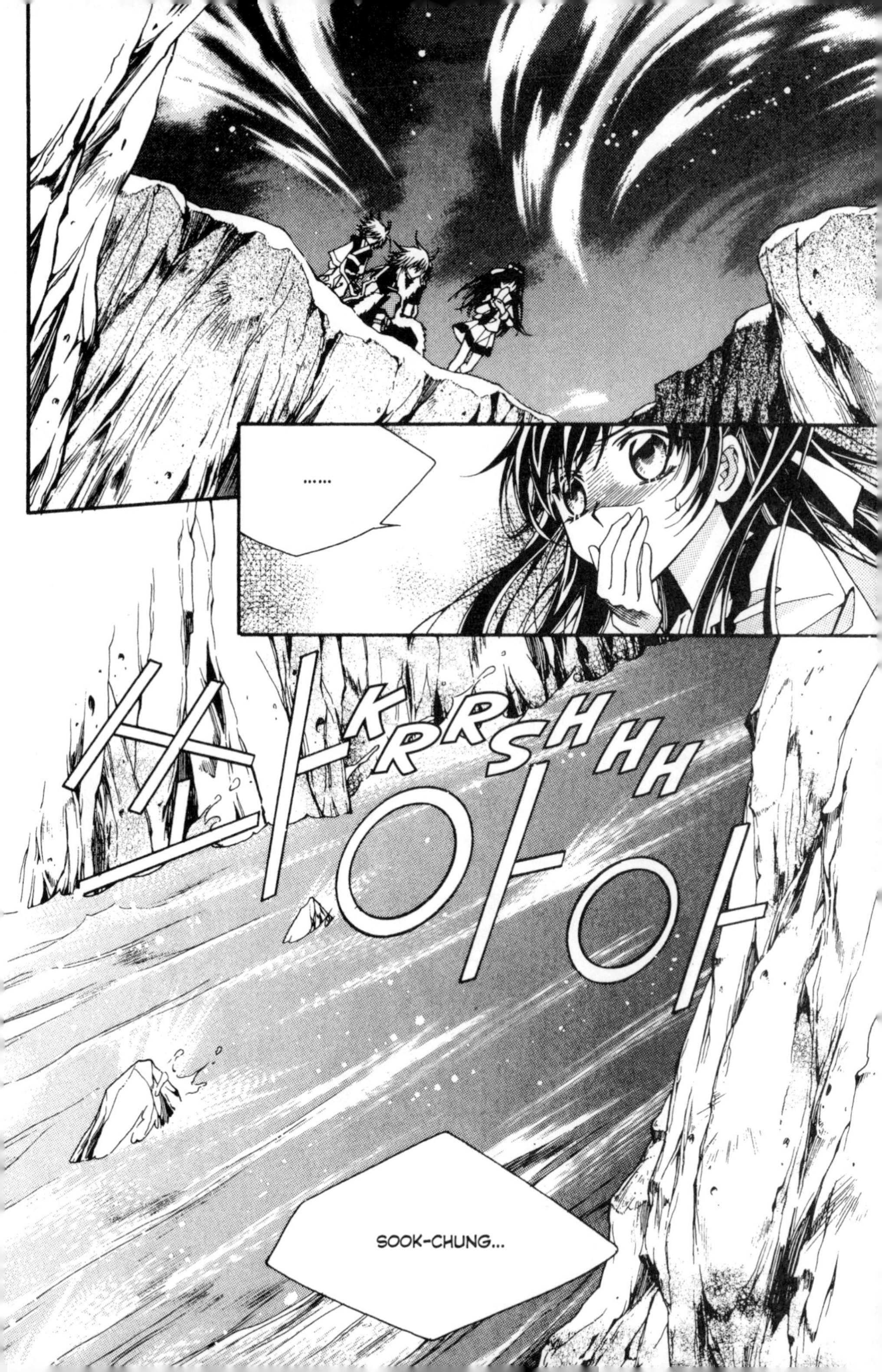
……
KRRSHHH
SOOK-CHUNG...

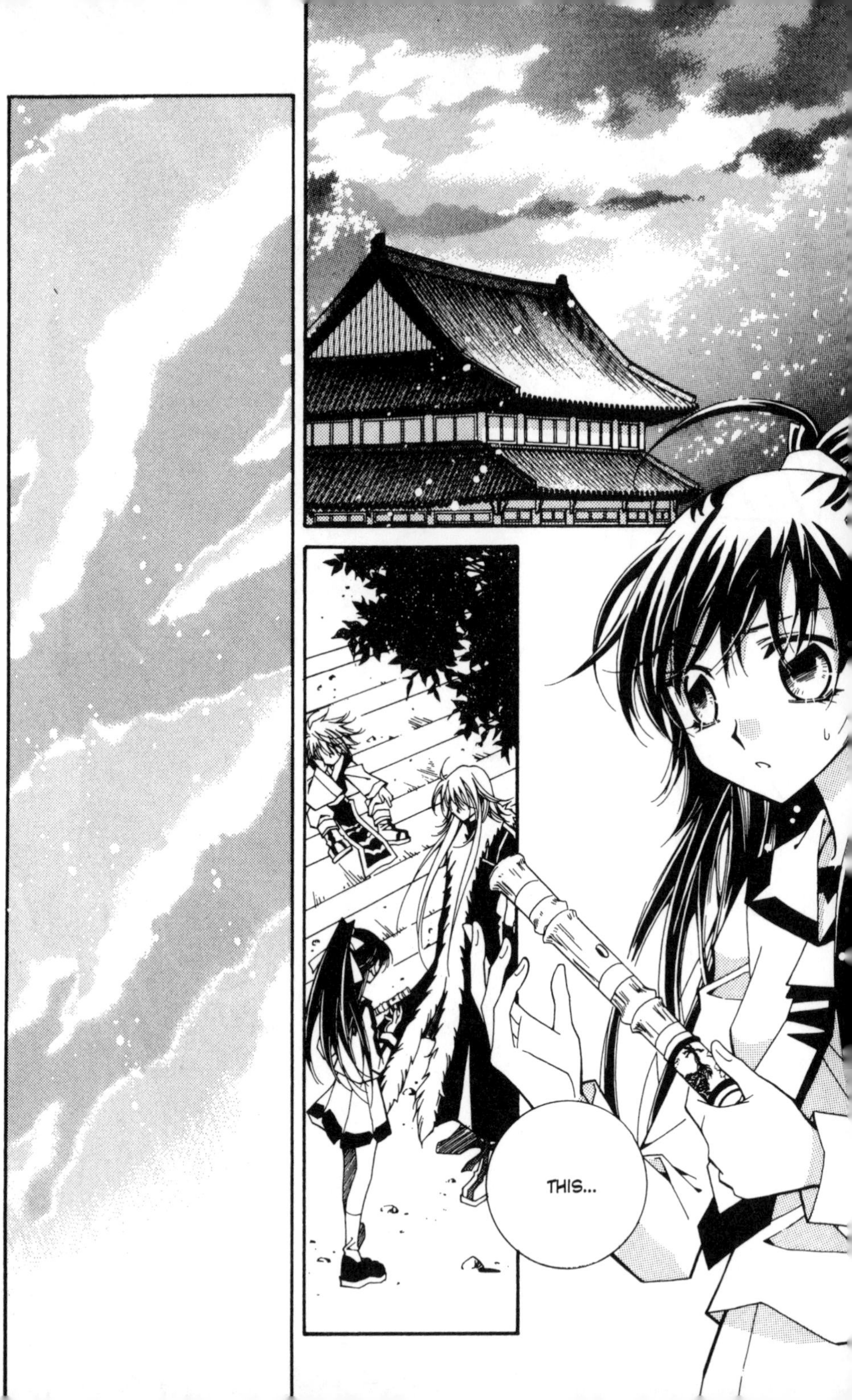
THIS...

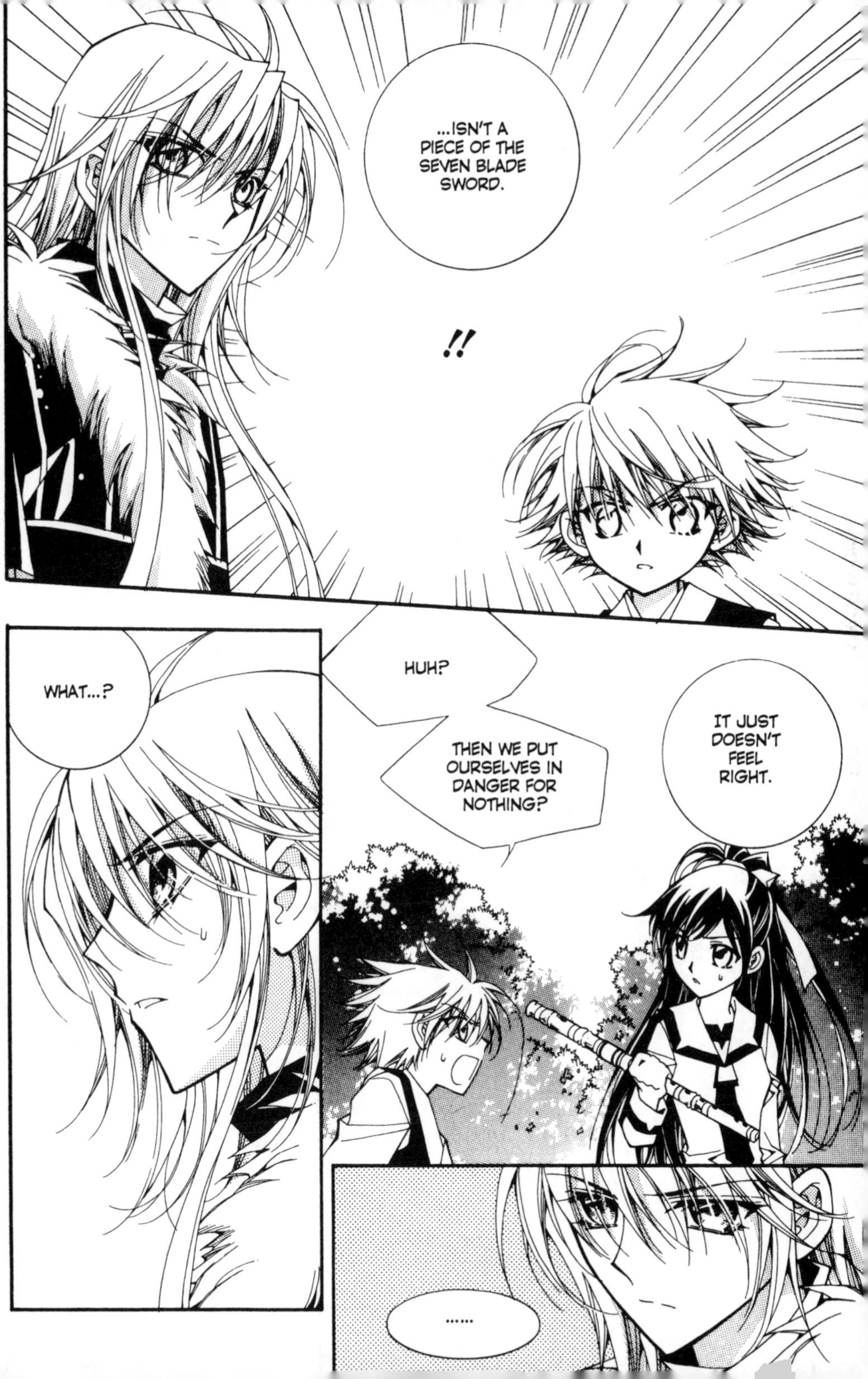
...ISN'T A PIECE OF THE SEVEN BLADE SWORD.
!!
WHAT...?
HUH?
THEN WE PUT OURSELVES IN DANGER FOR NOTHING?
IT JUST DOESN'T FEEL RIGHT.
......

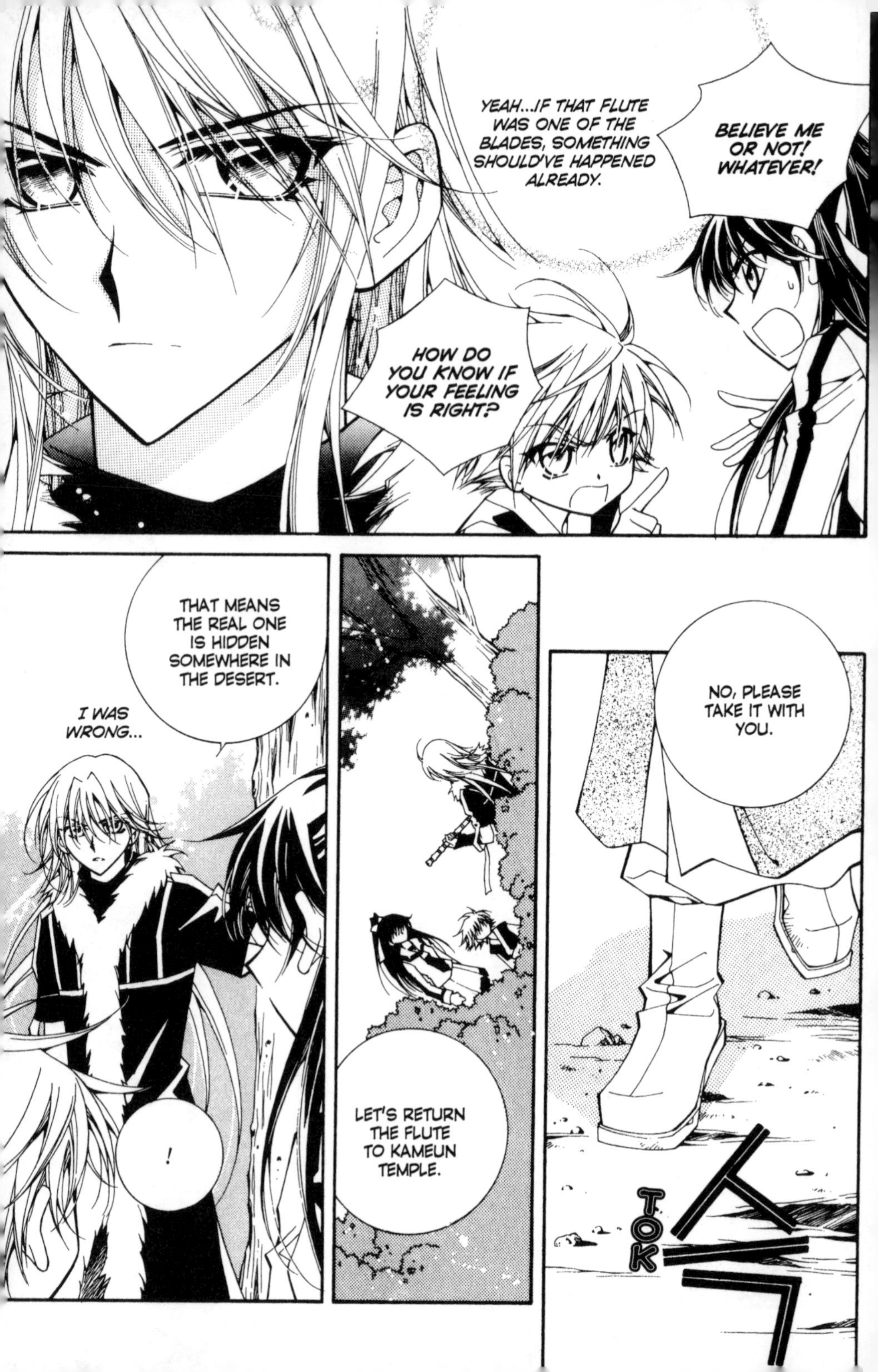
YEAH...IF THAT FLUTE WAS ONE OF THE BLADES, SOMETHING SHOULD'VE HAPPENED ALREADY.
BELIEVE ME OR NOT! WHATEVER!
HOW DO YOU KNOW IF YOUR FEELING IS RIGHT?
THAT MEANS THE REAL ONE IS HIDDEN SOMEWHERE IN THE DESERT.
I WAS WRONG...
!
LET'S RETURN THE FLUTE TO KAMEUN TEMPLE.
NO, PLEASE TAKE IT WITH YOU.
TOK

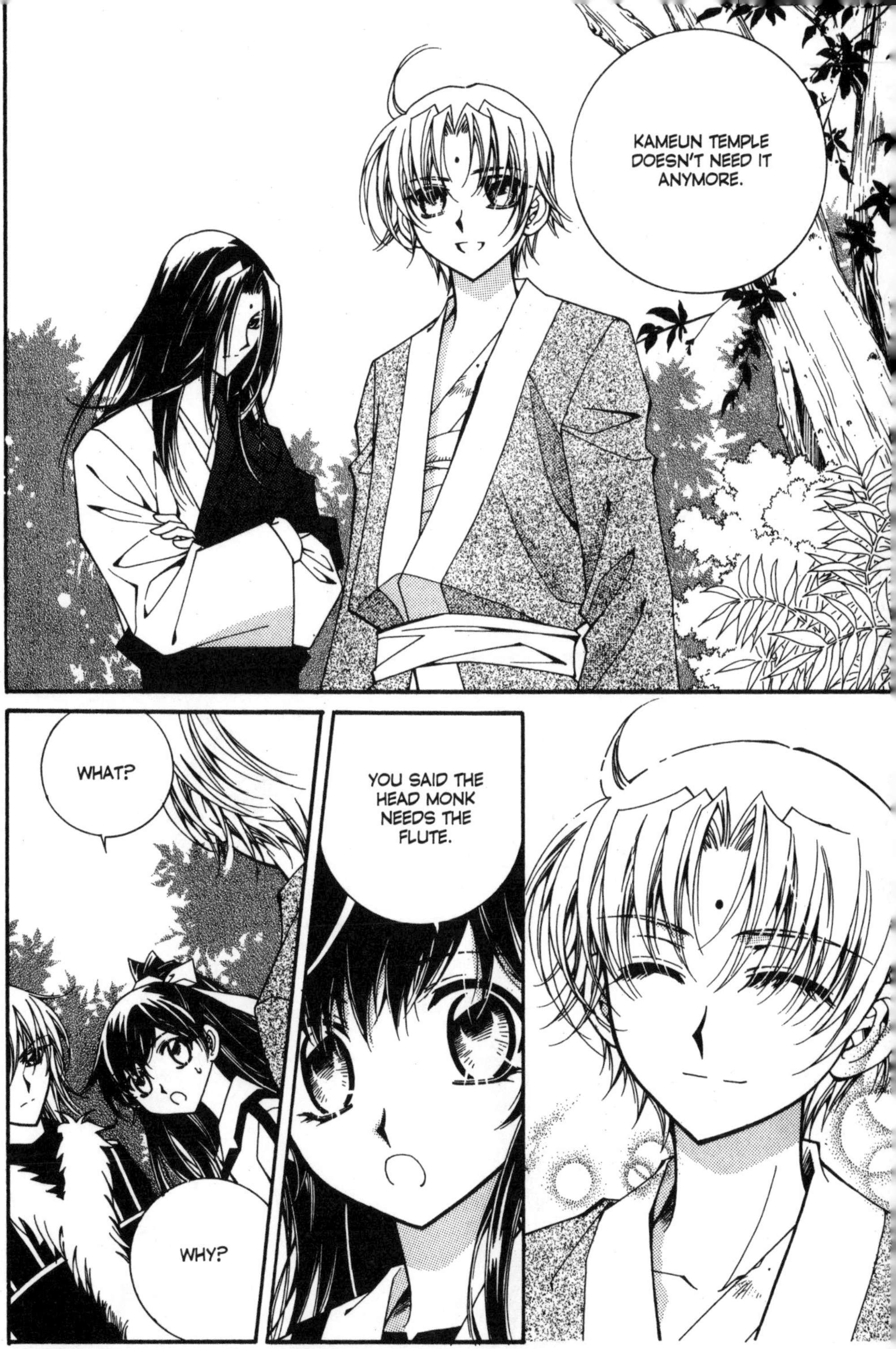
KAMEUN TEMPLE DOESN'T NEED IT ANYMORE.
WHAT?
WHY?
YOU SAID THE HEAD MONK NEEDS THE FLUTE.

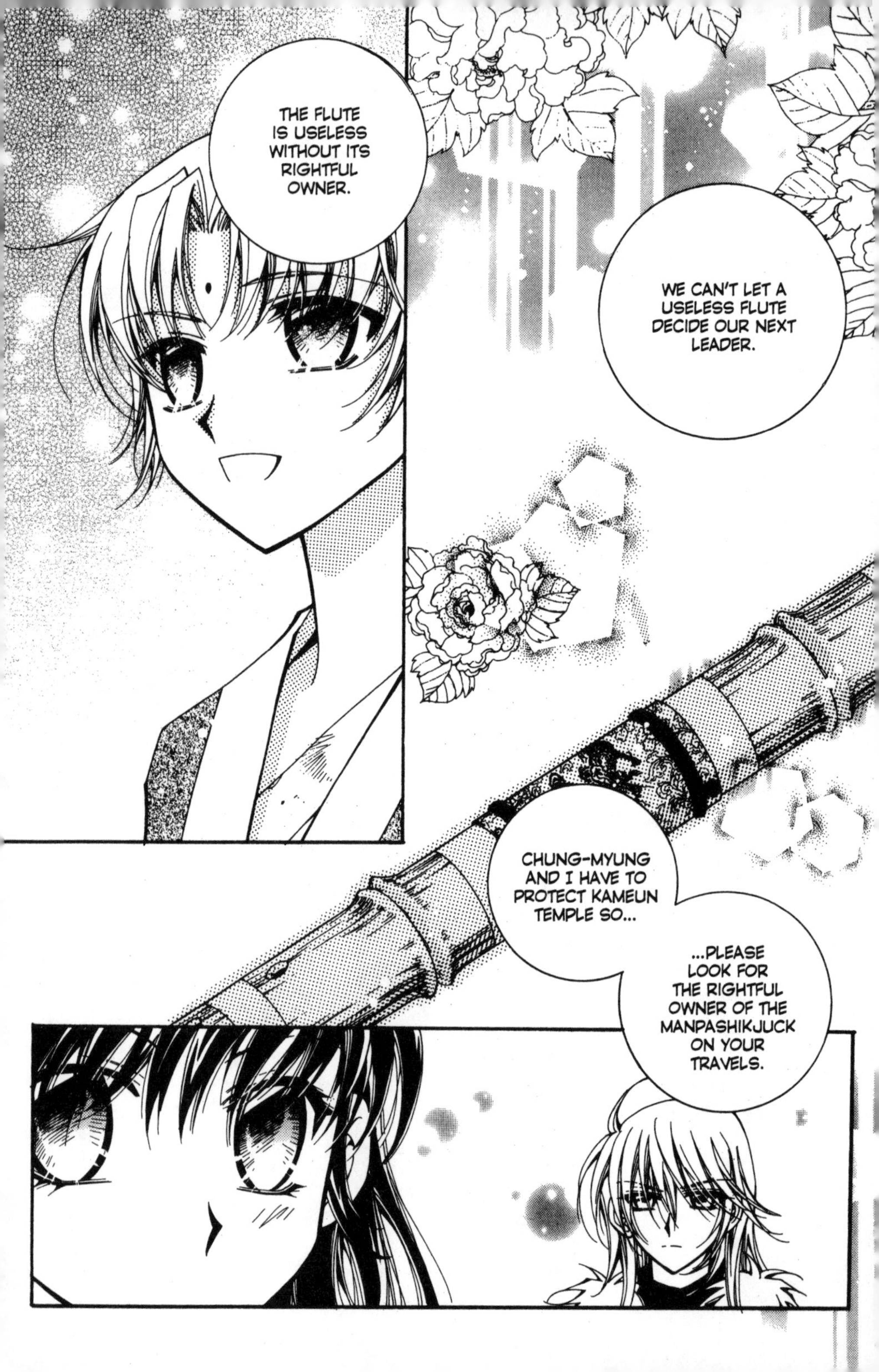
THE FLUTE IS USELESS WITHOUT ITS RIGHTFUL OWNER.
WE CAN'T LET A USELESS FLUTE DECIDE OUR NEXT LEADER.
CHUNG-MYUNG AND I HAVE TO PROTECT KAMEUN TEMPLE SO...
...PLEASE LOOK FOR THE RIGHTFUL OWNER OF THE MANPASHIKJUCK ON YOUR TRAVELS.

HAE-RANG AND CHUNG-MYUNG MADE UP. THAT'S GREAT.

AND WE HAVE THE FLUTE.

WE HOPE THE FLUTE WILL FIND ITS RIGHTFUL OWNER AND DO WHAT IT'S SUPPOSED TO DO.

I JUST REALIZED WE HAVEN'T SLEPT AT ALL.

I'M SO TIRED.

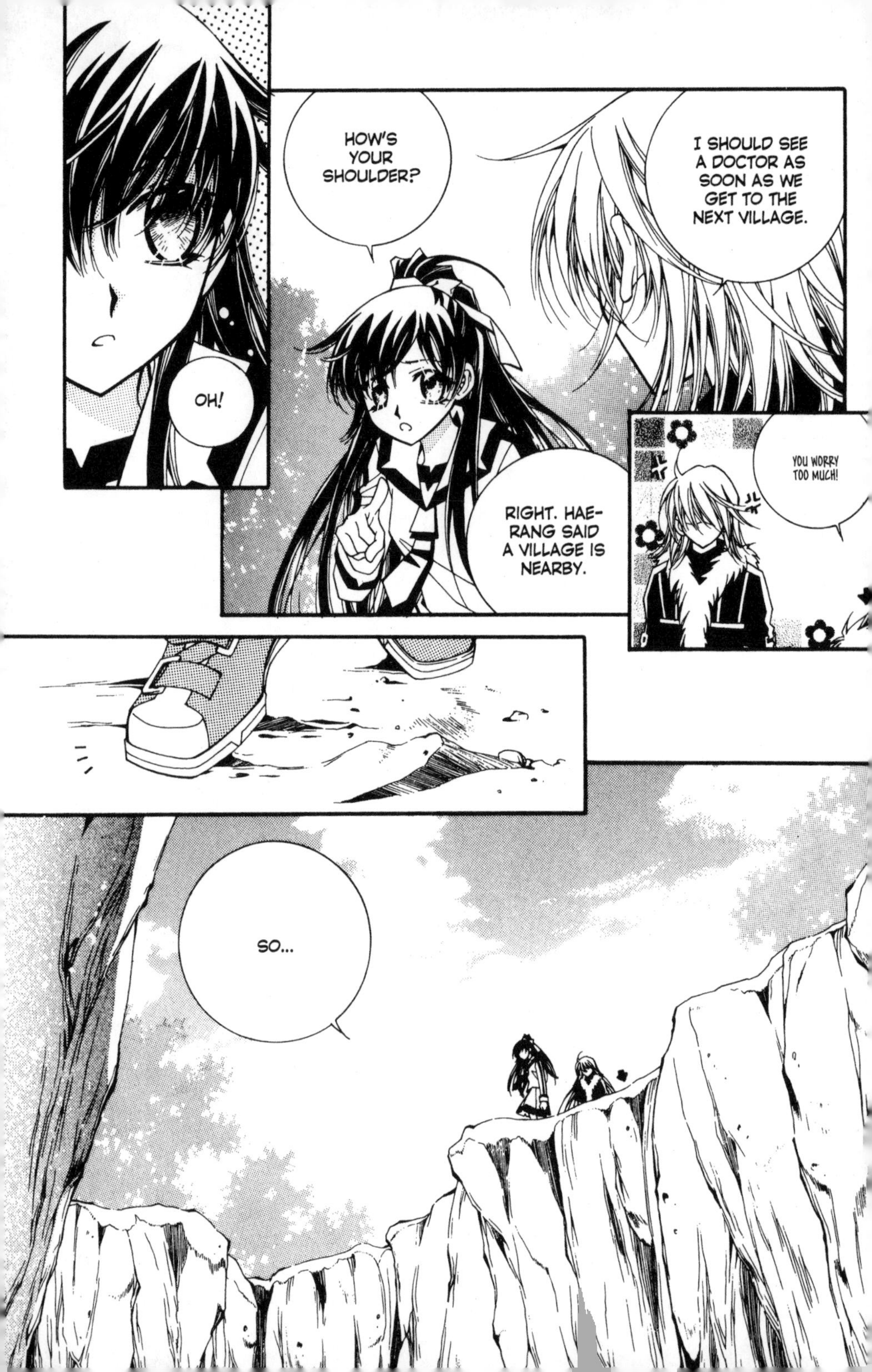
OH!
HOW'S YOUR SHOULDER?
I SHOULD SEE A DOCTOR AS SOON AS WE GET TO THE NEXT VILLAGE.
RIGHT. HAE-RANG SAID A VILLAGE IS NEARBY.
YOU WORRY TOO MUCH!
SO...

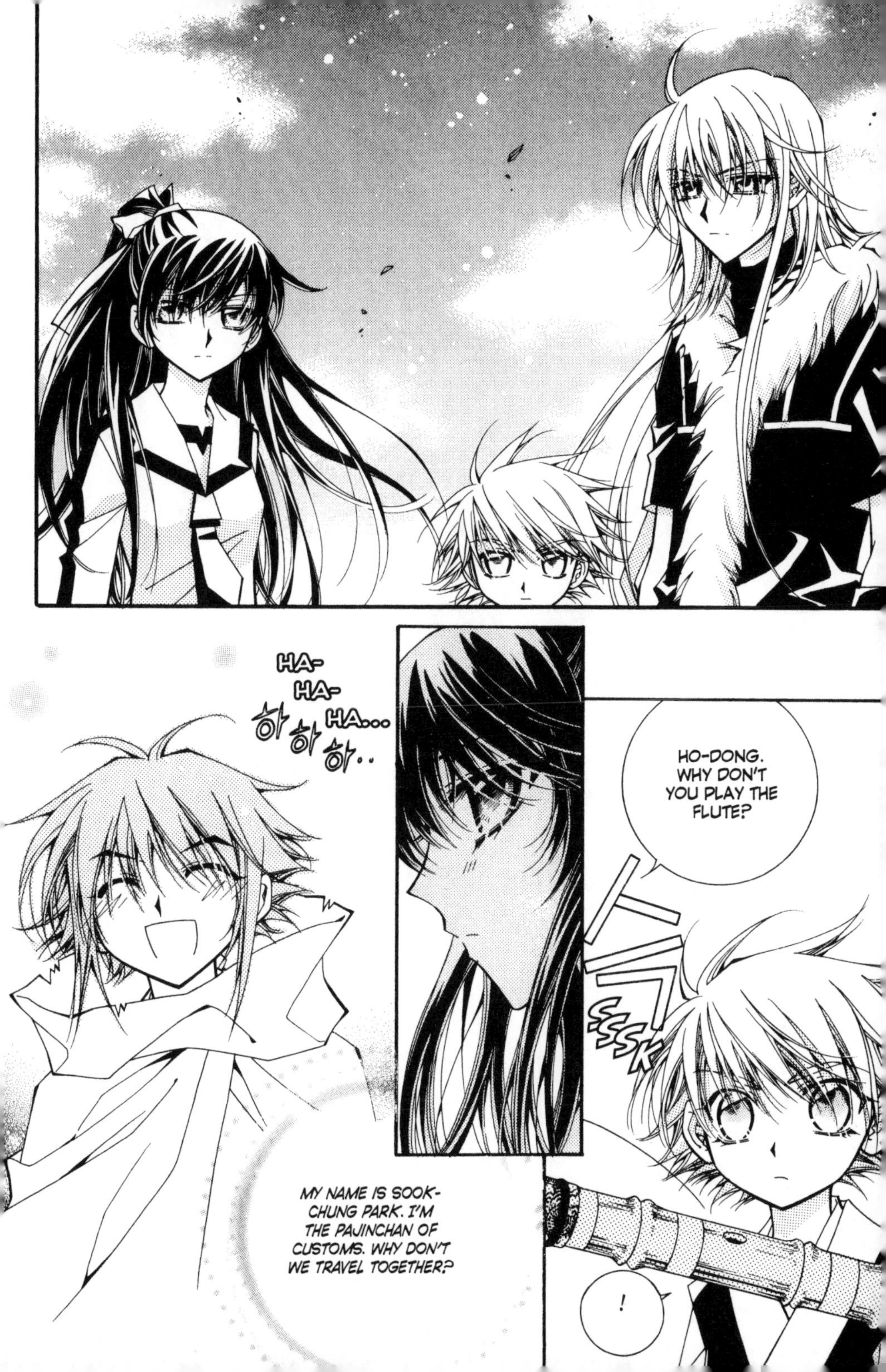
HA-HA-HA...
하하하..
MY NAME IS SOOK-CHUNG PARK. I'M THE PAJINCHAN OF CUSTOMS. WHY DON'T WE TRAVEL TOGETHER?
HO-DONG. WHY DON'T YOU PLAY THE FLUTE?
SSSK
!

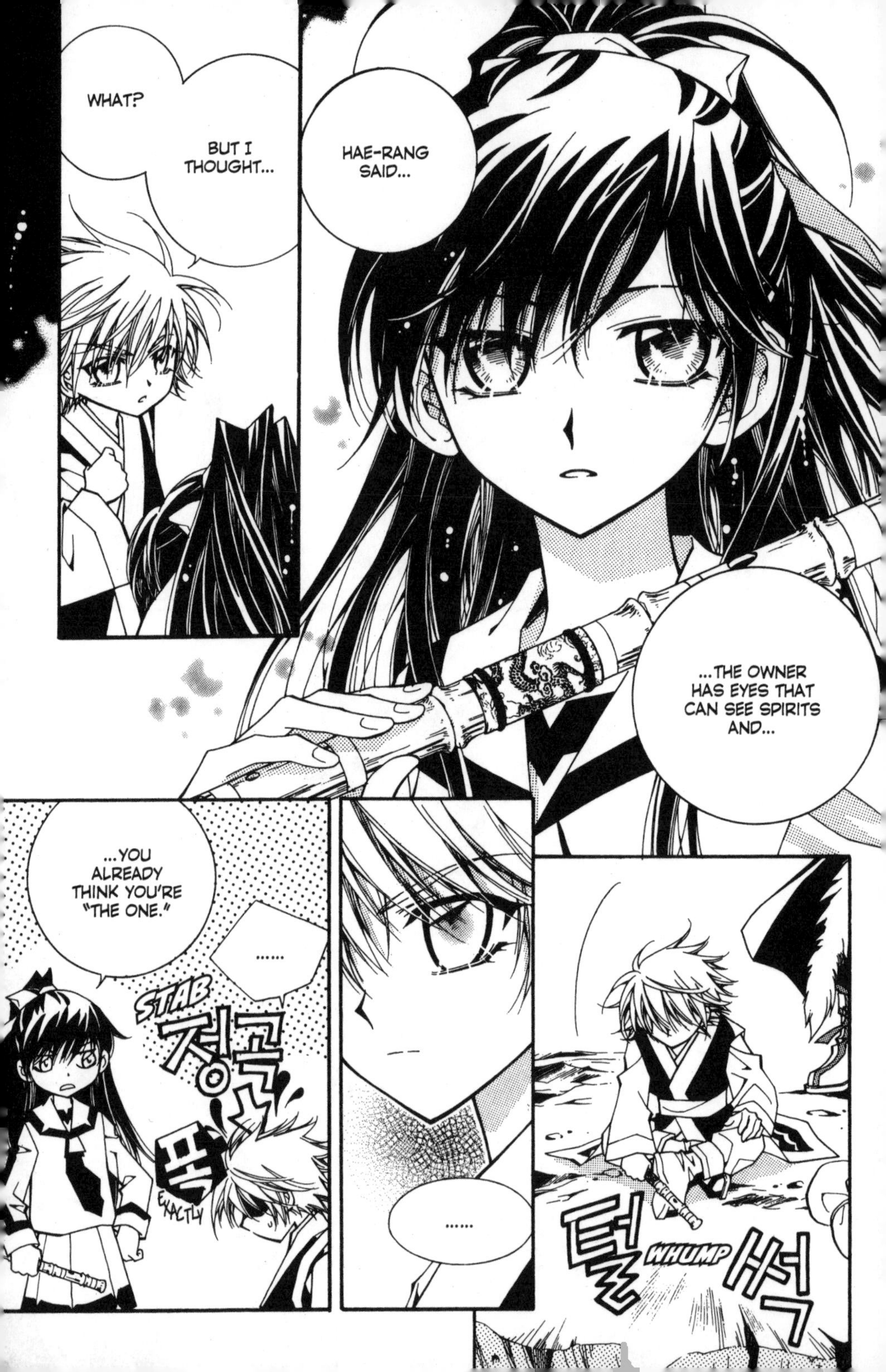
WHAT?
BUT I THOUGHT...
HAE-RANG SAID...
...THE OWNER HAS EYES THAT CAN SEE SPIRITS AND...
...YOU ALREADY THINK YOU'RE "THE ONE."
......
STAB
정곡
EXACTLY
푹
......
털썩
WHUMP

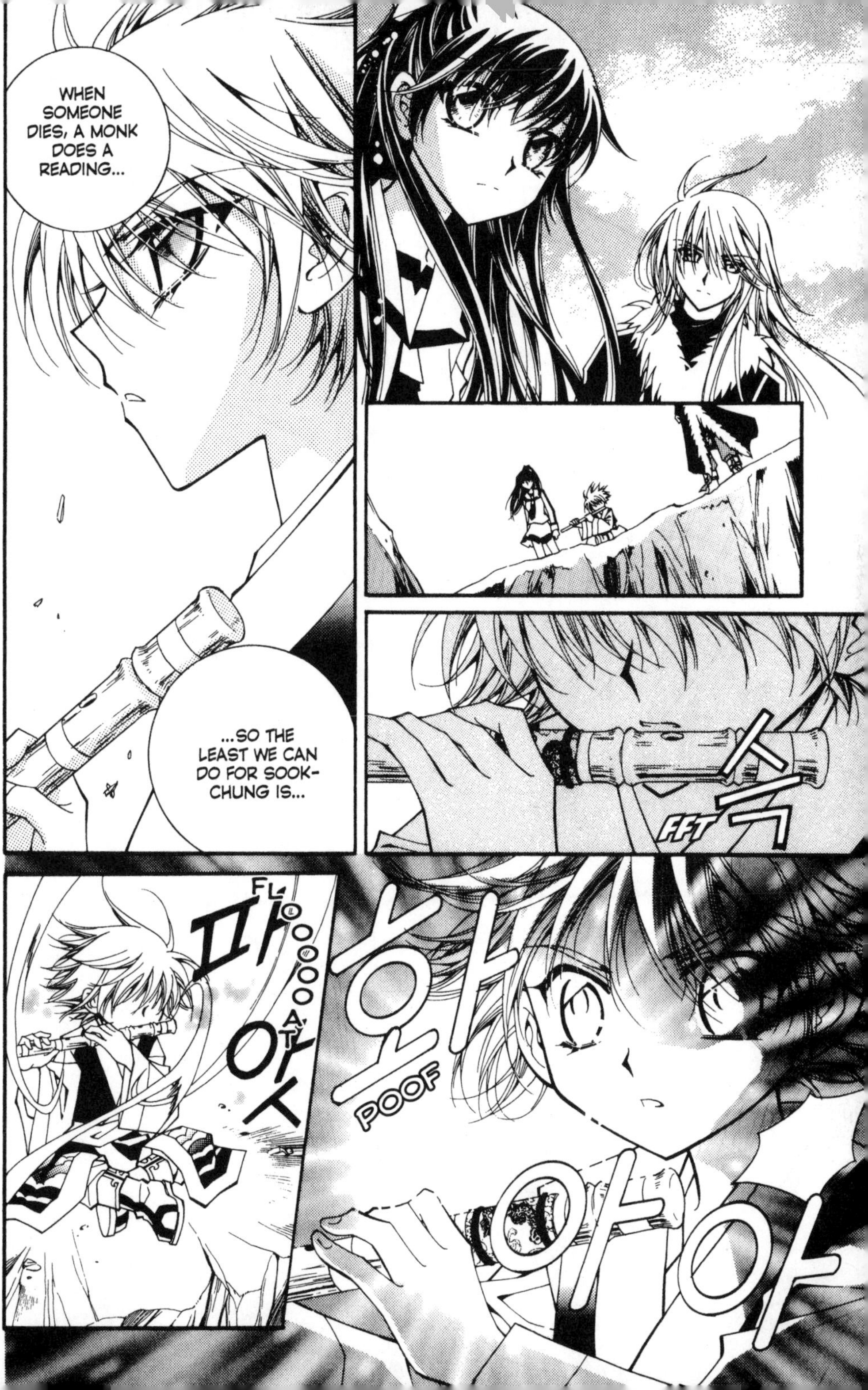
WHEN SOMEONE DIES, A MONK DOES A READING...
...SO THE LEAST WE CAN DO FOR SOOK-CHUNG IS...
FFT
FLOOOOOAT
POOF

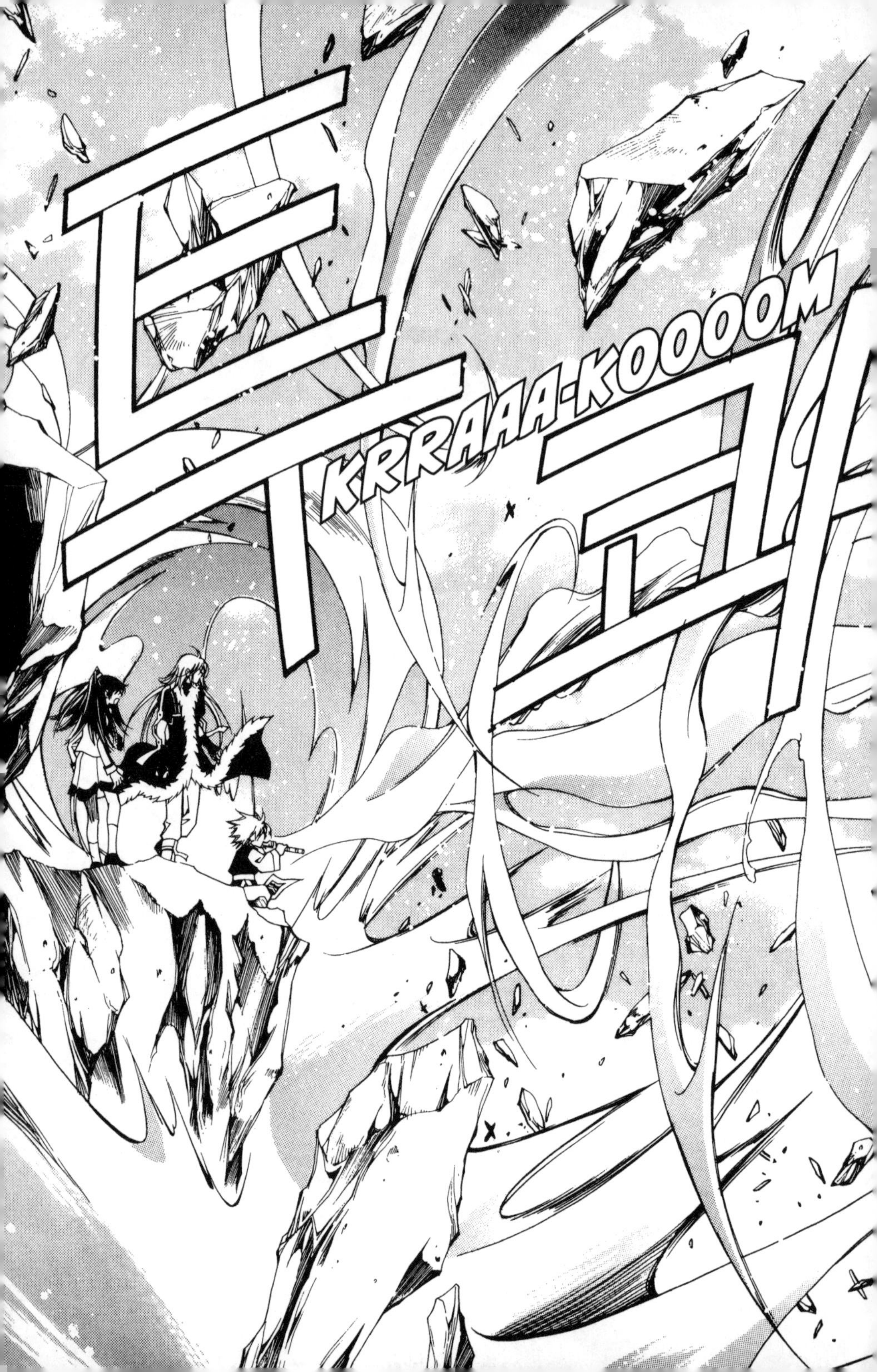
KRRAAA-KOOOOM

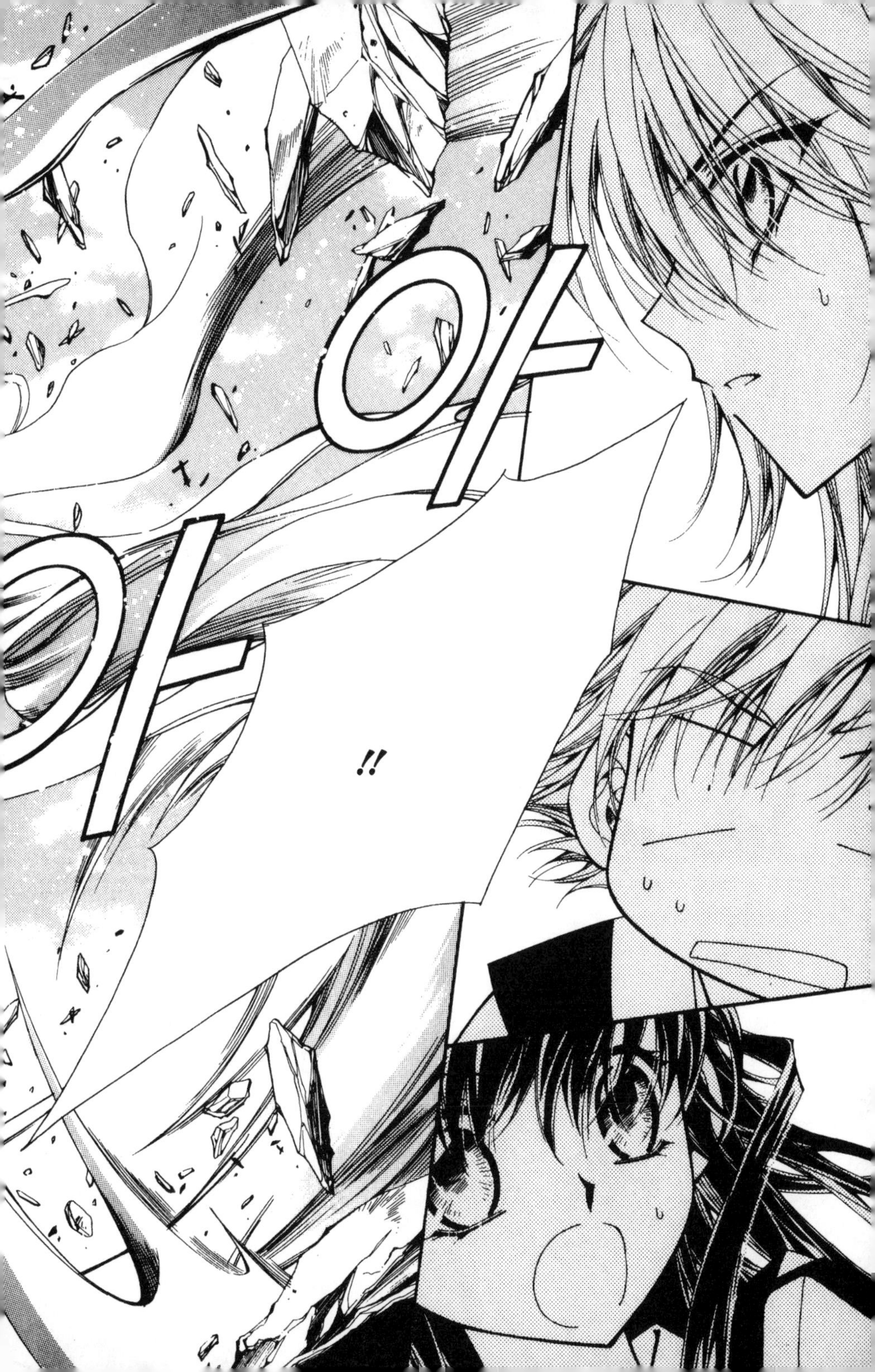
아아
!!

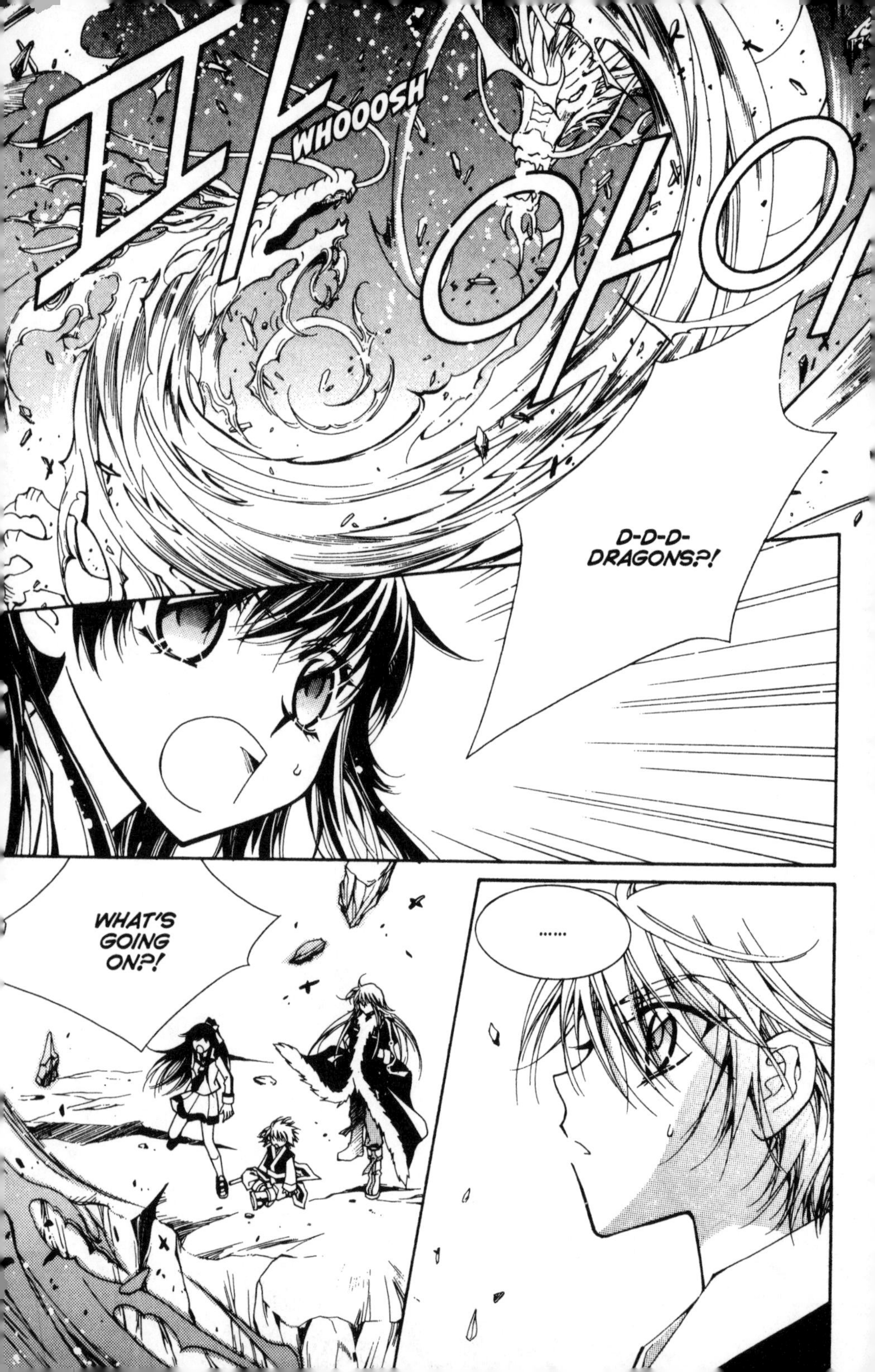

WHOOOSH
D-D-D-DRAGONS?!
WHAT'S GOING ON?!
......

HO-DONG...

...REALLY IS THE RIGHTFUL OWNER OF THE MANPASHIKJUCK!?

HAE-RANG SAID THAT TWO DRAGONS ARE SEALED WITHIN THE FLUTE!

......

OF COURSE I AM!

HE DOESN'T KNOW WHAT REALLY HAPPENED EITHER.

HA HA HA...

I HAVE MANY HIDDEN TALENTS!

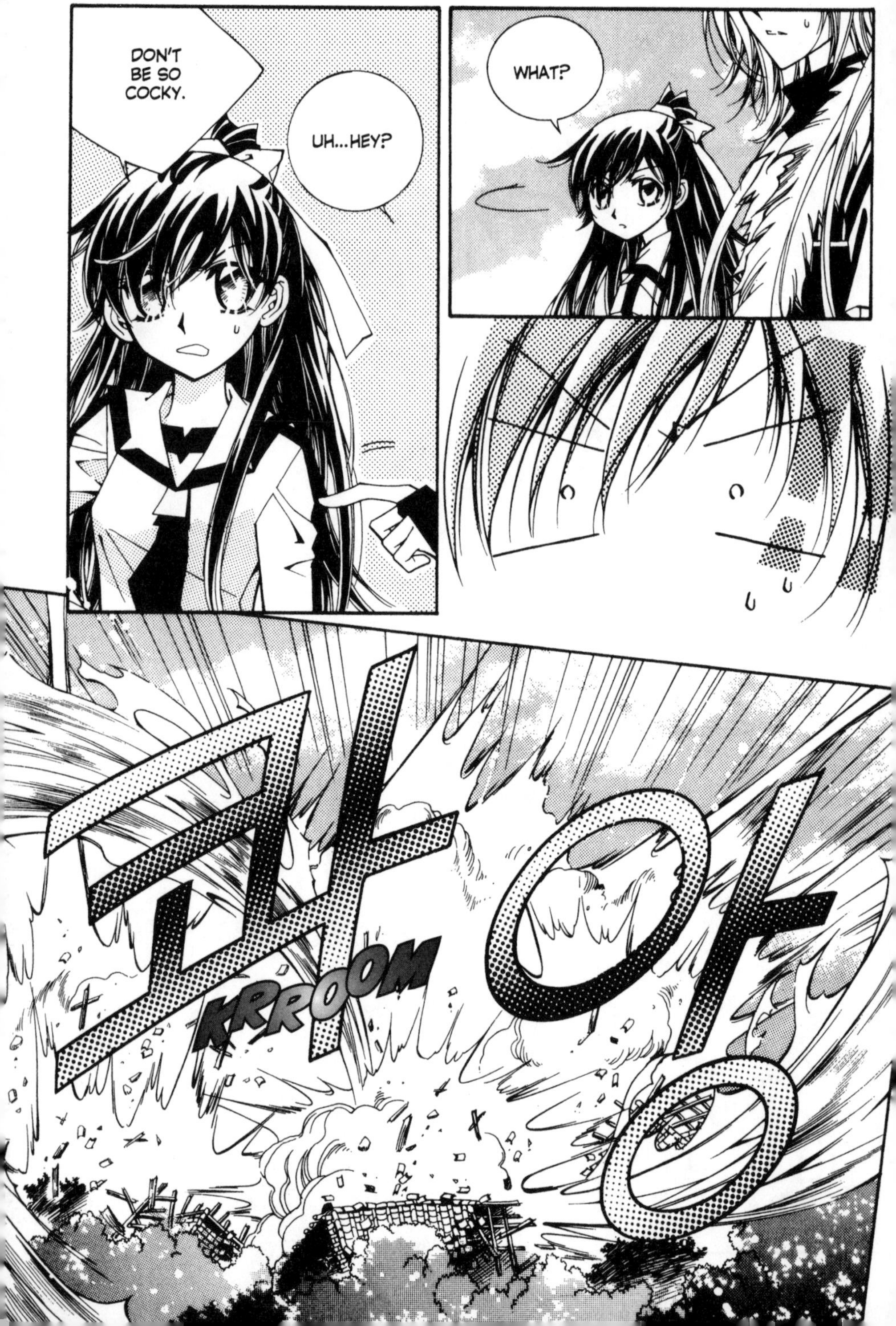
DON'T BE SO COCKY.
UH...HEY?
WHAT?
KRROOM

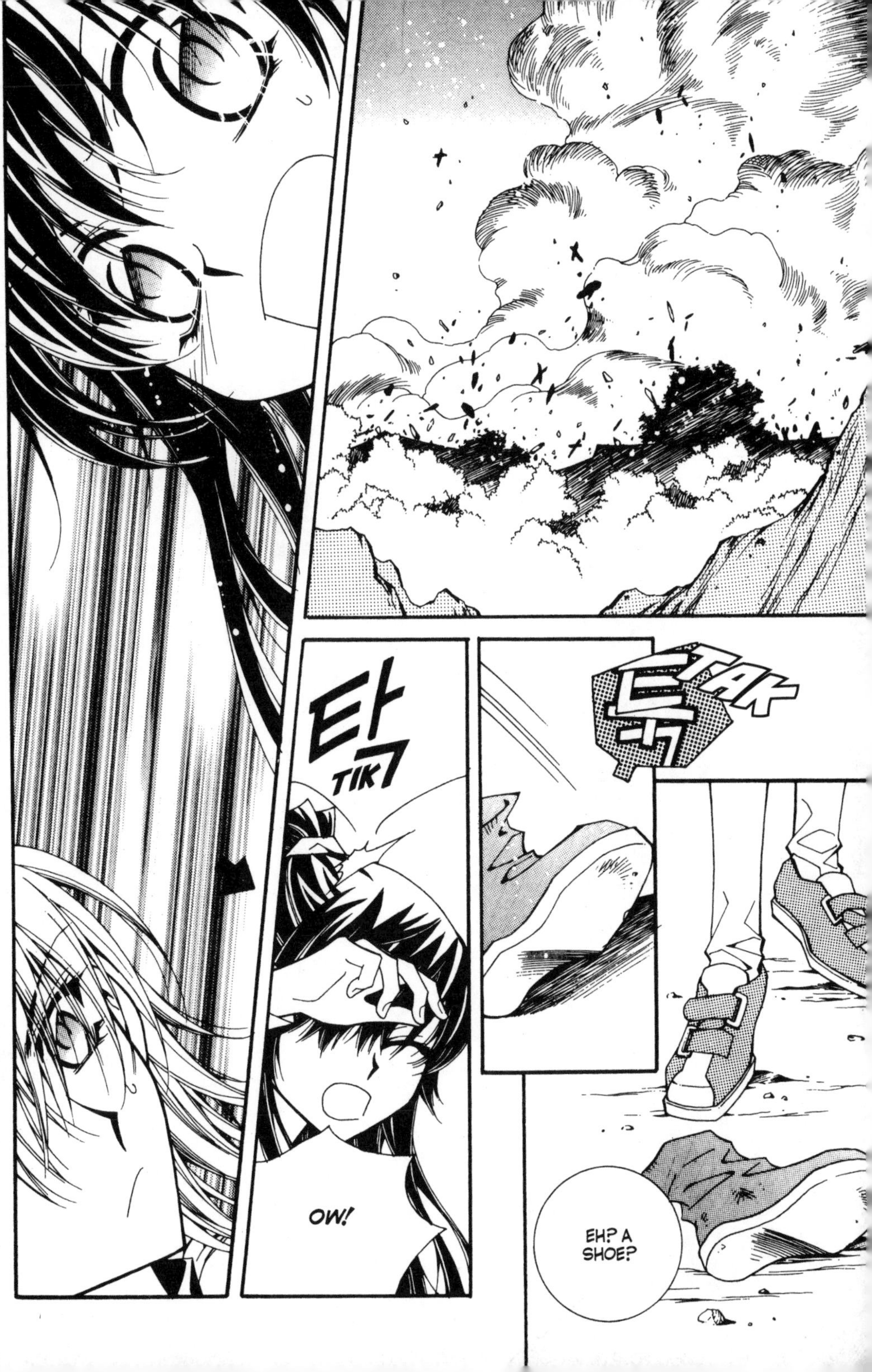
탁
TIK
OW!
탁
TAK
EH? A SHOE?

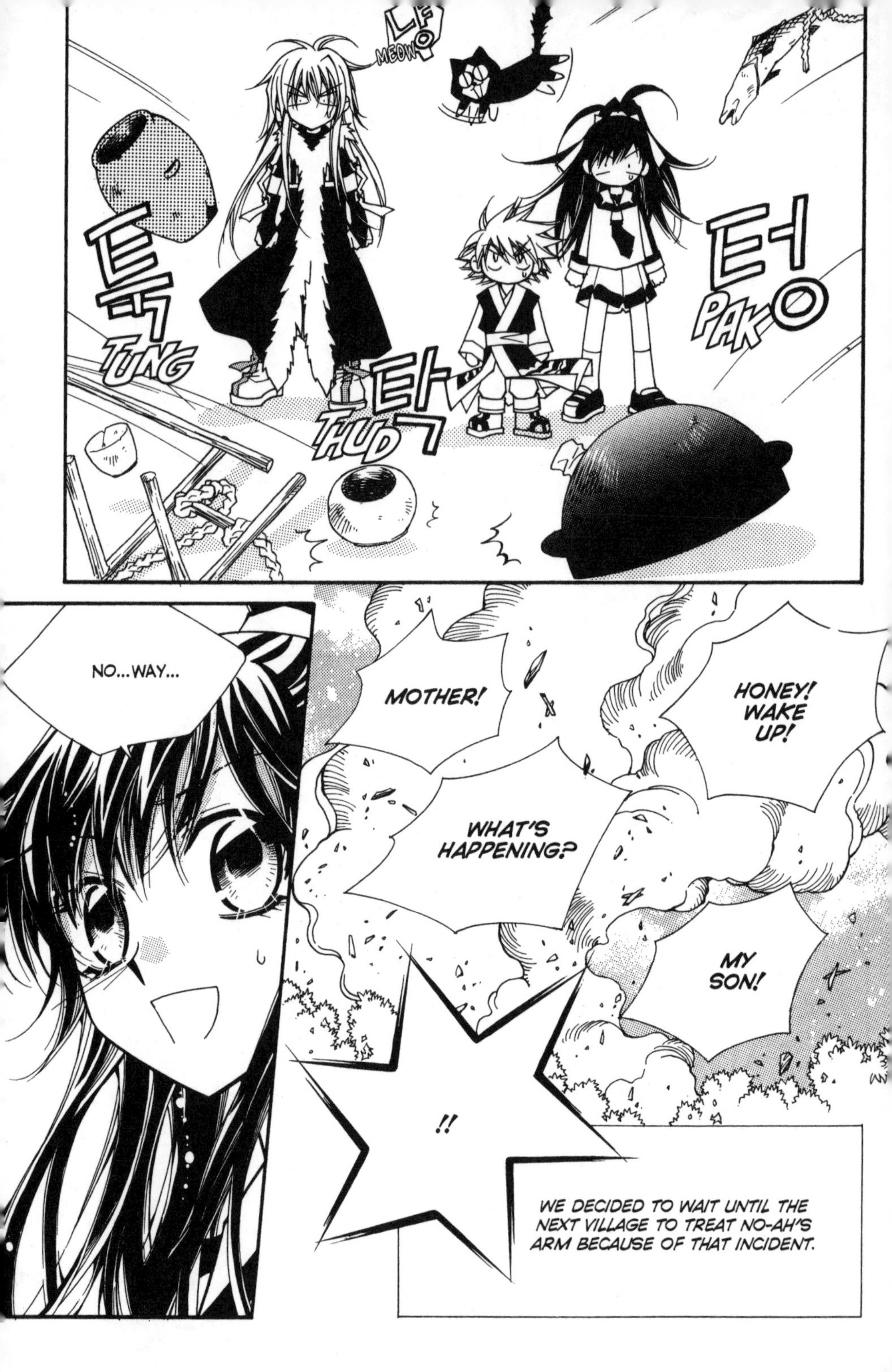
MEOW
TUNG
THUD
PAK
NO...WAY...
MOTHER!
HONEY! WAKE UP!
WHAT'S HAPPENING?
MY SON!
!!
WE DECIDED TO WAIT UNTIL THE NEXT VILLAGE TO TREAT NO-AH'S ARM BECAUSE OF THAT INCIDENT.

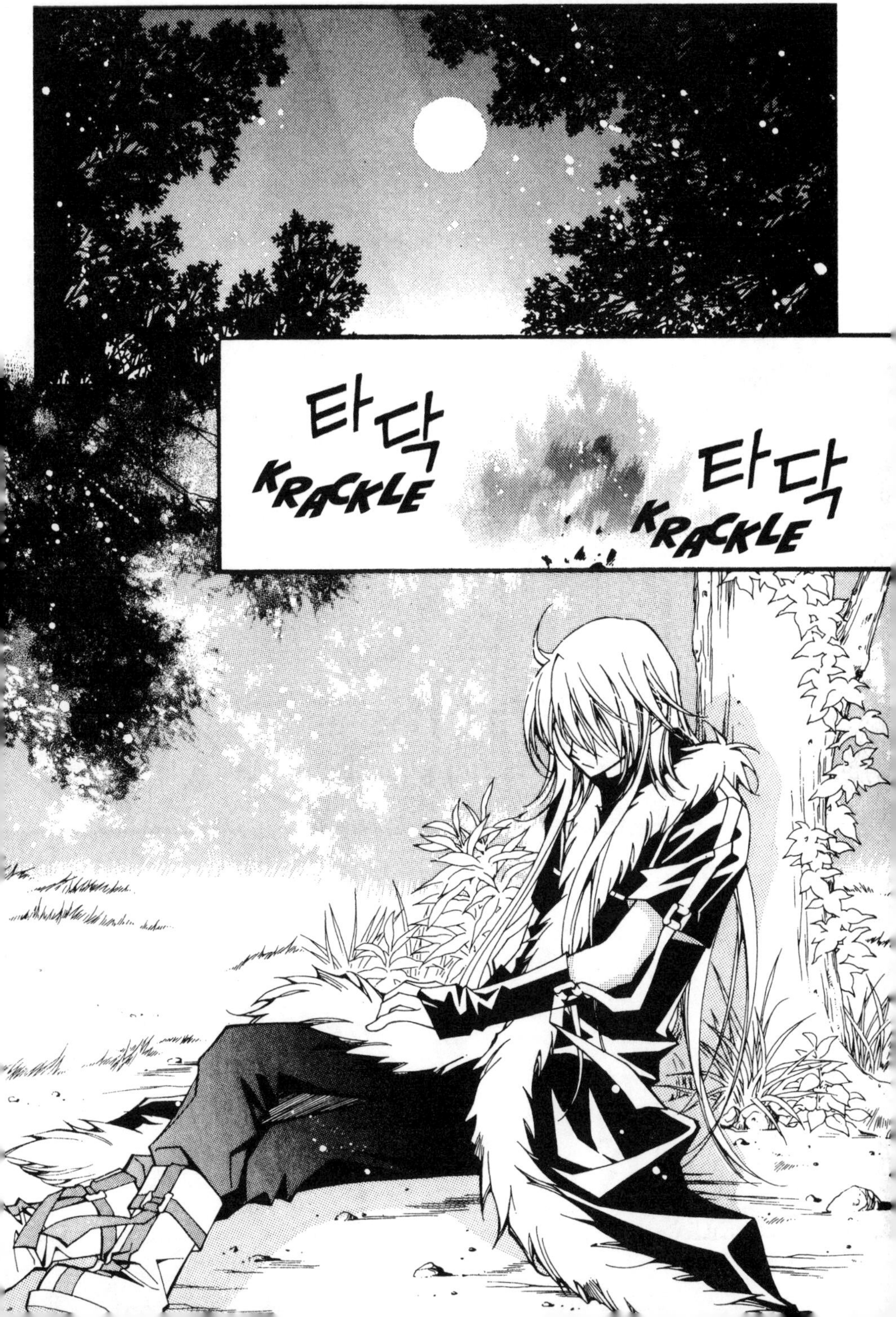
타닥
KRACKLE
타닥
KRACKLE

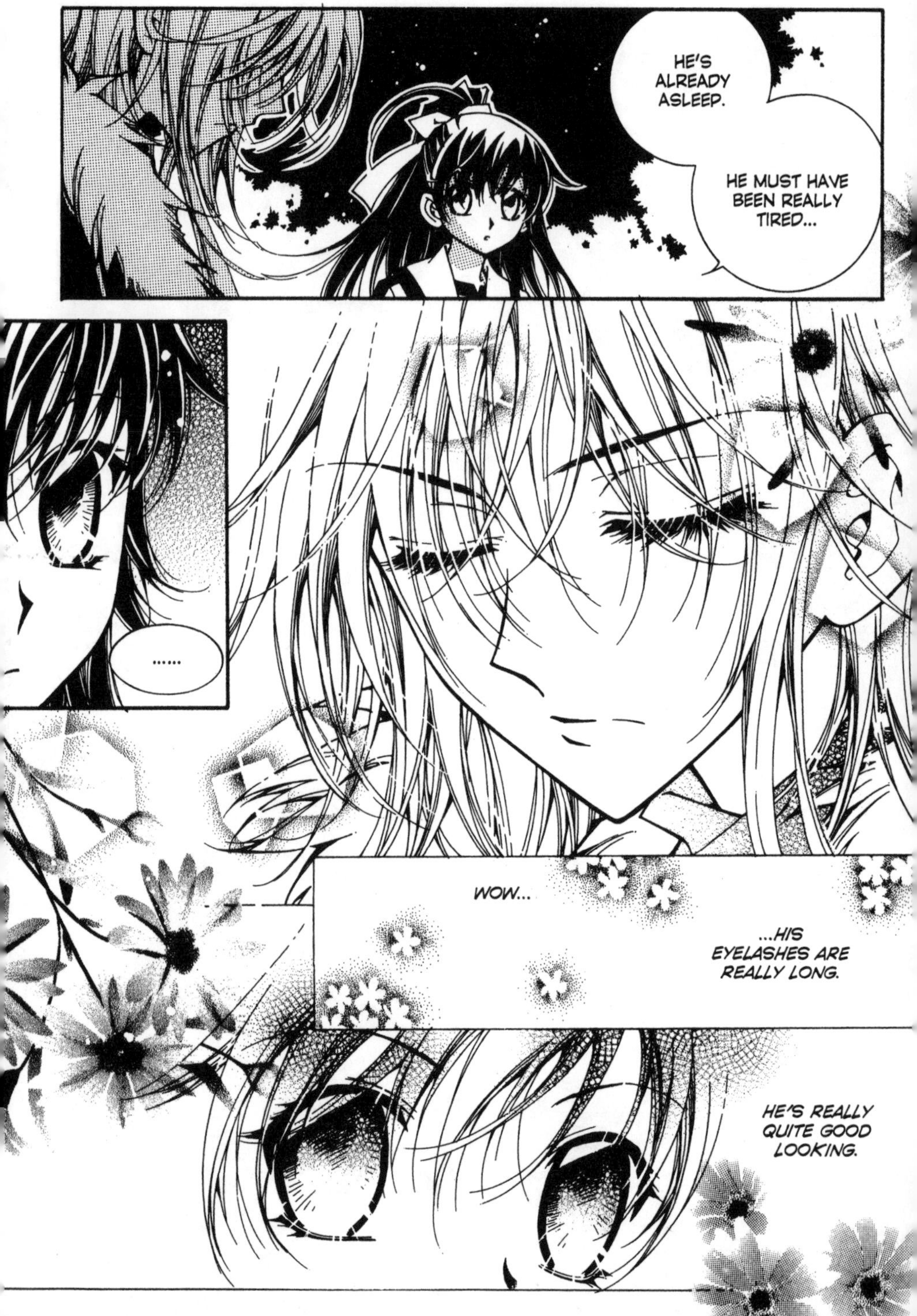
HE'S ALREADY ASLEEP.
HE MUST HAVE BEEN REALLY TIRED...
......
WOW...
...HIS EYELASHES ARE REALLY LONG.
HE'S REALLY QUITE GOOD LOOKING.

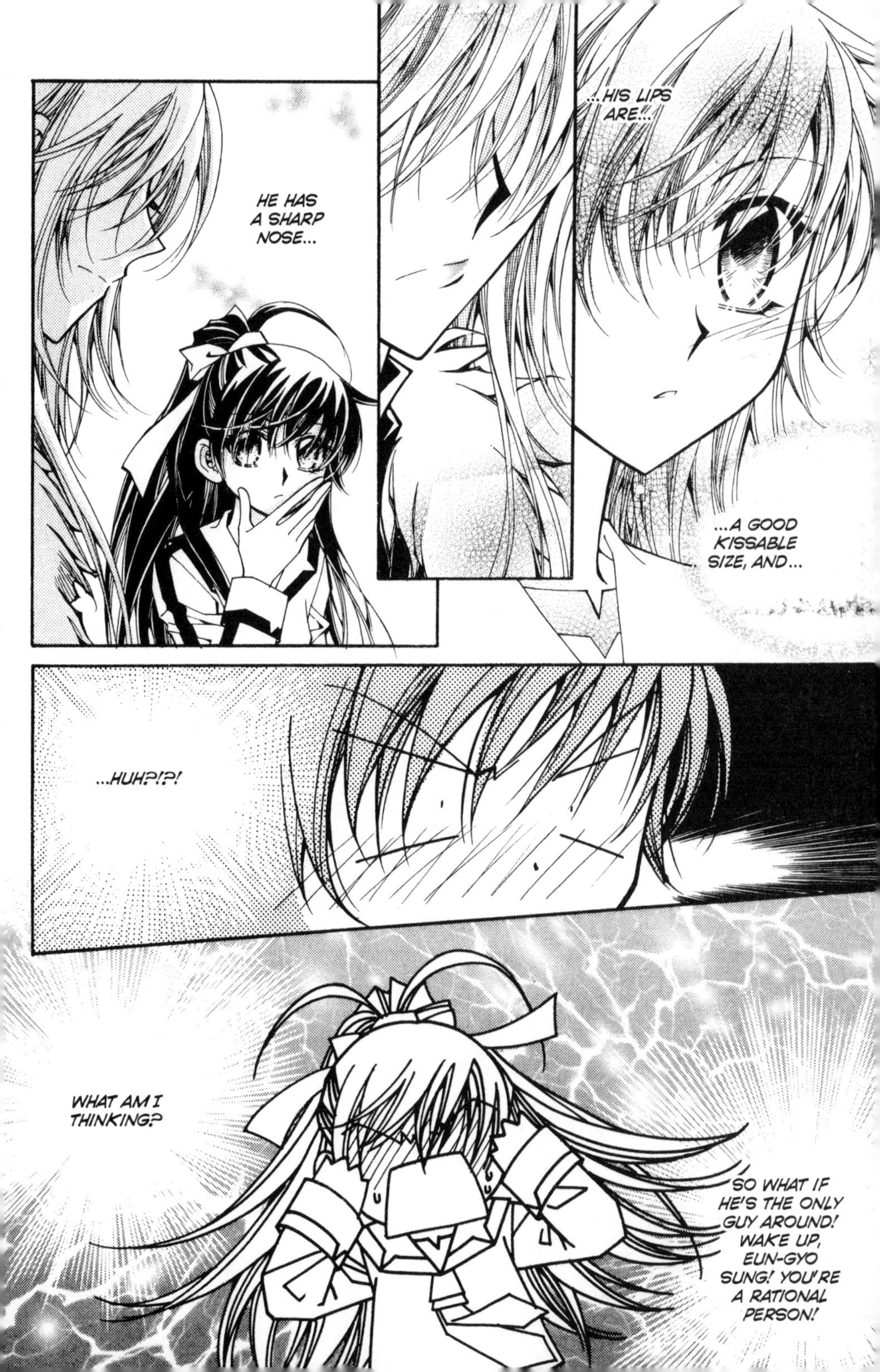
HE HAS A SHARP NOSE...
...HIS LIPS ARE...
...A GOOD KISSABLE SIZE, AND...
...HUH?!?!
WHAT AM I THINKING?
SO WHAT IF HE'S THE ONLY GUY AROUND! WAKE UP, EUN-GYO SUNG! YOU'RE A RATIONAL PERSON!

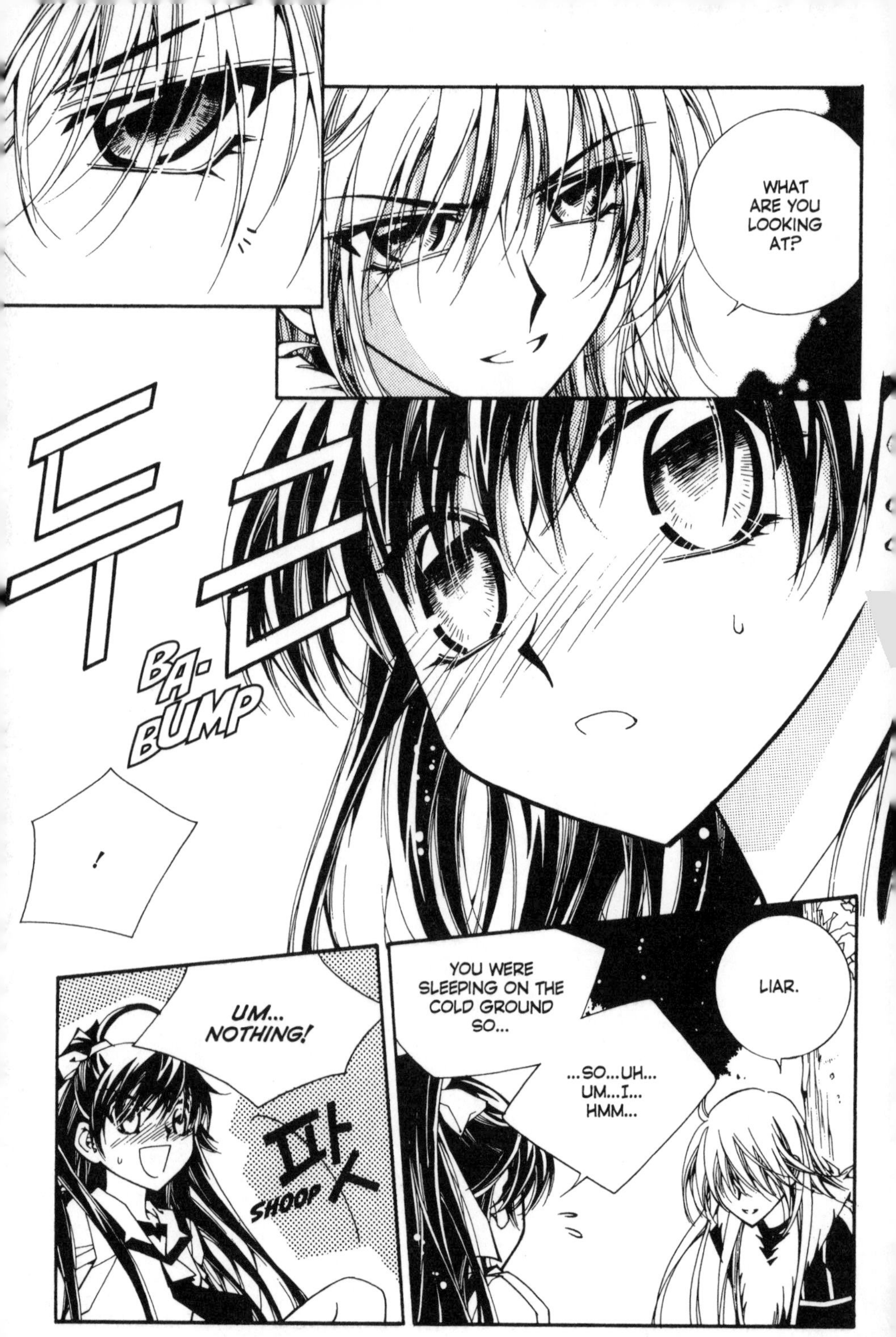
WHAT ARE YOU LOOKING AT?
BA-BUMP
!
UM... NOTHING!
SHOOP
YOU WERE SLEEPING ON THE COLD GROUND SO...
LIAR.
...SO...UH... UM...I... HMM...

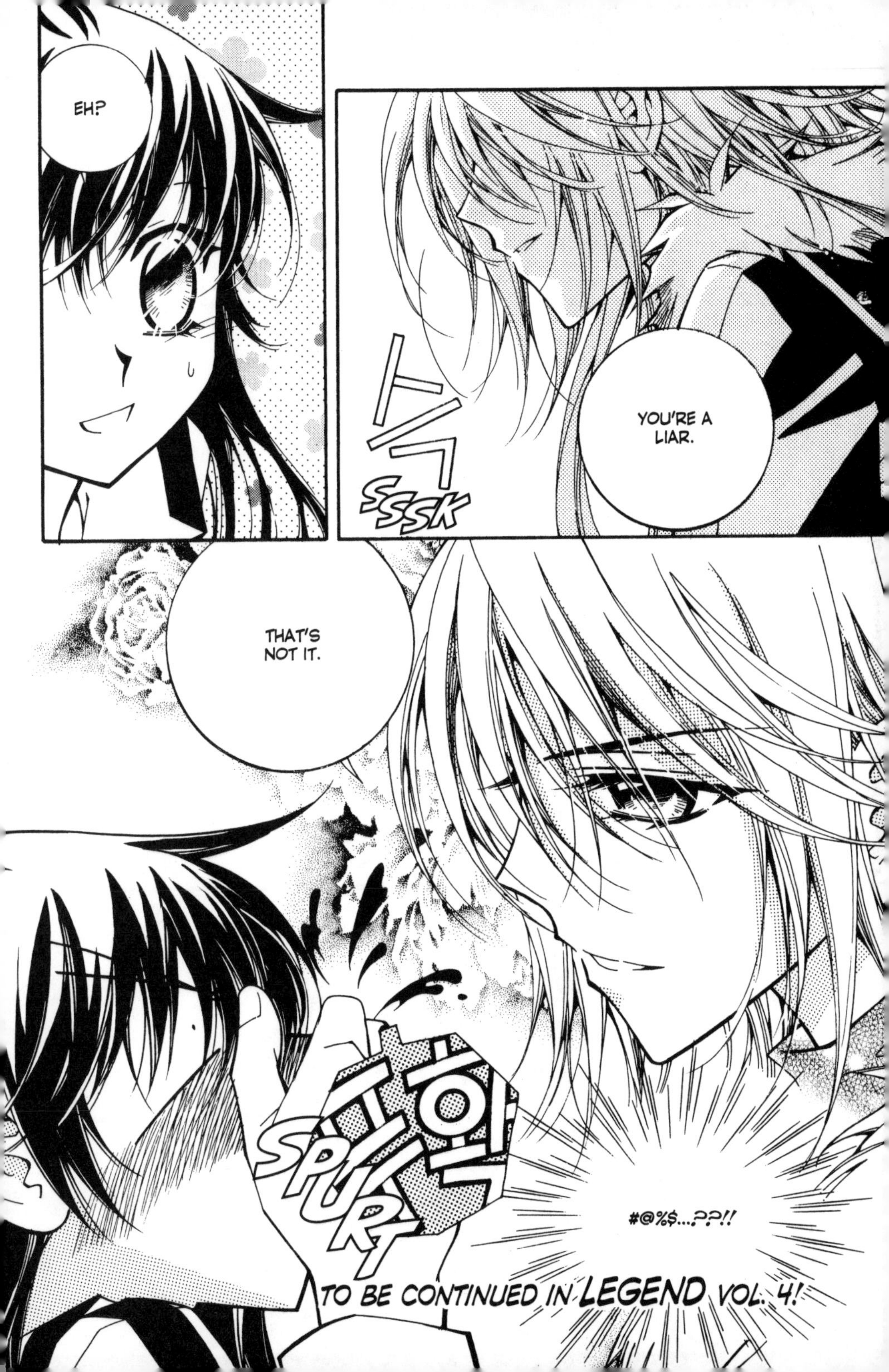
EH?
SSSK
YOU'RE A LIAR.
THAT'S NOT IT.
SPURT
#@%$...??!!
TO BE CONTINUED IN LEGEND VOL. 4!

AS I INTERPRET IT - BY ROMANTIC IMPERTINENT
〈THE MANPASHIKJUCK〉

THE MANPASHIKJUCK IS THE LEGENDRY FLUTE OF THE KINGDOM OF SHILA*. KING SHIN-MOON BUILT KAMEUN TEMPLE FOLLOWING THE WILL OF HIS FATHER, KING MOON-MOO. A HOLY MOUNT FLOATED FROM THE EAST SEA TO THE TEMPLE, AND THE MANPASHIKJUCK WAS MADE FROM THE BAMBOO FOUND THERE IN MAY OF THE YEAR AFTER THE TEMPLE WAS COMPLETED.

IF YOU ASK ME WHETHER OR NOT THE MANPASHIKJUCK REALLY EXISTED...I DON'T KNOW. EVEN THOUGH IT APPEARS THROUGHOUT HISTORY, THE STORY OF HOW MANPASHIKJUCK WAS CREATED IS TOO FANTASTIC. ACCORDING TO THE LEGEND, THE CHOON-CHOO KIM** BECAME DRAGON OF THE SEA AND YOO-SHIN KIM*** BECAME THE GOD OF HEAVEN WHEN THEY DIED. THE DRAGON OF THE SEA AND THE GOD OF HEAVEN WERE SEALED WITHIN THE MANPASHIKJUCK.

THE MANPASHIKJUCK WAS CONSIDERED A NATIONAL TREASURE. PLAYING THIS MAGIC FLUTE ENDED A WAR, PREVENTED THE SPREAD OF DISEASE, MADE IT RAIN DURING A DROUGHT, STOPPED THE RAIN DURING A FLOOD, AND EVEN CALMED THE WIND AND THE WAVES. (WOW!) CERTAINLY, HE WHO POSSESSED IT COULD RULE THE WORLD.

EXTRA INFO.

MANY READERS ARE CURIOUS WHETHER OR NOT THE SEVEN BLADE SWORD REALLY EXISTED. THE SEVEN BLADE SWORD REALLY EXISTS AND IS KEPT AT THE ISONOKAMI PALACE IN JAPAN. CHECK OUT SOME HISTORY BOOKS FOR ACTUAL PICTURES.

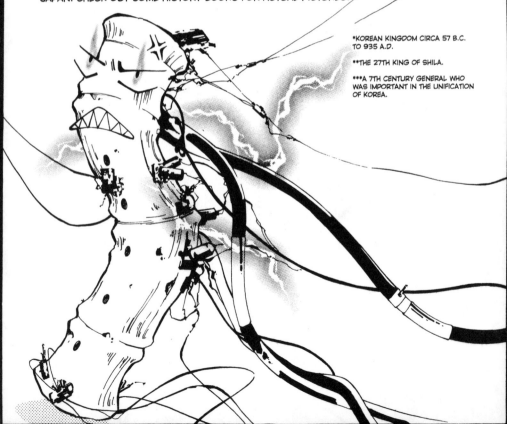

*KOREAN KINGDOM CIRCA 57 B.C. TO 935 A.D.

**THE 27TH KING OF SHILA.

***A 7TH CENTURY GENERAL WHO WAS IMPORTANT IN THE UNIFICATION OF KOREA.

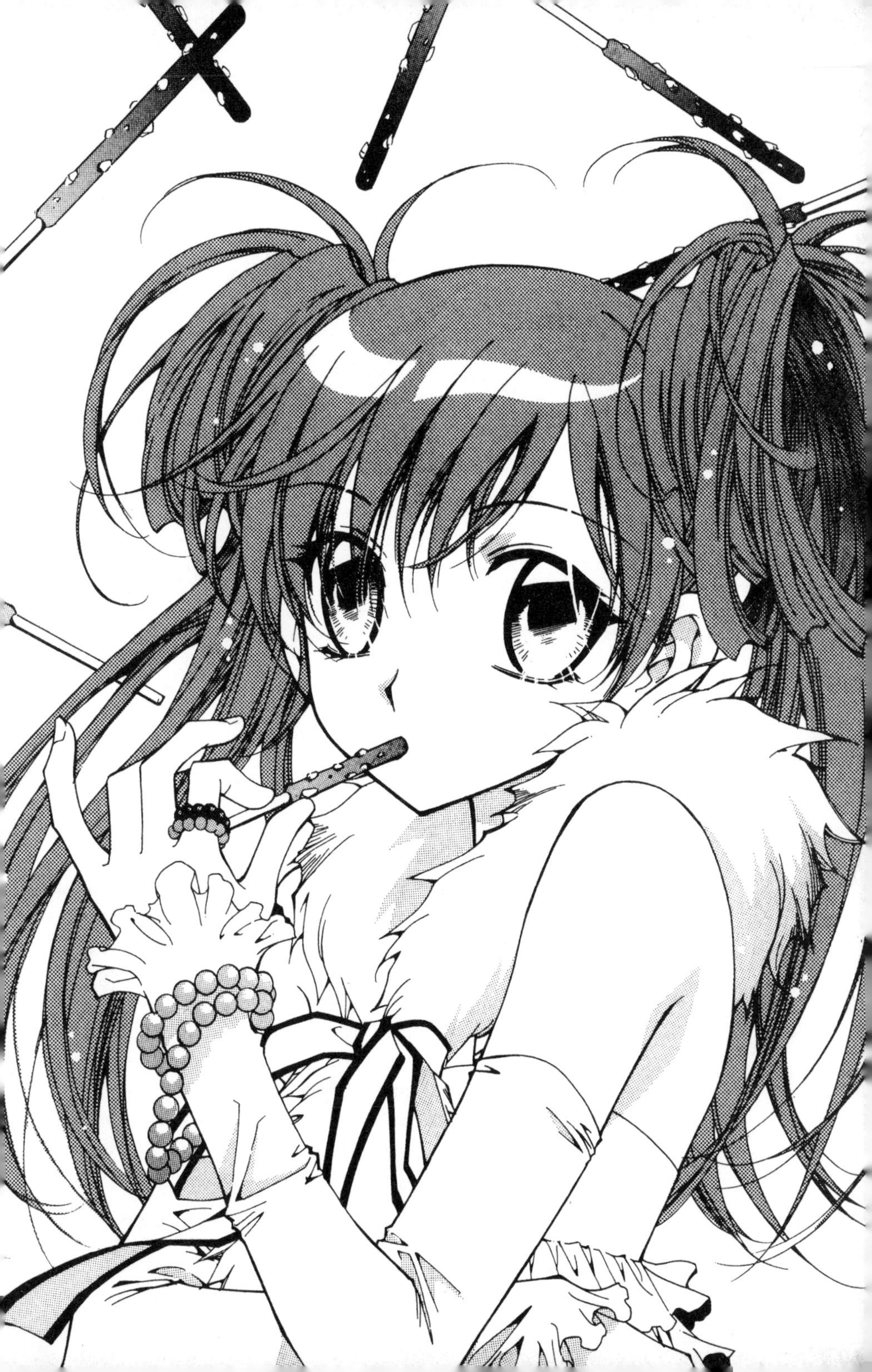

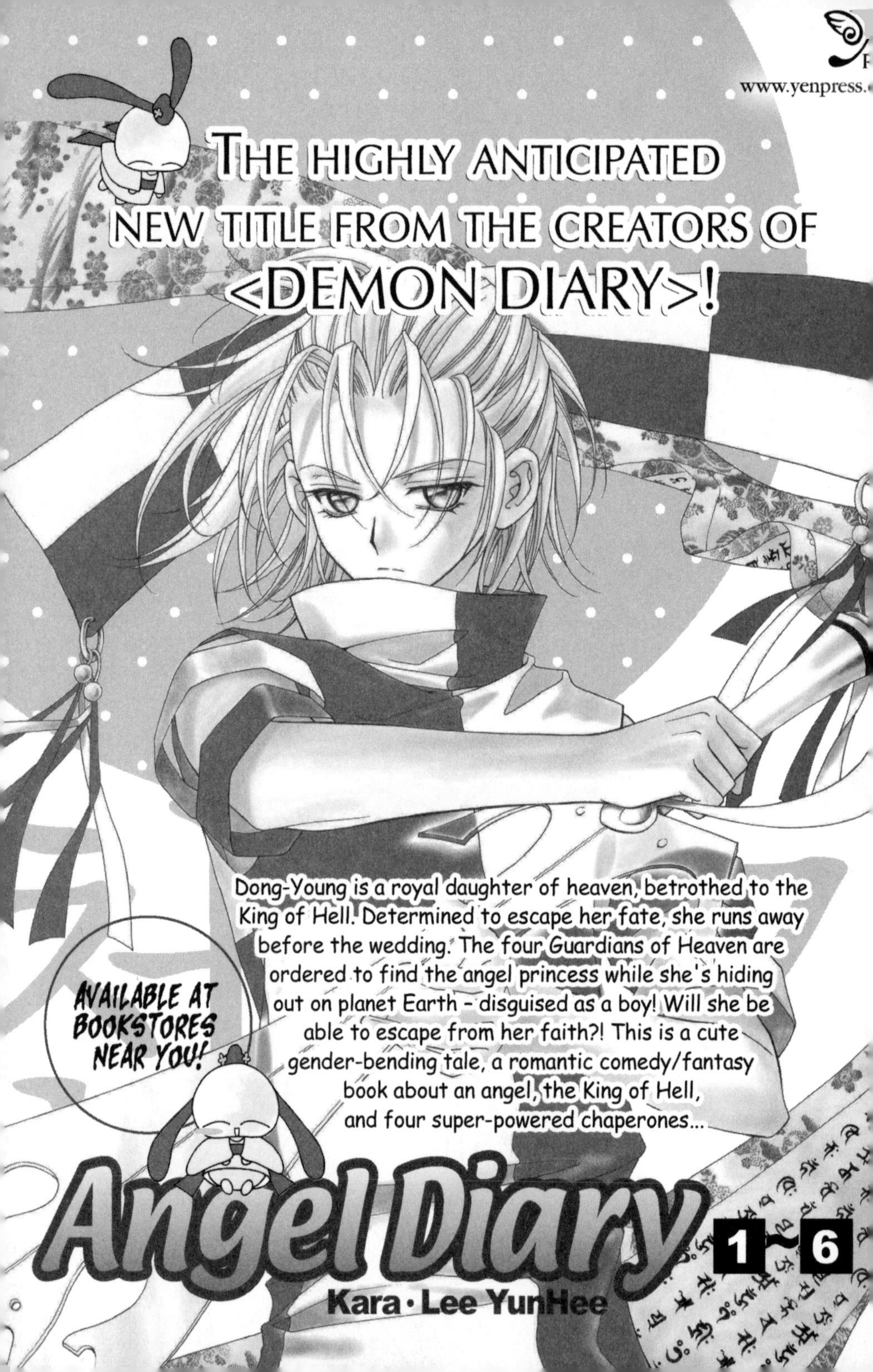
www.yenpress.
THE HIGHLY ANTICIPATED
NEW TITLE FROM THE CREATORS OF
<DEMON DIARY>!
Dong-Young is a royal daughter of heaven, betrothed to the King of Hell. Determined to escape her fate, she runs away before the wedding. The four Guardians of Heaven are ordered to find the angel princess while she's hiding out on planet Earth – disguised as a boy! Will she be able to escape from her faith?! This is a cute gender-bending tale, a romantic comedy/fantasy book about an angel, the King of Hell, and four super-powered chaperones...
AVAILABLE AT BOOKSTORES NEAR YOU!
Angel Diary
1~6
Kara · Lee YunHee

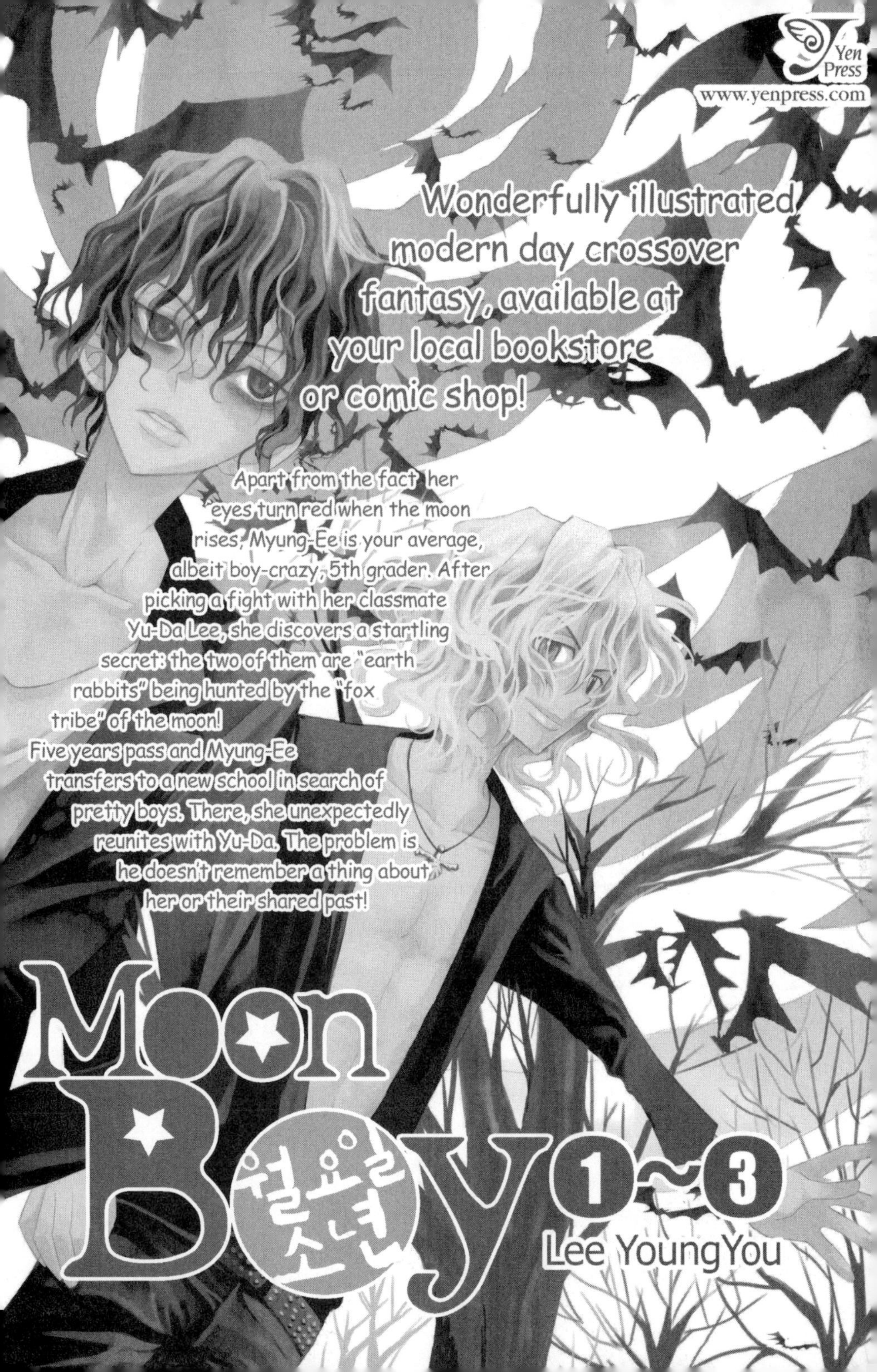
Yen Press
www.yenpress.com
Wonderfully illustrated modern day crossover fantasy, available at your local bookstore or comic shop!
Apart from the fact her eyes turn red when the moon rises, Myung-Ee is your average, albeit boy-crazy, 5th grader. After picking a fight with her classmate Yu-Da Lee, she discovers a startling secret: the two of them are "earth rabbits" being hunted by the "fox tribe" of the moon! Five years pass and Myung-Ee transfers to a new school in search of pretty boys. There, she unexpectedly reunites with Yu-Da. The problem is he doesn't remember a thing about her or their shared past!
Moon Boy
월요일 소녀
1~3
Lee YoungYou

Available at bookstores near you!

CHOCOLAT
1~5

Shin JiSang · Geo

Kum-ji was a little late getting under the spell
of the chart-topping band, DDL. Unable to
join the DDL fan club, she almost gives up
on meeting her idols, until she develops a
cunning plan–to become a member of a
rival fan club for the brand-new boy band
Yo-I. This way she can act as Yo-I's fan
club member and also be near Yo-I,

How far would you
go to meet your
favorite boy band?

who always seem to be in the
same shows as DDL. Perfect
plan...except being a fanatic is a lot
more complicated than she
expects. Especially when you're
actually a fan of someone else. This
full-blown love comedy about a fan
club will make you laugh, cry, and
laugh some more.

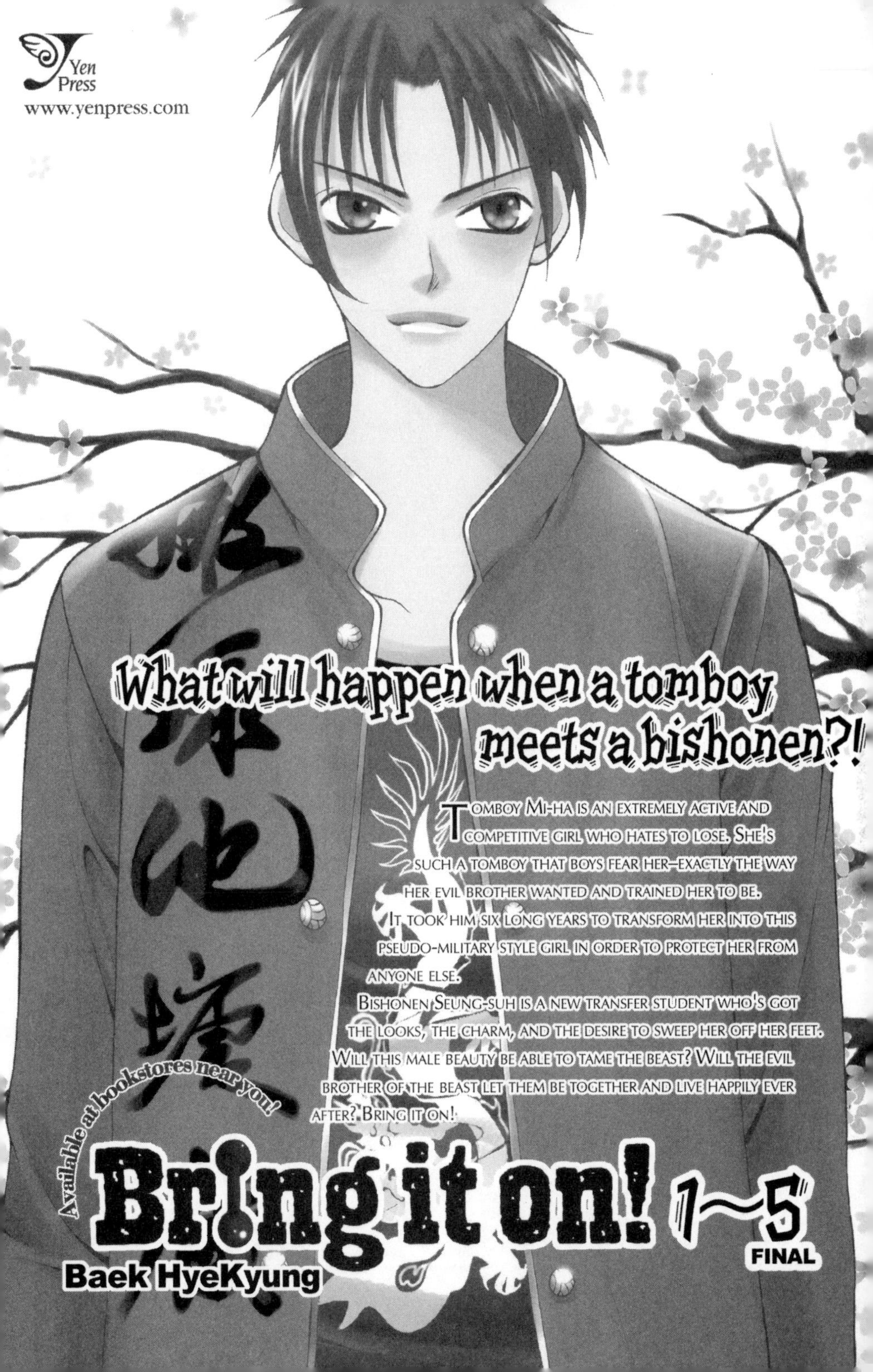
Yen Press
www.yenpress.com
What will happen when a tomboy meets a bishonen?!
Tomboy Mi-ha is an extremely active and competitive girl who hates to lose. She's such a tomboy that boys fear her—exactly the way her evil brother wanted and trained her to be. It took him six long years to transform her into this pseudo-military style girl in order to protect her from anyone else. Bishonen Seung-suh is a new transfer student who's got the looks, the charm, and the desire to sweep her off her feet. Will this male beauty be able to tame the beast? Will the evil brother of the beast let them be together and live happily ever after?. Bring it on!
Available at bookstores near you!
Bring it on! 1~5
FINAL
Baek HyeKyung

Yen Press
www.yenpress.com

Becoming the princess... Isn't that every girl's dream?!

Monarchy rule ended long ago in Korea, but there are still other countries with kings, queens, princes and princesses. What if Korea had continued monarchism? What if all the beautiful palaces, which are now only historical relics, were actually filled with people? What if the glamorous royal family still maintained the palace customs? Welcome to a world where Korea still has the royal family living in their everyday lives! Only for this one high school girl, Chae-Kyung, is this a tragedy, since she has to marry the prince — who apparently is a total bastard!

THE ROYAL PALACE
Goong
vol.1~2

Park SoHee

Sometimes, just being a teenager is hard enough.

Da-Eh, an aspiring manhwa artist who lives with her father and her little brother, comes across Sun-Nam, a softie whose ultimate goal is simply to become a "Tough guy." Whenever these two meet, trouble follows. Meanwhile, Ta-Jun, the hottest guy in town, finds himself drawn to the one girl that his killer smile does not work on—Da-Eh. With their complicated family history hanging on their shoulders, watch how these three teenagers find their way out into the world!

Available at bookstores near you!

HISSING 1~4

Kang EunYoung

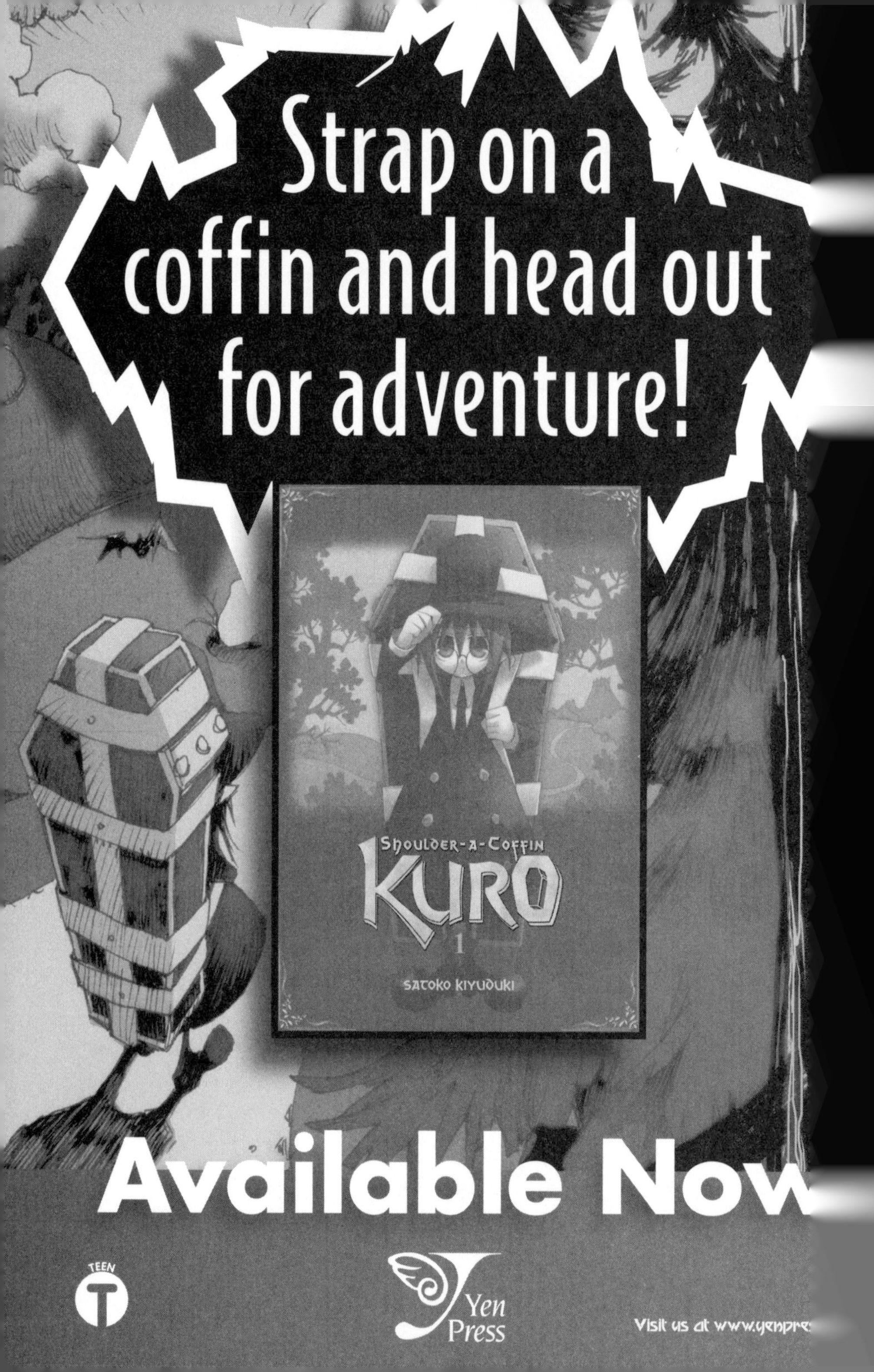
Strap on a coffin and head out for adventure!
SHOULDER-A-COFFIN
KURO
1
SATOKO KIYUDUKI
Available Now
TEEN
T
Yen Press
Visit us at www.yenpres

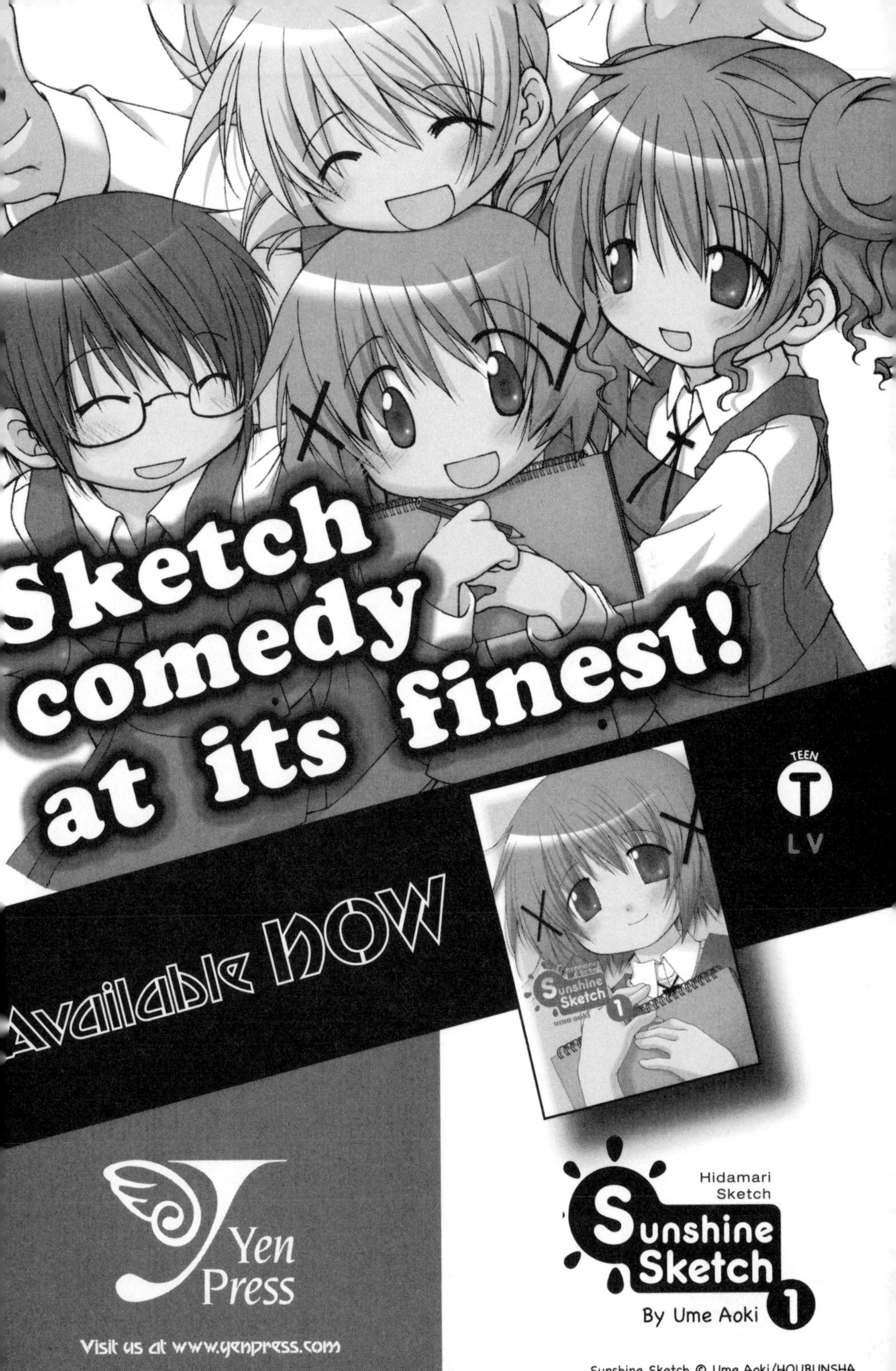
Sketch
comedy
at its finest!
TEEN
T
LV
Available NOW
Yen Press
Visit us at www.yenpress.com
Hidamari Sketch
Sunshine Sketch 1
By Ume Aoki

This one will make you PURR!
Suzunari!
By Shoko Iwami
OLDER TEEN
OT
Yen Press
Visit us at www.yenpress.com
Suzunari
1
Shoko Iwami

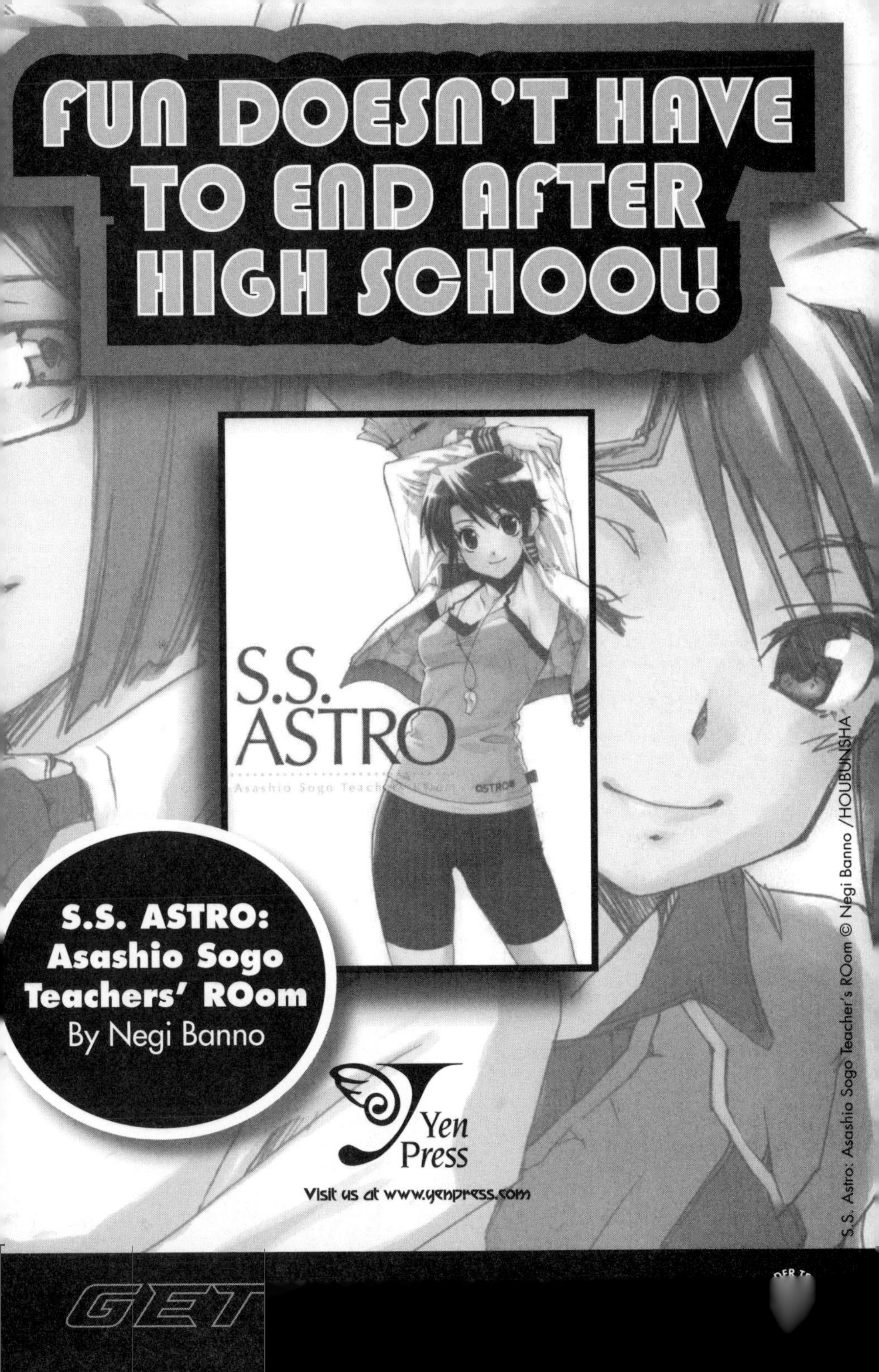
FUN DOESN'T HAVE TO END AFTER HIGH SCHOOL!
S.S. ASTRO
Asashio Sogo Teacher's ROom
ASTRO
S.S. ASTRO:
Asashio Sogo Teachers' ROom
By Negi Banno
Yen Press
Visit us at www.yenpress.com
S.S. Astro: Asashio Sogo Teacher's ROom © Negi Banno /HOUBUNSHA
GET

Legend vol. 3

Story by SooJung Woo
Art by Kara

Translation: HyeYoung Im
English Adaptation: J. Torres
Lettering: Erika T.

Legend, Vol. 3 © 2005 Kara · SooJung Woo. All rights reserved. First published in Korea in 2005 by Seoul Cultural Publishers, Inc. English translation rights arranged by Seoul Cultural Publishers, Inc.

English translation © 2008 Hachette Book Group USA, Inc.

Yen Press
Hachette Book Group USA
237 Park Avenue, New York, NY 10017

Visit our Web sites at www.HachetteBookGroupUSA.com and www.YenPress.com.

Yen Press is an imprint of Hachette Book Group USA, Inc. The Yen Press name and logo are trademarks of Hachette Book Group USA, Inc.

First Yen Press Edition: August 2008

ISBN-10: 0-7595-2869-1
ISBN-13: 978-0-7595-2869-7

10 9 8 7 6 5 4 3 2 1

BVG

Printed in the United States of America

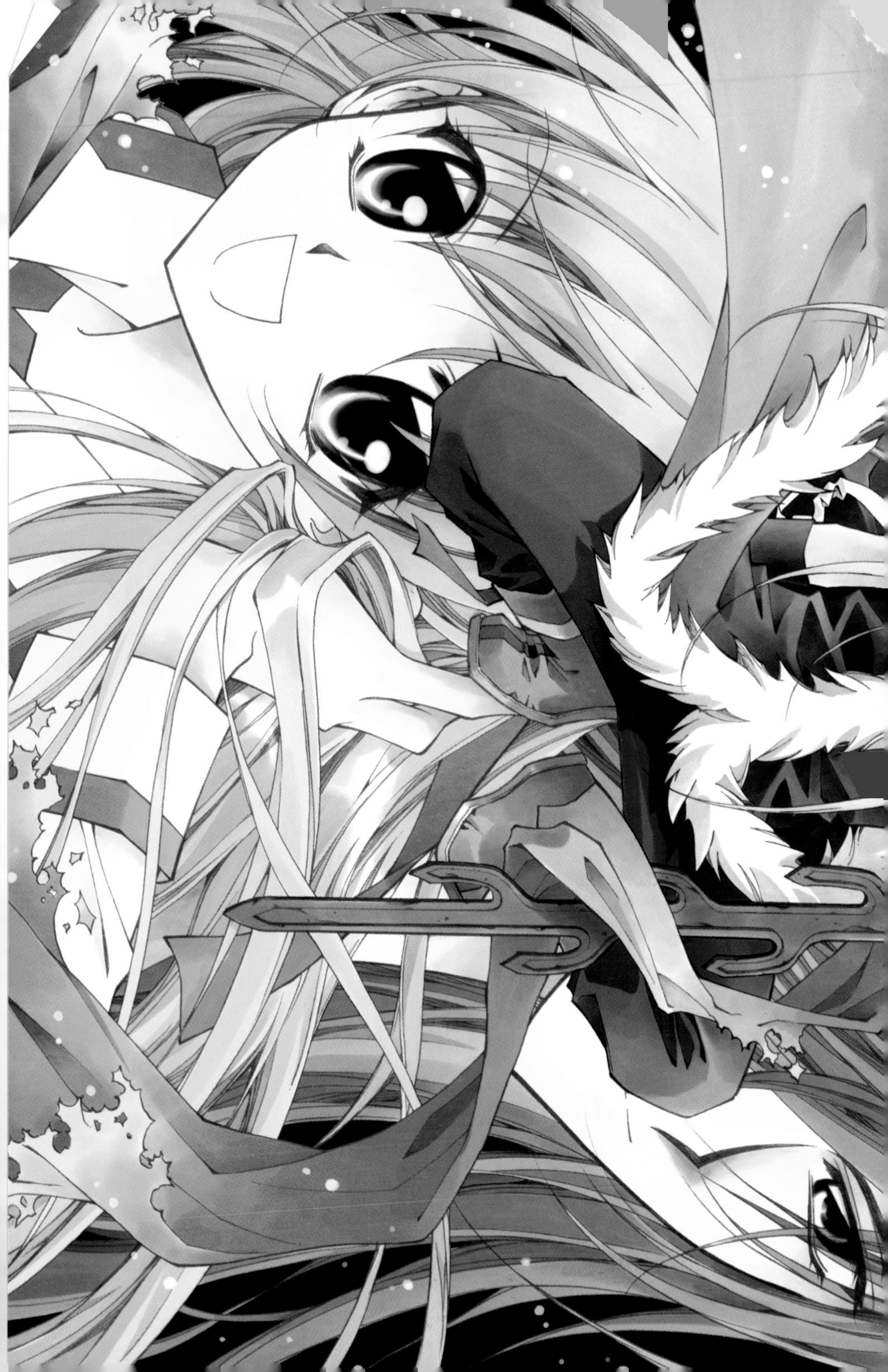

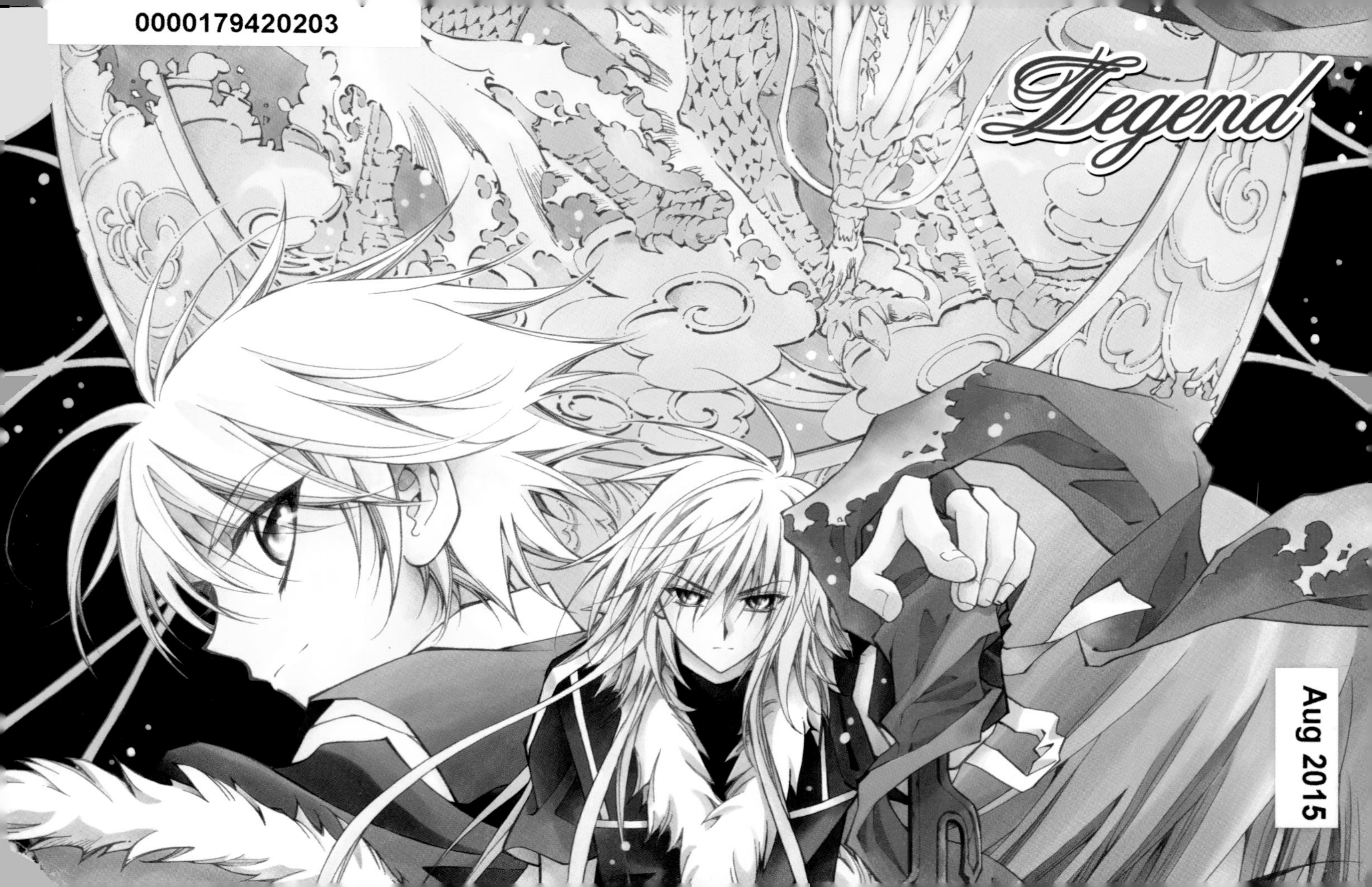
Legend